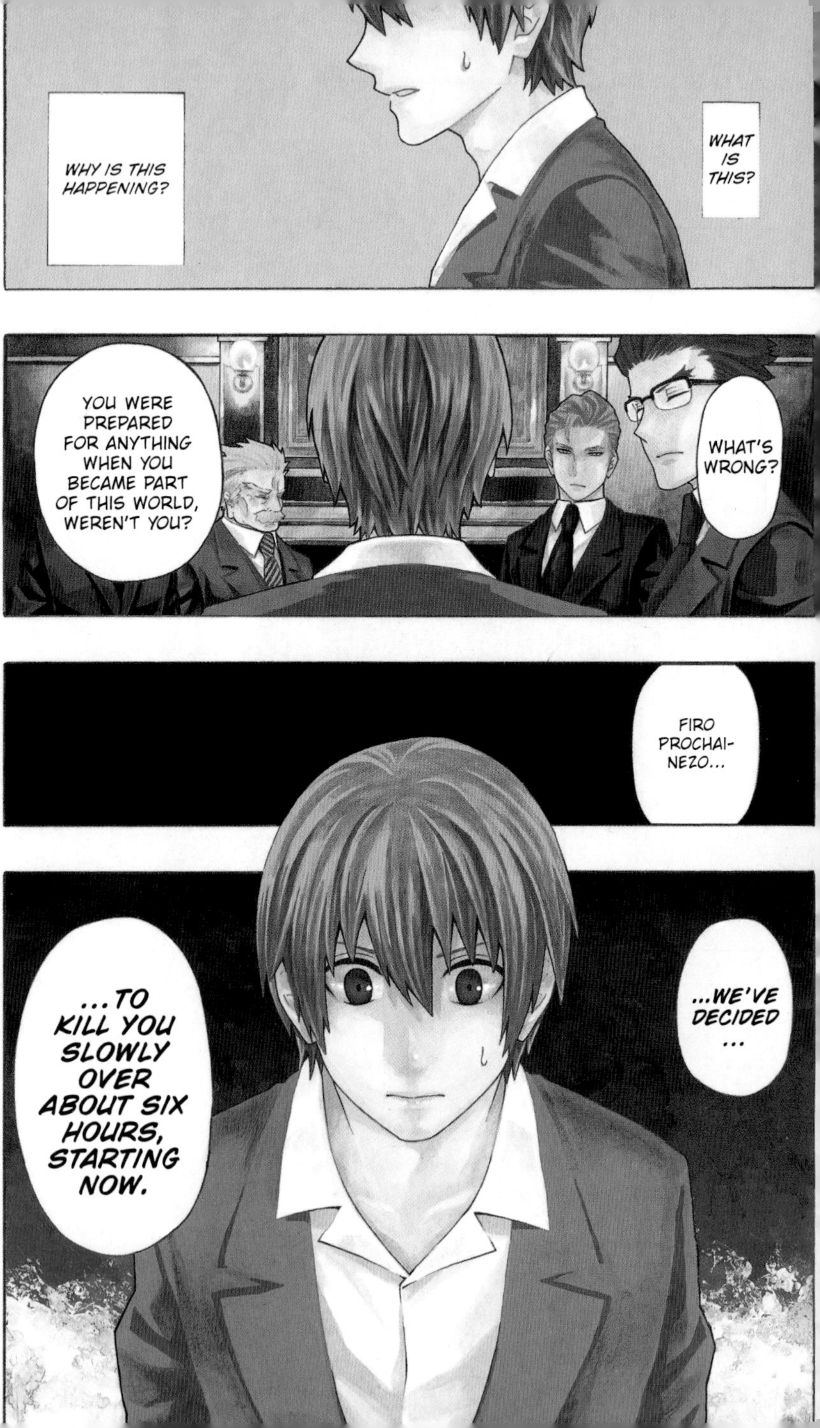
WHAT IS THIS?
WHY IS THIS HAPPENING?
WHAT'S WRONG?
YOU WERE PREPARED FOR ANYTHING WHEN YOU BECAME PART OF THIS WORLD, WEREN'T YOU?
FIRO PROCHAI-NEZO...
...WE'VE DECIDED ...
...TO KILL YOU SLOWLY OVER ABOUT SIX HOURS, STARTING NOW.

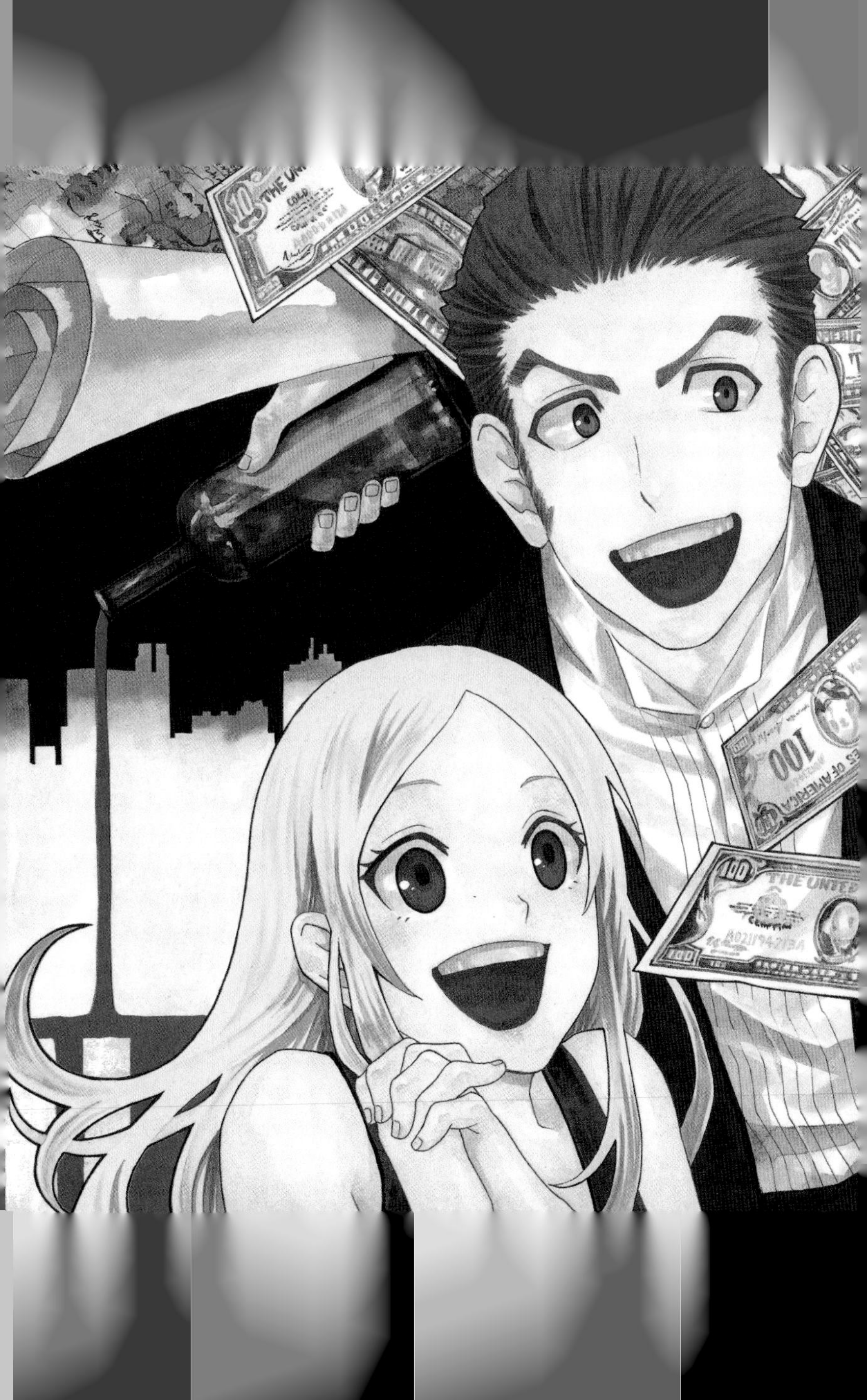
THE UNITED
100

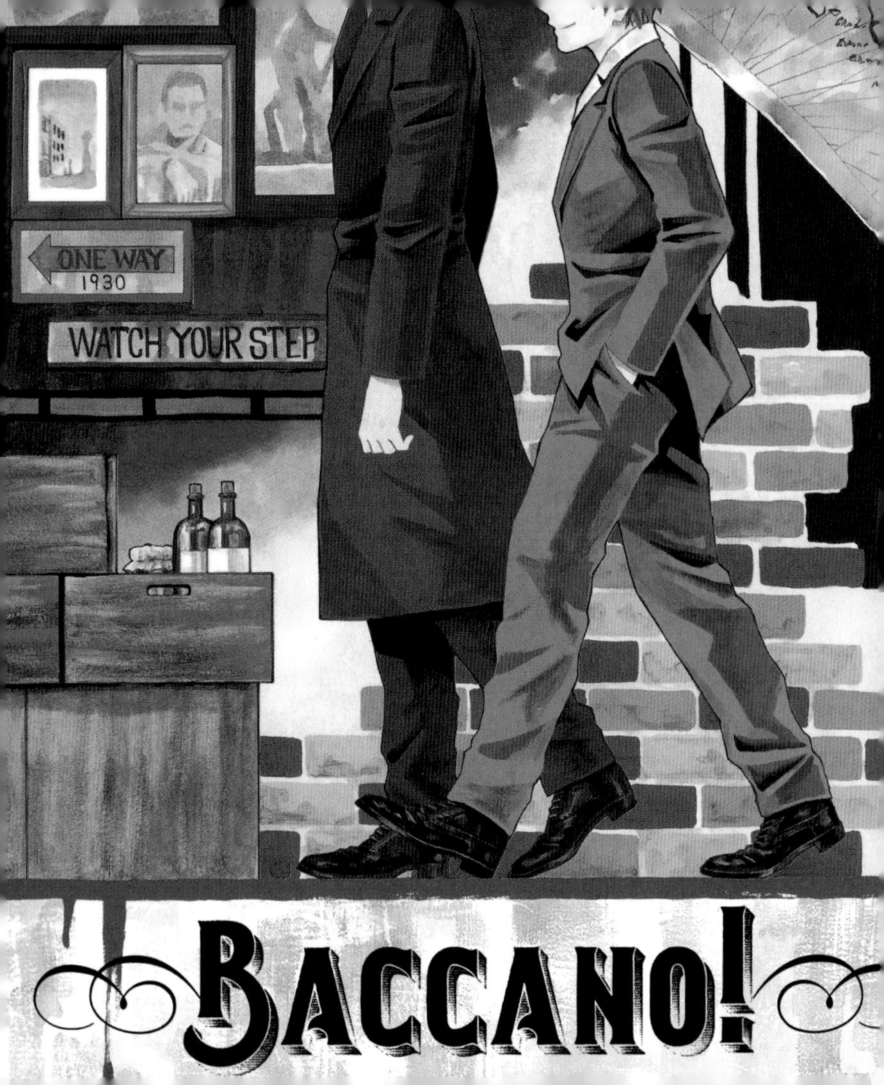
ONE WAY
1930
WATCH YOUR STEP
BACCANO!

Since 1930

BACCANO!

Vol. 2

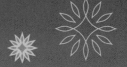

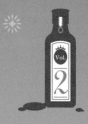

BACCANO!

Original Story *Ryohgo Narita*

Art
Shinta Fujimoto

Character Design
Katsumi Enami

2

ALVEARE

BACCANO! 2

Contents

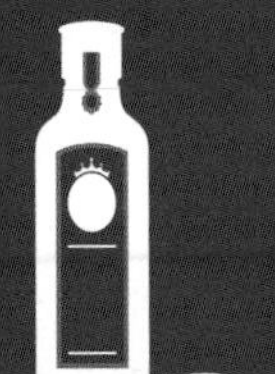

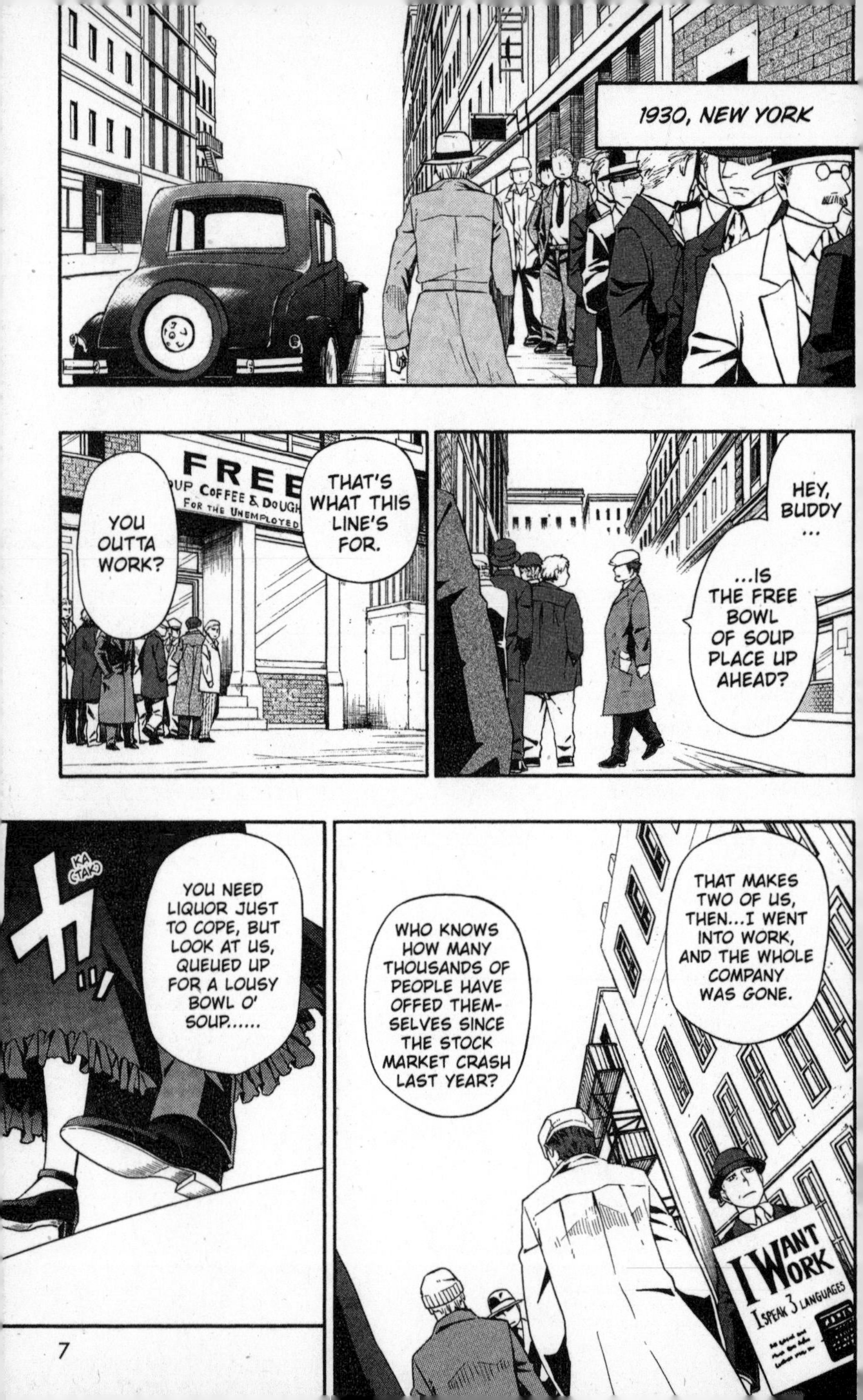
1930, NEW YORK
HEY, BUDDY ...
...IS THE FREE BOWL OF SOUP PLACE UP AHEAD?
FREE
UP COFFEE & DOUGH
FOR THE UNEMPLOYED
THAT'S WHAT THIS LINE'S FOR.
YOU OUTTA WORK?
THAT MAKES TWO OF US, THEN...I WENT INTO WORK, AND THE WHOLE COMPANY WAS GONE.
WHO KNOWS HOW MANY THOUSANDS OF PEOPLE HAVE OFFED THEM-SELVES SINCE THE STOCK MARKET CRASH LAST YEAR?
I WANT WORK
I SPEAK 3 LANGUAGES
KA CTAK
YOU NEED LIQUOR JUST TO COPE, BUT LOOK AT US, QUEUED UP FOR A LOUSY BOWL O' SOUP......

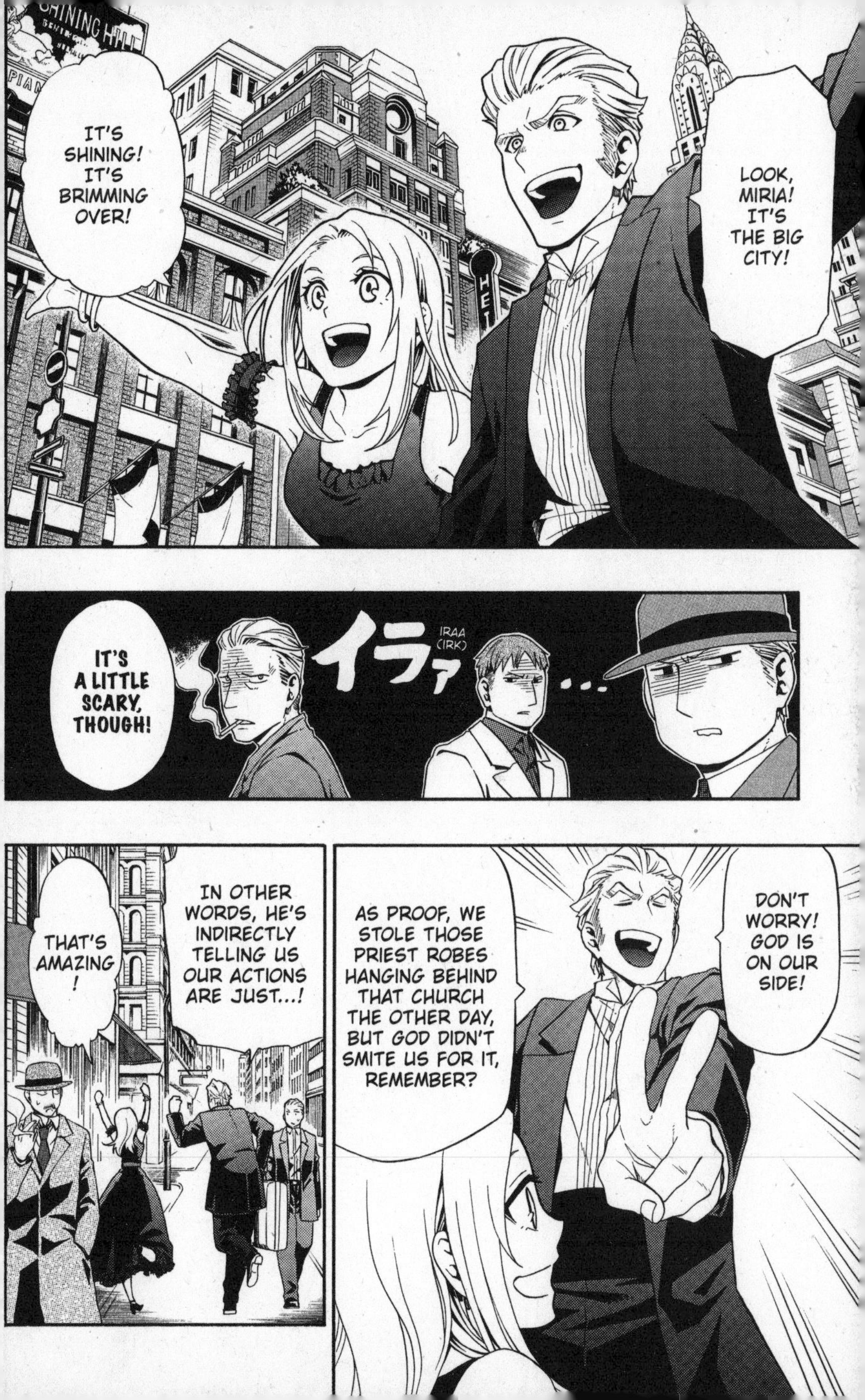
LOOK, MIRIA! IT'S THE BIG CITY!
IT'S SHINING! IT'S BRIMMING OVER!
...
イラァ
IRAA (IRK)
IT'S A LITTLE SCARY, THOUGH!
DON'T WORRY! GOD IS ON OUR SIDE!
AS PROOF, WE STOLE THOSE PRIEST ROBES HANGING BEHIND THAT CHURCH THE OTHER DAY, BUT GOD DIDN'T SMITE US FOR IT, REMEMBER?
IN OTHER WORDS, HE'S INDIRECTLY TELLING US OUR ACTIONS ARE JUST...!
THAT'S AMAZING!

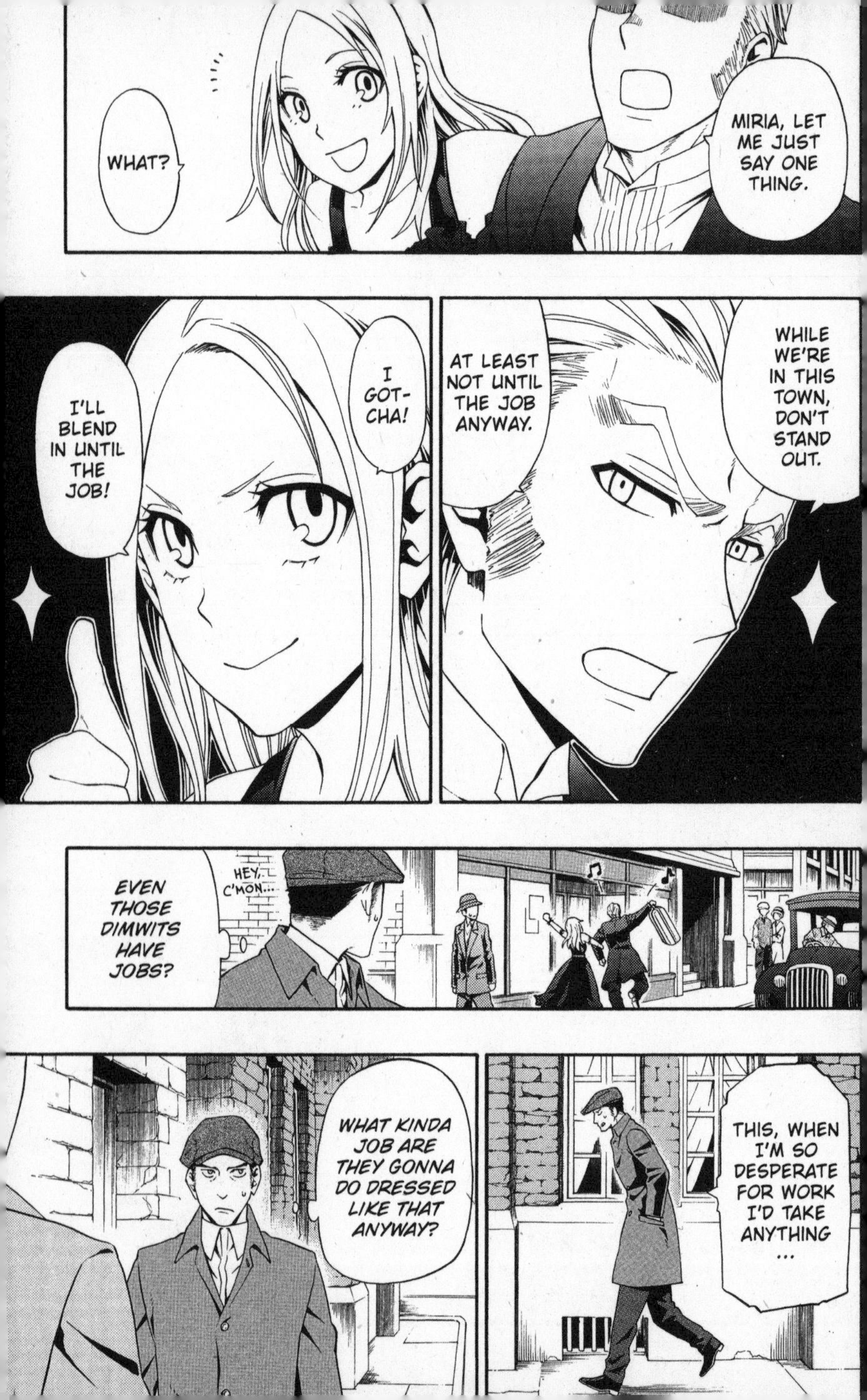
MIRIA, LET ME JUST SAY ONE THING.
WHAT?
WHILE WE'RE IN THIS TOWN, DON'T STAND OUT.
AT LEAST NOT UNTIL THE JOB ANYWAY.
I GOT-CHA!
I'LL BLEND IN UNTIL THE JOB!
HEY, C'MON...
EVEN THOSE DIMWITS HAVE JOBS?
THIS, WHEN I'M SO DESPERATE FOR WORK I'D TAKE ANYTHING ...
WHAT KINDA JOB ARE THEY GONNA DO DRESSED LIKE THAT ANYWAY?

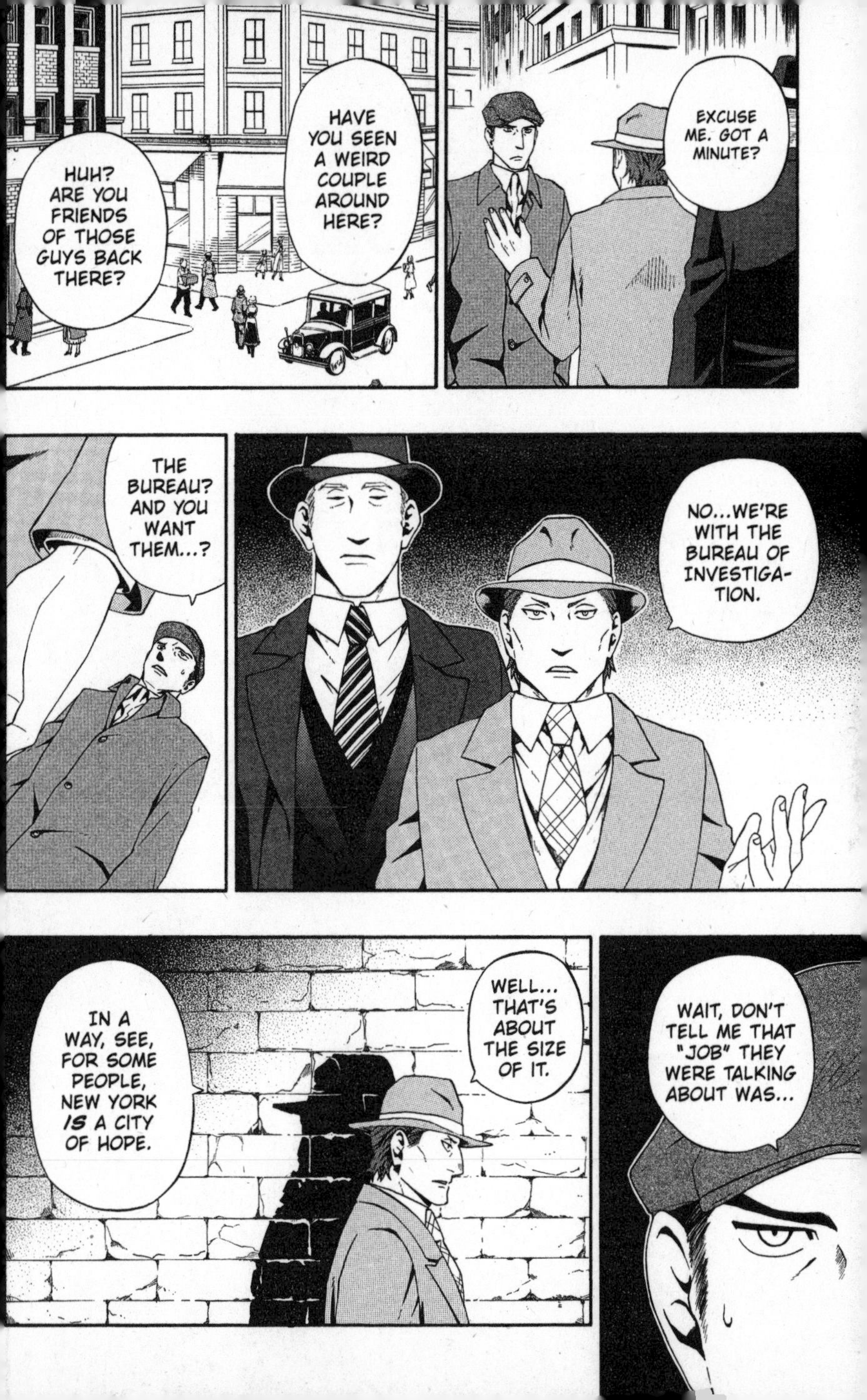
EXCUSE ME. GOT A MINUTE?
HAVE YOU SEEN A WEIRD COUPLE AROUND HERE?
HUH? ARE YOU FRIENDS OF THOSE GUYS BACK THERE?
NO...WE'RE WITH THE BUREAU OF INVESTIGATION.
THE BUREAU? AND YOU WANT THEM...?
WAIT, DON'T TELL ME THAT "JOB" THEY WERE TALKING ABOUT WAS...
WELL... THAT'S ABOUT THE SIZE OF IT.
IN A WAY, SEE, FOR SOME PEOPLE, NEW YORK *IS* A CITY OF HOPE.

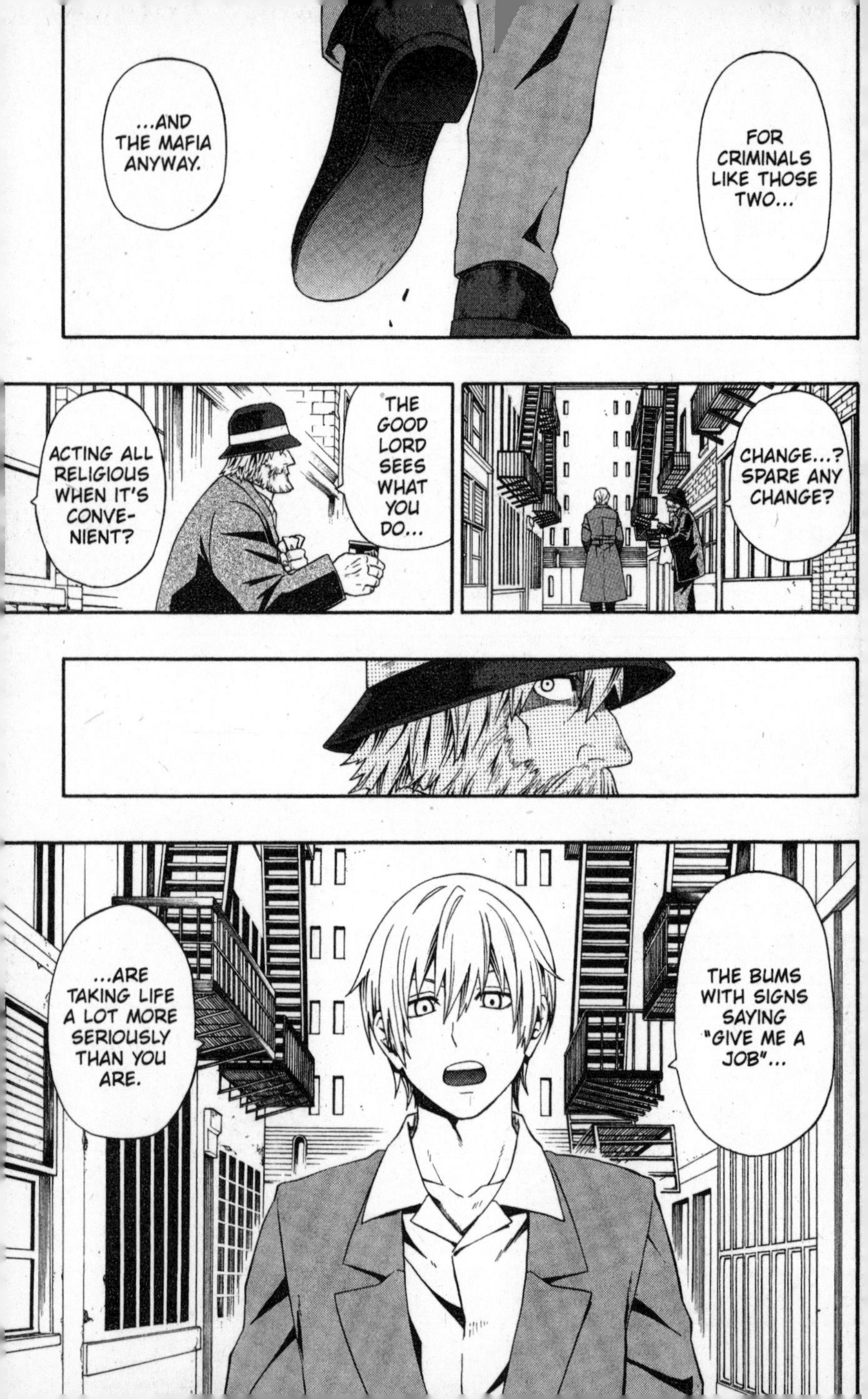
FOR CRIMINALS LIKE THOSE TWO...
...AND THE MAFIA ANYWAY.
CHANGE...? SPARE ANY CHANGE?
THE GOOD LORD SEES WHAT YOU DO...
ACTING ALL RELIGIOUS WHEN IT'S CONVE-NIENT?
THE BUMS WITH SIGNS SAYING "GIVE ME A JOB"...
...ARE TAKING LIFE A LOT MORE SERIOUSLY THAN YOU ARE.

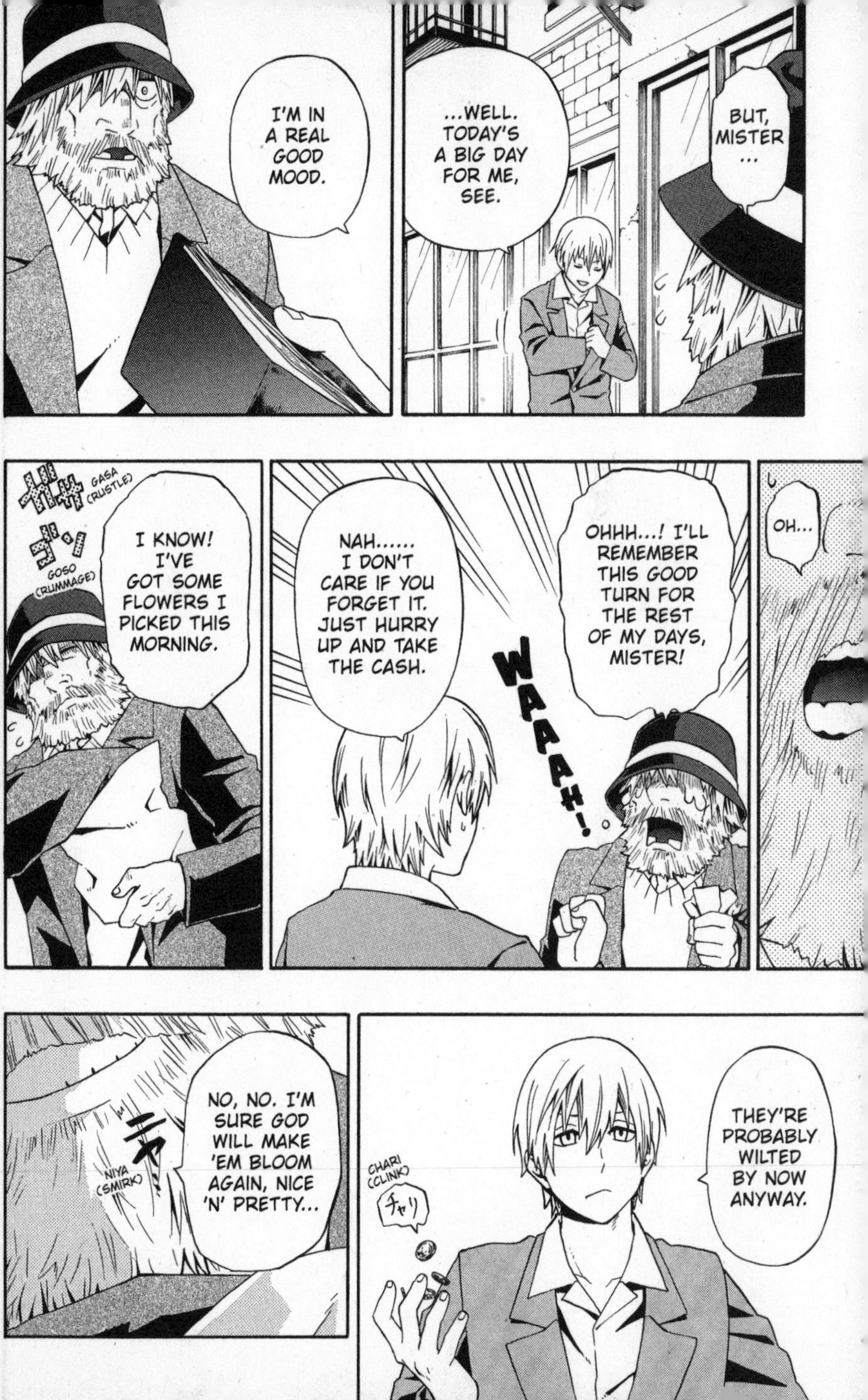
BUT, MISTER ...
...WELL. TODAY'S A BIG DAY FOR ME, SEE.
I'M IN A REAL GOOD MOOD.
OH...
OHHH...! I'LL REMEMBER THIS GOOD TURN FOR THE REST OF MY DAYS, MISTER!
WAAAAH!
NAH...... I DON'T CARE IF YOU FORGET IT. JUST HURRY UP AND TAKE THE CASH.
GASA (RUSTLE)
GOSO (RUMMAGE)
I KNOW! I'VE GOT SOME FLOWERS I PICKED THIS MORNING.
THEY'RE PROBABLY WILTED BY NOW ANYWAY.
チャリ
CHARI (CLINK)
NO, NO. I'M SURE GOD WILL MAKE 'EM BLOOM AGAIN, NICE 'N' PRETTY...
ニヤ
NIYA (SMIRK)

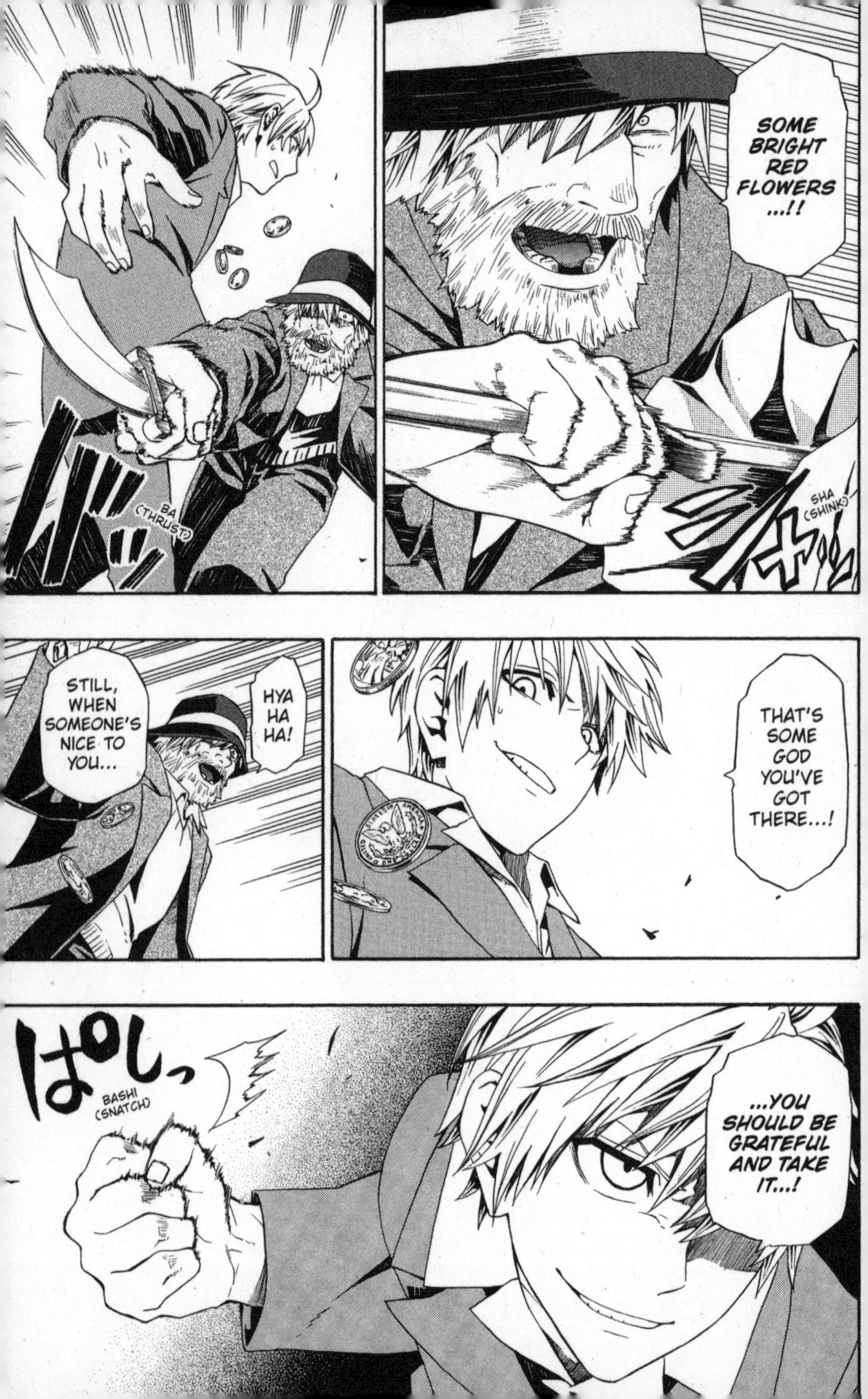
SOME BRIGHT RED FLOWERS ...!!
SHA (SHINK!)
BA (THRUST!)
THAT'S SOME GOD YOU'VE GOT THERE...!
HYA HA HA!
STILL, WHEN SOMEONE'S NICE TO YOU...
...YOU SHOULD BE GRATEFUL AND TAKE IT...!
ぱしっ
BASHI (SNATCH)

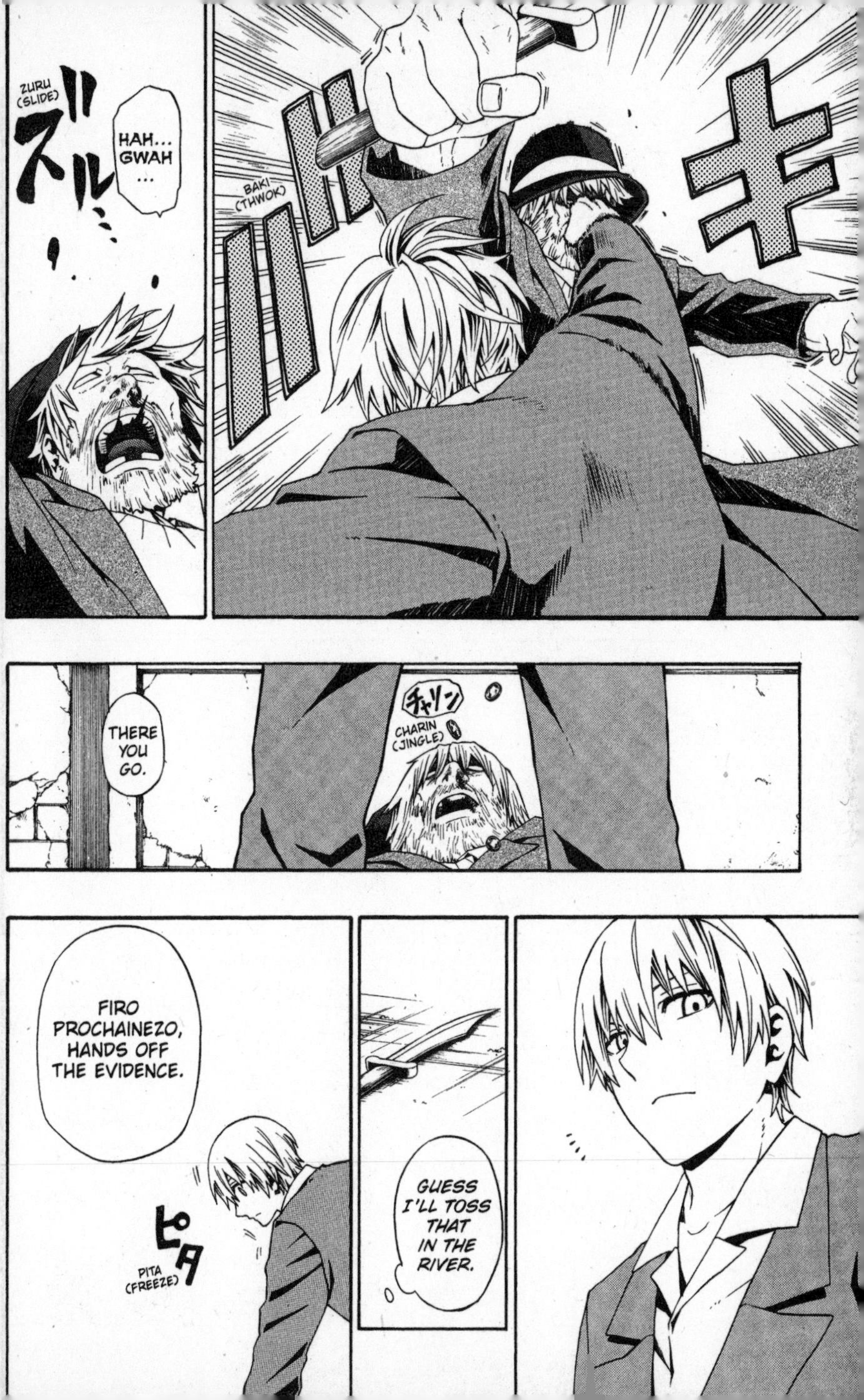
BAKI (THWOK)
ズル
ZURU (SLIDE)
HAH... GWAH ...
チャリン
CHARIN (JINGLE)
THERE YOU GO.
GUESS I'LL TOSS THAT IN THE RIVER.
FIRO PROCHAINEZO, HANDS OFF THE EVIDENCE.
ピタ
PITA (FREEZE)

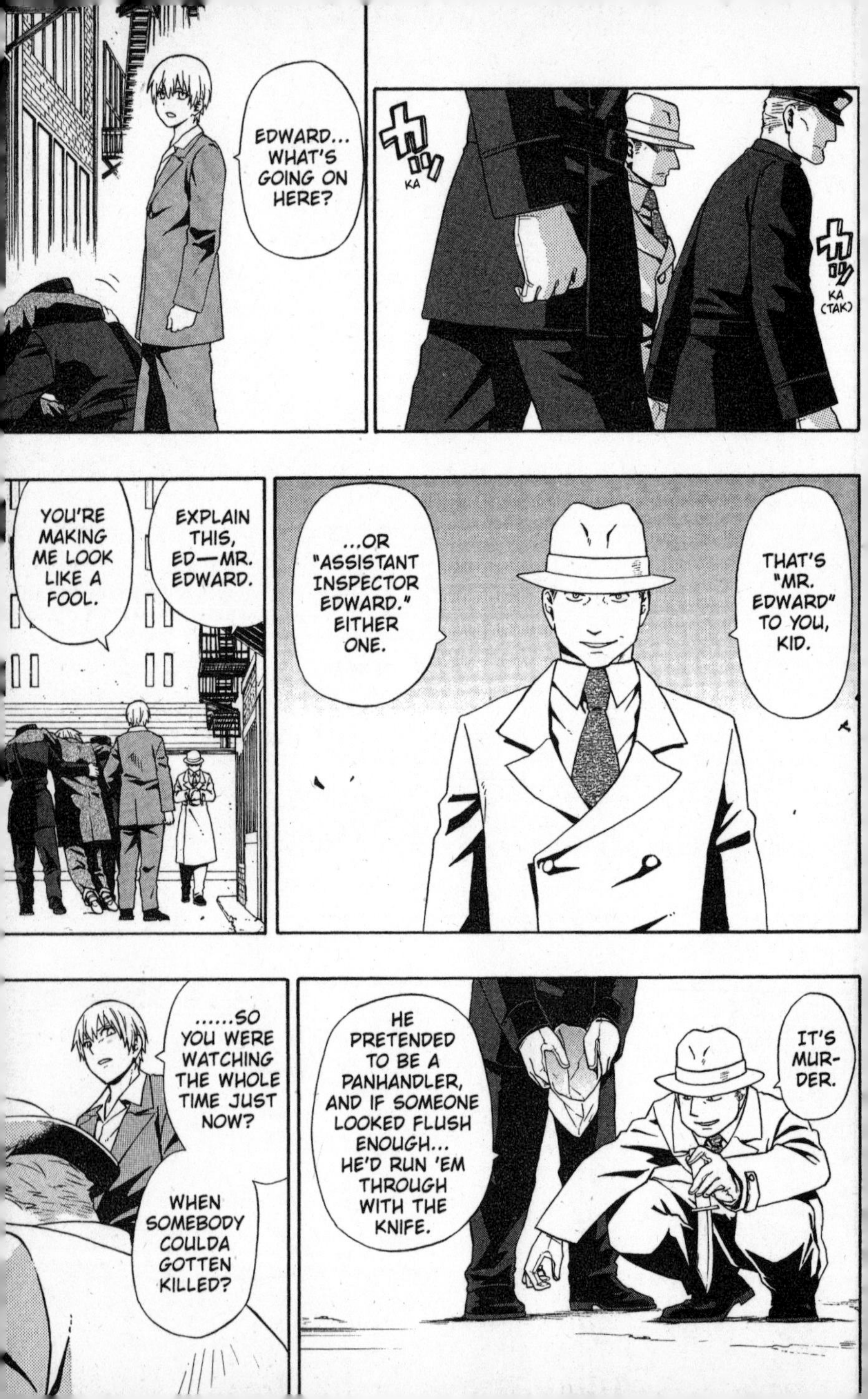

カッ
KA
カッ
KA (TAK)
EDWARD... WHAT'S GOING ON HERE?
THAT'S "MR. EDWARD" TO YOU, KID.
...OR "ASSISTANT INSPECTOR EDWARD." EITHER ONE.
EXPLAIN THIS, ED—MR. EDWARD.
YOU'RE MAKING ME LOOK LIKE A FOOL.
IT'S MURDER.
HE PRETENDED TO BE A PANHANDLER, AND IF SOMEONE LOOKED FLUSH ENOUGH... HE'D RUN 'EM THROUGH WITH THE KNIFE.
......SO YOU WERE WATCHING THE WHOLE TIME JUST NOW?
WHEN SOMEBODY COULDA GOTTEN KILLED?

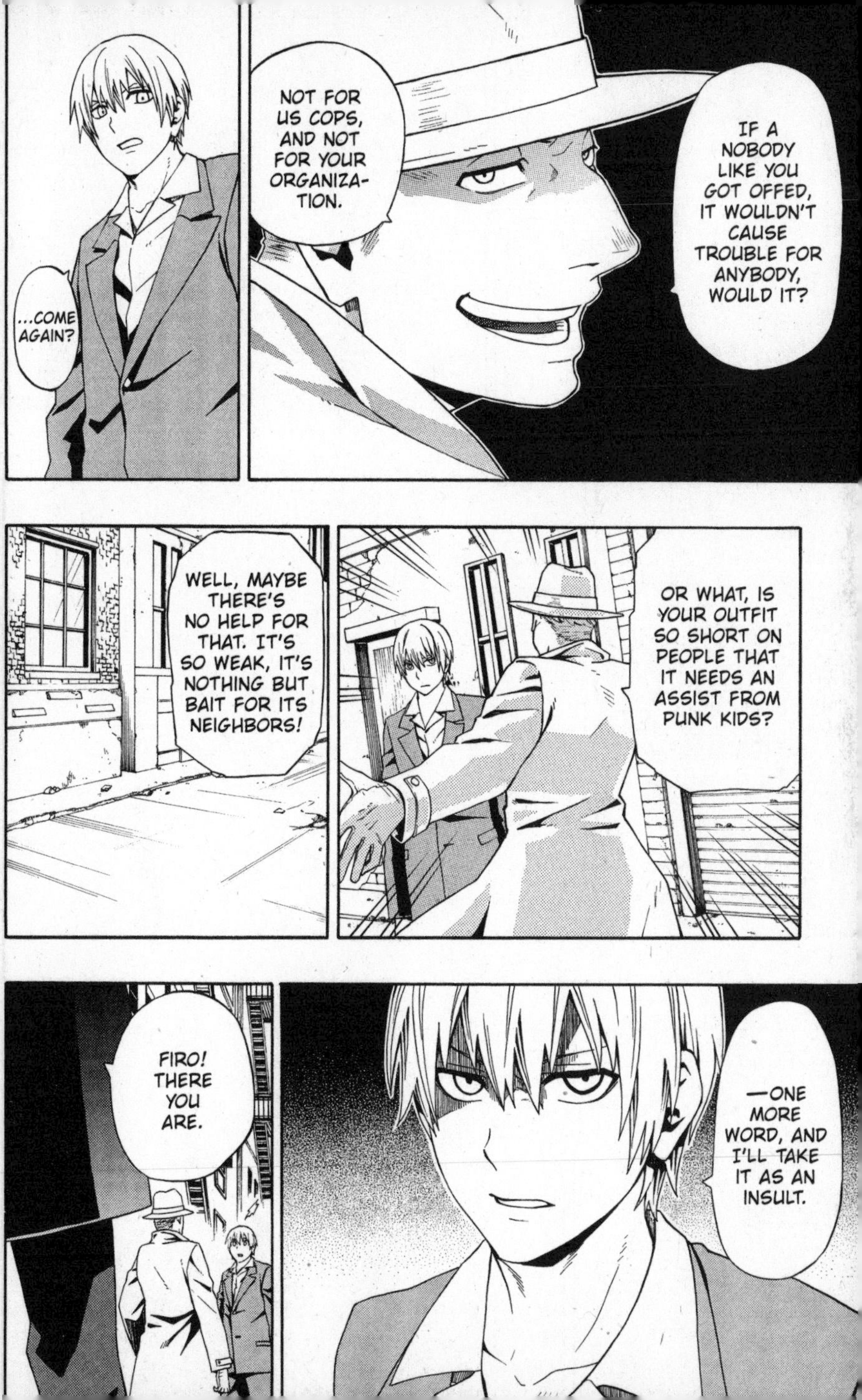
IF A NOBODY LIKE YOU GOT OFFED, IT WOULDN'T CAUSE TROUBLE FOR ANYBODY, WOULD IT?
NOT FOR US COPS, AND NOT FOR YOUR ORGANIZA-TION.
...COME AGAIN?
OR WHAT, IS YOUR OUTFIT SO SHORT ON PEOPLE THAT IT NEEDS AN ASSIST FROM PUNK KIDS?
WELL, MAYBE THERE'S NO HELP FOR THAT. IT'S SO WEAK, IT'S NOTHING BUT BAIT FOR ITS NEIGHBORS!
—ONE MORE WORD, AND I'LL TAKE IT AS AN INSULT.
FIRO! THERE YOU ARE.

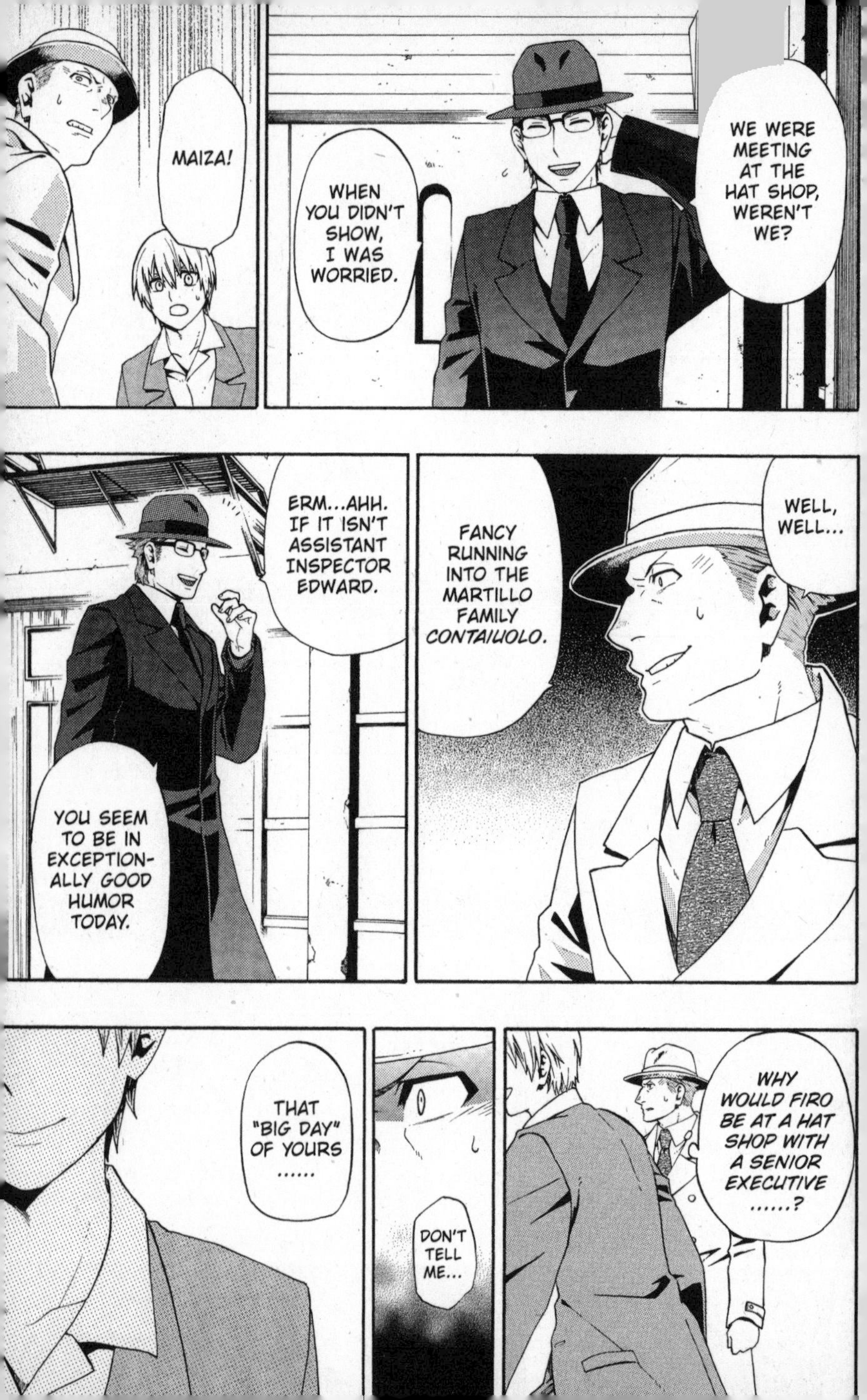
WE WERE MEETING AT THE HAT SHOP, WEREN'T WE?
WHEN YOU DIDN'T SHOW, I WAS WORRIED.
MAIZA!
WELL, WELL...
FANCY RUNNING INTO THE MARTILLO FAMILY CONTAIUOLO.
ERM...AHH. IF IT ISN'T ASSISTANT INSPECTOR EDWARD.
YOU SEEM TO BE IN EXCEPTION-ALLY GOOD HUMOR TODAY.
WHY WOULD FIRO BE AT A HAT SHOP WITH A SENIOR EXECUTIVE ......?
DON'T TELL ME...
THAT "BIG DAY" OF YOURS ......

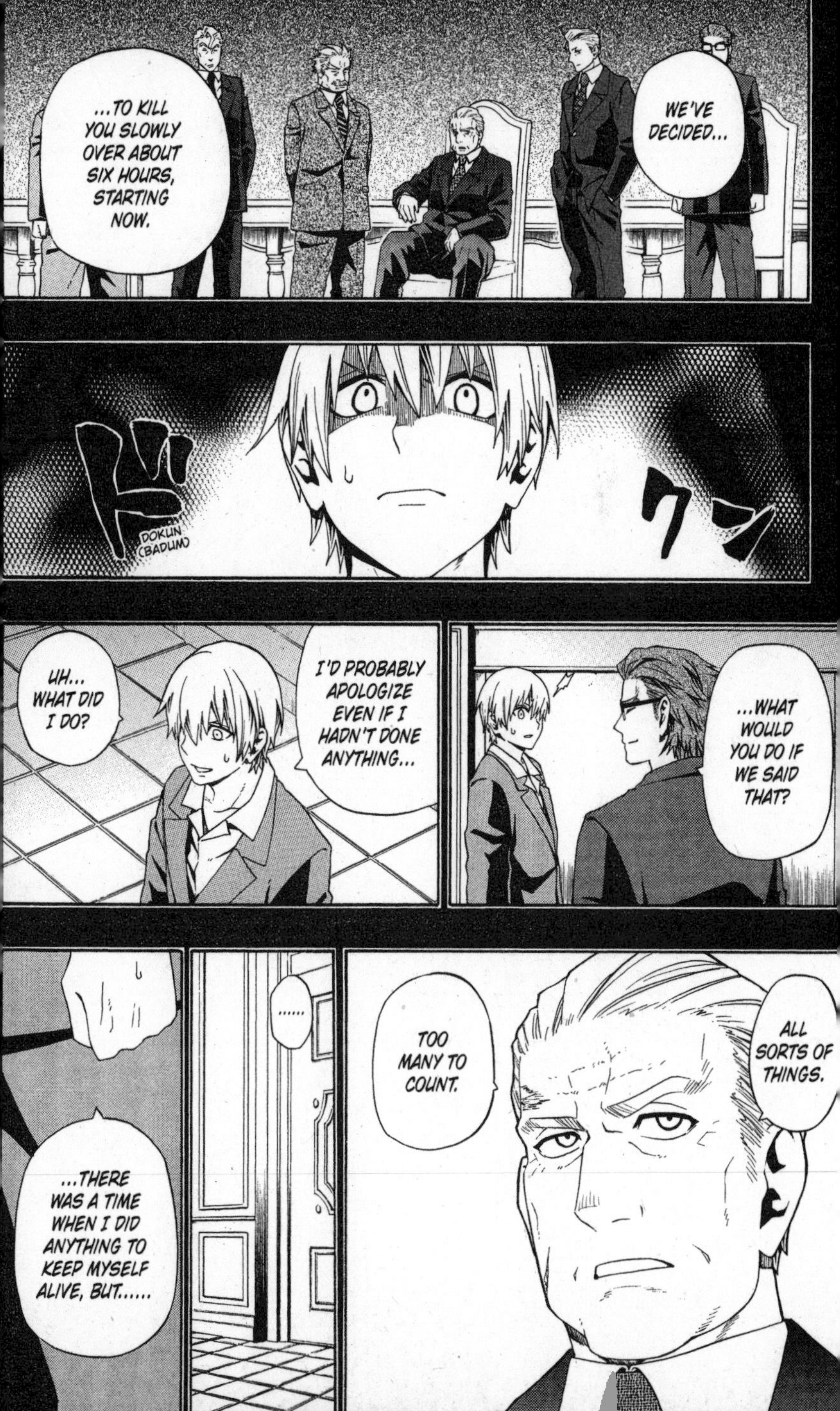
WE'VE DECIDED...
...TO KILL YOU SLOWLY OVER ABOUT SIX HOURS, STARTING NOW.
DOKUN (BADUM)
...WHAT WOULD YOU DO IF WE SAID THAT?
I'D PROBABLY APOLOGIZE EVEN IF I HADN'T DONE ANYTHING...
UH... WHAT DID I DO?
ALL SORTS OF THINGS.
TOO MANY TO COUNT.
......
...THERE WAS A TIME WHEN I DID ANYTHING TO KEEP MYSELF ALIVE, BUT.....

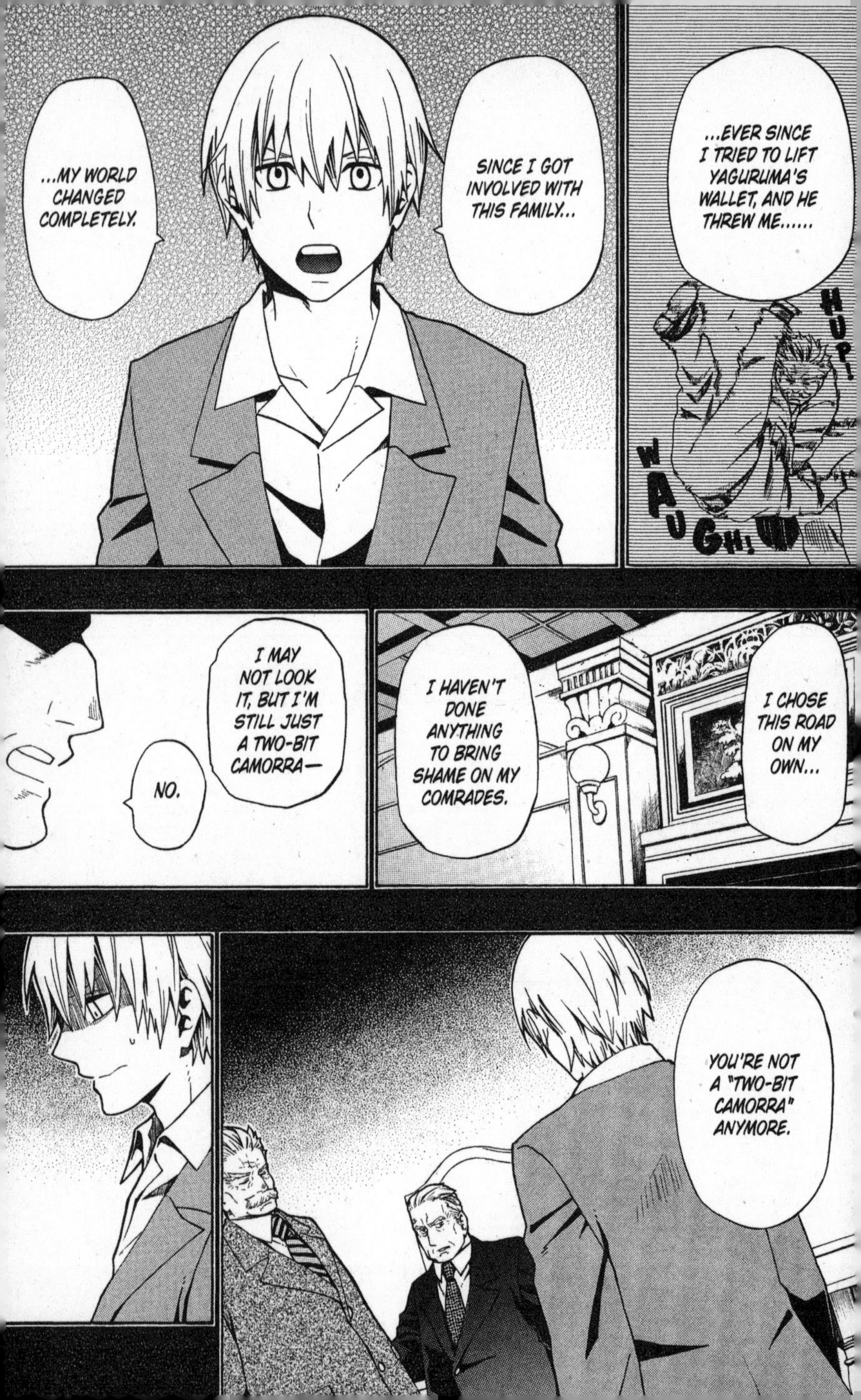
...EVER SINCE I TRIED TO LIFT YAGURUMA'S WALLET, AND HE THREW ME......
HUP!
WAUGH!
SINCE I GOT INVOLVED WITH THIS FAMILY...
...MY WORLD CHANGED COMPLETELY.
I CHOSE THIS ROAD ON MY OWN...
I HAVEN'T DONE ANYTHING TO BRING SHAME ON MY COMRADES.
I MAY NOT LOOK IT, BUT I'M STILL JUST A TWO-BIT CAMORRA—
NO.
YOU'RE NOT A "TWO-BIT CAMORRA" ANYMORE.

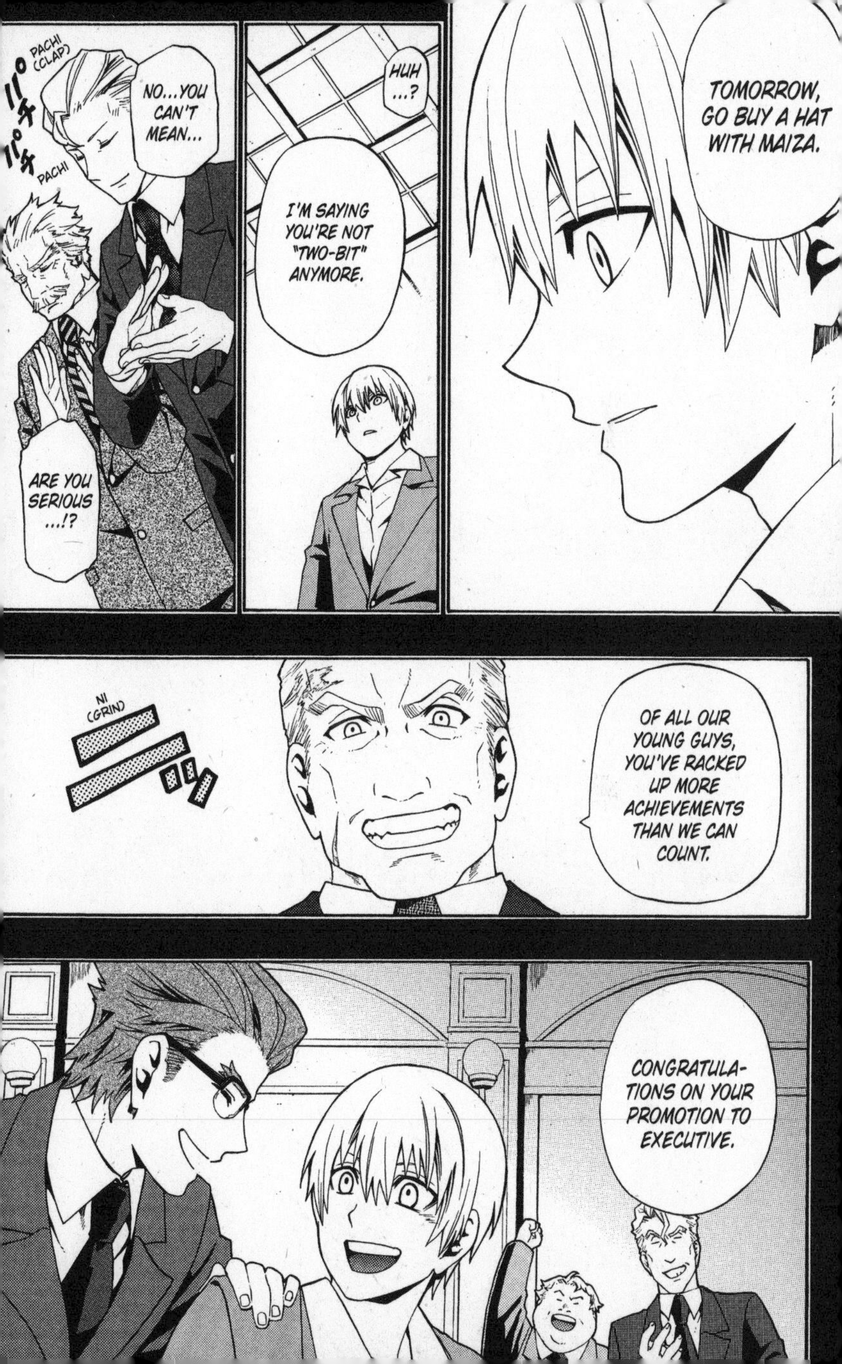
TOMORROW, GO BUY A HAT WITH MAIZA.
HUH ...?
I'M SAYING YOU'RE NOT "TWO-BIT" ANYMORE.
PACHI (CLAP)
PACHI
NO...YOU CAN'T MEAN...
ARE YOU SERIOUS ...!?
OF ALL OUR YOUNG GUYS, YOU'VE RACKED UP MORE ACHIEVEMENTS THAN WE CAN COUNT.
NI (GRIN)
CONGRATULATIONS ON YOUR PROMOTION TO EXECUTIVE.

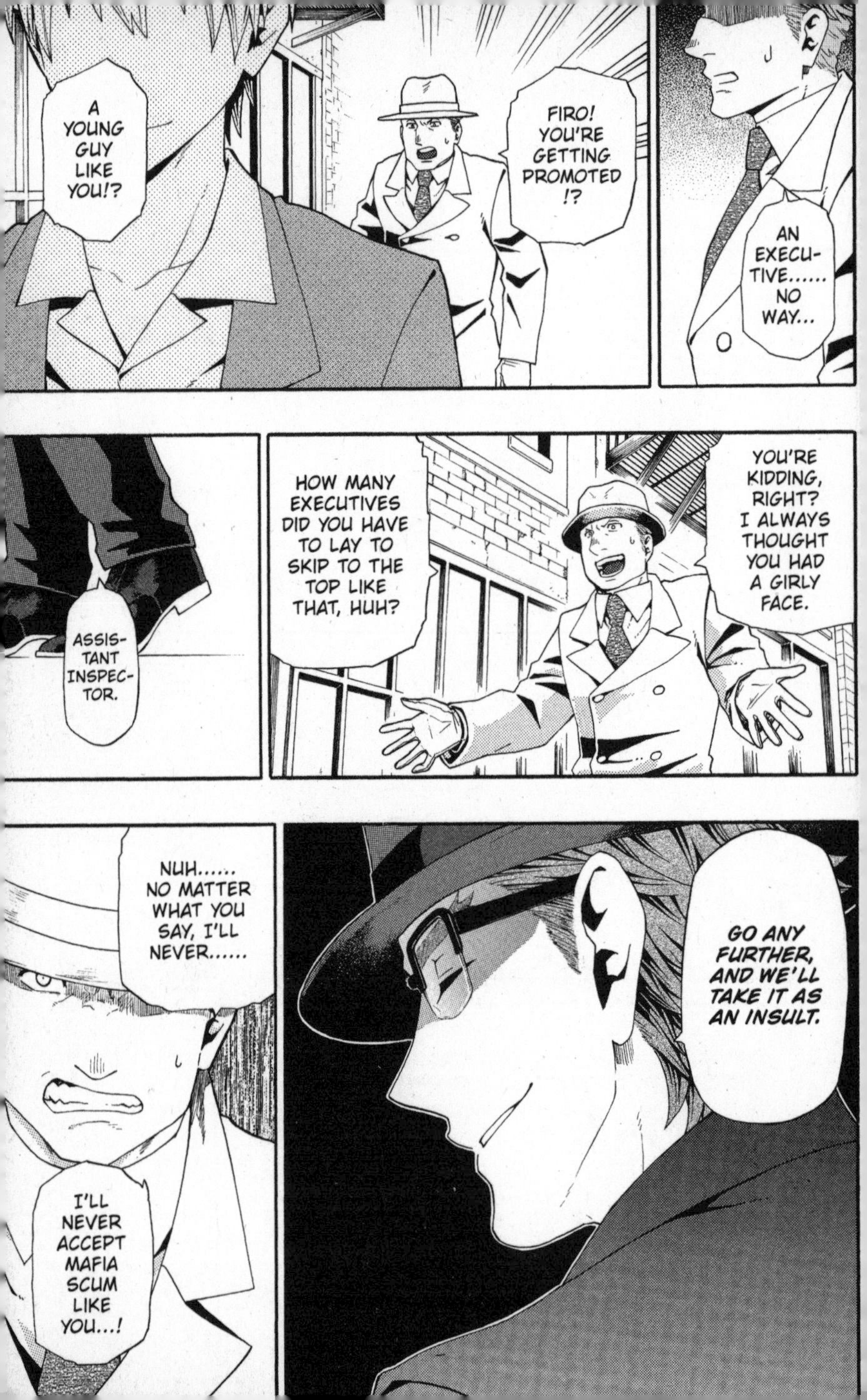
AN EXECUTIVE...... NO WAY...
FIRO! YOU'RE GETTING PROMOTED !?
A YOUNG GUY LIKE YOU!?
YOU'RE KIDDING, RIGHT? I ALWAYS THOUGHT YOU HAD A GIRLY FACE.
HOW MANY EXECUTIVES DID YOU HAVE TO LAY TO SKIP TO THE TOP LIKE THAT, HUH?
ASSISTANT INSPECTOR.
GO ANY FURTHER, AND WE'LL TAKE IT AS AN INSULT.
NUH...... NO MATTER WHAT YOU SAY, I'LL NEVER......
I'LL NEVER ACCEPT MAFIA SCUM LIKE YOU...!

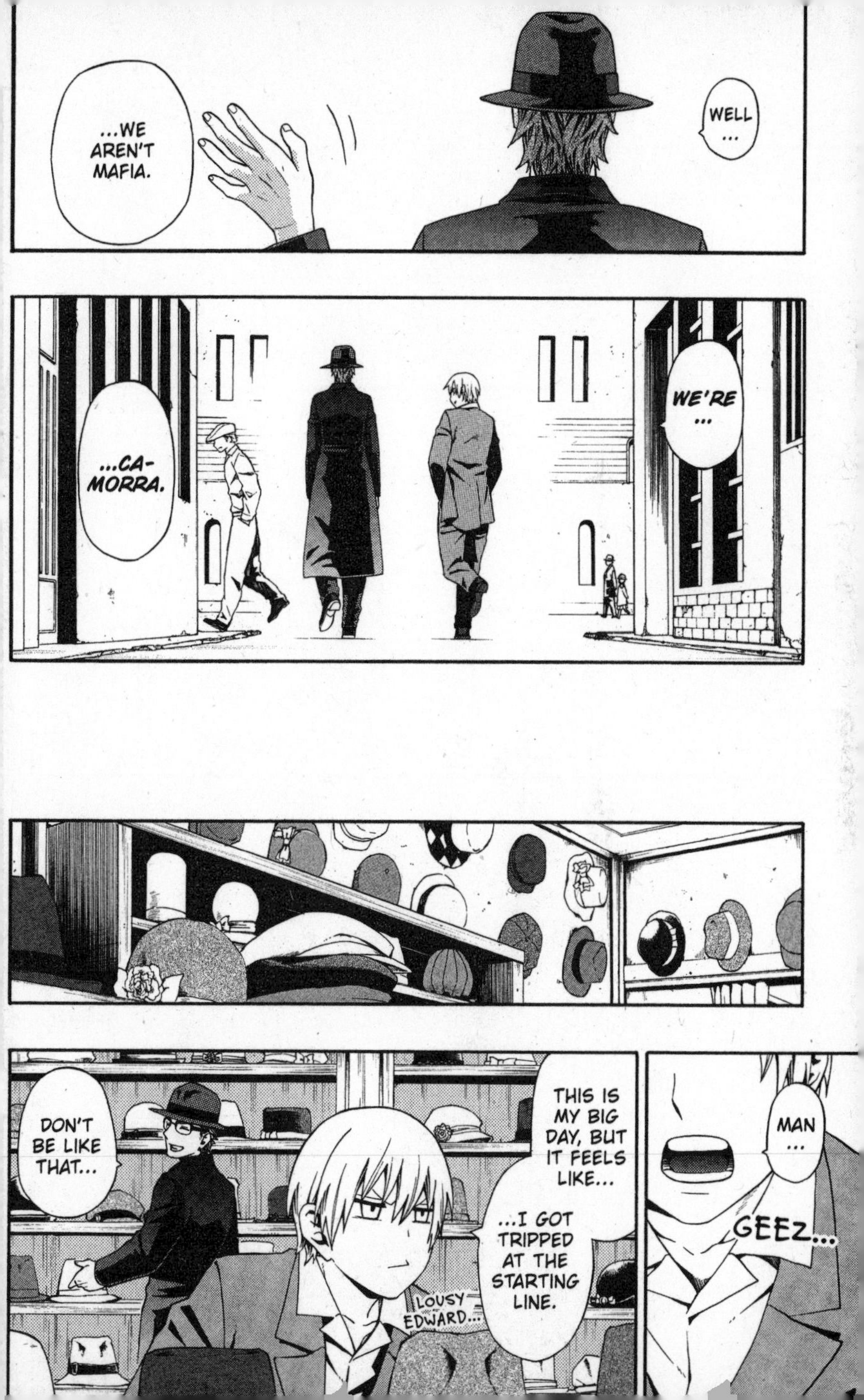
WELL ...
...WE AREN'T MAFIA.
WE'RE ...
...CA-MORRA.
MAN ...
GEEZ...
THIS IS MY BIG DAY, BUT IT FEELS LIKE...
...I GOT TRIPPED AT THE STARTING LINE.
LOUSY EDWARD...
DON'T BE LIKE THAT...

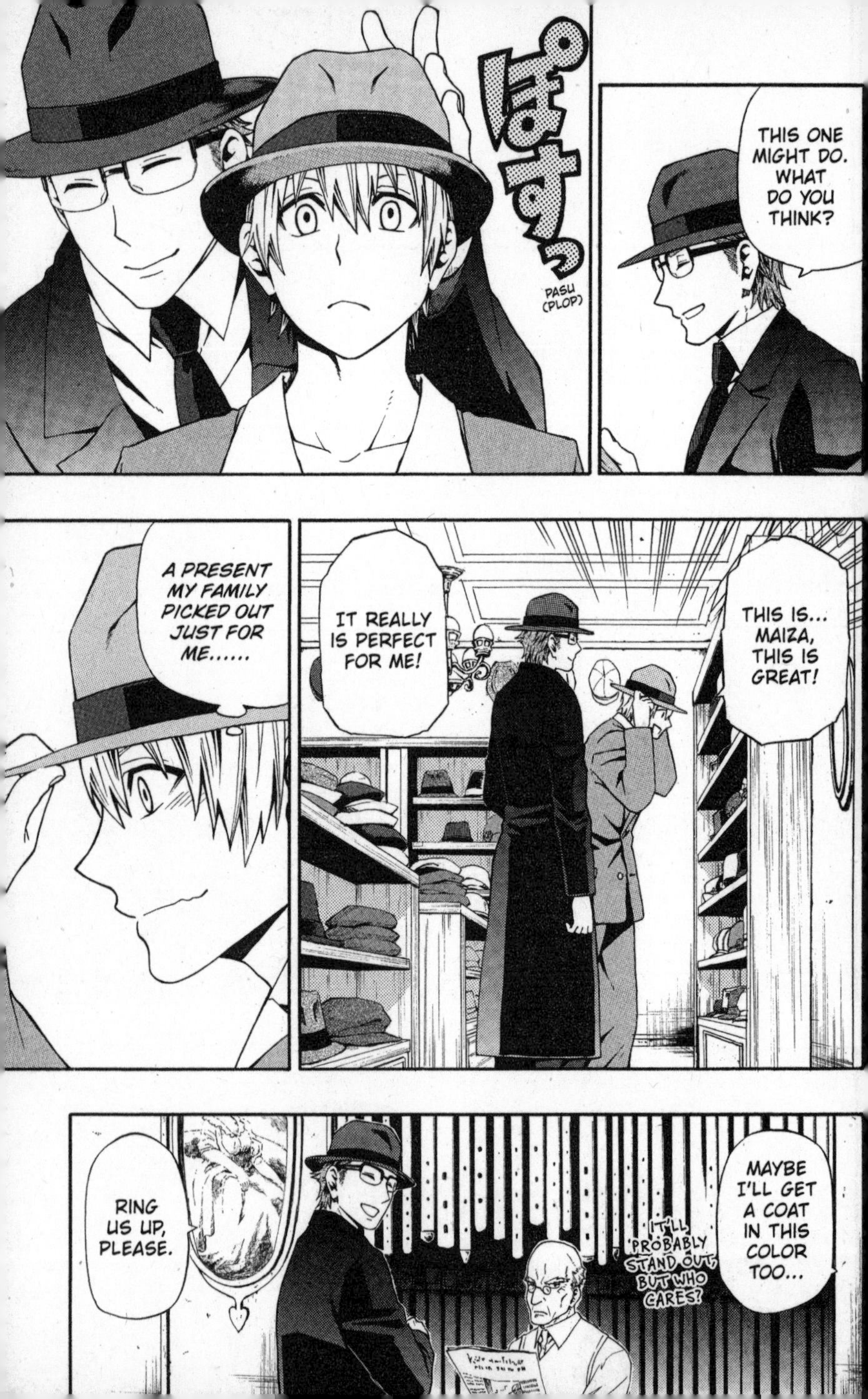
THIS ONE MIGHT DO. WHAT DO YOU THINK?
ぽすっ
PASU (PLOP)
THIS IS... MAIZA, THIS IS GREAT!
IT REALLY IS PERFECT FOR ME!
A PRESENT MY FAMILY PICKED OUT JUST FOR ME......
MAYBE I'LL GET A COAT IN THIS COLOR TOO...
IT'LL PROBABLY STAND OUT, BUT WHO CARES?
RING US UP, PLEASE.

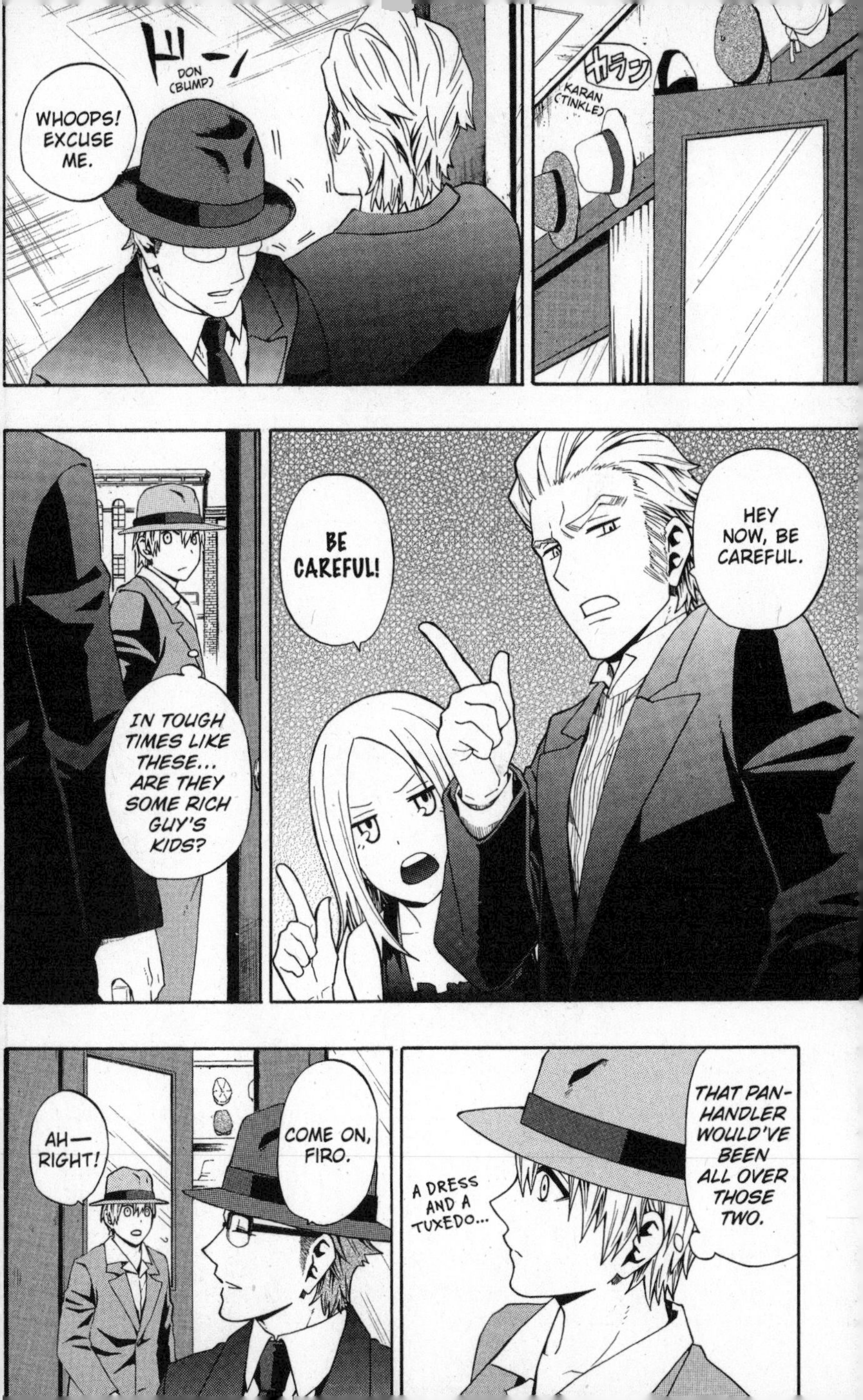
カラン
KARAN (TINKLE)
ドーン
DON (BUMP)
WHOOPS! EXCUSE ME.
HEY NOW, BE CAREFUL.
BE CAREFUL!
IN TOUGH TIMES LIKE THESE... ARE THEY SOME RICH GUY'S KIDS?
THAT PAN-HANDLER WOULD'VE BEEN ALL OVER THOSE TWO.
A DRESS AND A TUXEDO...
COME ON, FIRO.
AH—RIGHT!

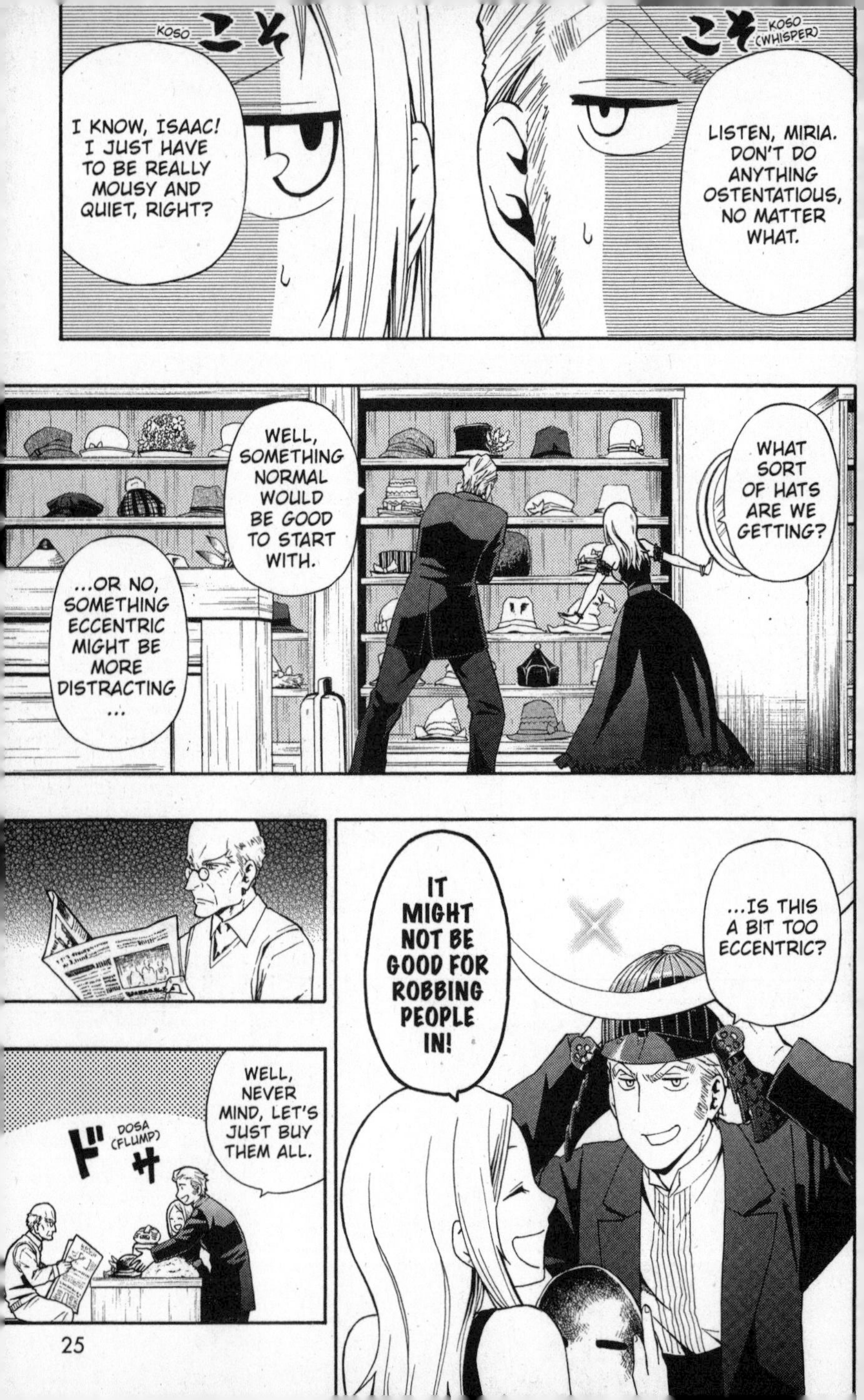
こそ KOSO (WHISPER)
LISTEN, MIRIA. DON'T DO ANYTHING OSTENTATIOUS, NO MATTER WHAT.
こそ KOSO
I KNOW, ISAAC! I JUST HAVE TO BE REALLY MOUSY AND QUIET, RIGHT?
WHAT SORT OF HATS ARE WE GETTING?
WELL, SOMETHING NORMAL WOULD BE GOOD TO START WITH.
...OR NO, SOMETHING ECCENTRIC MIGHT BE MORE DISTRACTING...
...IS THIS A BIT TOO ECCENTRIC?
IT MIGHT NOT BE GOOD FOR ROBBING PEOPLE IN!
WELL, NEVER MIND, LET'S JUST BUY THEM ALL.
ドサ DOSA (FLUMP)

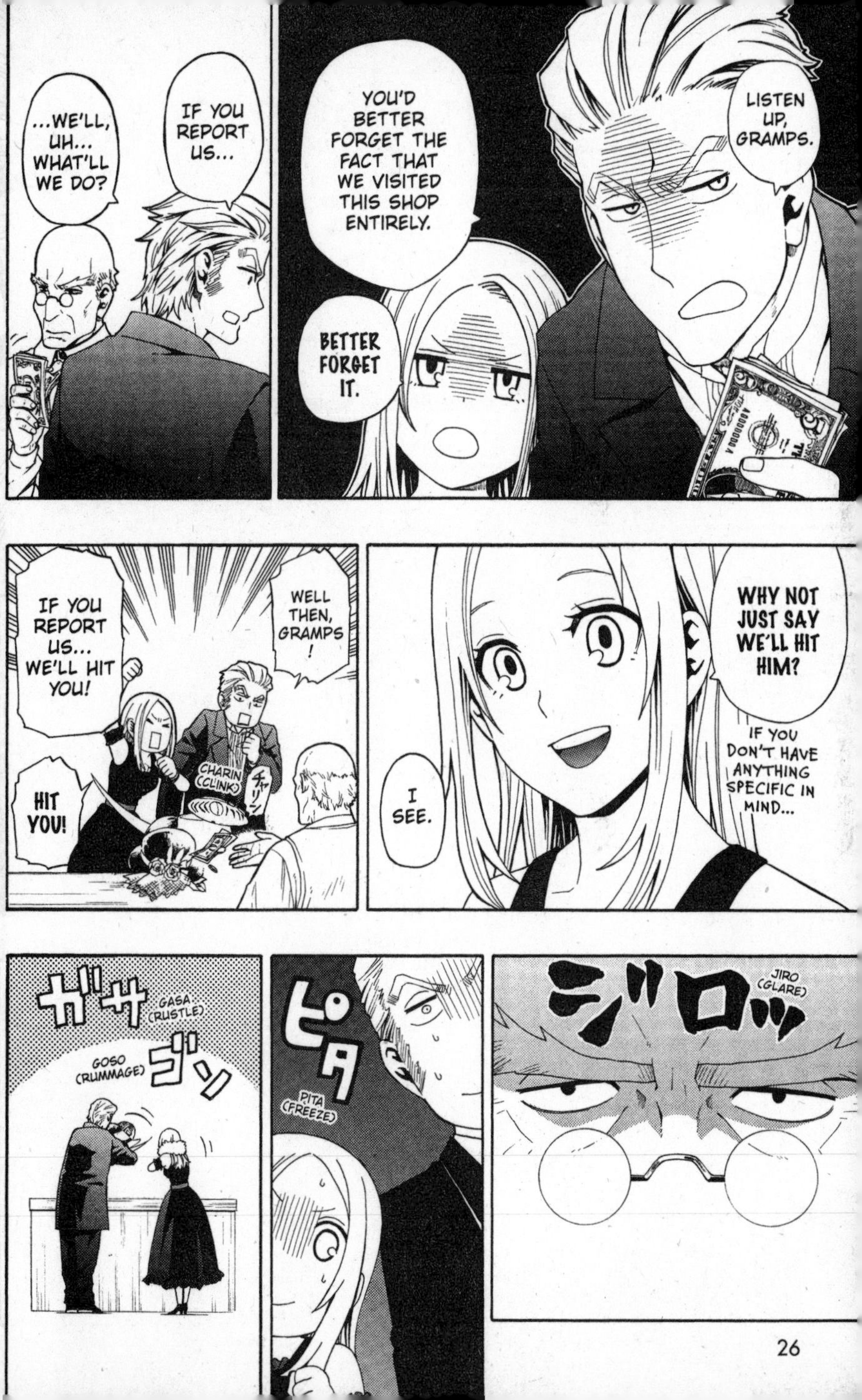
LISTEN UP, GRAMPS.
YOU'D BETTER FORGET THE FACT THAT WE VISITED THIS SHOP ENTIRELY.
BETTER FORGET IT.
IF YOU REPORT US...
...WE'LL, UH... WHAT'LL WE DO?
WHY NOT JUST SAY WE'LL HIT HIM?
IF YOU DON'T HAVE ANYTHING SPECIFIC IN MIND...
I SEE.
WELL THEN, GRAMPS!
IF YOU REPORT US... WE'LL HIT YOU!
チャリン
CHARIN (CLINK)
HIT YOU!
ジロッ
JIRO (GLARE)
ピタ
PITA (FREEZE)
ガサ
GASA (RUSTLE)
ゴソッ
GOSO (RUMMAGE)

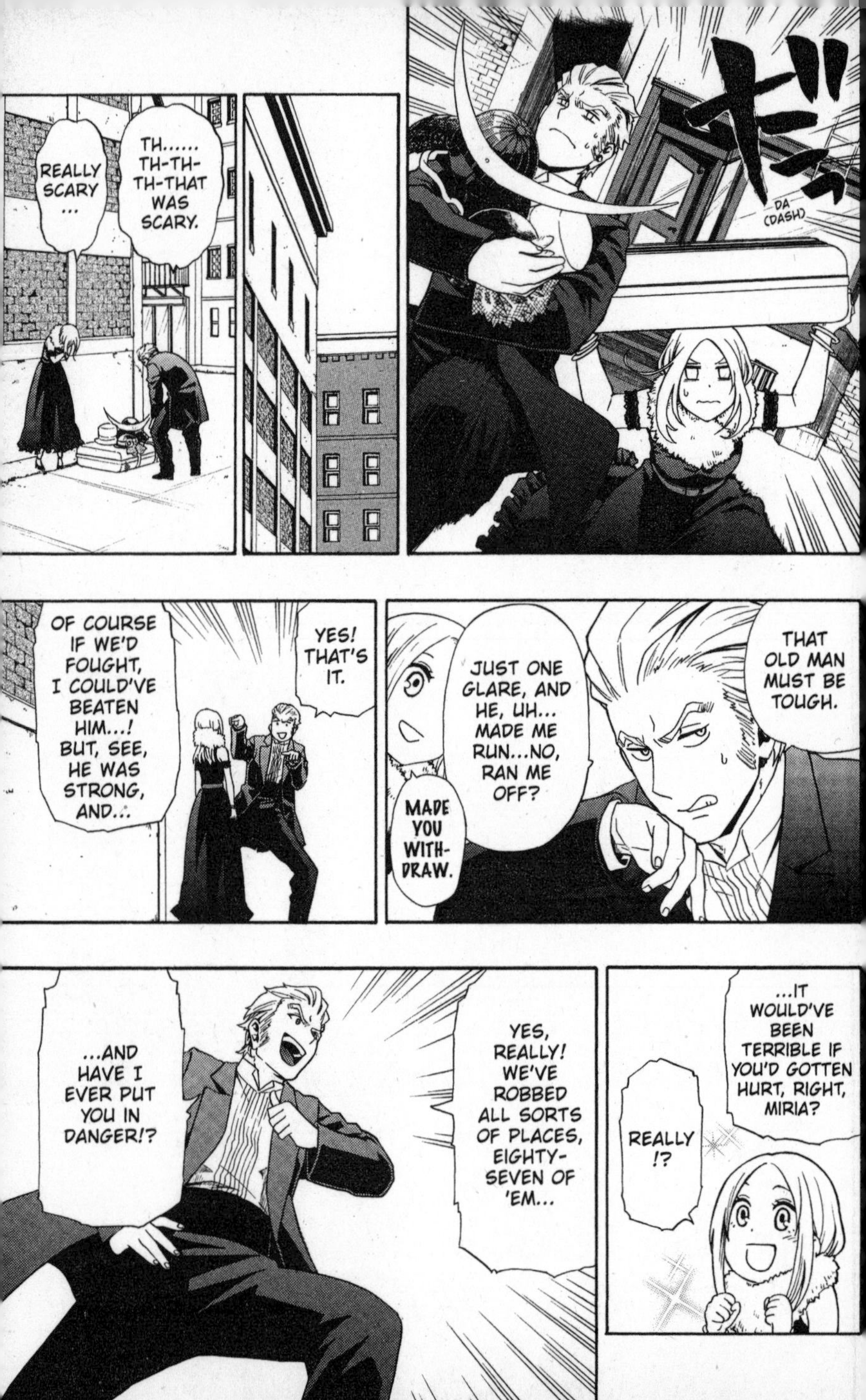
DA (DASH)
TH...... TH-TH-TH-THAT WAS SCARY.
REALLY SCARY ...
THAT OLD MAN MUST BE TOUGH.
JUST ONE GLARE, AND HE, UH... MADE ME RUN...NO, RAN ME OFF?
MADE YOU WITH-DRAW.
YES! THAT'S IT.
OF COURSE IF WE'D FOUGHT, I COULD'VE BEATEN HIM...! BUT, SEE, HE WAS STRONG, AND...
...IT WOULD'VE BEEN TERRIBLE IF YOU'D GOTTEN HURT, RIGHT, MIRIA?
REALLY !?
YES, REALLY! WE'VE ROBBED ALL SORTS OF PLACES, EIGHTY-SEVEN OF 'EM...
...AND HAVE I EVER PUT YOU IN DANGER!?

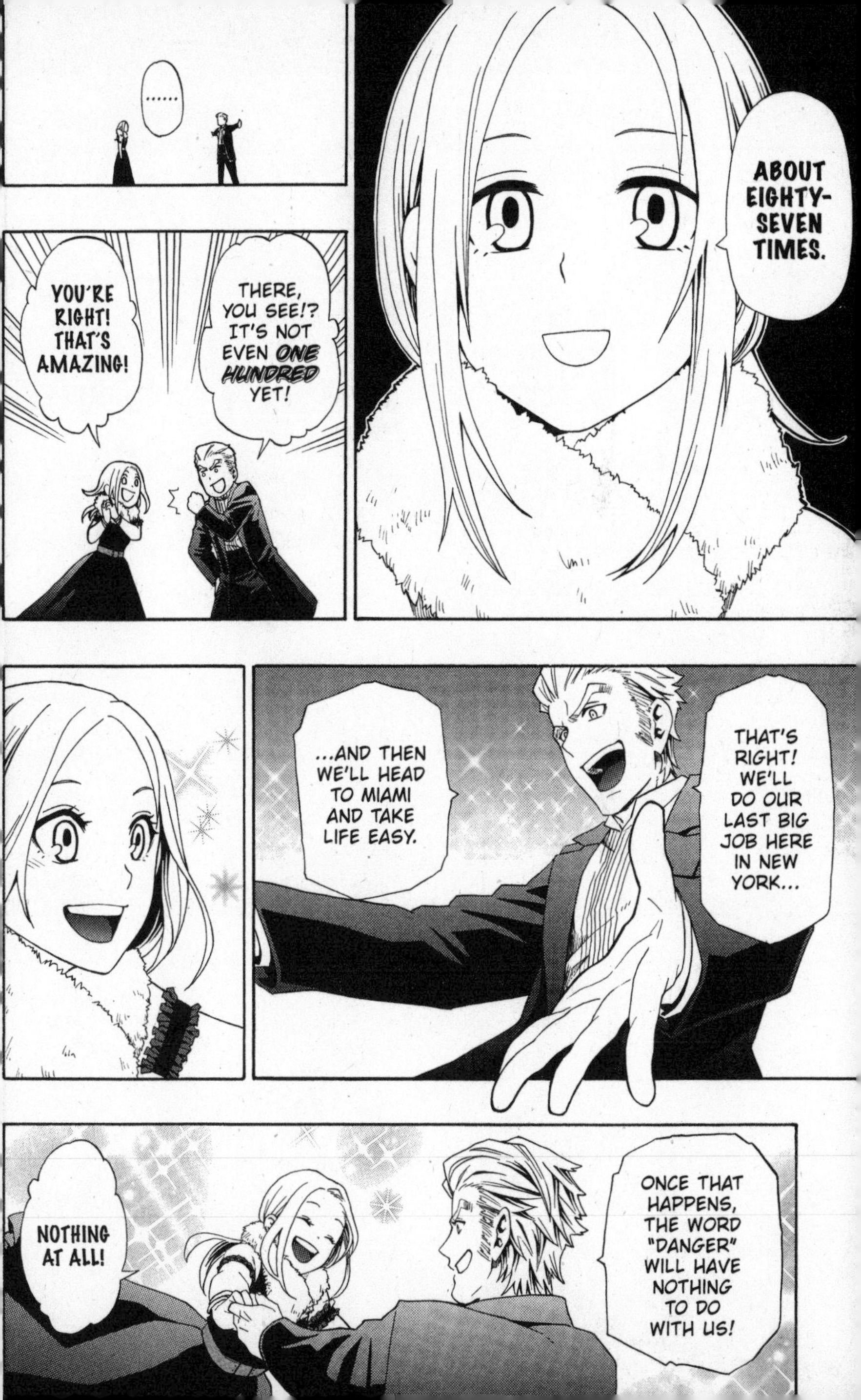
ABOUT EIGHTY-SEVEN TIMES.
......
THERE, YOU SEE!? IT'S NOT EVEN ONE HUNDRED YET!
YOU'RE RIGHT! THAT'S AMAZING!
THAT'S RIGHT! WE'LL DO OUR LAST BIG JOB HERE IN NEW YORK...
...AND THEN WE'LL HEAD TO MIAMI AND TAKE LIFE EASY.
ONCE THAT HAPPENS, THE WORD "DANGER" WILL HAVE NOTHING TO DO WITH US!
NOTHING AT ALL!

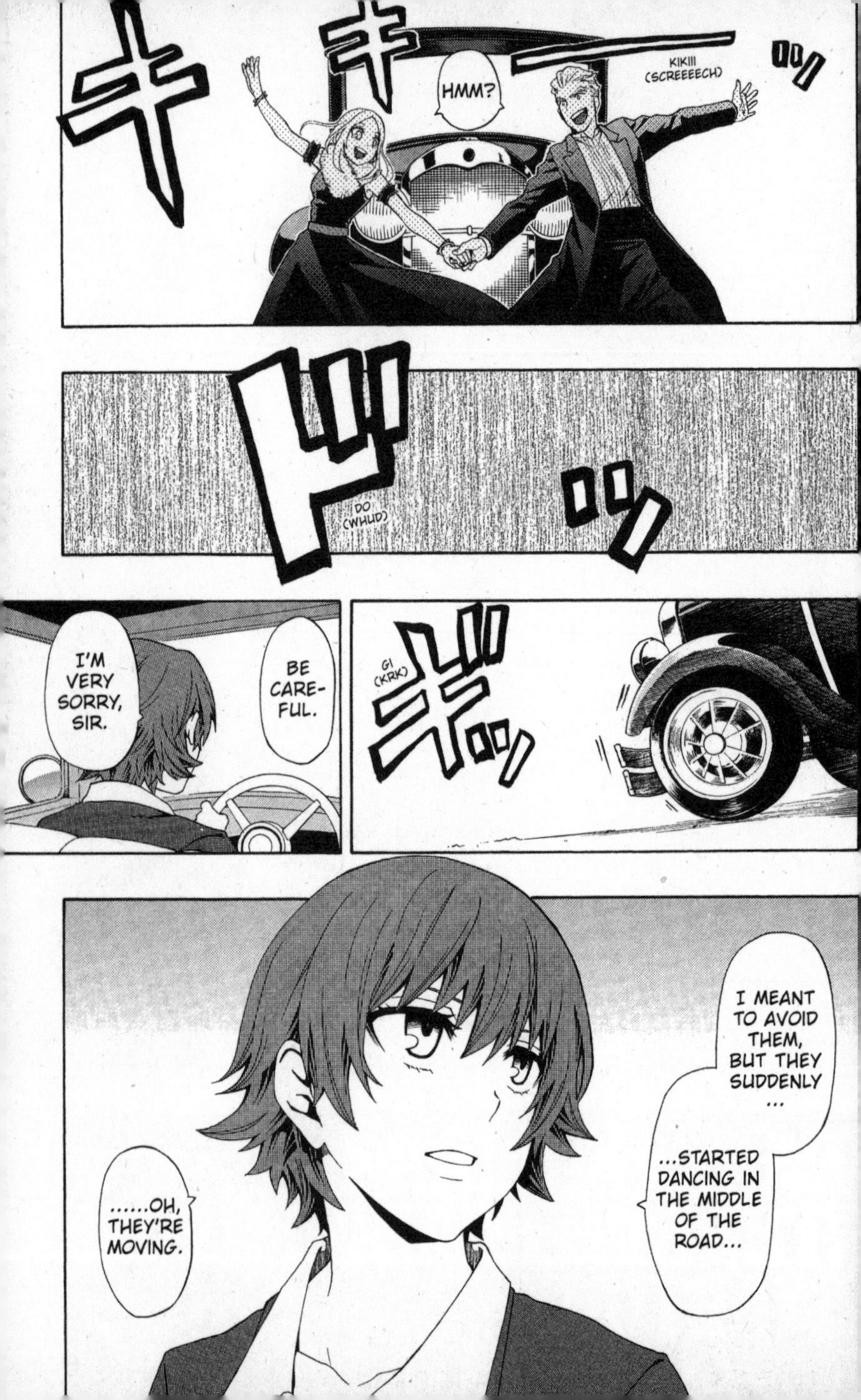
KIKIII (SCREEEECH)
HMM?
DO (WHUD)
GI (KRK)
BE CARE-FUL.
I'M VERY SORRY, SIR.
I MEANT TO AVOID THEM, BUT THEY SUDDENLY...
...STARTED DANCING IN THE MIDDLE OF THE ROAD...
......OH, THEY'RE MOVING.

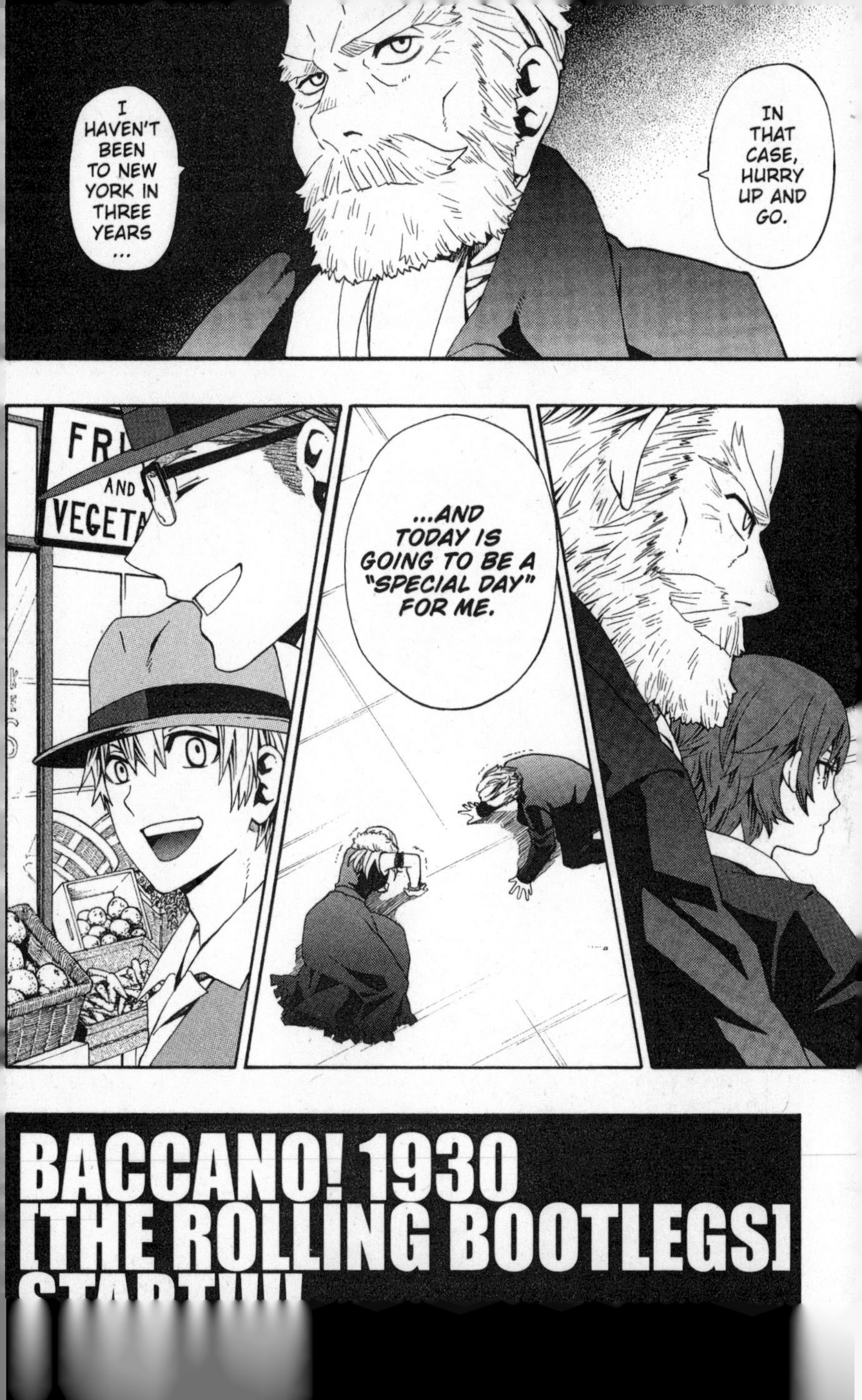
IN THAT CASE, HURRY UP AND GO.
I HAVEN'T BEEN TO NEW YORK IN THREE YEARS...
...AND TODAY IS GOING TO BE A "SPECIAL DAY" FOR ME.

BACCANO! 1930 [THE ROLLING BOOTLEGS] START!!!

#7 Encounter

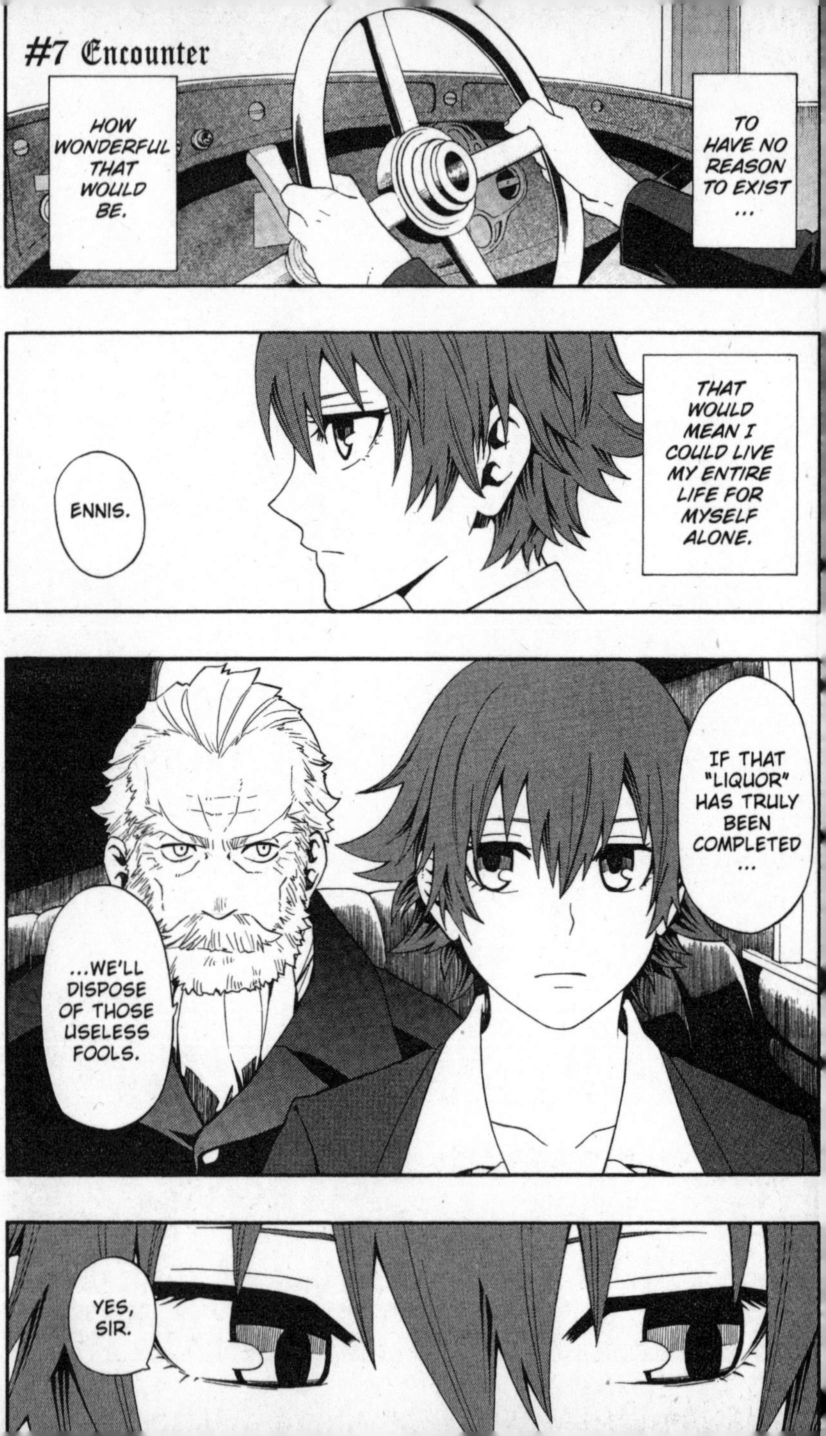
TO HAVE NO REASON TO EXIST...
HOW WONDERFUL THAT WOULD BE.
THAT WOULD MEAN I COULD LIVE MY ENTIRE LIFE FOR MYSELF ALONE.
ENNIS.
IF THAT "LIQUOR" HAS TRULY BEEN COMPLETED...
...WE'LL DISPOSE OF THOSE USELESS FOOLS.
YES, SIR.

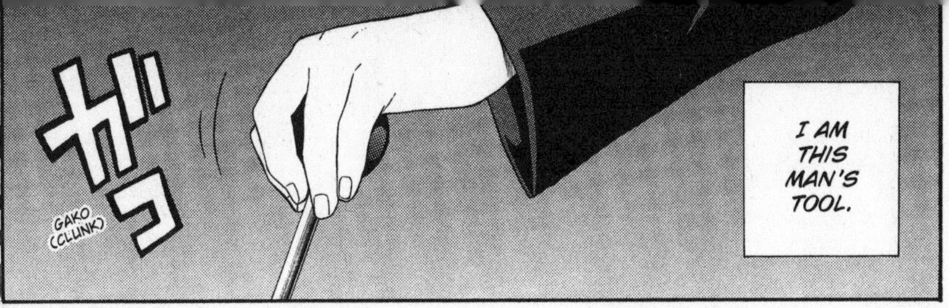
I AM THIS MAN'S TOOL.
ガコ
GAKO (CLUNK)

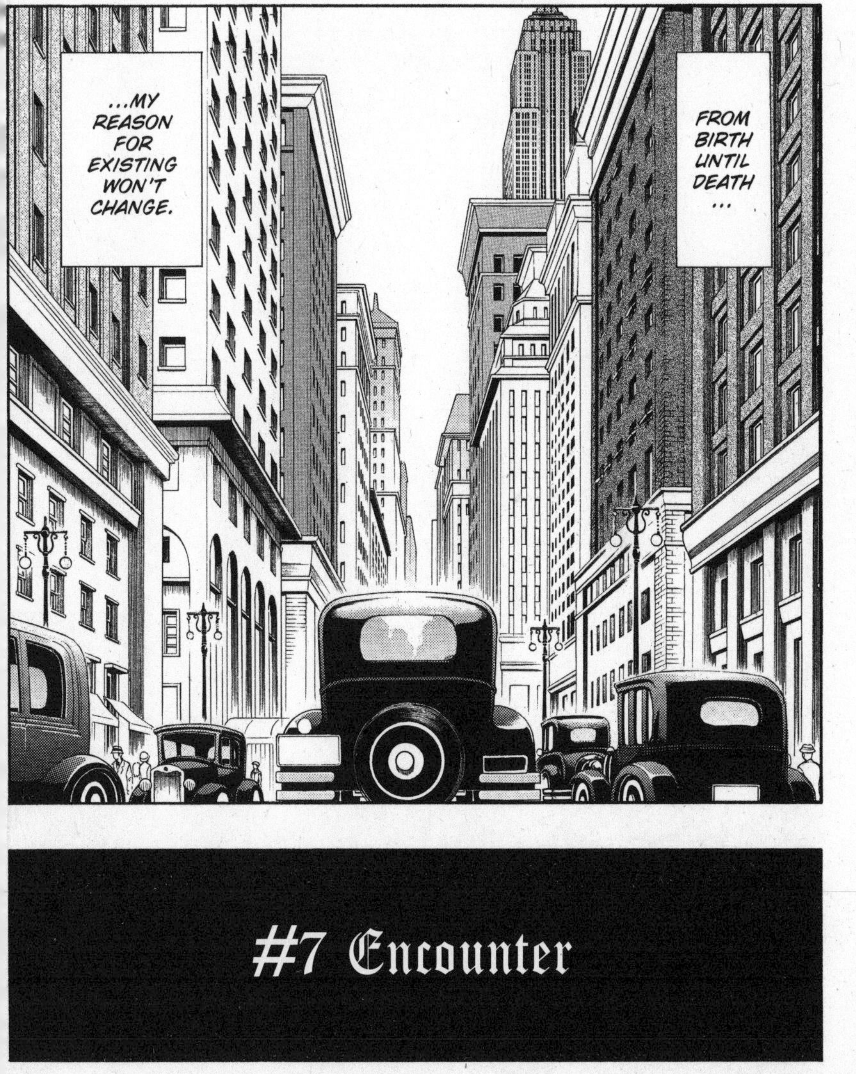
FROM BIRTH UNTIL DEATH ...
...MY REASON FOR EXISTING WON'T CHANGE.

#7 Encounter

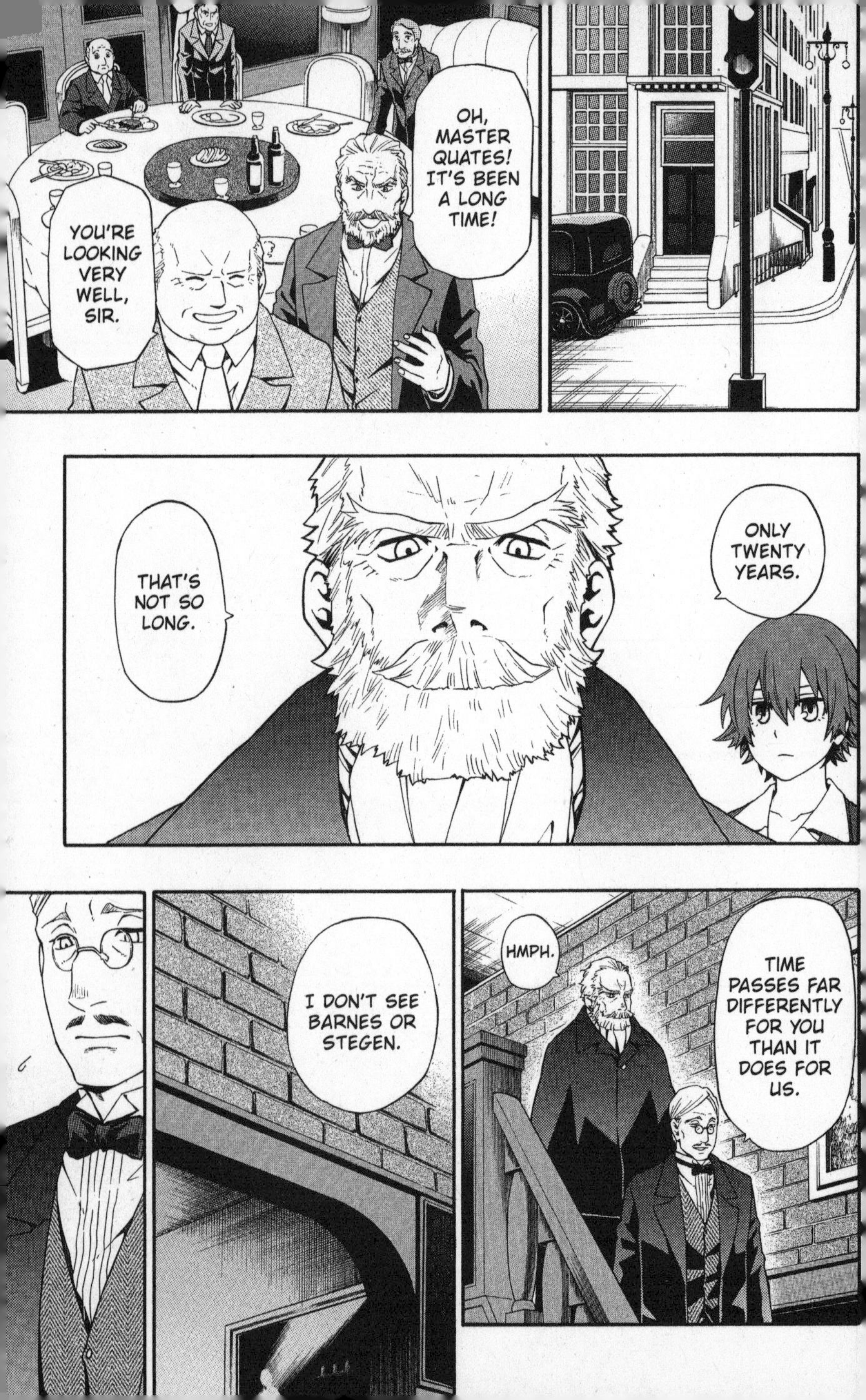
OH, MASTER QUATES! IT'S BEEN A LONG TIME!
YOU'RE LOOKING VERY WELL, SIR.
ONLY TWENTY YEARS.
THAT'S NOT SO LONG.
TIME PASSES FAR DIFFERENTLY FOR YOU THAN IT DOES FOR US.
HMPH.
I DON'T SEE BARNES OR STEGEN.

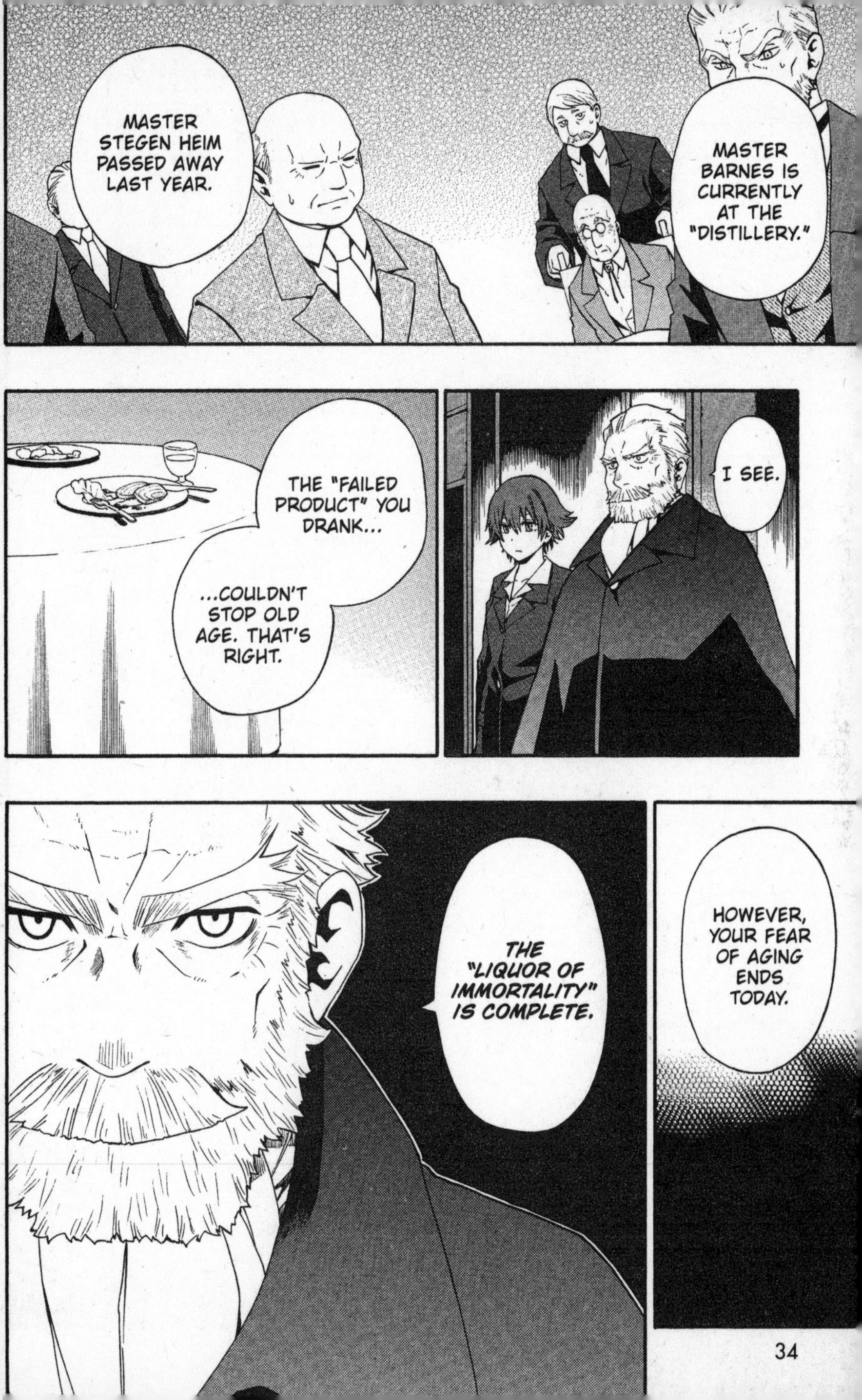
MASTER BARNES IS CURRENTLY AT THE "DISTILLERY."
MASTER STEGEN HEIM PASSED AWAY LAST YEAR.
I SEE.
THE "FAILED PRODUCT" YOU DRANK...
...COULDN'T STOP OLD AGE. THAT'S RIGHT.
HOWEVER, YOUR FEAR OF AGING ENDS TODAY.
THE "LIQUOR OF IMMORTALITY" IS COMPLETE.

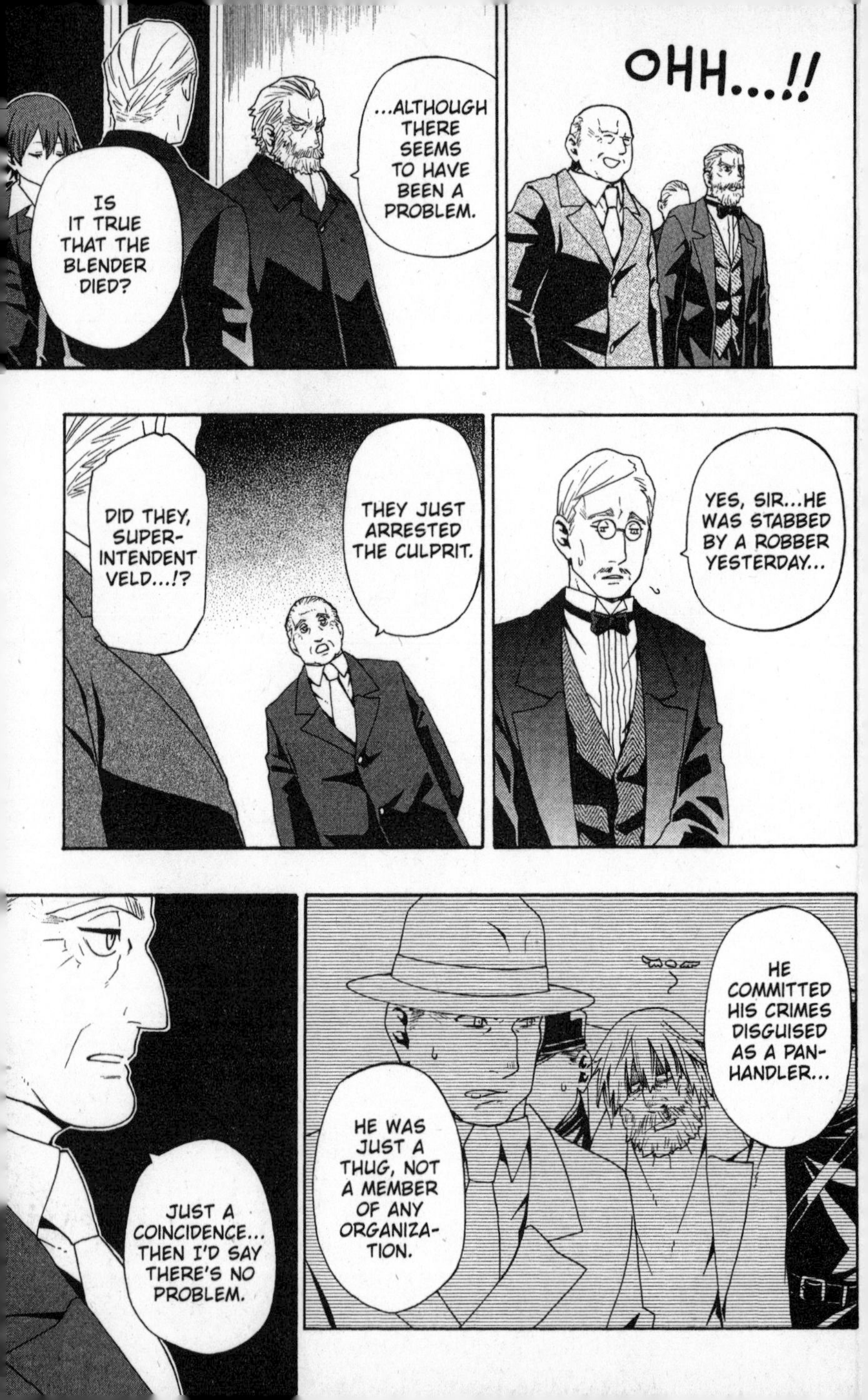
OHH...!!
...ALTHOUGH THERE SEEMS TO HAVE BEEN A PROBLEM.
IS IT TRUE THAT THE BLENDER DIED?
YES, SIR...HE WAS STABBED BY A ROBBER YESTERDAY...
THEY JUST ARRESTED THE CULPRIT.
DID THEY, SUPER-INTENDENT VELD...!?
HE COMMITTED HIS CRIMES DISGUISED AS A PAN-HANDLER...
HE WAS JUST A THUG, NOT A MEMBER OF ANY ORGANIZA-TION.
JUST A COINCIDENCE... THEN I'D SAY THERE'S NO PROBLEM.

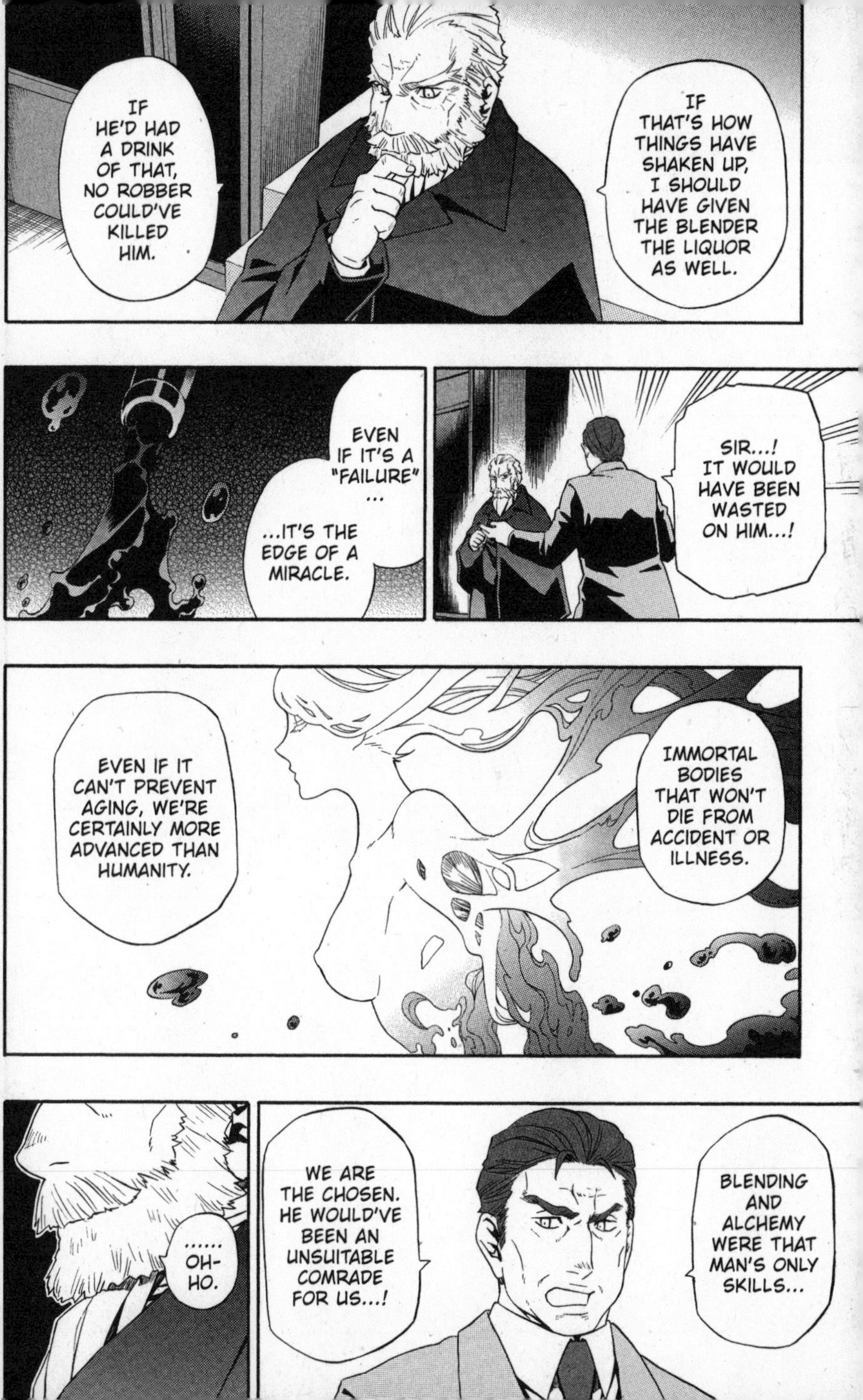
IF THAT'S HOW THINGS HAVE SHAKEN UP, I SHOULD HAVE GIVEN THE BLENDER THE LIQUOR AS WELL.
IF HE'D HAD A DRINK OF THAT, NO ROBBER COULD'VE KILLED HIM.
SIR...! IT WOULD HAVE BEEN WASTED ON HIM...!
EVEN IF IT'S A "FAILURE"...
...IT'S THE EDGE OF A MIRACLE.
IMMORTAL BODIES THAT WON'T DIE FROM ACCIDENT OR ILLNESS.
EVEN IF IT CAN'T PREVENT AGING, WE'RE CERTAINLY MORE ADVANCED THAN HUMANITY.
BLENDING AND ALCHEMY WERE THAT MAN'S ONLY SKILLS...
WE ARE THE CHOSEN. HE WOULD'VE BEEN AN UNSUITABLE COMRADE FOR US...!
......OH-HO.

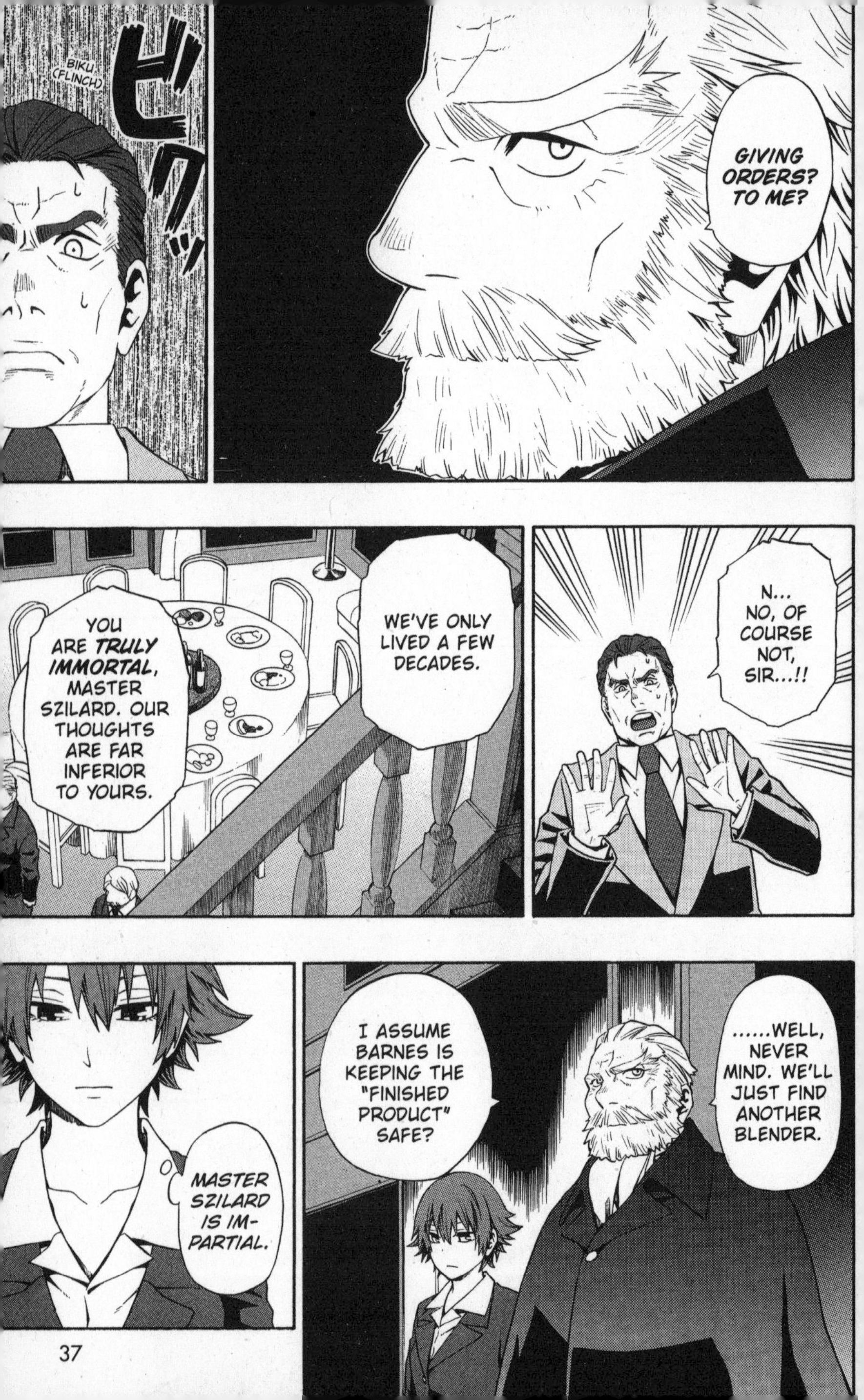
GIVING ORDERS? TO ME?
BIKU (FLINCH)
N... NO, OF COURSE NOT, SIR...!!
WE'VE ONLY LIVED A FEW DECADES.
YOU ARE TRULY IMMORTAL, MASTER SZILARD. OUR THOUGHTS ARE FAR INFERIOR TO YOURS.
......WELL, NEVER MIND. WE'LL JUST FIND ANOTHER BLENDER.
I ASSUME BARNES IS KEEPING THE "FINISHED PRODUCT" SAFE?
MASTER SZILARD IS IM-PARTIAL.

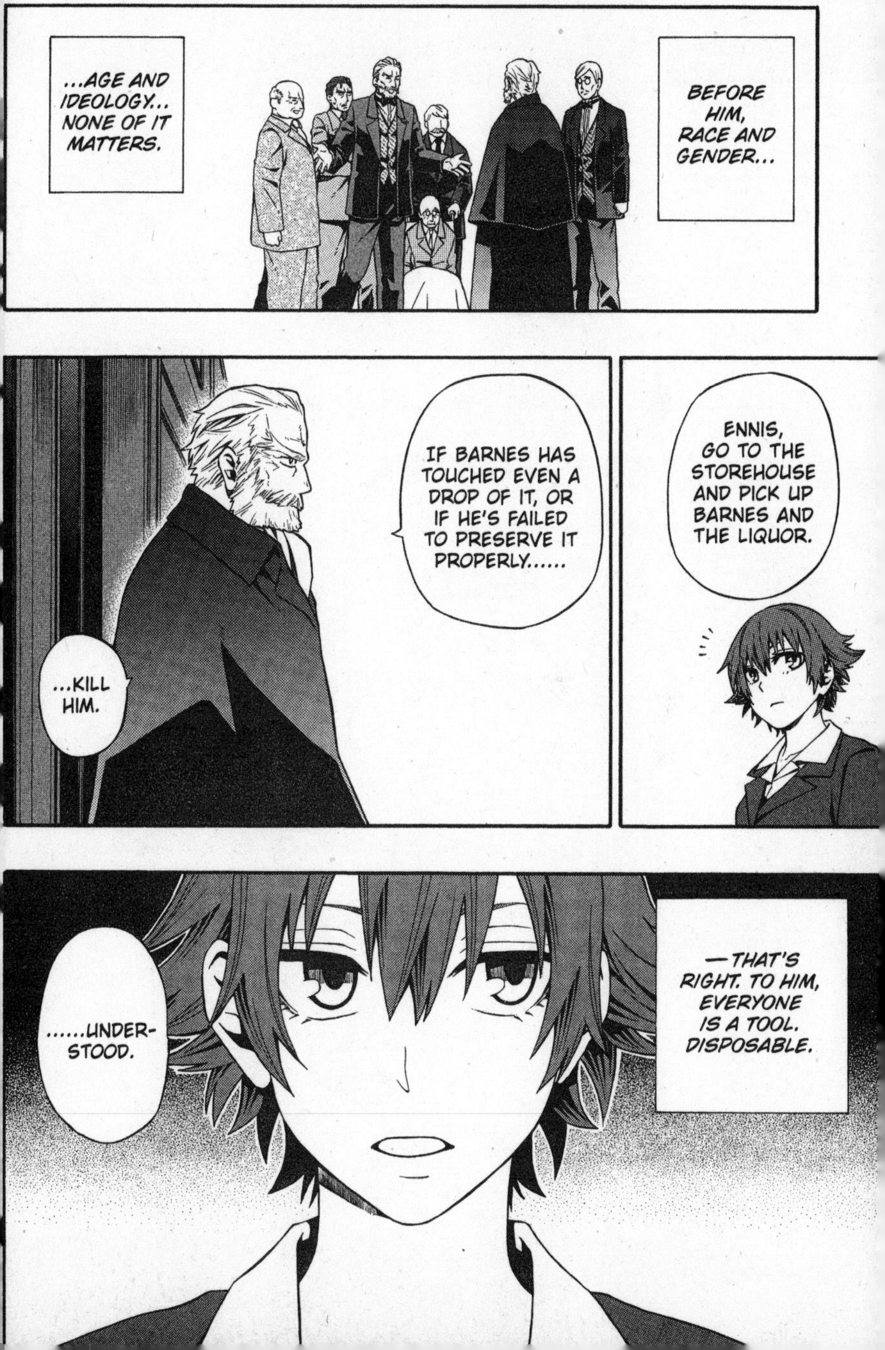
BEFORE HIM, RACE AND GENDER...
...AGE AND IDEOLOGY... NONE OF IT MATTERS.
ENNIS, GO TO THE STOREHOUSE AND PICK UP BARNES AND THE LIQUOR.
IF BARNES HAS TOUCHED EVEN A DROP OF IT, OR IF HE'S FAILED TO PRESERVE IT PROPERLY......
...KILL HIM.
—THAT'S RIGHT. TO HIM, EVERYONE IS A TOOL. DISPOSABLE.
......UNDER-STOOD.

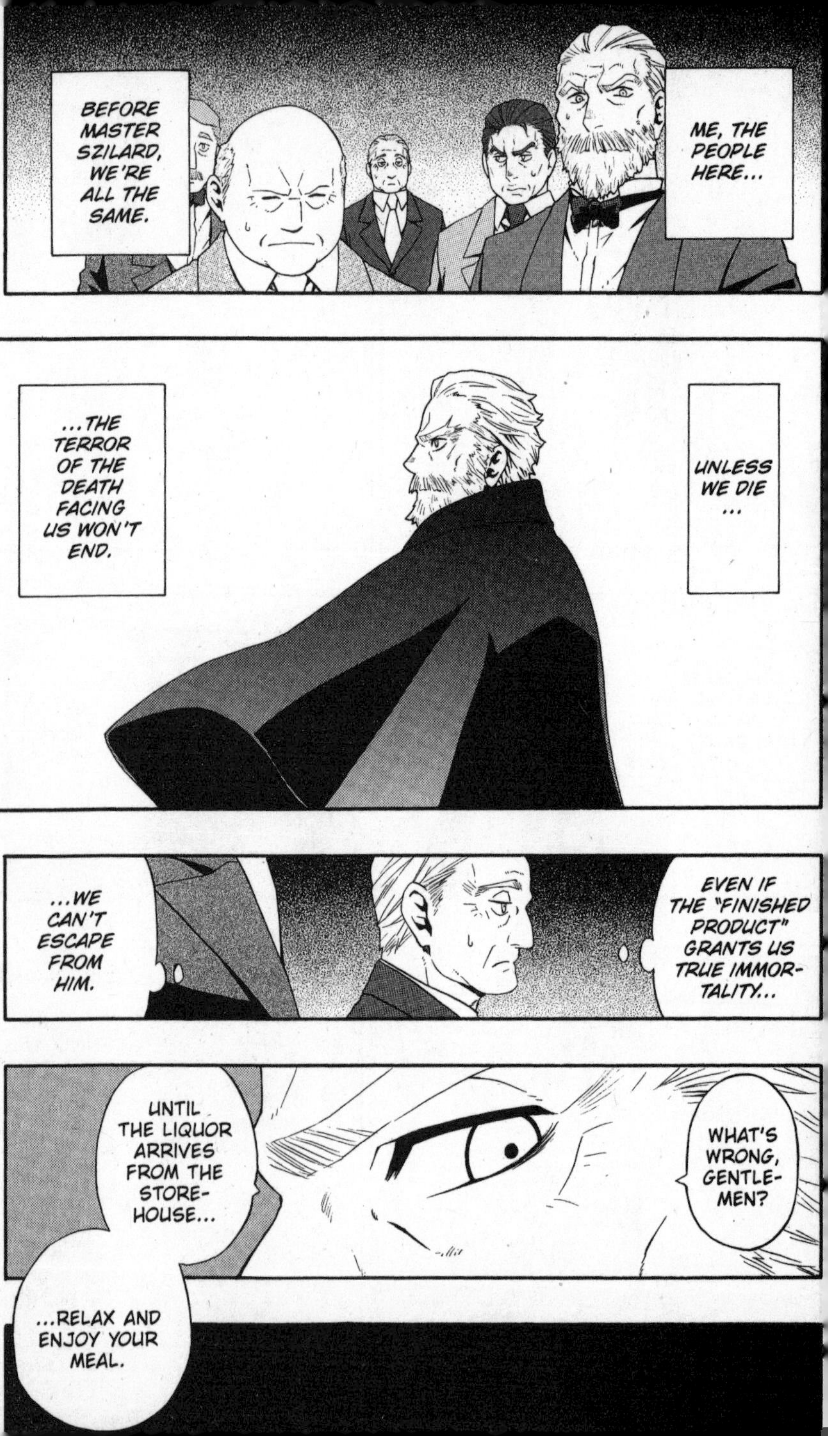
ME, THE PEOPLE HERE...
BEFORE MASTER SZILARD, WE'RE ALL THE SAME.
UNLESS WE DIE ...
...THE TERROR OF THE DEATH FACING US WON'T END.
EVEN IF THE "FINISHED PRODUCT" GRANTS US TRUE IMMORTALITY...
...WE CAN'T ESCAPE FROM HIM.
WHAT'S WRONG, GENTLEMEN?
UNTIL THE LIQUOR ARRIVES FROM THE STOREHOUSE...
...RELAX AND ENJOY YOUR MEAL.

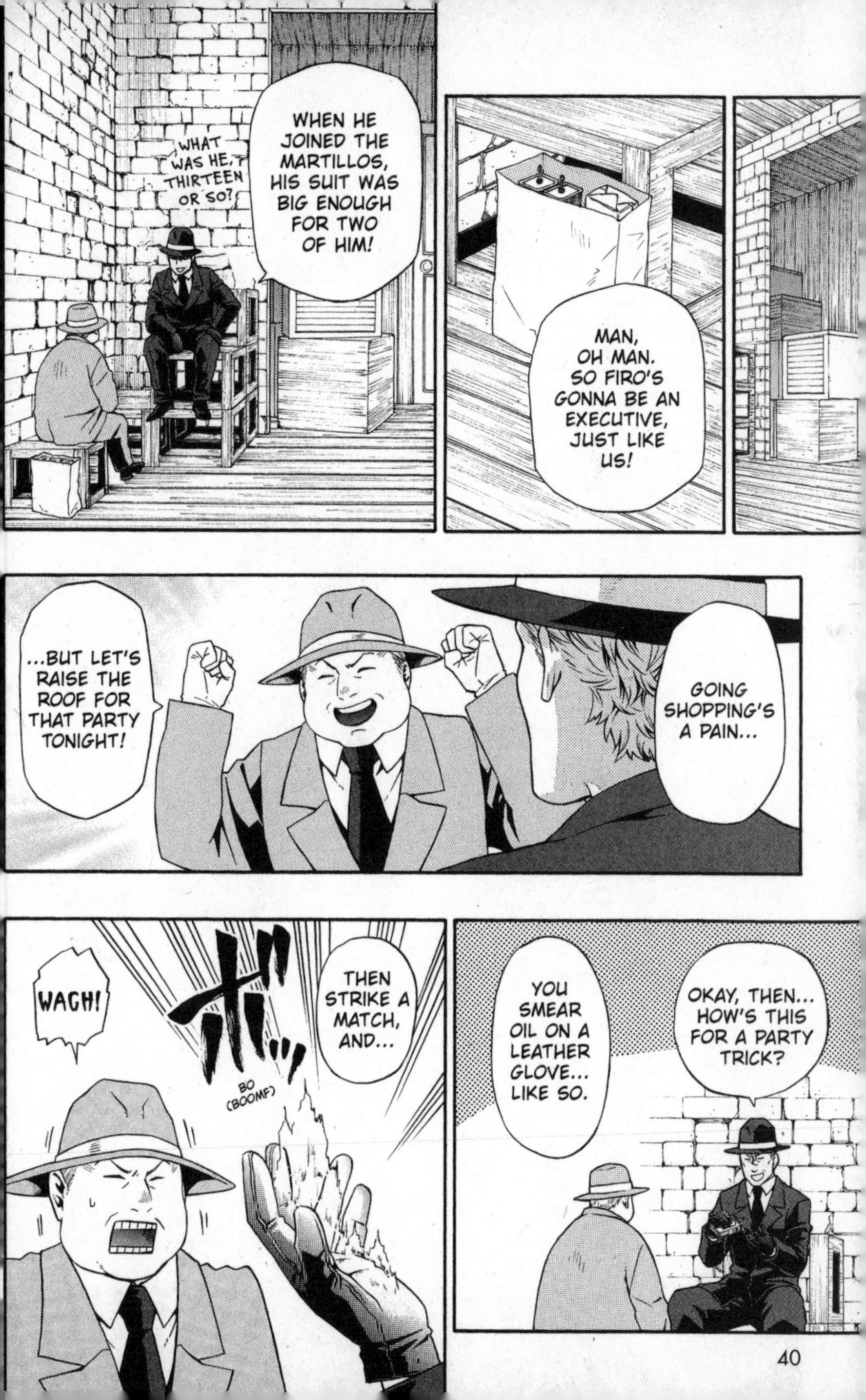
MAN, OH MAN. SO FIRO'S GONNA BE AN EXECUTIVE, JUST LIKE US!
WHEN HE JOINED THE MARTILLOS, HIS SUIT WAS BIG ENOUGH FOR TWO OF HIM!
WHAT WAS HE, THIRTEEN OR SO?
GOING SHOPPING'S A PAIN...
...BUT LET'S RAISE THE ROOF FOR THAT PARTY TONIGHT!
OKAY, THEN... HOW'S THIS FOR A PARTY TRICK?
YOU SMEAR OIL ON A LEATHER GLOVE... LIKE SO.
THEN STRIKE A MATCH, AND...
BO (BOOMF)
WAGH!

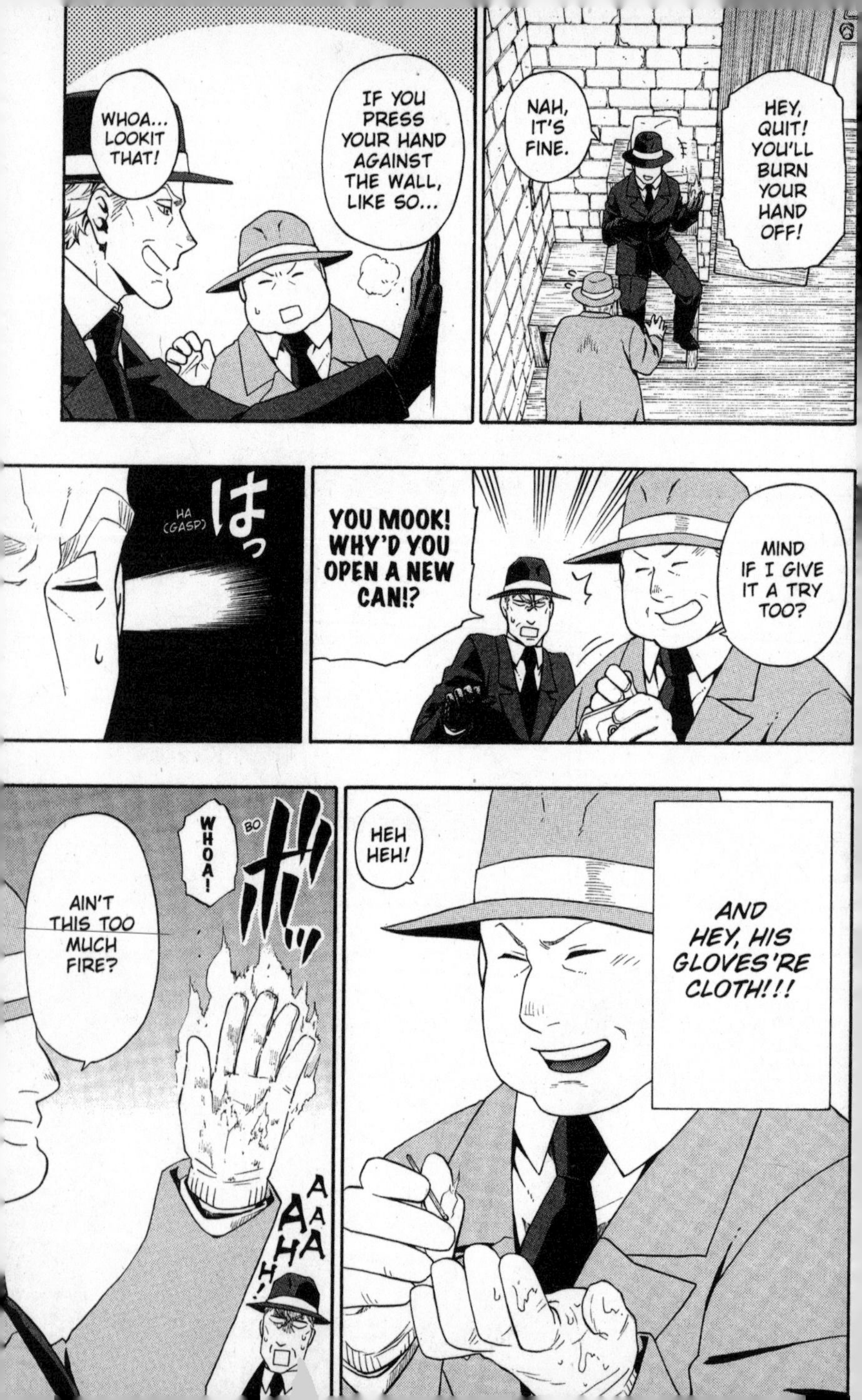

HEY, QUIT! YOU'LL BURN YOUR HAND OFF!
NAH, IT'S FINE.
IF YOU PRESS YOUR HAND AGAINST THE WALL, LIKE SO...
WHOA... LOOKIT THAT!
MIND IF I GIVE IT A TRY TOO?
YOU MOOK! WHY'D YOU OPEN A NEW CAN!?
はっ
HA (GASP)
AND HEY, HIS GLOVES'RE CLOTH!!!
HEH HEH!
WHOA!
ボッ
BO
AIN'T THIS TOO MUCH FIRE?
AAAAHH!

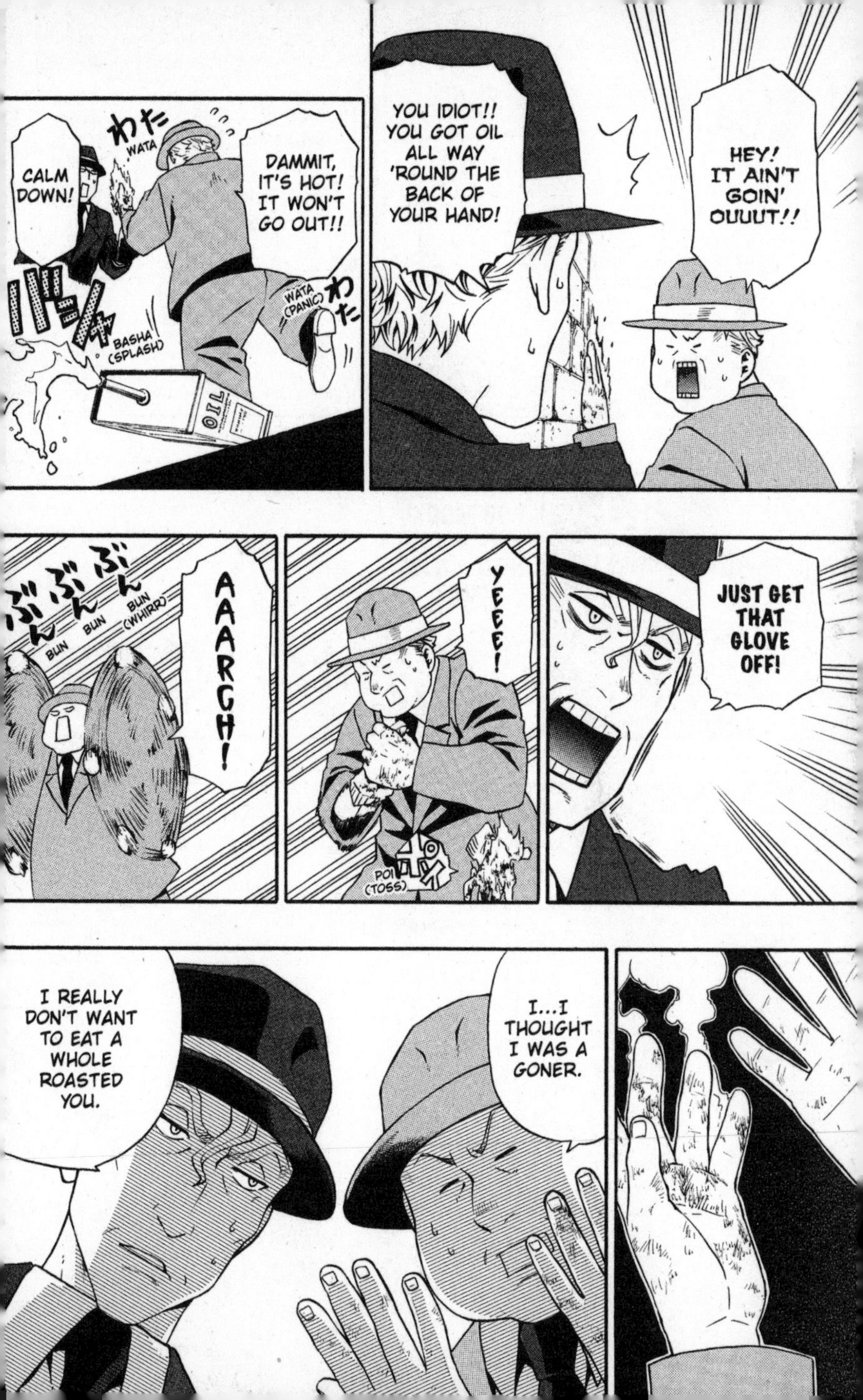

HEY! IT AIN'T GOIN' OUUUT!!
YOU IDIOT!! YOU GOT OIL ALL WAY 'ROUND THE BACK OF YOUR HAND!
DAMMIT, IT'S HOT! IT WON'T GO OUT!!
わた
WATA
CALM DOWN!
わた
WATA (PANIC)
BASHA (SPLASH)
OIL
JUST GET THAT GLOVE OFF!
YEEE!
POI (TOSS)
AAARGH!
ぶん
BUN (WHIRR)
ぶん
BUN
ぶん
BUN
I...I THOUGHT I WAS A GONER.
I REALLY DON'T WANT TO EAT A WHOLE ROASTED YOU.

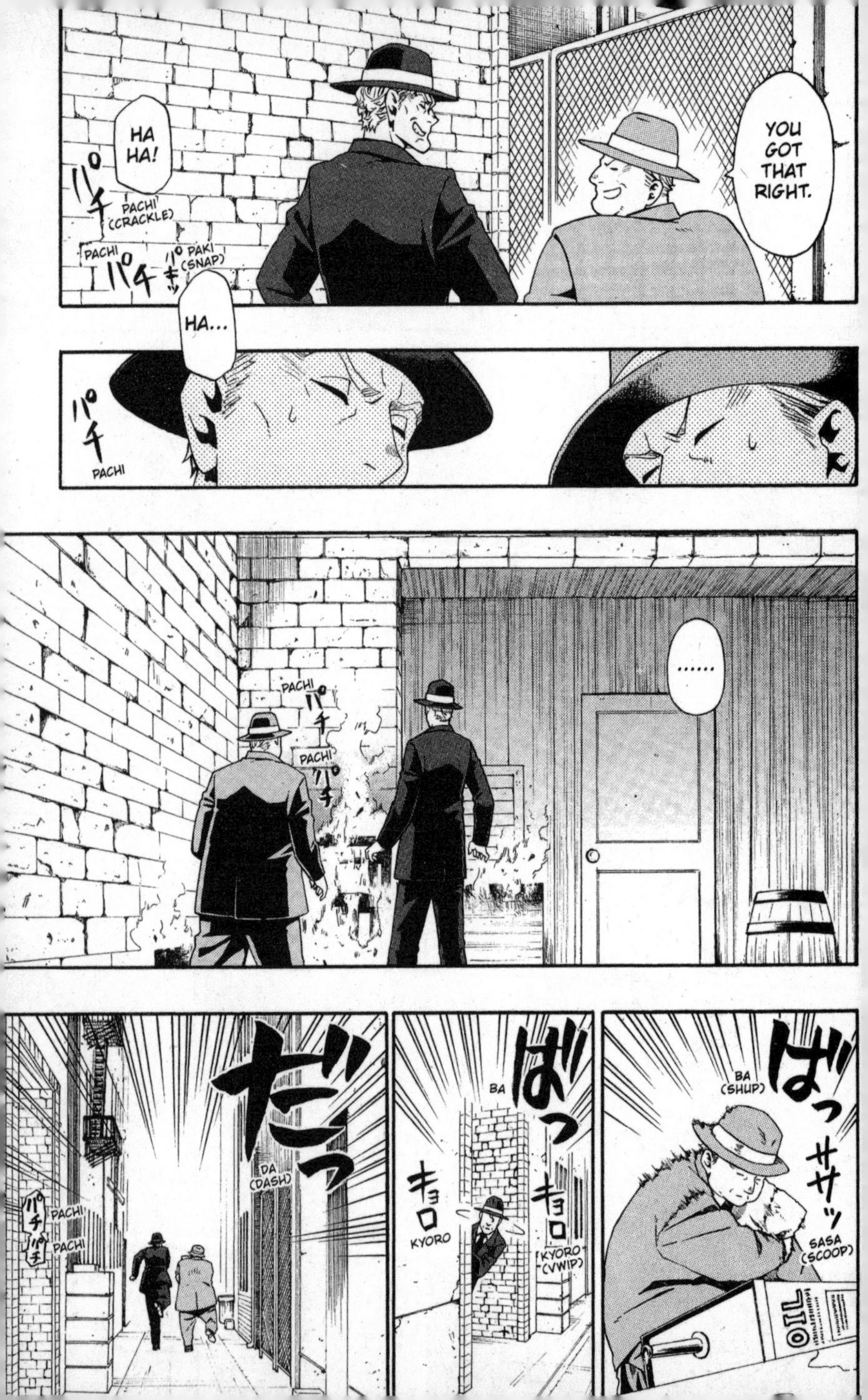
YOU GOT THAT RIGHT.
HA HA!
パチ
PACHI (CRACKLE)
PACHI パチ
パキッ PAKI (SNAP)
HA...
パチ PACHI
......
PACHI パチ
PACHI パチ
ばっ
BA (SHUP)
ササッ
SASA (SCOOP)
OIL
BA ばっ
キョロ
KYORO (VWIP)
キョロ
KYORO
だっ
DA (DASH)
パチ PACHI
パチ PACHI

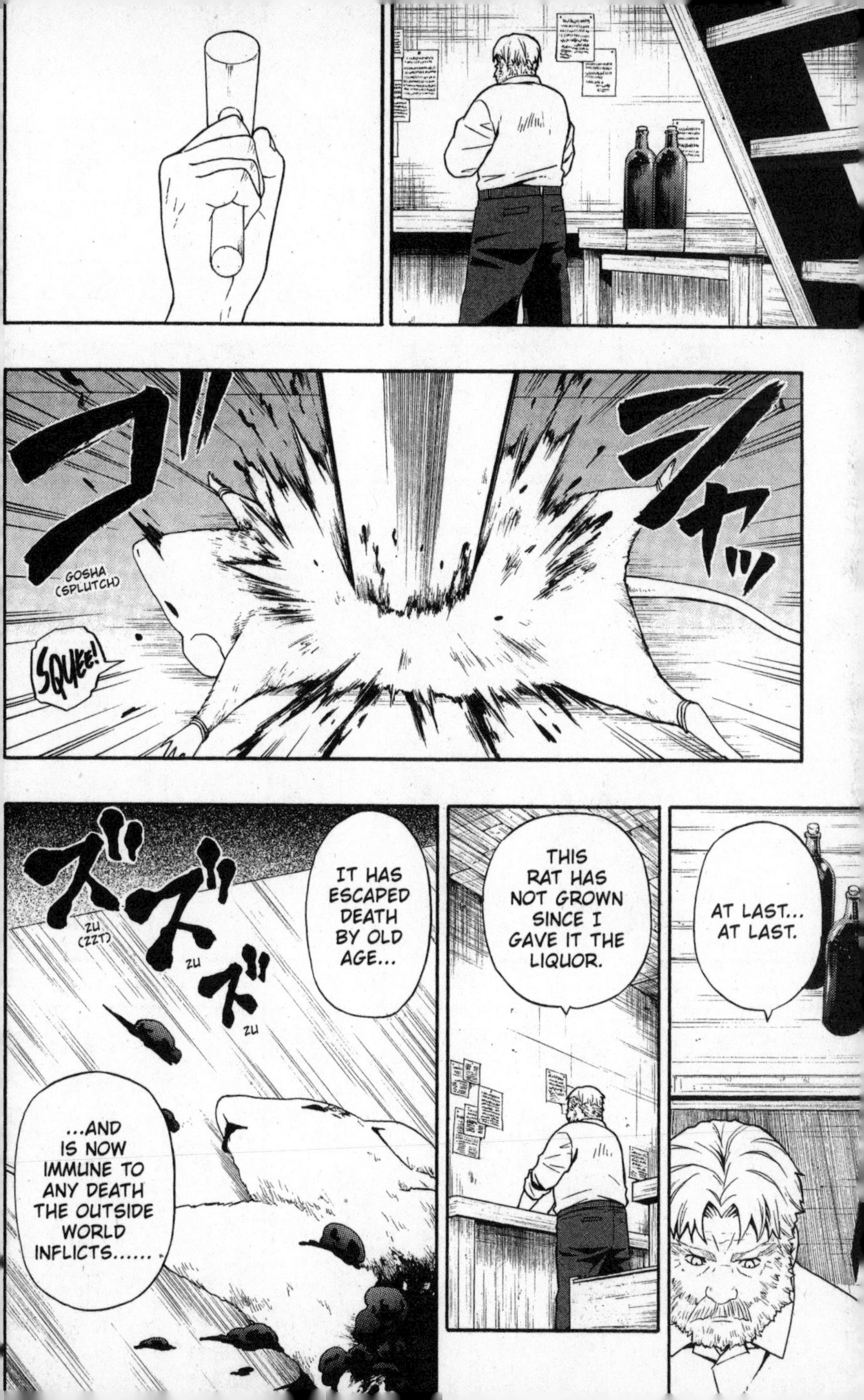
GOSHA (SPLUTCH)
SQUEEE!
AT LAST... AT LAST.
THIS RAT HAS NOT GROWN SINCE I GAVE IT THE LIQUOR.
IT HAS ESCAPED DEATH BY OLD AGE...
ZU (ZZT)
ZU
ZU
...AND IS NOW IMMUNE TO ANY DEATH THE OUTSIDE WORLD INFLICTS......

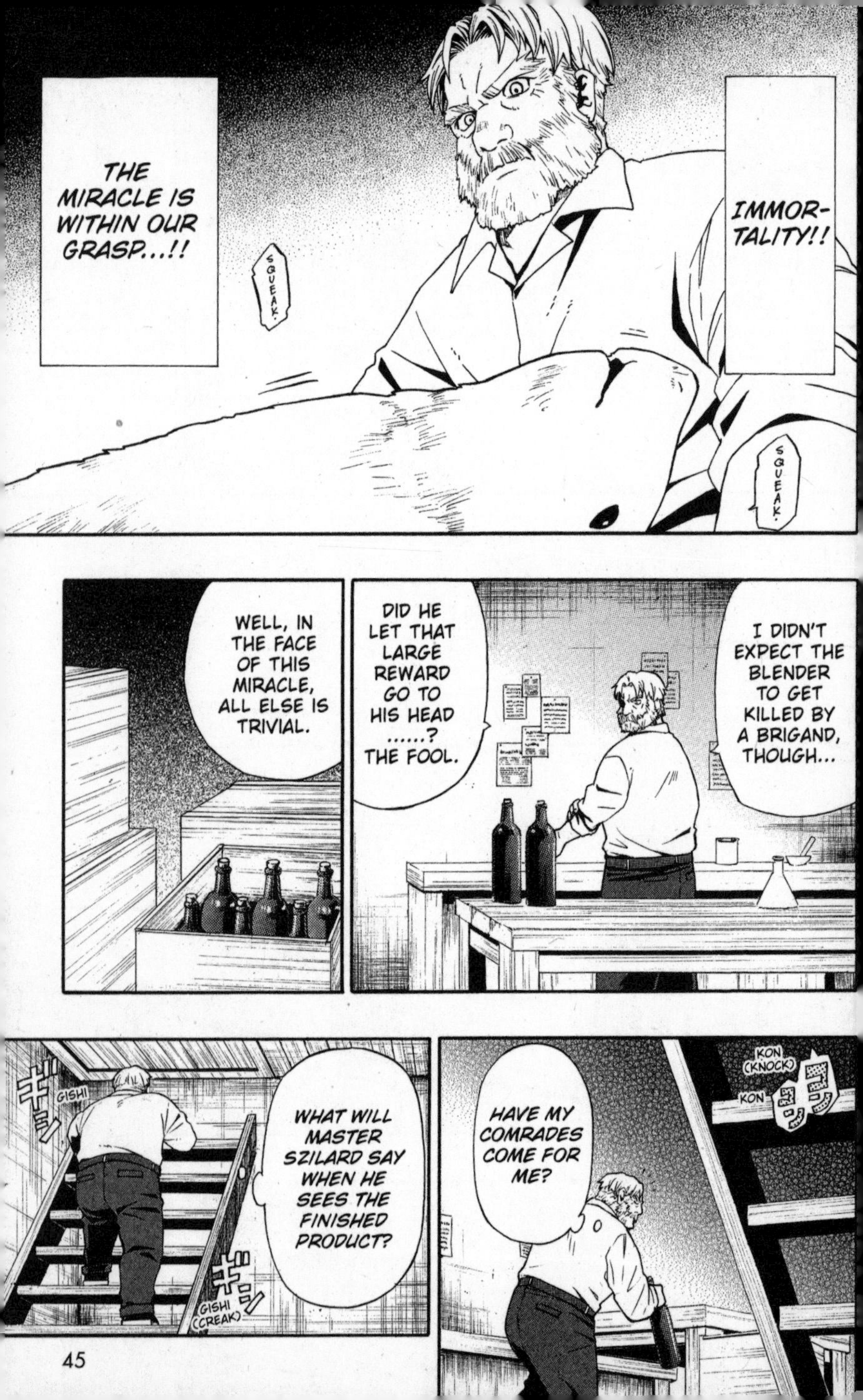
IMMOR-TALITY!!
SQUEAK.
THE MIRACLE IS WITHIN OUR GRASP...!!
SQUEAK.
I DIDN'T EXPECT THE BLENDER TO GET KILLED BY A BRIGAND, THOUGH...
DID HE LET THAT LARGE REWARD GO TO HIS HEAD ......? THE FOOL.
WELL, IN THE FACE OF THIS MIRACLE, ALL ELSE IS TRIVIAL.
KON (KNOCK)
KON
HAVE MY COMRADES COME FOR ME?
WHAT WILL MASTER SZILARD SAY WHEN HE SEES THE FINISHED PRODUCT?
GISHI
GISHI (CREAK)

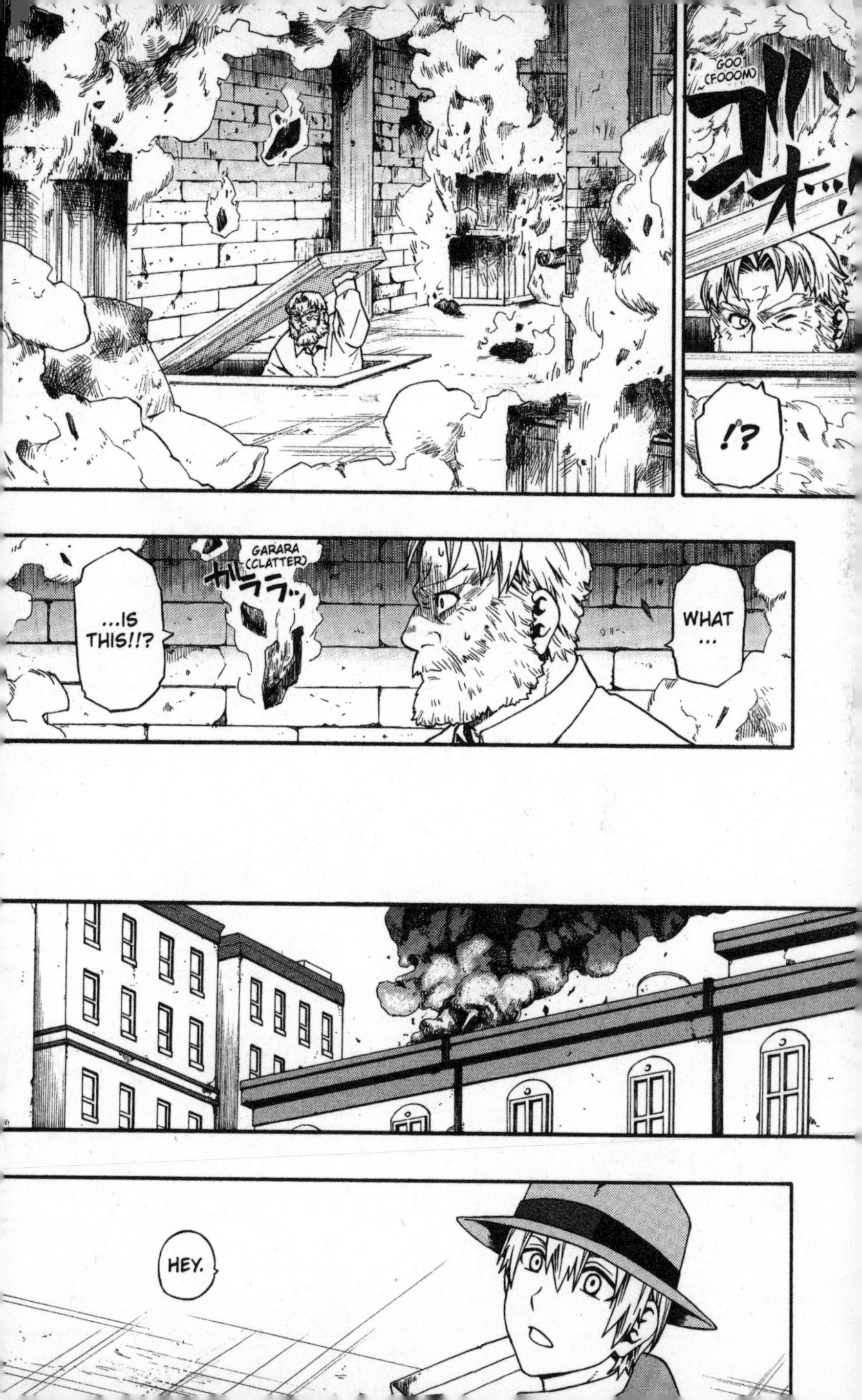
GOO (FOOOM)
!?
WHAT ...
GARARA (CLATTER)
...IS THIS!!?
HEY.

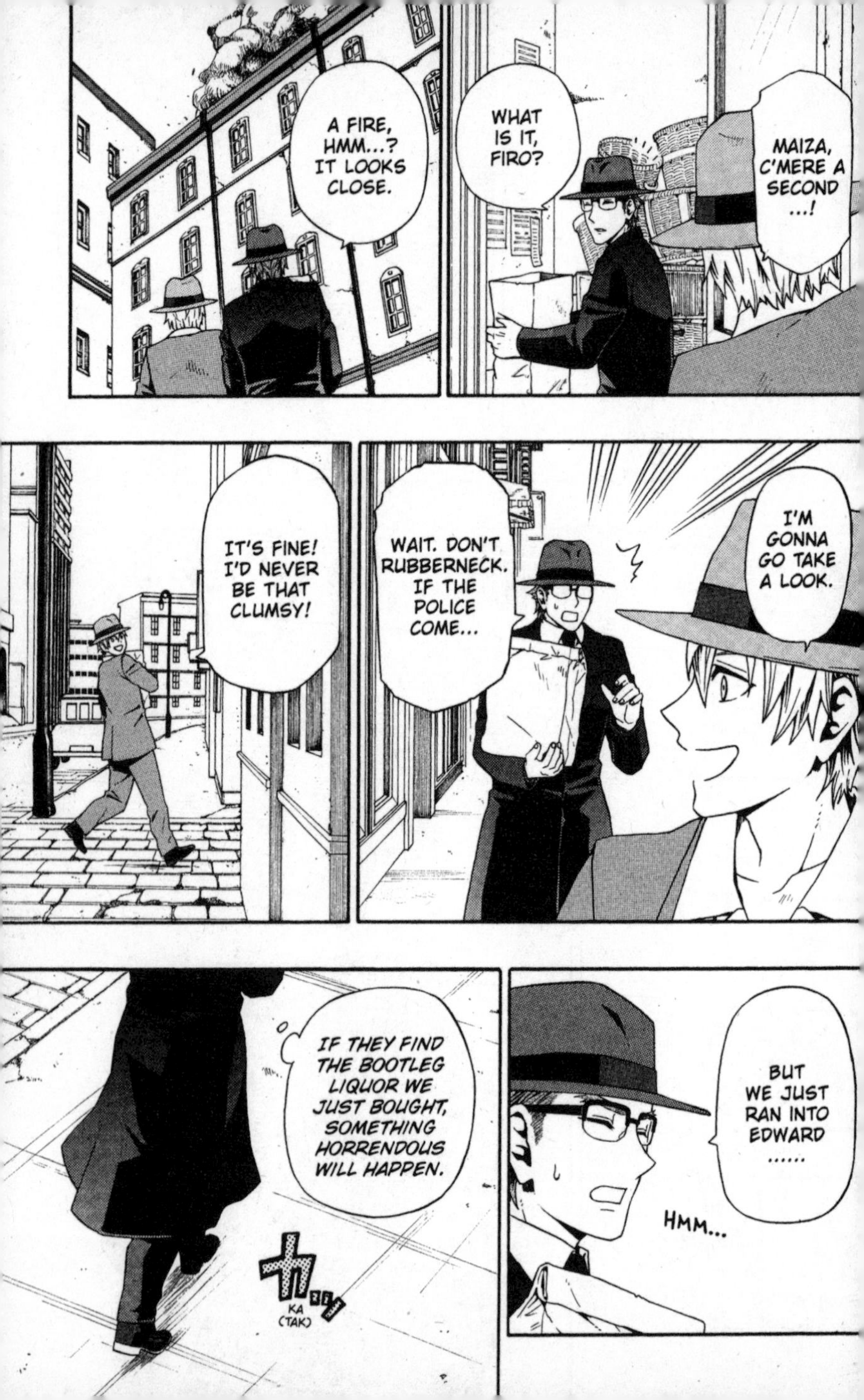
MAIZA, C'MERE A SECOND ...!
WHAT IS IT, FIRO?
A FIRE, HMM...? IT LOOKS CLOSE.
I'M GONNA GO TAKE A LOOK.
WAIT. DON'T RUBBERNECK. IF THE POLICE COME...
IT'S FINE! I'D NEVER BE THAT CLUMSY!
BUT WE JUST RAN INTO EDWARD ......
HMM...
IF THEY FIND THE BOOTLEG LIQUOR WE JUST BOUGHT, SOMETHING HORRENDOUS WILL HAPPEN.
カッ
KA (TAK)

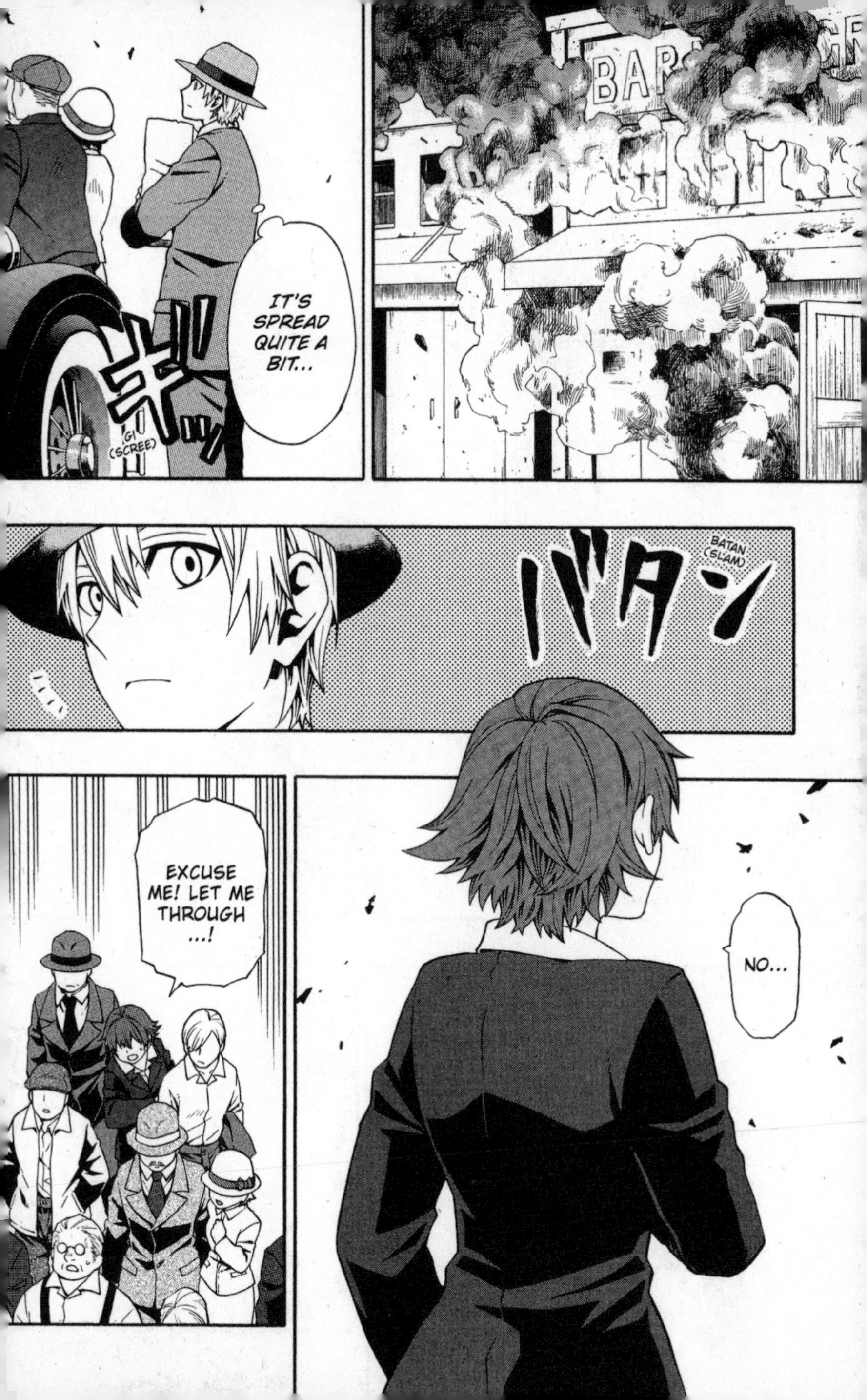
IT'S SPREAD QUITE A BIT...
GI (SCREE)
BATAN (SLAM)
NO...
EXCUSE ME! LET ME THROUGH ...!

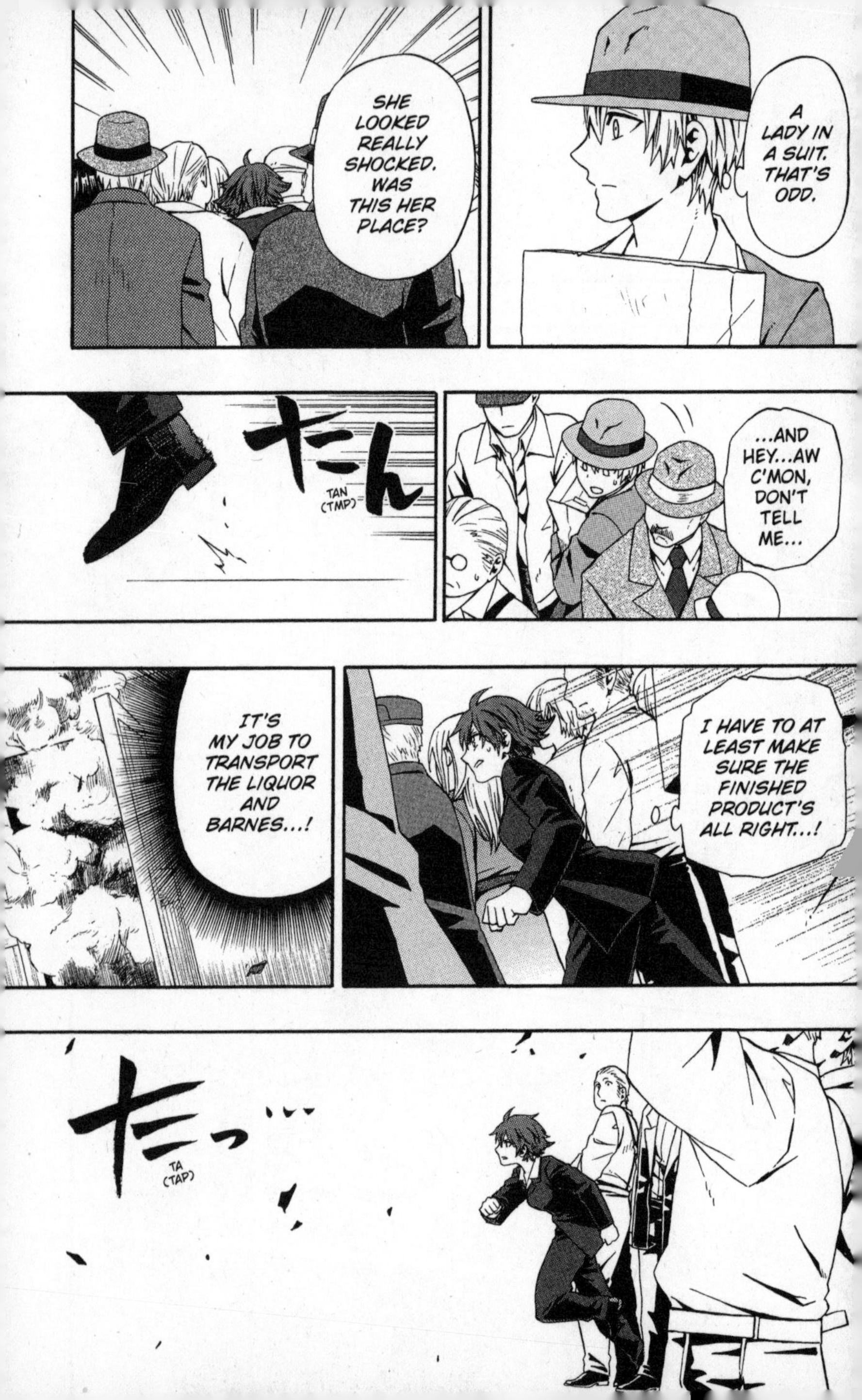
A LADY IN A SUIT. THAT'S ODD.
SHE LOOKED REALLY SHOCKED. WAS THIS HER PLACE?
...AND HEY...AW C'MON, DON'T TELL ME...
たん
TAN (TMP)
I HAVE TO AT LEAST MAKE SURE THE FINISHED PRODUCT'S ALL RIGHT...!
IT'S MY JOB TO TRANSPORT THE LIQUOR AND BARNES...!
たっ
TA (TAP)

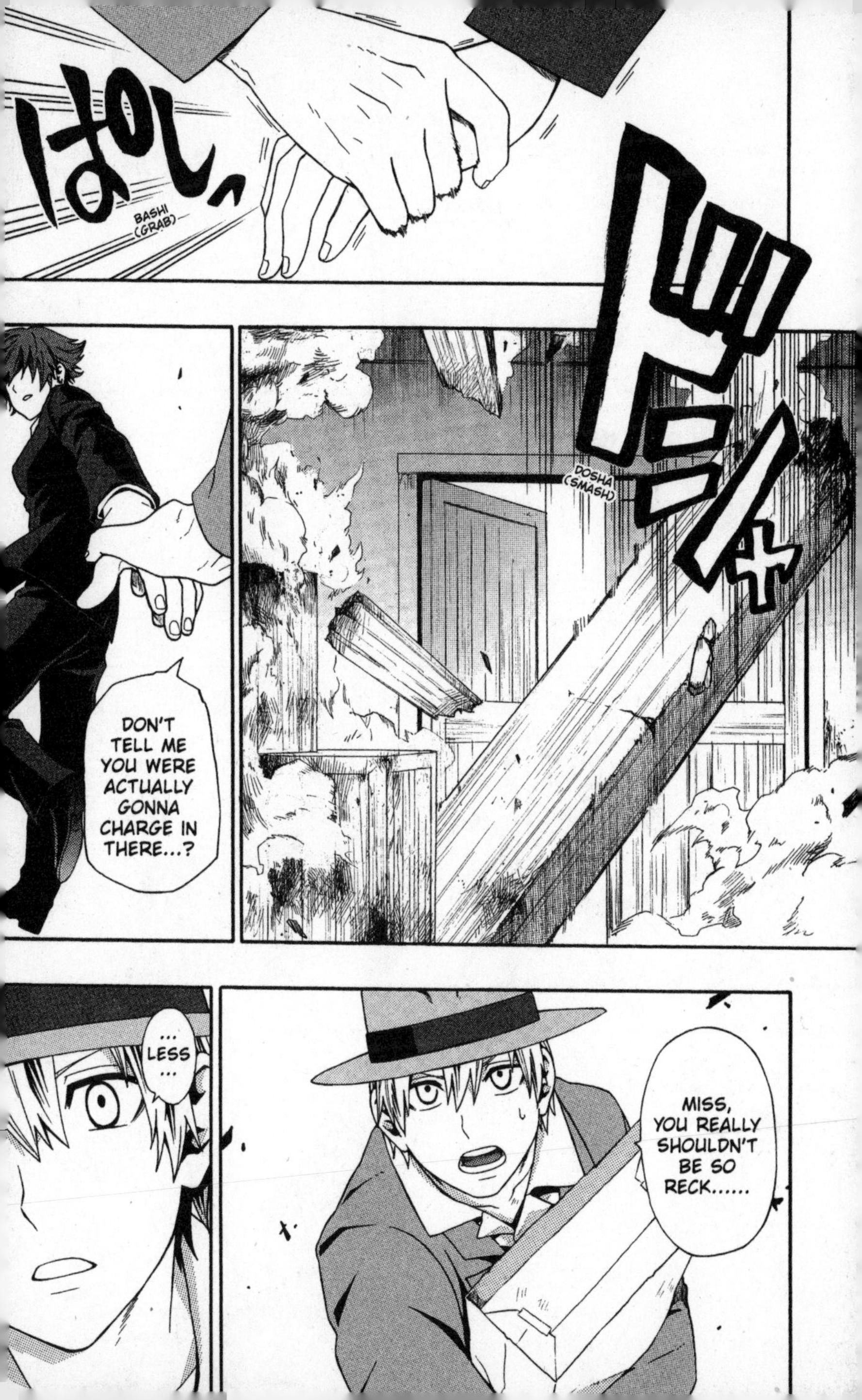
ぱしっ
BASHI (GRAB)
ドシャッ
DOSHA (SMASH)
DON'T TELL ME YOU WERE ACTUALLY GONNA CHARGE IN THERE...?
MISS, YOU REALLY SHOULDN'T BE SO RECK......
...LESS...

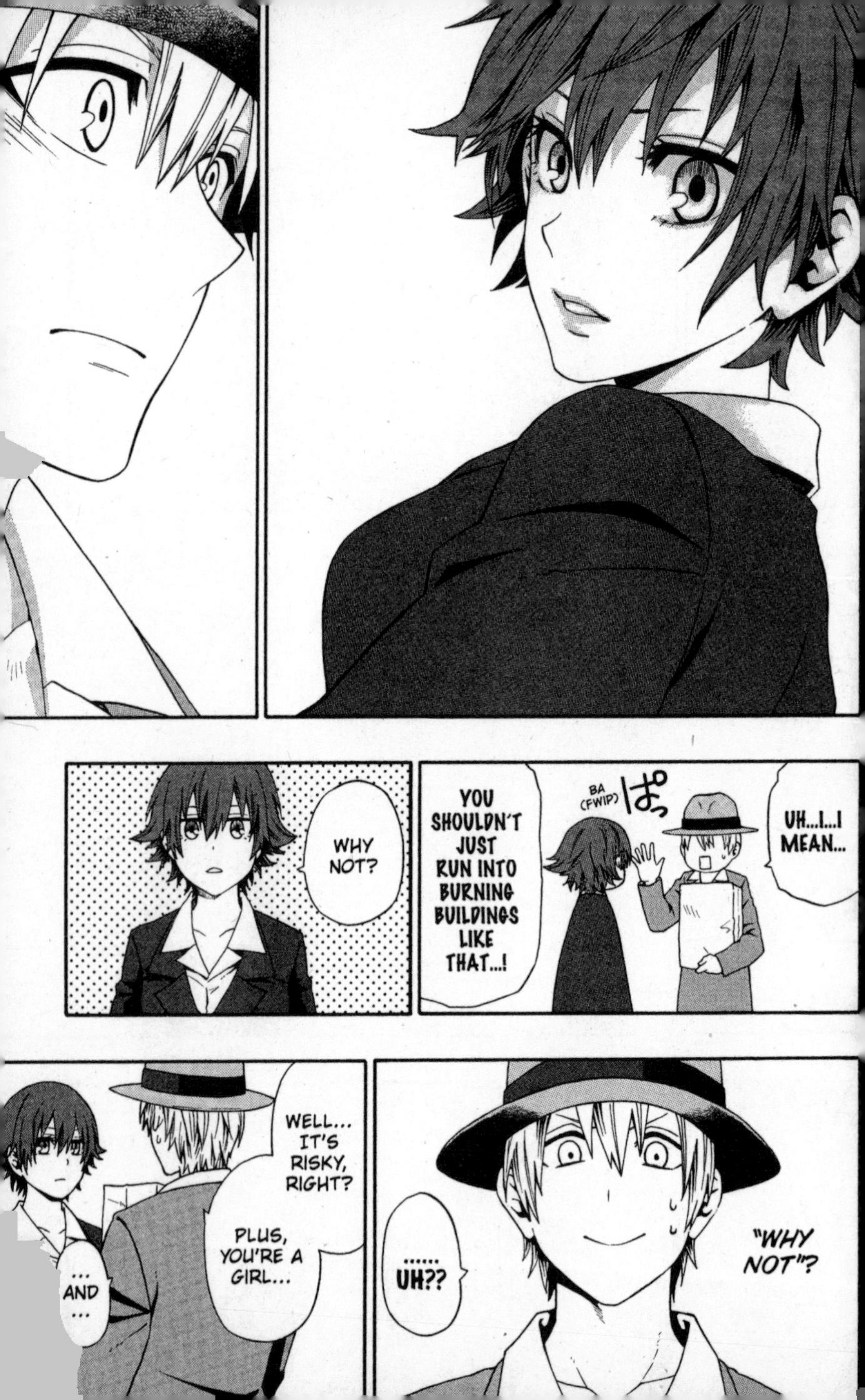
UH...I...I MEAN...
BA (FWIP) ぱっ
YOU SHOULDN'T JUST RUN INTO BURNING BUILDINGS LIKE THAT...!
WHY NOT?
"WHY NOT"?
......UH??
WELL... IT'S RISKY, RIGHT?
PLUS, YOU'RE A GIRL...
...AND...

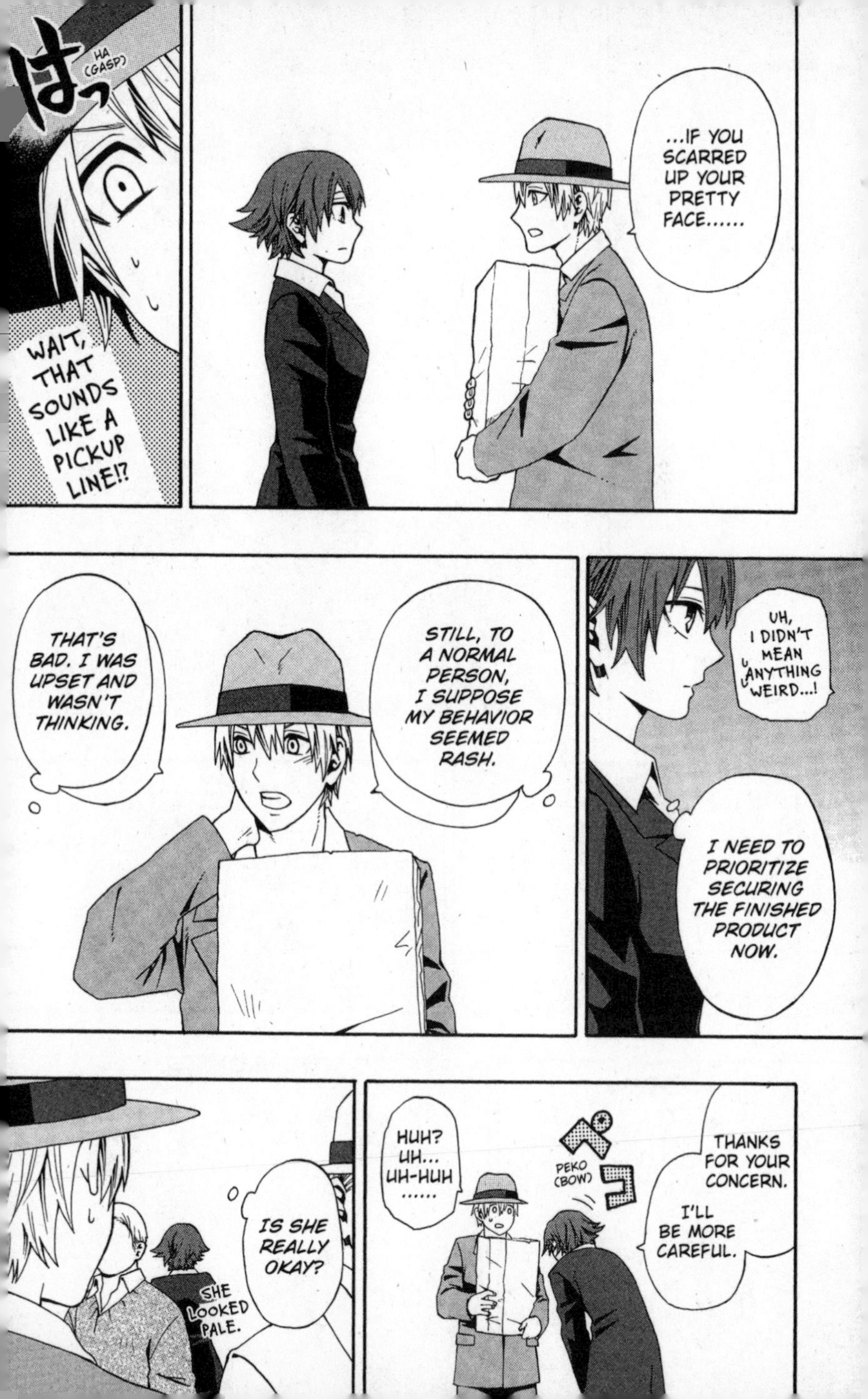
...IF YOU SCARRED UP YOUR PRETTY FACE......
はっ
HA (GASP)
WAIT, THAT SOUNDS LIKE A PICKUP LINE!?
UH, I DIDN'T MEAN ANYTHING WEIRD...!
I NEED TO PRIORITIZE SECURING THE FINISHED PRODUCT NOW.
STILL, TO A NORMAL PERSON, I SUPPOSE MY BEHAVIOR SEEMED RASH.
THAT'S BAD. I WAS UPSET AND WASN'T THINKING.
THANKS FOR YOUR CONCERN.
I'LL BE MORE CAREFUL.
ペコっ
PEKO (BOW)
HUH? UH... UH-HUH ......
IS SHE REALLY OKAY?
SHE LOOKED PALE.

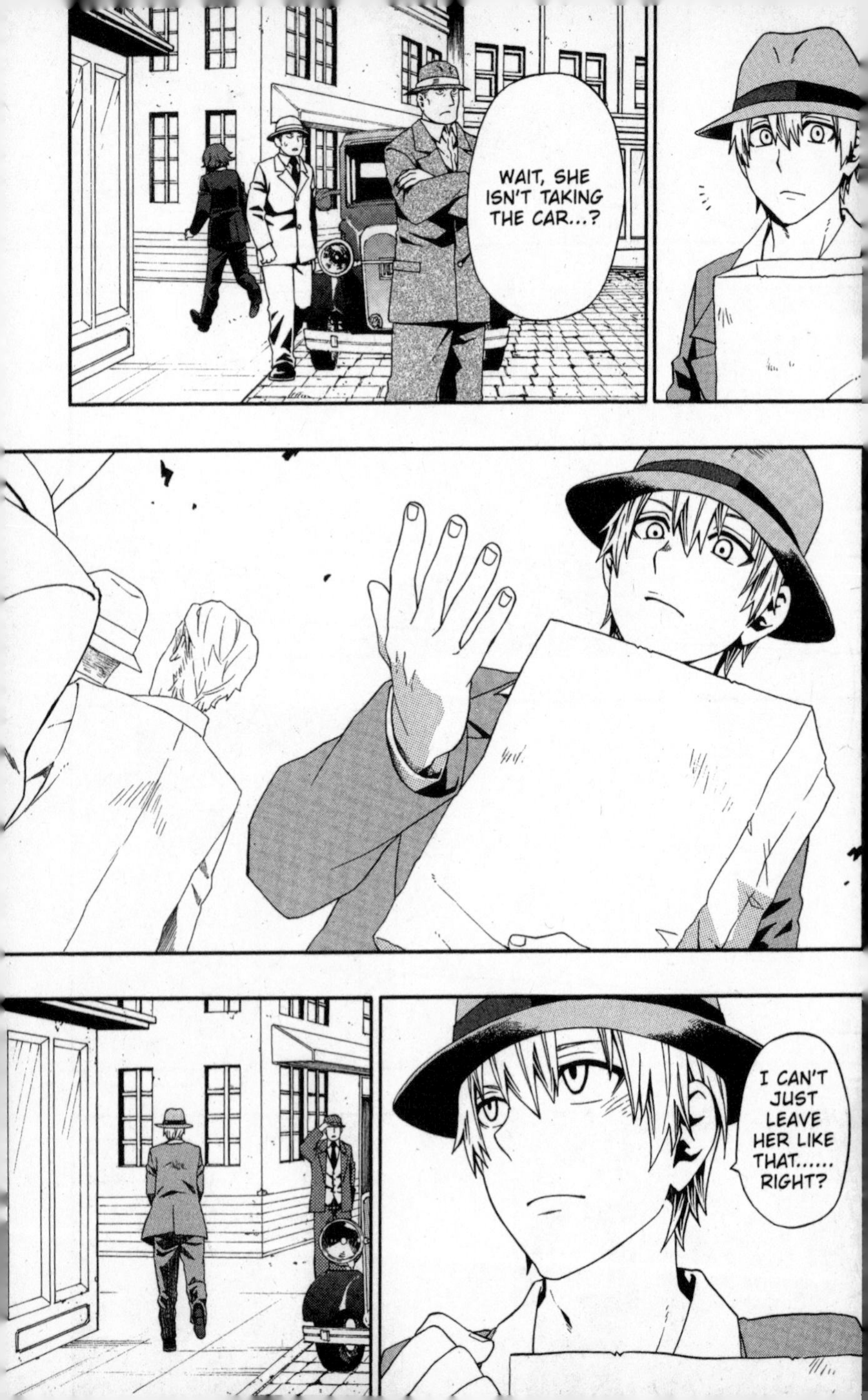
WAIT, SHE ISN'T TAKING THE CAR...?
I CAN'T JUST LEAVE HER LIKE THAT...... RIGHT?

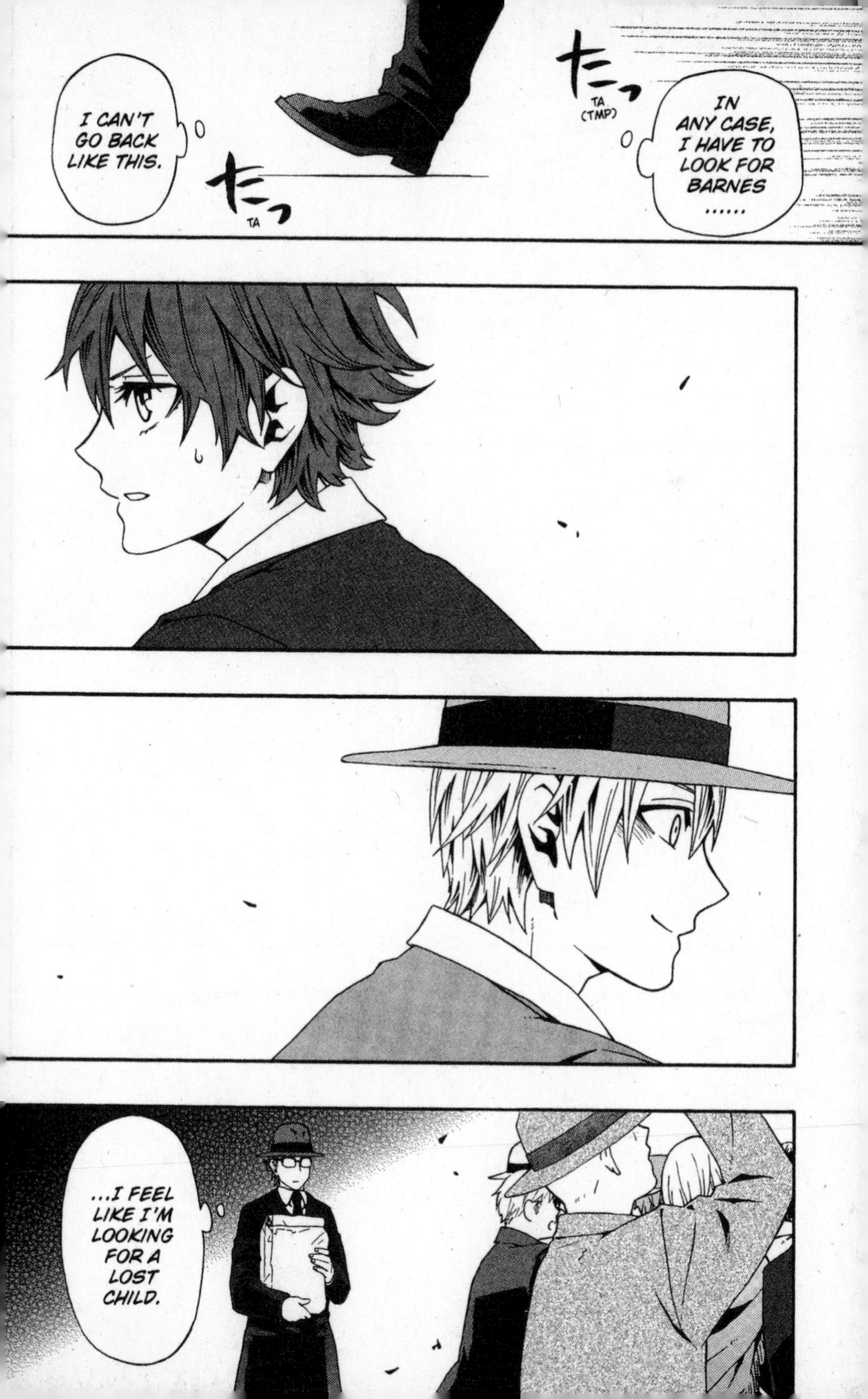

TA (TMP)
IN ANY CASE, I HAVE TO LOOK FOR BARNES ......
TA
I CAN'T GO BACK LIKE THIS.
...I FEEL LIKE I'M LOOKING FOR A LOST CHILD.

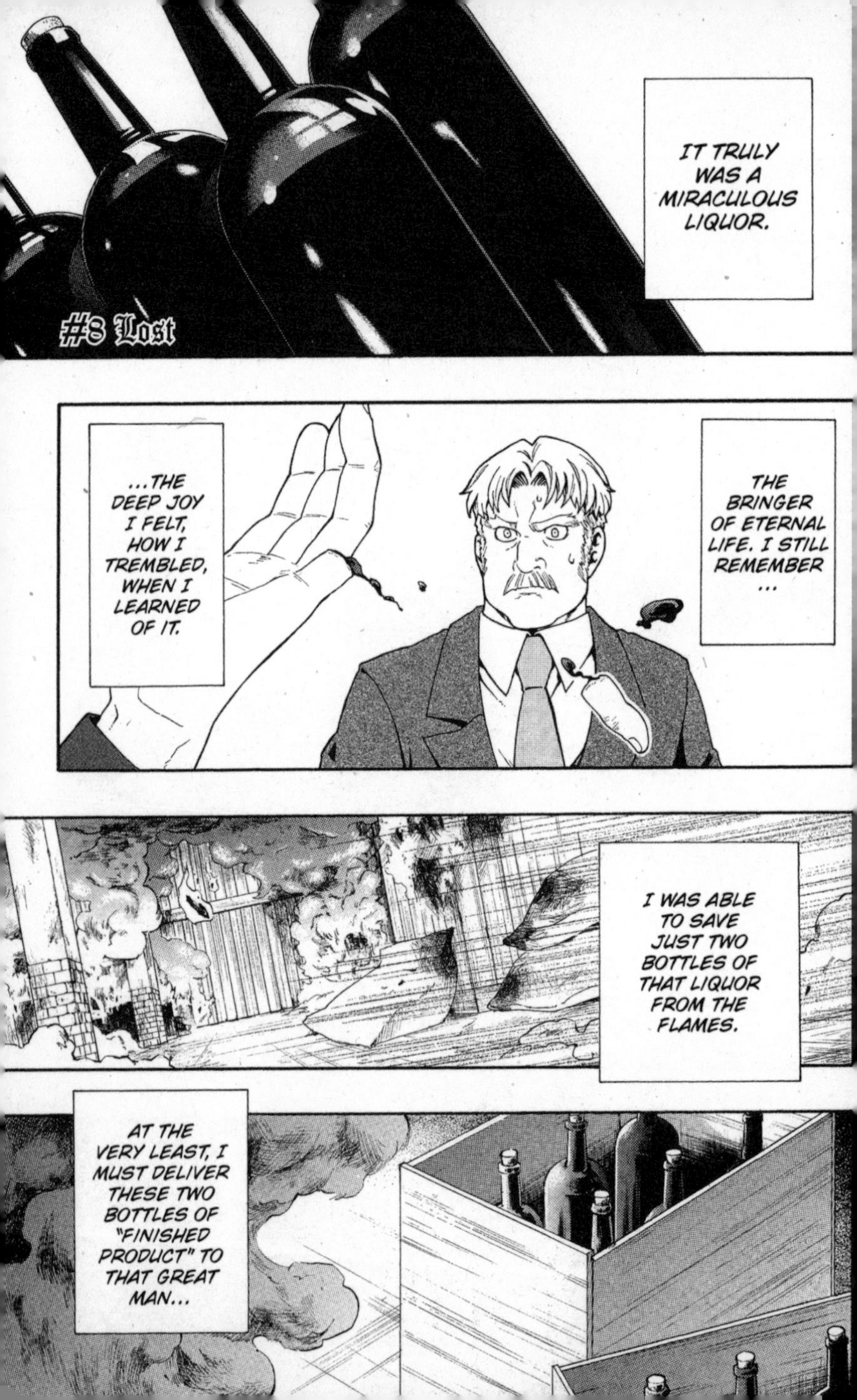
IT TRULY WAS A MIRACULOUS LIQUOR.
#8 Lost
THE BRINGER OF ETERNAL LIFE. I STILL REMEMBER ...
...THE DEEP JOY I FELT, HOW I TREMBLED, WHEN I LEARNED OF IT.
I WAS ABLE TO SAVE JUST TWO BOTTLES OF THAT LIQUOR FROM THE FLAMES.
AT THE VERY LEAST, I MUST DELIVER THESE TWO BOTTLES OF "FINISHED PRODUCT" TO THAT GREAT MAN...

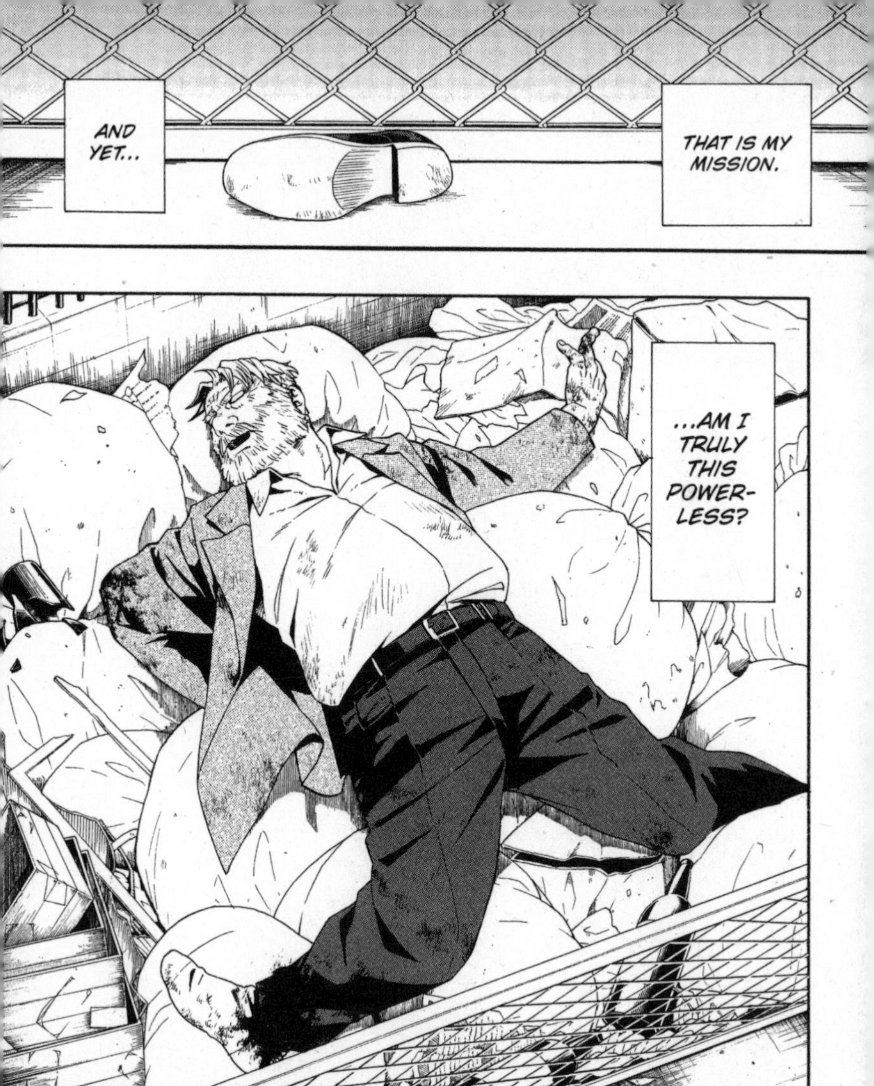
THAT IS MY MISSION.
AND YET...
...AM I TRULY THIS POWER-LESS?

#8 Lost

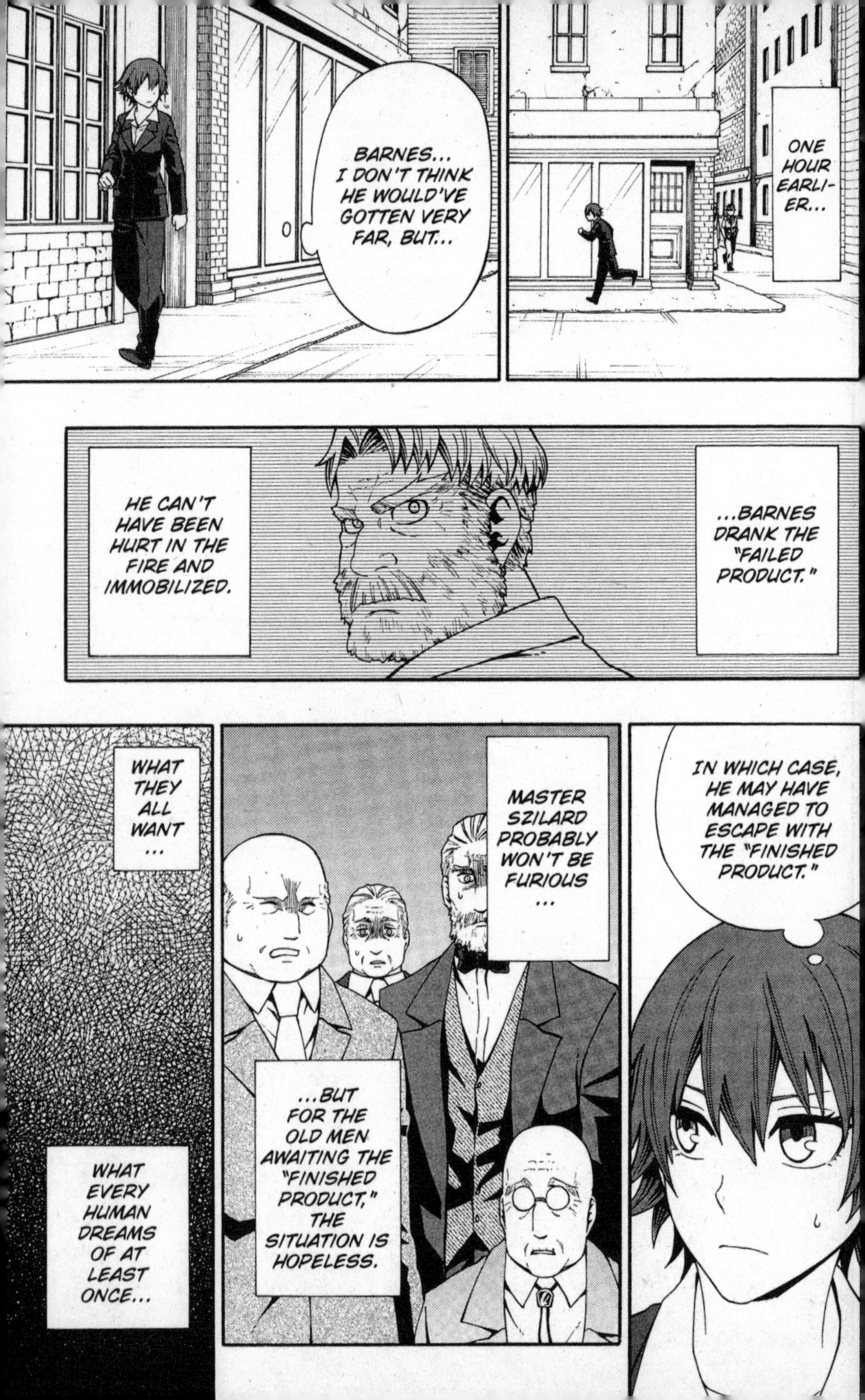
ONE HOUR EARLIER...
BARNES... I DON'T THINK HE WOULD'VE GOTTEN VERY FAR, BUT...
...BARNES DRANK THE "FAILED PRODUCT."
HE CAN'T HAVE BEEN HURT IN THE FIRE AND IMMOBILIZED.
IN WHICH CASE, HE MAY HAVE MANAGED TO ESCAPE WITH THE "FINISHED PRODUCT."
MASTER SZILARD PROBABLY WON'T BE FURIOUS...
...BUT FOR THE OLD MEN AWAITING THE "FINISHED PRODUCT," THE SITUATION IS HOPELESS.
WHAT THEY ALL WANT...
WHAT EVERY HUMAN DREAMS OF AT LEAST ONCE...

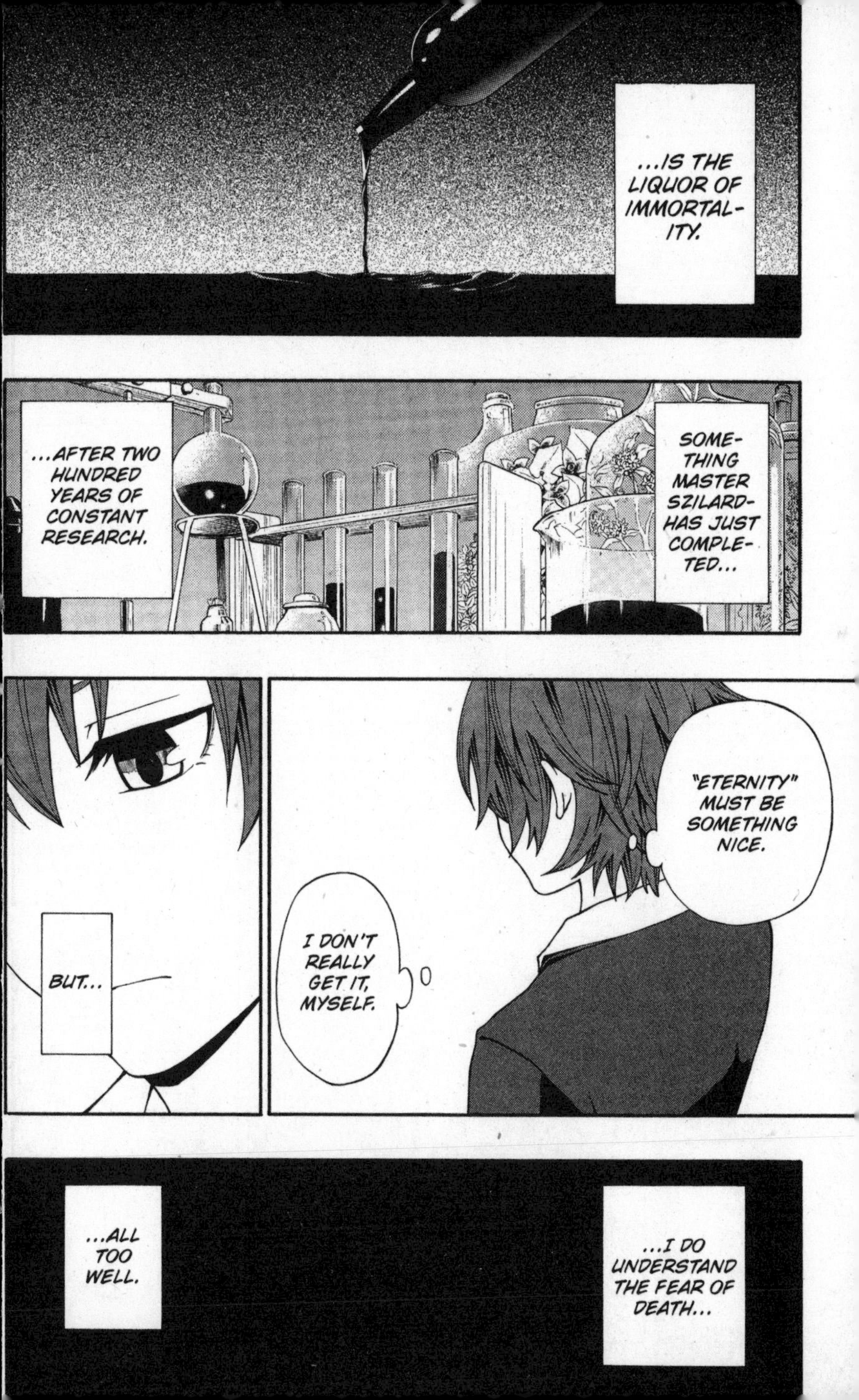
...IS THE LIQUOR OF IMMORTALITY.
SOMETHING MASTER SZILARD HAS JUST COMPLETED...
...AFTER TWO HUNDRED YEARS OF CONSTANT RESEARCH.
"ETERNITY" MUST BE SOMETHING NICE.
I DON'T REALLY GET IT, MYSELF.
BUT...
...I DO UNDERSTAND THE FEAR OF DEATH...
...ALL TOO WELL.

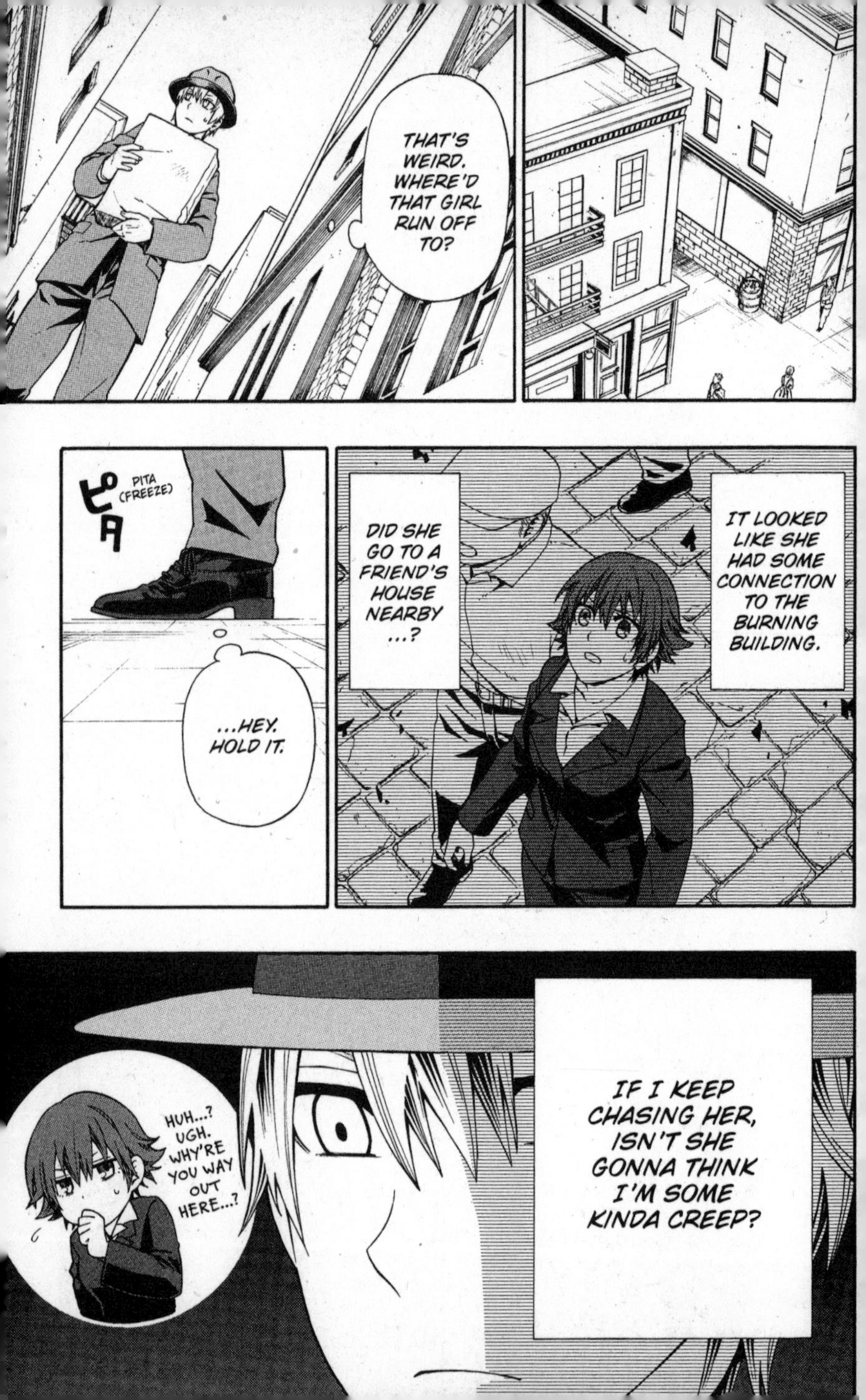
THAT'S WEIRD. WHERE'D THAT GIRL RUN OFF TO?
IT LOOKED LIKE SHE HAD SOME CONNECTION TO THE BURNING BUILDING.
DID SHE GO TO A FRIEND'S HOUSE NEARBY ...?
ピタ
PITA (FREEZE)
...HEY. HOLD IT.
IF I KEEP CHASING HER, ISN'T SHE GONNA THINK I'M SOME KINDA CREEP?
HUH...? UGH. WHY'RE YOU WAY OUT HERE...?

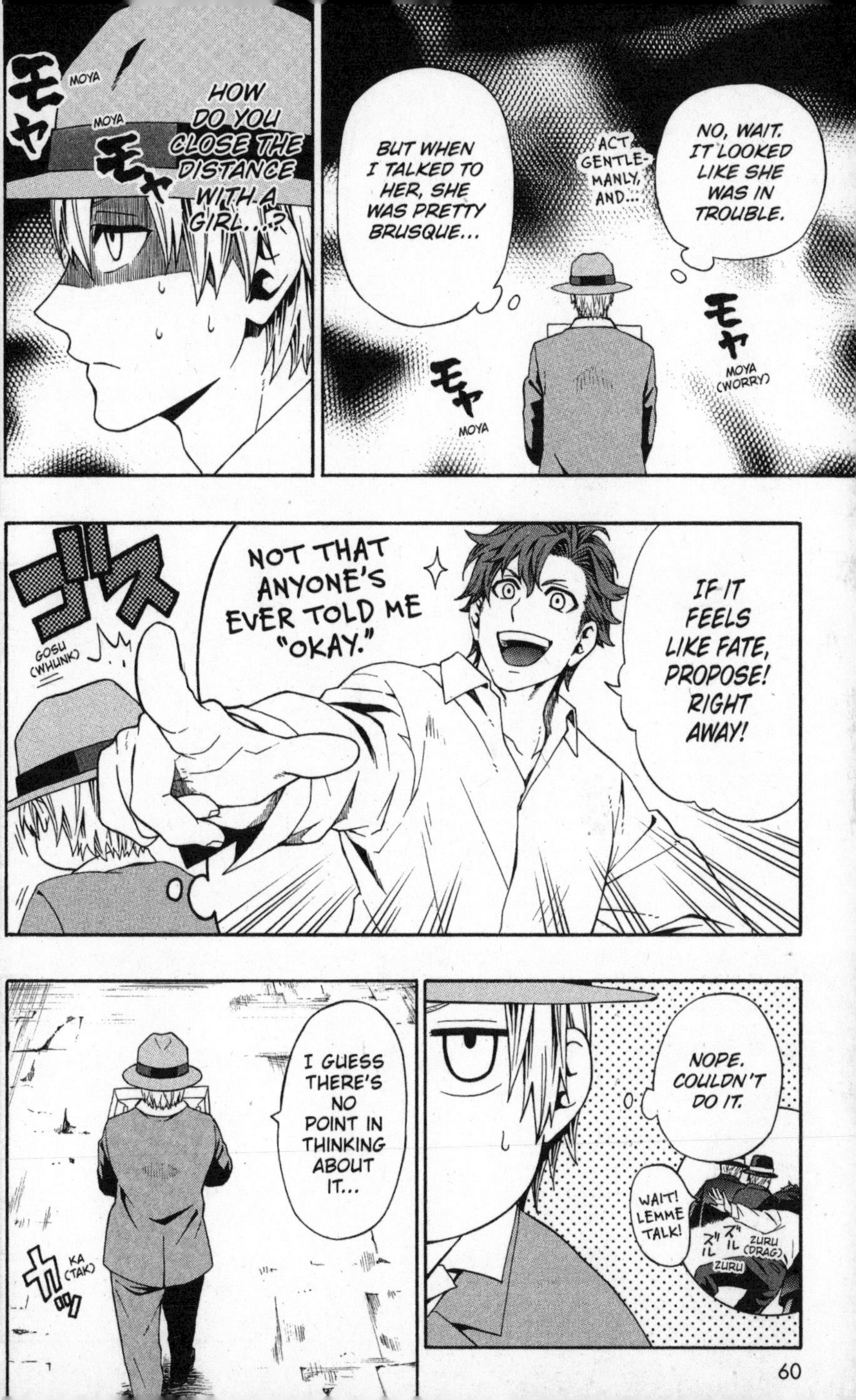
モヤ
MOYA (WORRY)
NO, WAIT. IT LOOKED LIKE SHE WAS IN TROUBLE.
ACT GENTLEMANLY, AND...
BUT WHEN I TALKED TO HER, SHE WAS PRETTY BRUSQUE...
モヤ
MOYA
モヤ
MOYA
モヤ
MOYA
HOW DO YOU CLOSE THE DISTANCE WITH A GIRL...?
IF IT FEELS LIKE FATE, PROPOSE! RIGHT AWAY!
NOT THAT ANYONE'S EVER TOLD ME "OKAY."
ゴス
GOSU (WHUNK)
NOPE. COULDN'T DO IT.
WAIT! LEMME TALK!
ズル ズル
ZURU (DRAG)
ZURU
I GUESS THERE'S NO POINT IN THINKING ABOUT IT...
カッ
KA (TAK)

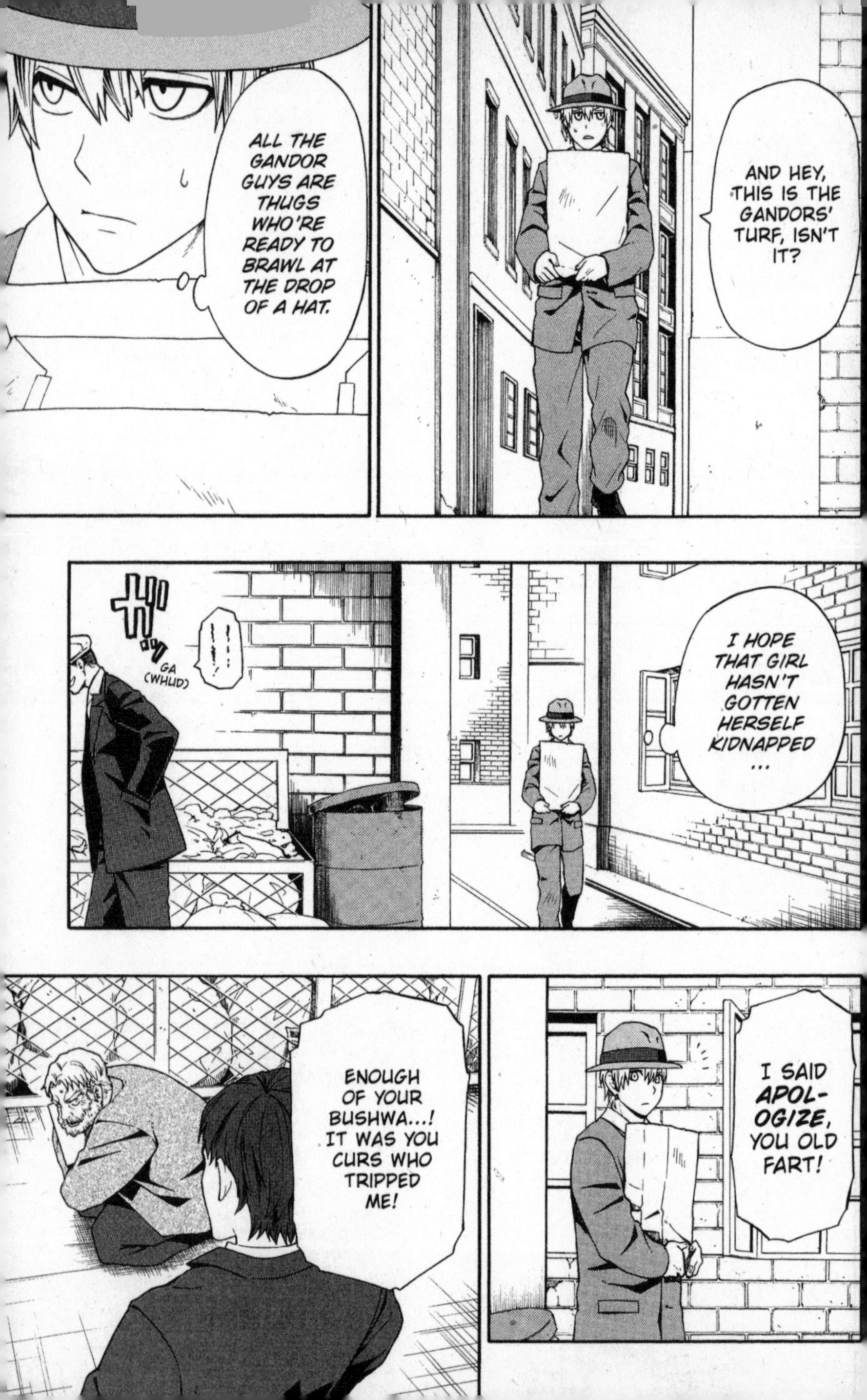
AND HEY, THIS IS THE GANDORS' TURF, ISN'T IT?
ALL THE GANDOR GUYS ARE THUGS WHO'RE READY TO BRAWL AT THE DROP OF A HAT.
I HOPE THAT GIRL HASN'T GOTTEN HERSELF KIDNAPPED...
ガッ
GA (WHUD)
I SAID APOLOGIZE, YOU OLD FART!
ENOUGH OF YOUR BUSHWA...! IT WAS YOU CURS WHO TRIPPED ME!

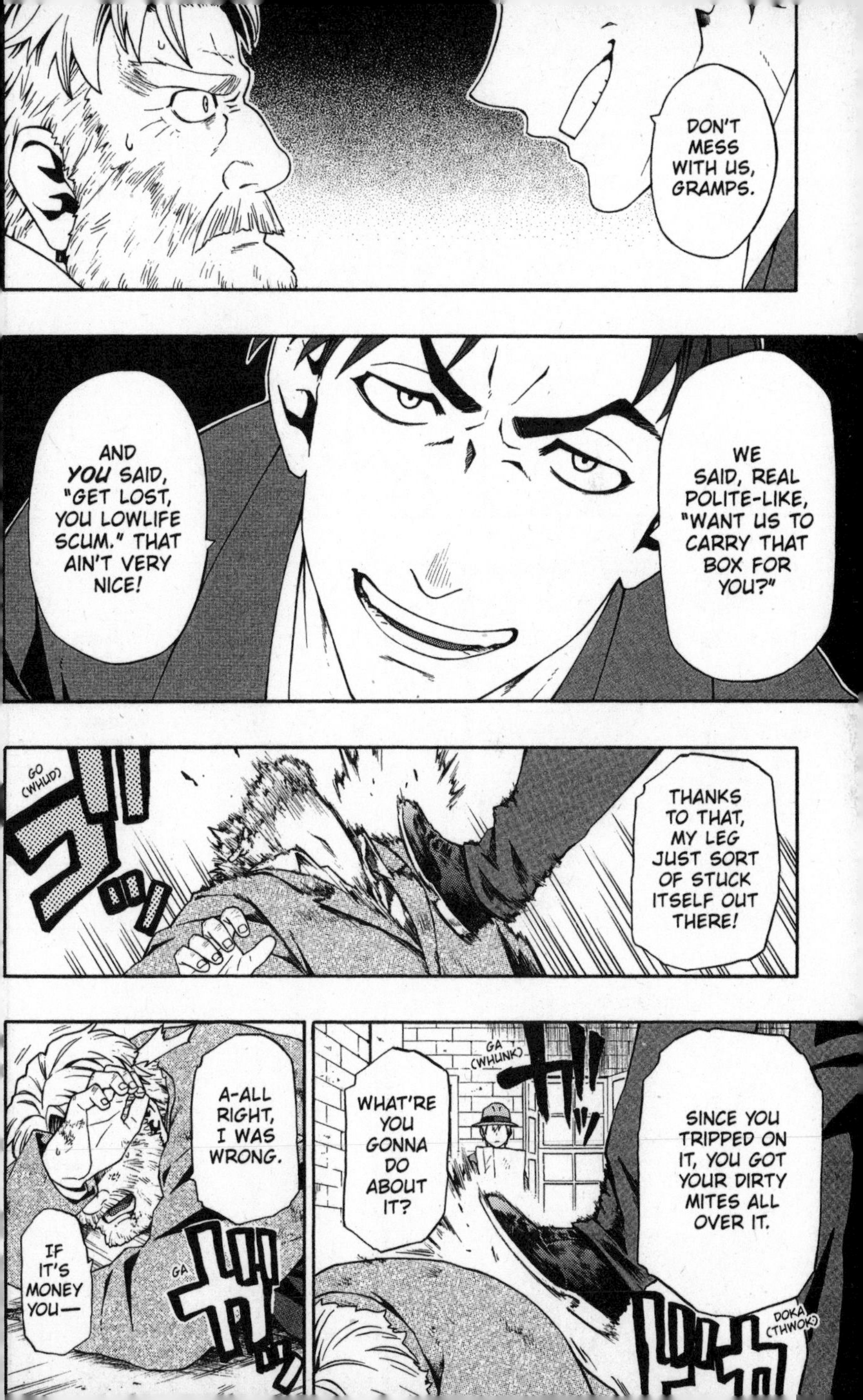
DON'T MESS WITH US, GRAMPS.
WE SAID, REAL POLITE-LIKE, "WANT US TO CARRY THAT BOX FOR YOU?"
AND *YOU* SAID, "GET LOST, YOU LOWLIFE SCUM." THAT AIN'T VERY NICE!
THANKS TO THAT, MY LEG JUST SORT OF STUCK ITSELF OUT THERE!
GO (WHUD)
SINCE YOU TRIPPED ON IT, YOU GOT YOUR DIRTY MITES ALL OVER IT.
GA (WHUNK)
WHAT'RE YOU GONNA DO ABOUT IT?
DOKA (THWOK)
A-ALL RIGHT, I WAS WRONG.
IF IT'S MONEY YOU—
GA

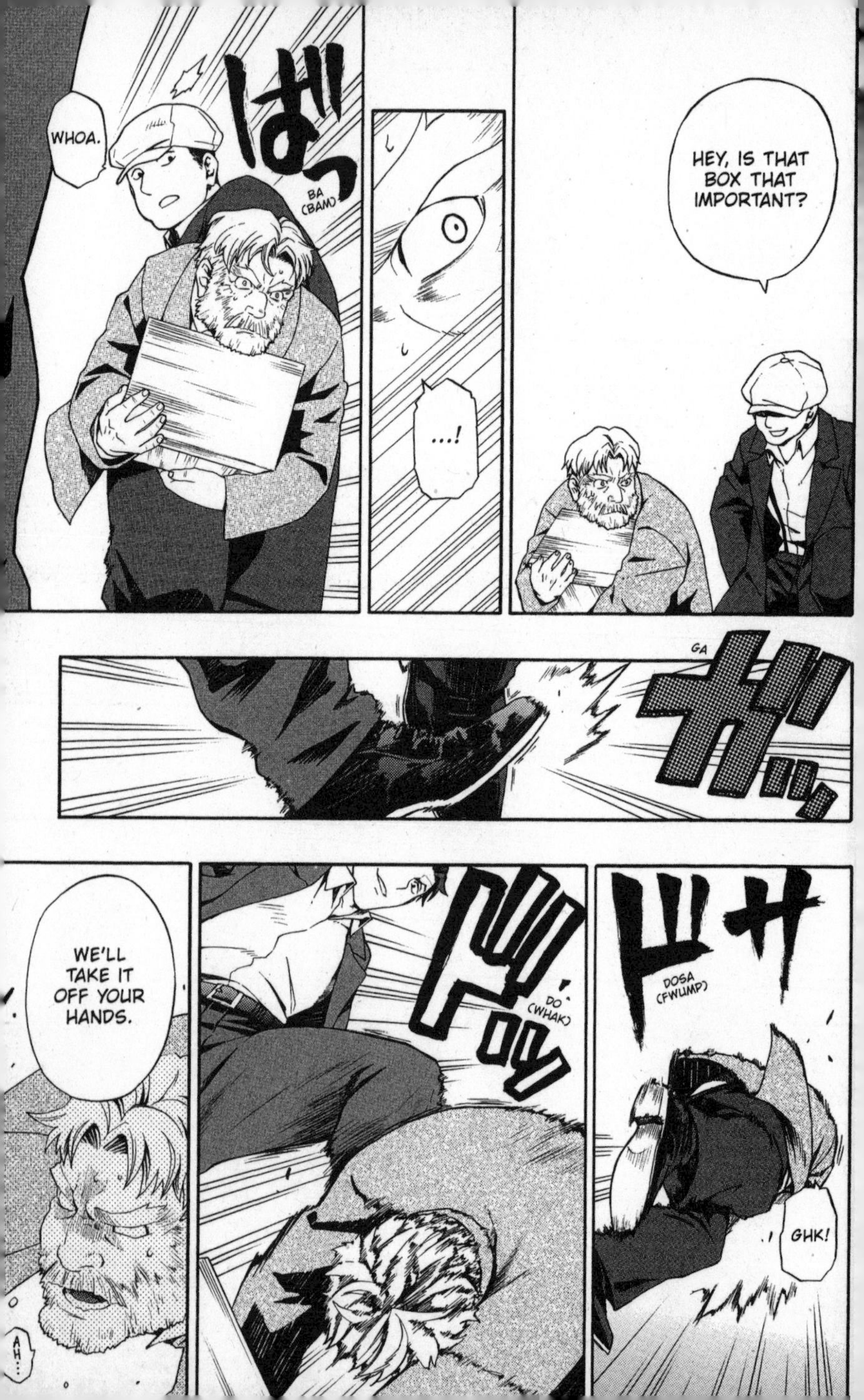
HEY, IS THAT BOX THAT IMPORTANT?
...!
BA (BAM)
WHOA.
GA
DOSA (FWUMP)
GHK!
DO (WHAK)
WE'LL TAKE IT OFF YOUR HANDS.
AH...

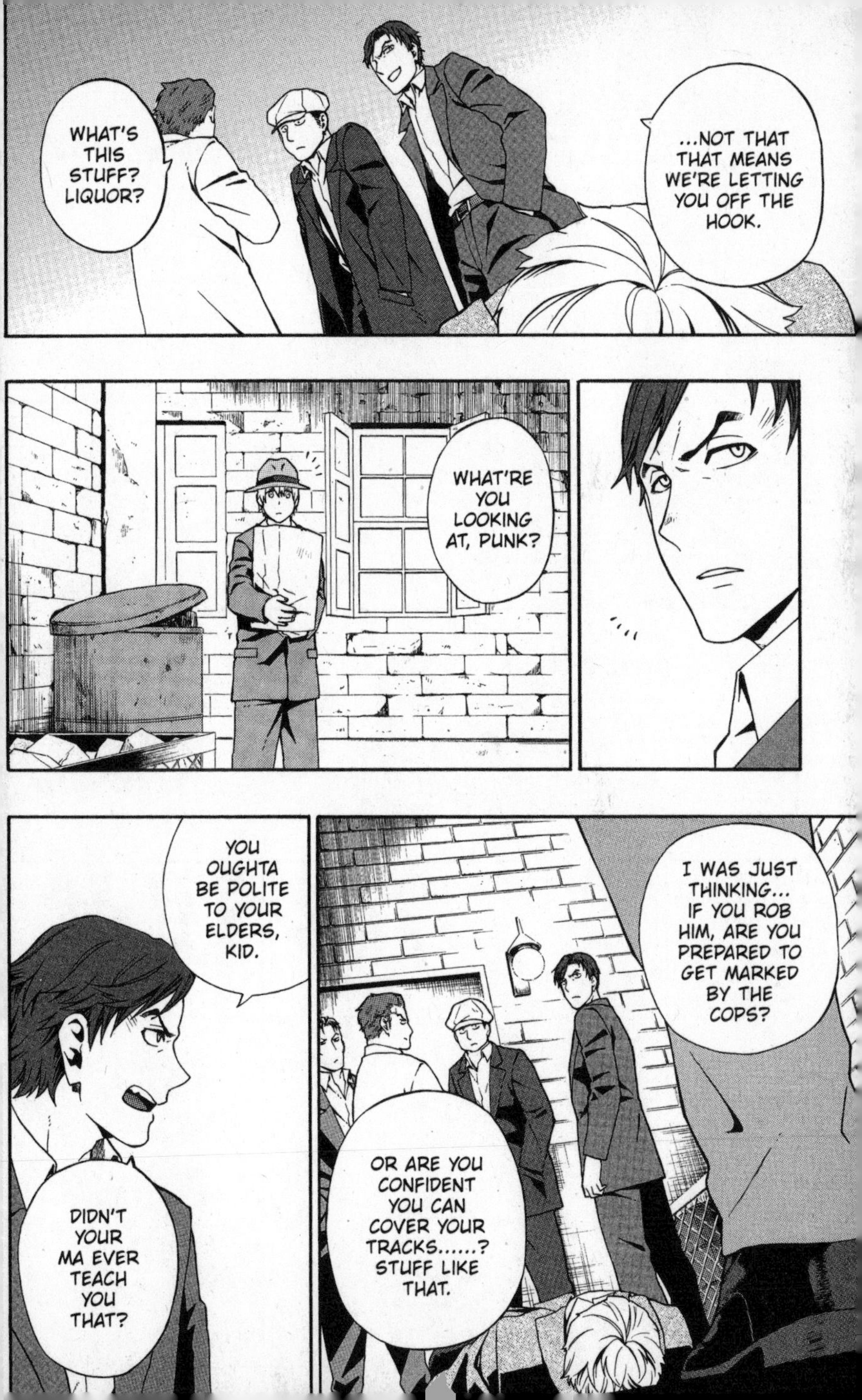
...NOT THAT THAT MEANS WE'RE LETTING YOU OFF THE HOOK.
WHAT'S THIS STUFF? LIQUOR?
WHAT'RE YOU LOOKING AT, PUNK?
I WAS JUST THINKING... IF YOU ROB HIM, ARE YOU PREPARED TO GET MARKED BY THE COPS?
OR ARE YOU CONFIDENT YOU CAN COVER YOUR TRACKS......? STUFF LIKE THAT.
YOU OUGHTA BE POLITE TO YOUR ELDERS, KID.
DIDN'T YOUR MA EVER TEACH YOU THAT?

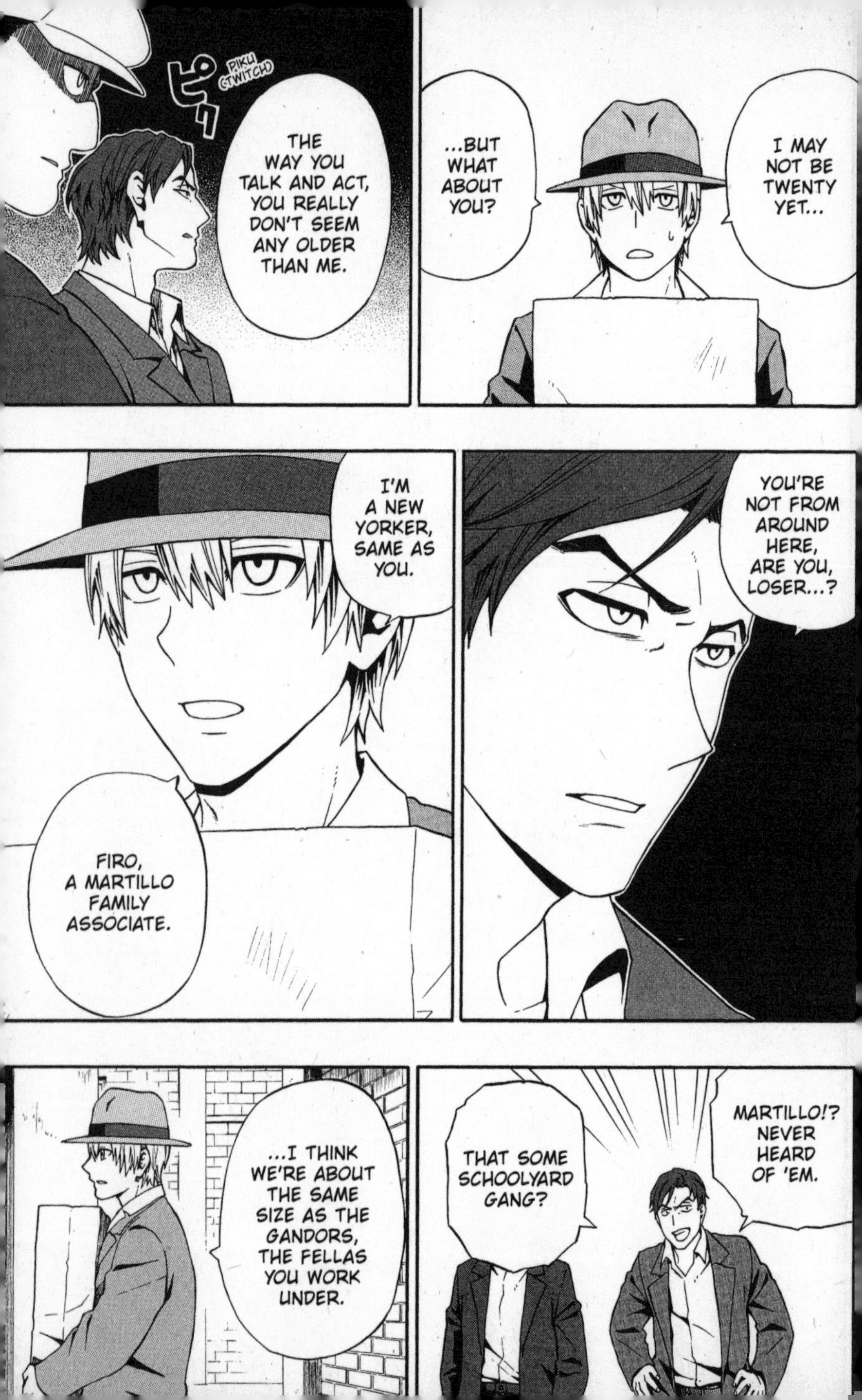
I MAY NOT BE TWENTY YET...
...BUT WHAT ABOUT YOU?
ピク
PIKU (TWITCH)
THE WAY YOU TALK AND ACT, YOU REALLY DON'T SEEM ANY OLDER THAN ME.
YOU'RE NOT FROM AROUND HERE, ARE YOU, LOSER...?
I'M A NEW YORKER, SAME AS YOU.
FIRO, A MARTILLO FAMILY ASSOCIATE.
MARTILLO!? NEVER HEARD OF 'EM.
THAT SOME SCHOOLYARD GANG?
...I THINK WE'RE ABOUT THE SAME SIZE AS THE GANDORS, THE FELLAS YOU WORK UNDER.

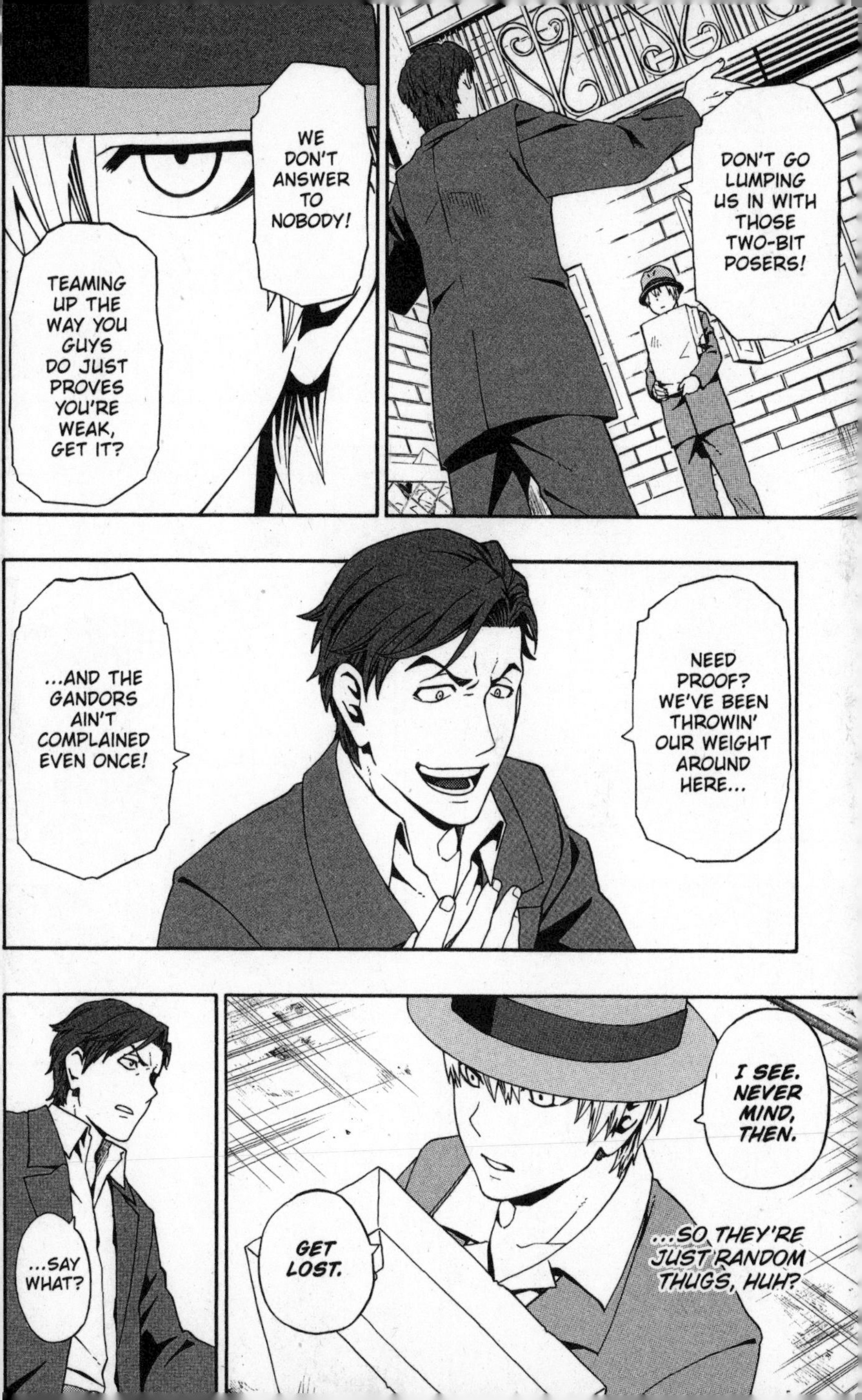
DON'T GO LUMPING US IN WITH THOSE TWO-BIT POSERS!
WE DON'T ANSWER TO NOBODY!
TEAMING UP THE WAY YOU GUYS DO JUST PROVES YOU'RE WEAK, GET IT?
NEED PROOF? WE'VE BEEN THROWIN' OUR WEIGHT AROUND HERE...
...AND THE GANDORS AIN'T COMPLAINED EVEN ONCE!
I SEE. NEVER MIND, THEN.
...SO THEY'RE JUST RANDOM THUGS, HUH?
GET LOST.
...SAY WHAT?

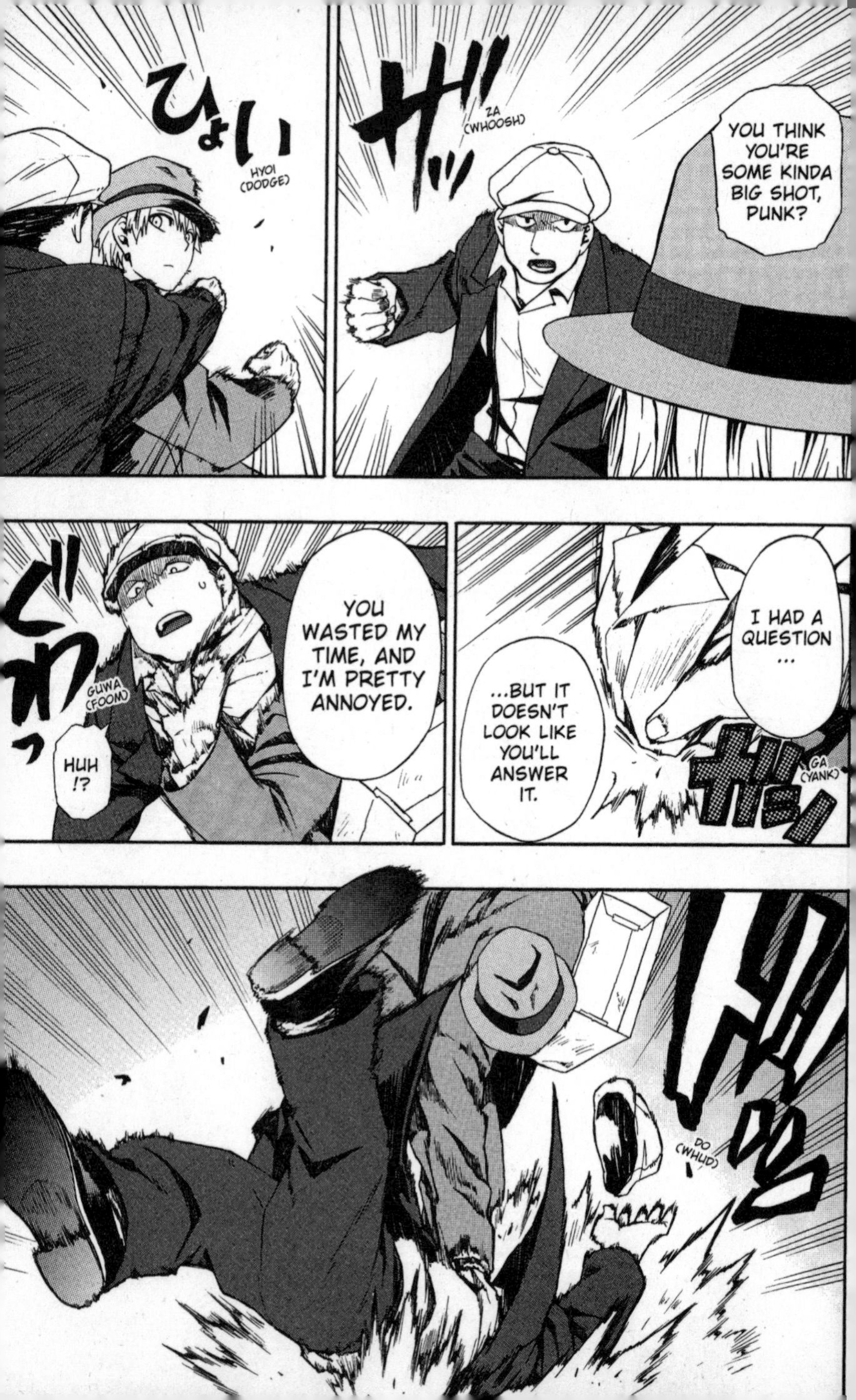

ザッ
ZA (WHOOSH)
YOU THINK YOU'RE SOME KINDA BIG SHOT, PUNK?
ひょい
HYOI (DODGE)
I HAD A QUESTION...
...BUT IT DOESN'T LOOK LIKE YOU'LL ANSWER IT.
GA (YANK)
YOU WASTED MY TIME, AND I'M PRETTY ANNOYED.
GUWA (FOOM)
HUH!?
DO (WHUD)

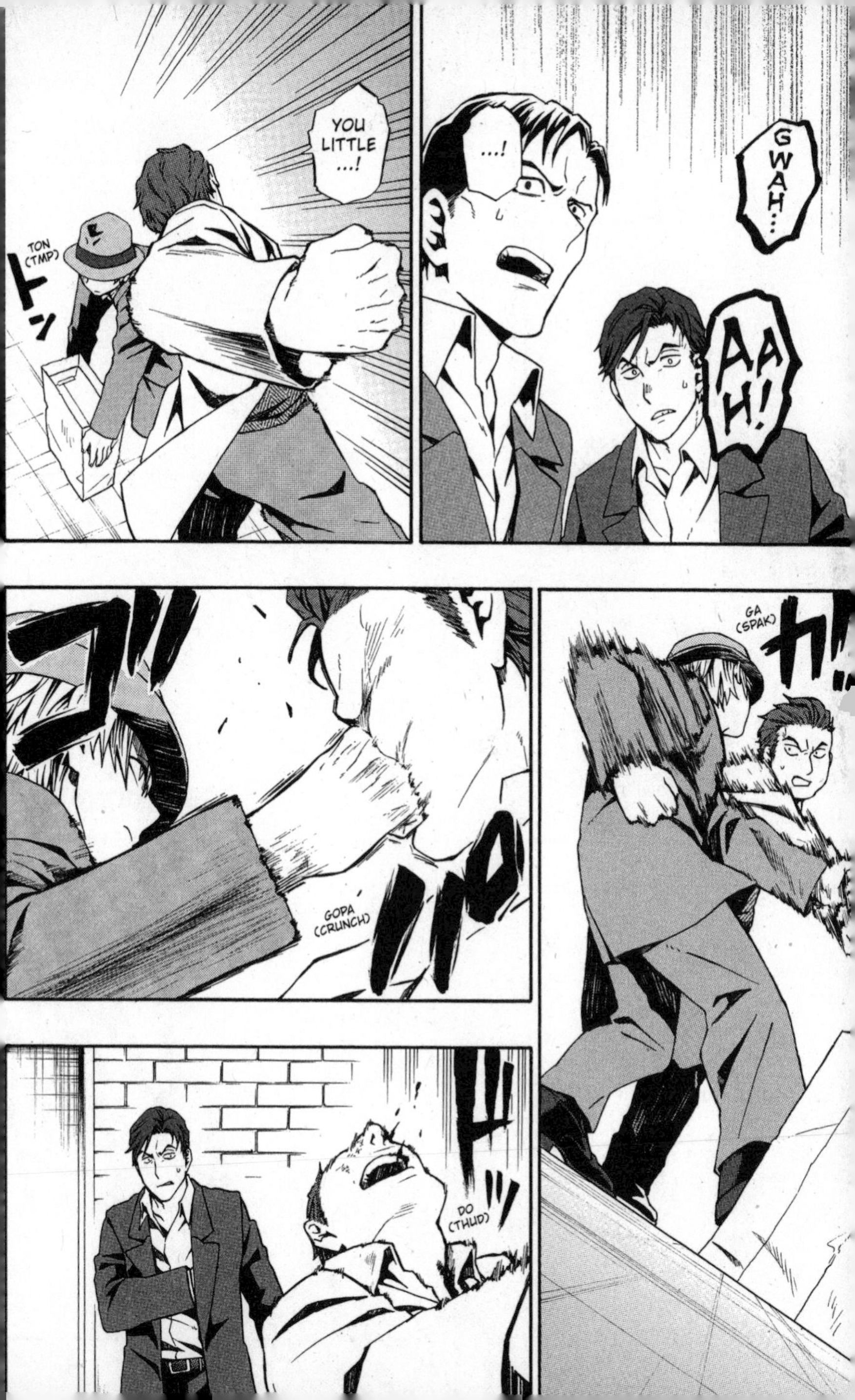

GWAH...
...!
AAH!
YOU LITTLE ...!
TON (TMP)
トン
GA (SPAK)
ガッ
ゴパッ
GOPA (CRUNCH)
ドッ
DO (THUD)

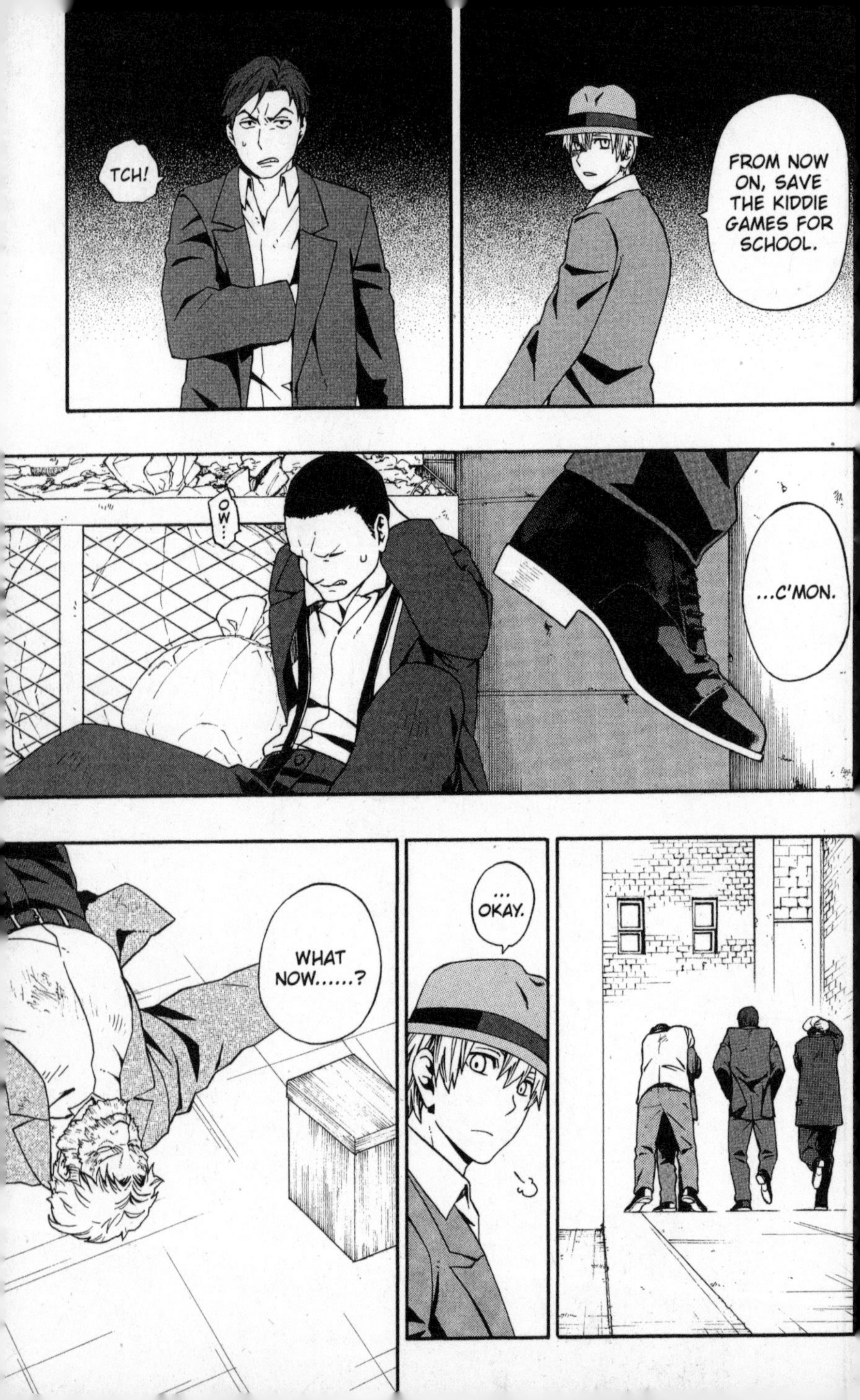
FROM NOW ON, SAVE THE KIDDIE GAMES FOR SCHOOL.
TCH!
...C'MON.
OW...
...OKAY.
WHAT NOW......?

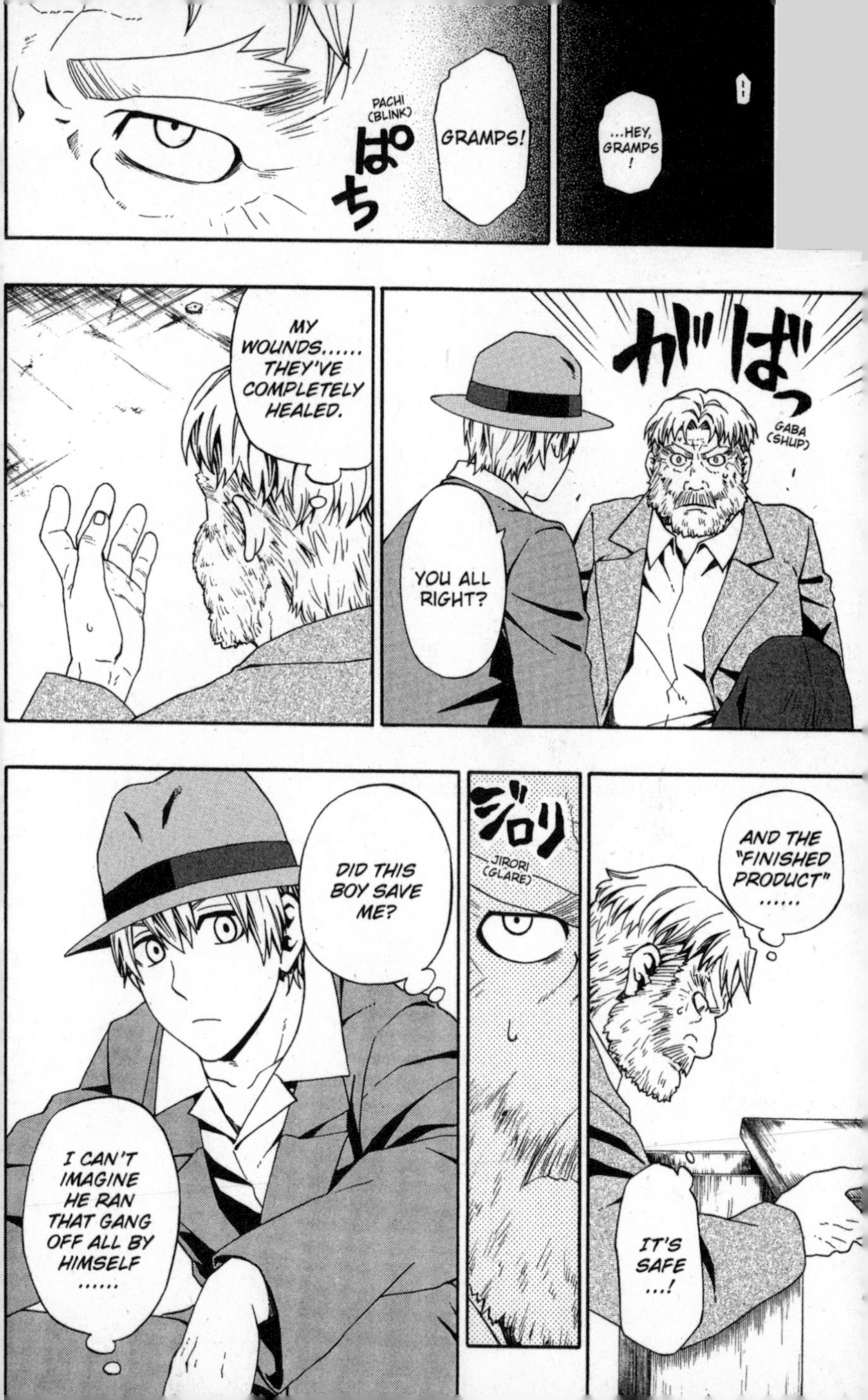
!!
...HEY, GRAMPS!
GRAMPS!
ぱち
PACHI (BLINK)
がばっ
GABA (SHUP)
!
YOU ALL RIGHT?
MY WOUNDS...... THEY'VE COMPLETELY HEALED.
AND THE "FINISHED PRODUCT"......
IT'S SAFE...!
ジロリ
JIRORI (GLARE)
DID THIS BOY SAVE ME?
I CAN'T IMAGINE HE RAN THAT GANG OFF ALL BY HIMSELF......

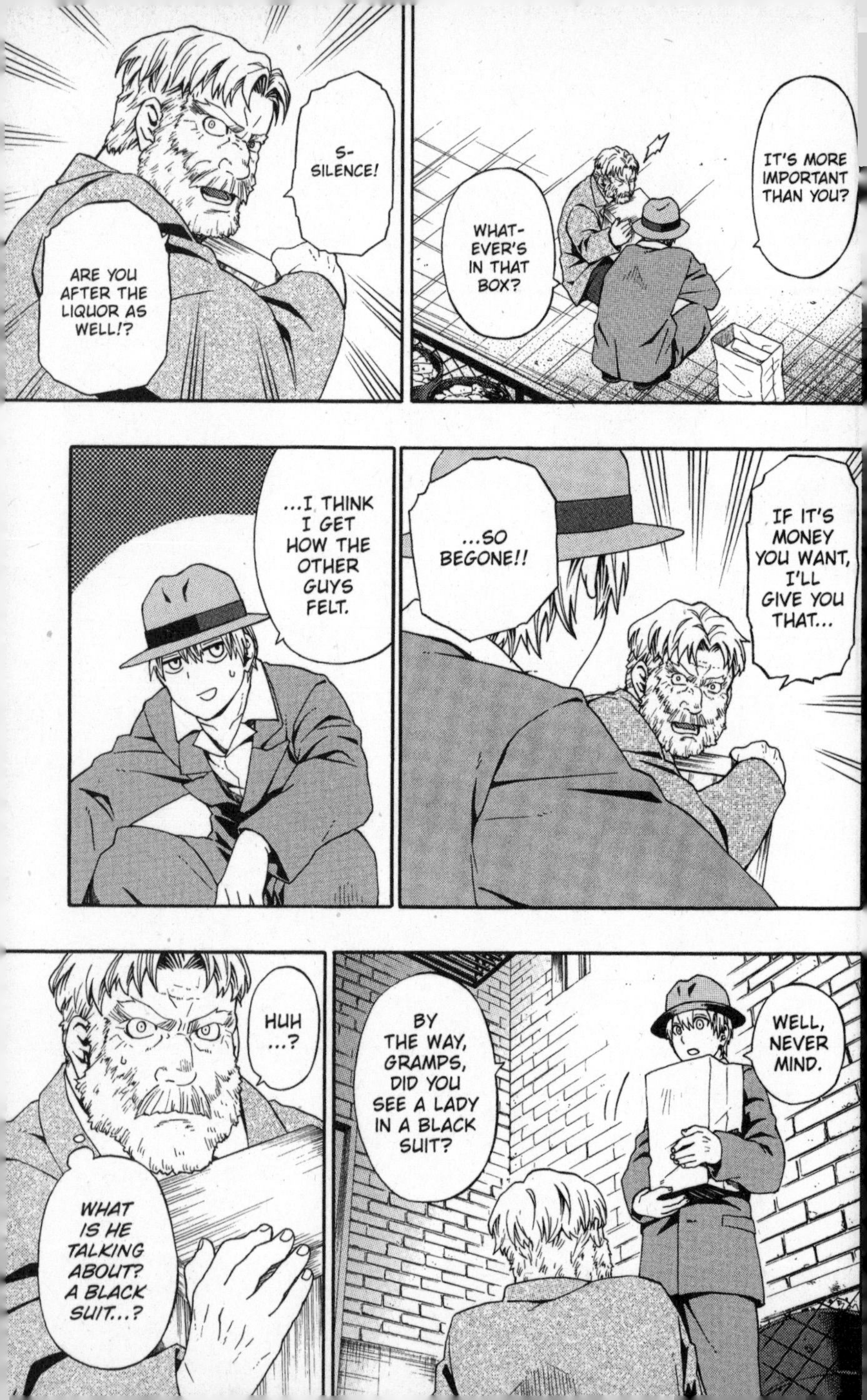
IT'S MORE IMPORTANT THAN YOU?
WHAT-EVER'S IN THAT BOX?
S-SILENCE!
ARE YOU AFTER THE LIQUOR AS WELL!?
IF IT'S MONEY YOU WANT, I'LL GIVE YOU THAT...
...SO BEGONE!!
...I THINK I GET HOW THE OTHER GUYS FELT.
WELL, NEVER MIND.
BY THE WAY, GRAMPS, DID YOU SEE A LADY IN A BLACK SUIT?
HUH...?
WHAT IS HE TALKING ABOUT? A BLACK SUIT...?

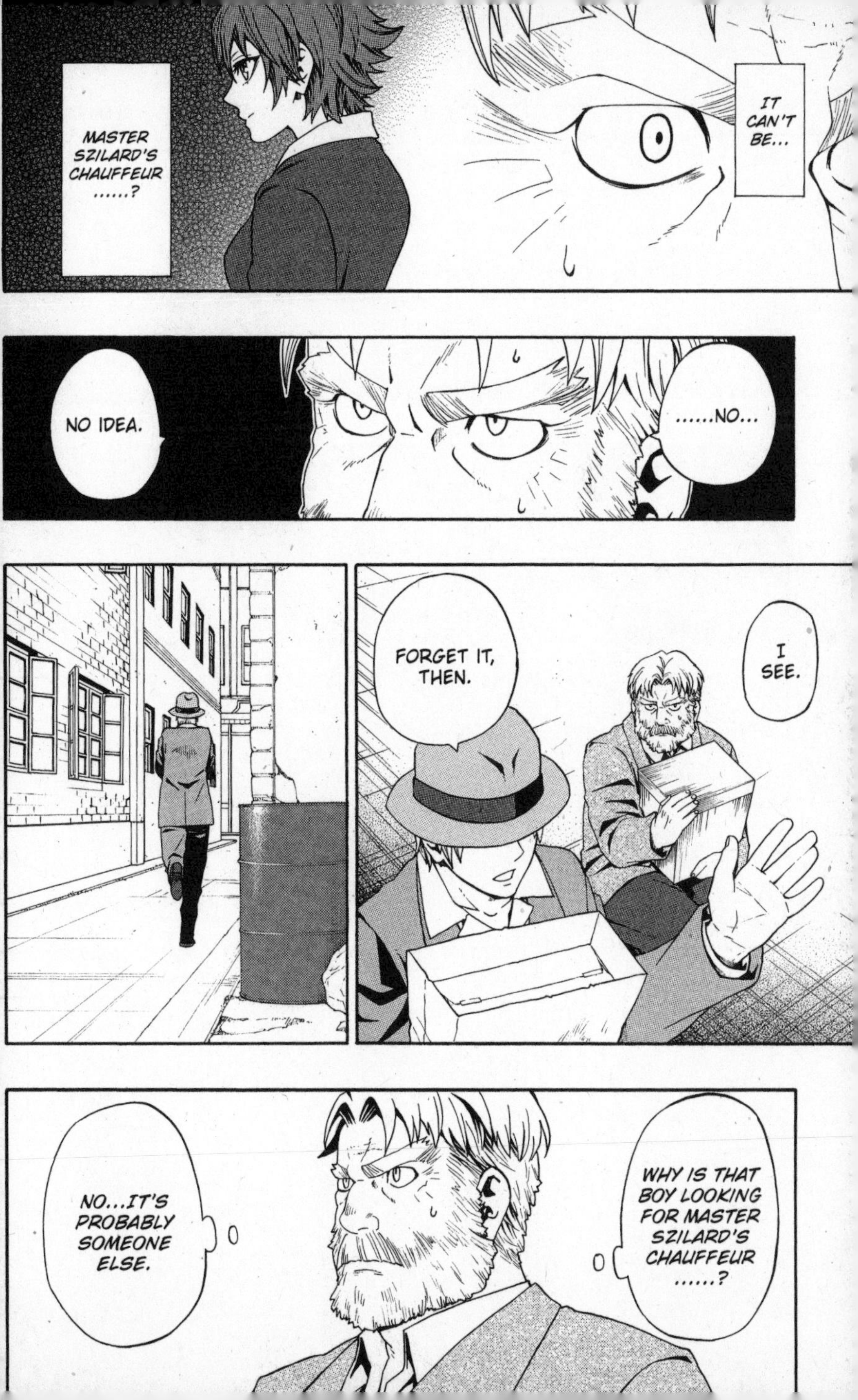
IT CAN'T BE...
MASTER SZILARD'S CHAUFFEUR ......?
......NO...
NO IDEA.
I SEE.
FORGET IT, THEN.
WHY IS THAT BOY LOOKING FOR MASTER SZILARD'S CHAUFFEUR ......?
NO...IT'S PROBABLY SOMEONE ELSE.

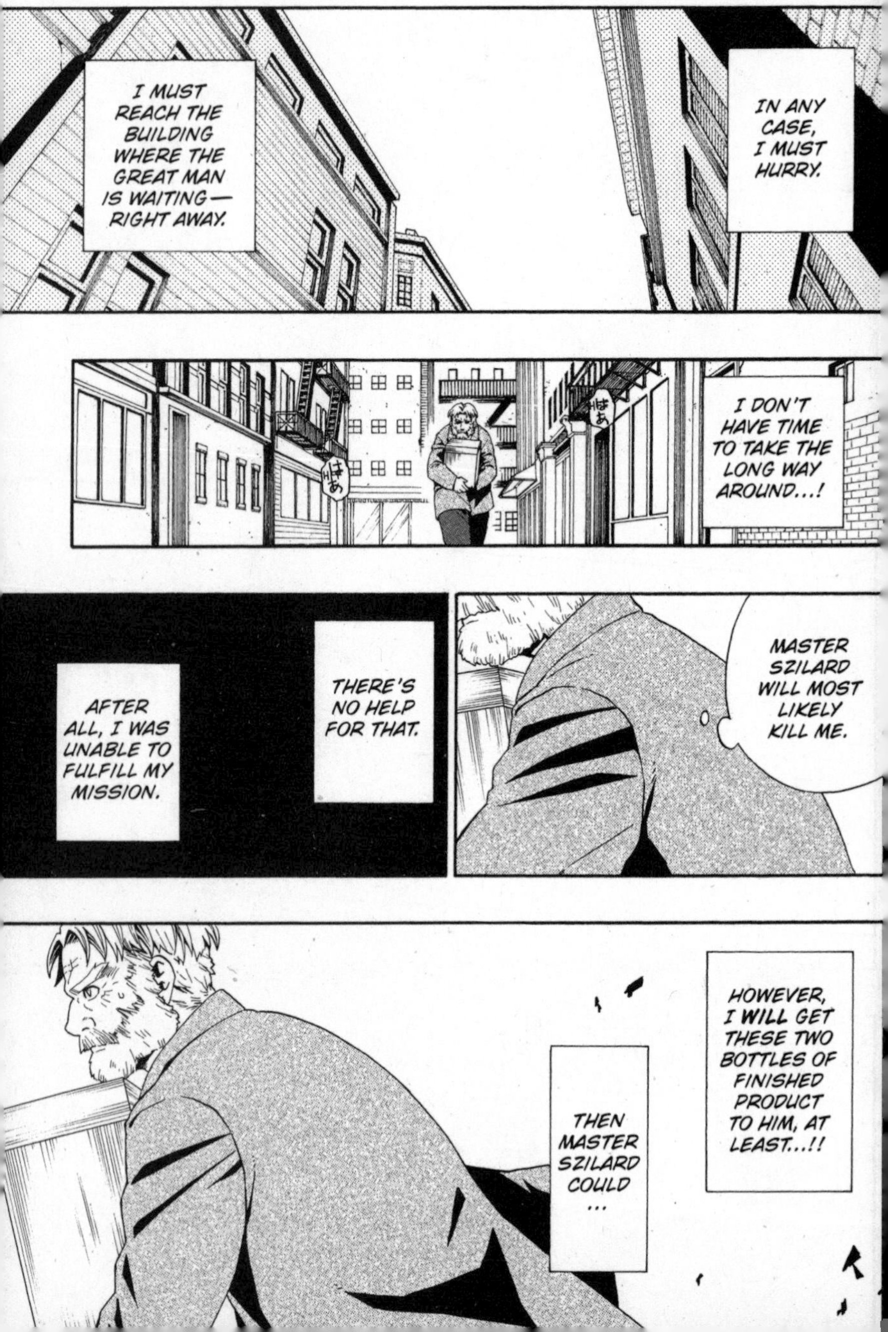
IN ANY CASE, I MUST HURRY.
I MUST REACH THE BUILDING WHERE THE GREAT MAN IS WAITING—RIGHT AWAY.
I DON'T HAVE TIME TO TAKE THE LONG WAY AROUND...!
はぁ
はぁ
MASTER SZILARD WILL MOST LIKELY KILL ME.
THERE'S NO HELP FOR THAT.
AFTER ALL, I WAS UNABLE TO FULFILL MY MISSION.
HOWEVER, I **WILL** GET THESE TWO BOTTLES OF FINISHED PRODUCT TO HIM, AT LEAST...!!
THEN MASTER SZILARD COULD...

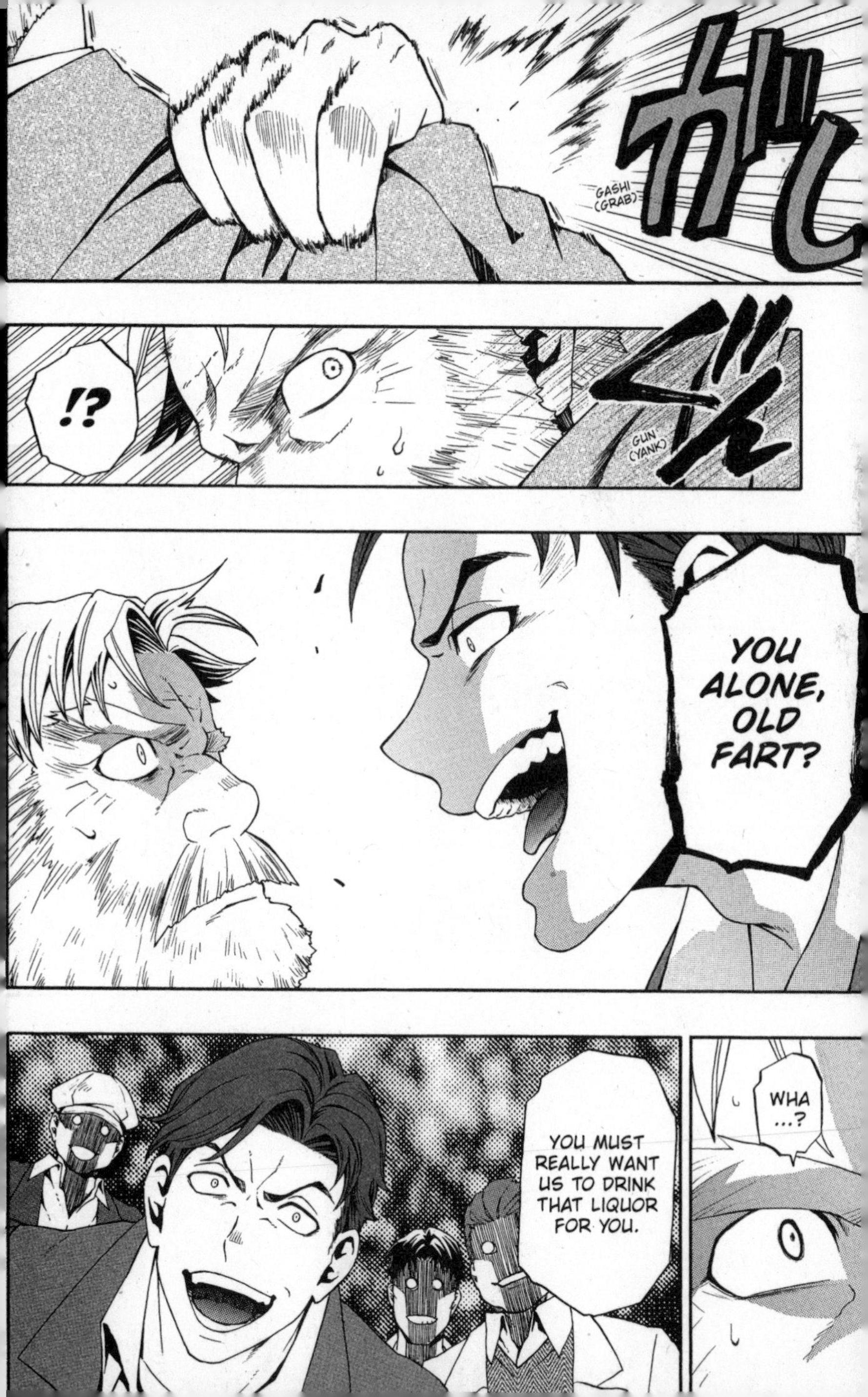
がし
GASHI (GRAB)
ぐぃ
GUN (YANK)
!?
YOU ALONE, OLD FART?
WHA ...?
YOU MUST REALLY WANT US TO DRINK THAT LIQUOR FOR YOU.

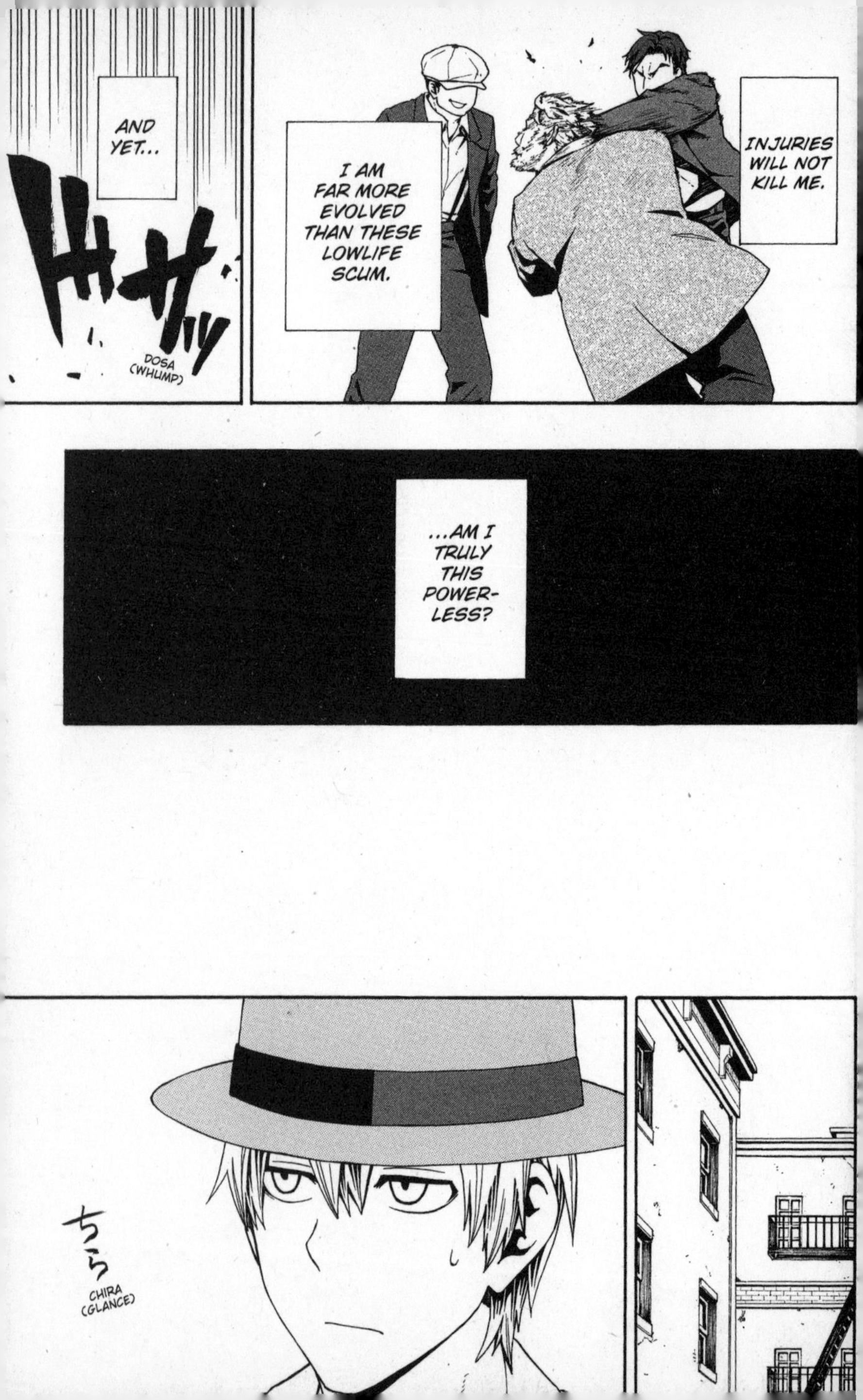
INJURIES WILL NOT KILL ME.
I AM FAR MORE EVOLVED THAN THESE LOWLIFE SCUM.
AND YET...
DOSA (WHUMP)
...AM I TRULY THIS POWER-LESS?
ちら
CHIRA (GLANCE)

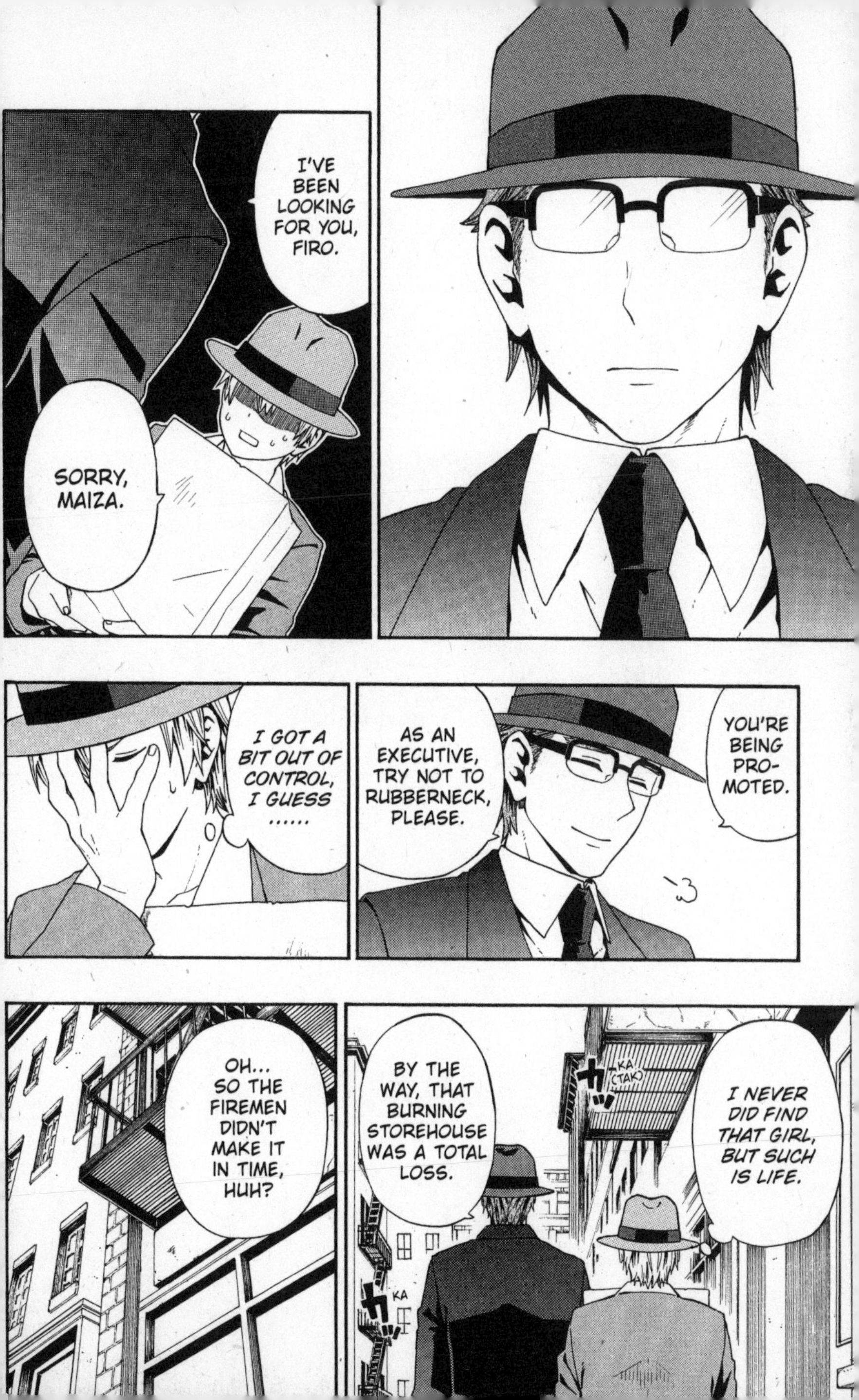
I'VE BEEN LOOKING FOR YOU, FIRO.
SORRY, MAIZA.
YOU'RE BEING PRO-MOTED.
AS AN EXECUTIVE, TRY NOT TO RUBBERNECK, PLEASE.
I GOT A BIT OUT OF CONTROL, I GUESS ......
I NEVER DID FIND THAT GIRL, BUT SUCH IS LIFE.
KA (TAK)
BY THE WAY, THAT BURNING STOREHOUSE WAS A TOTAL LOSS.
KA
OH... SO THE FIREMEN DIDN'T MAKE IT IN TIME, HUH?

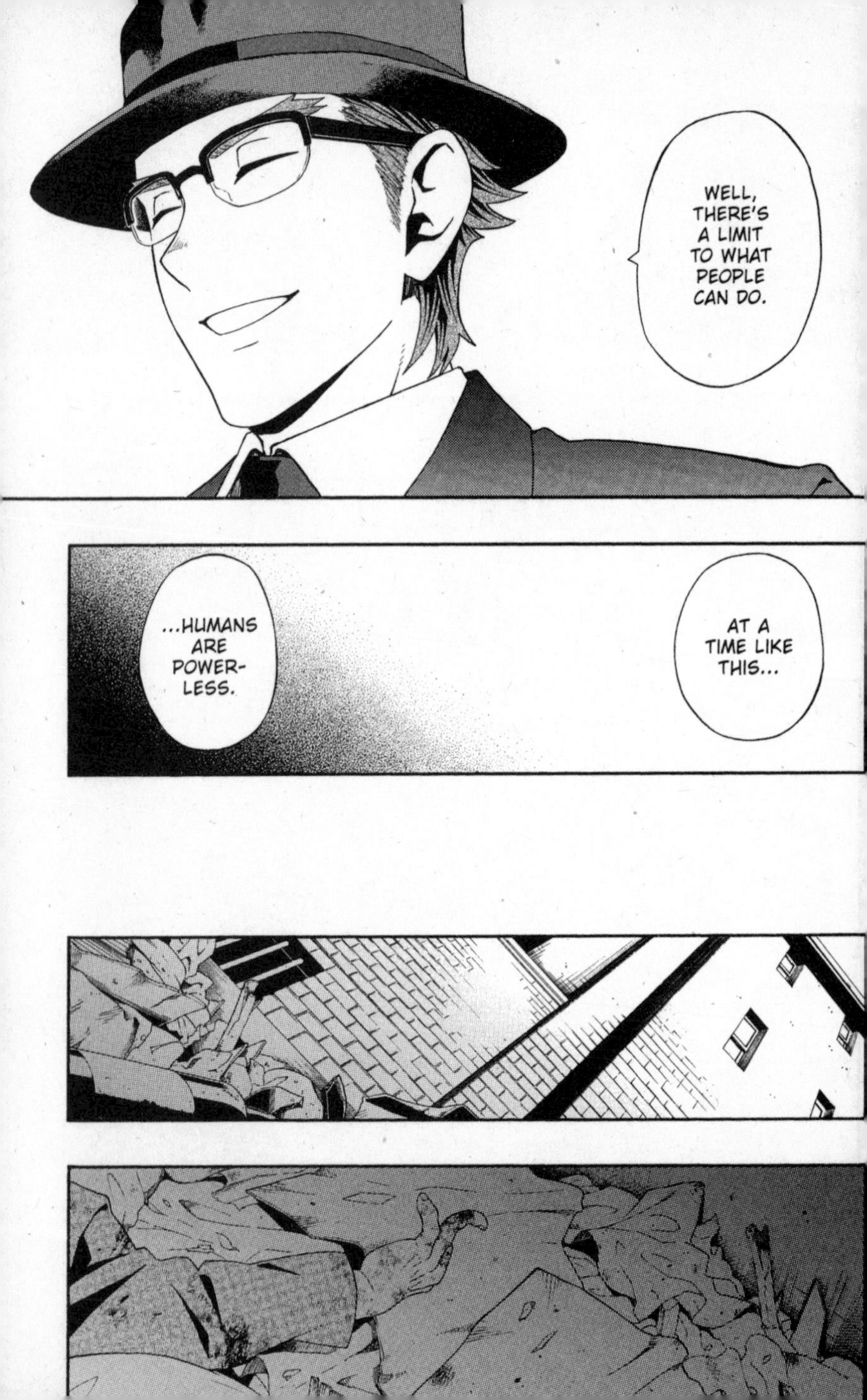
WELL, THERE'S A LIMIT TO WHAT PEOPLE CAN DO.
AT A TIME LIKE THIS...
...HUMANS ARE POWER-LESS.

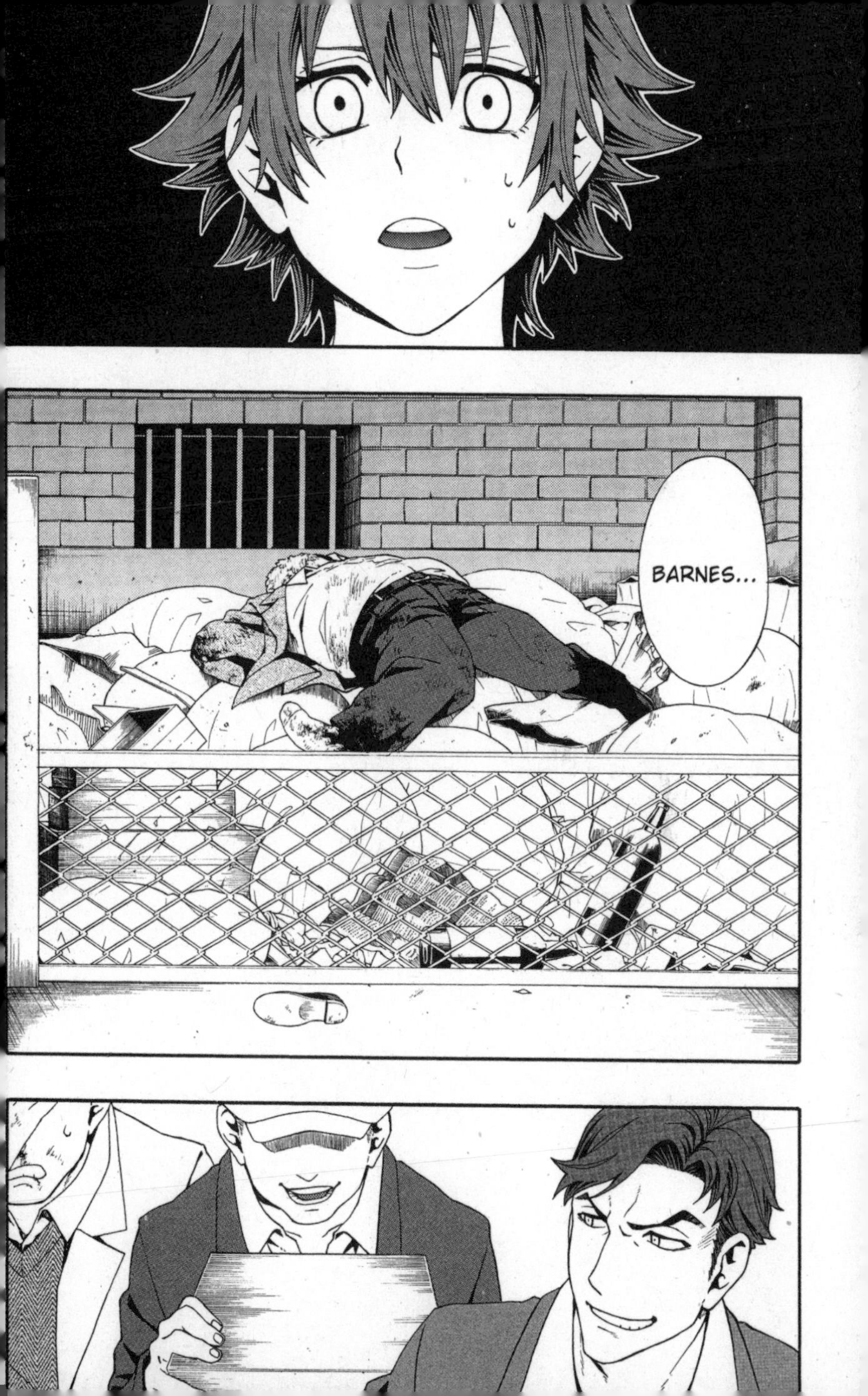
BARNES...

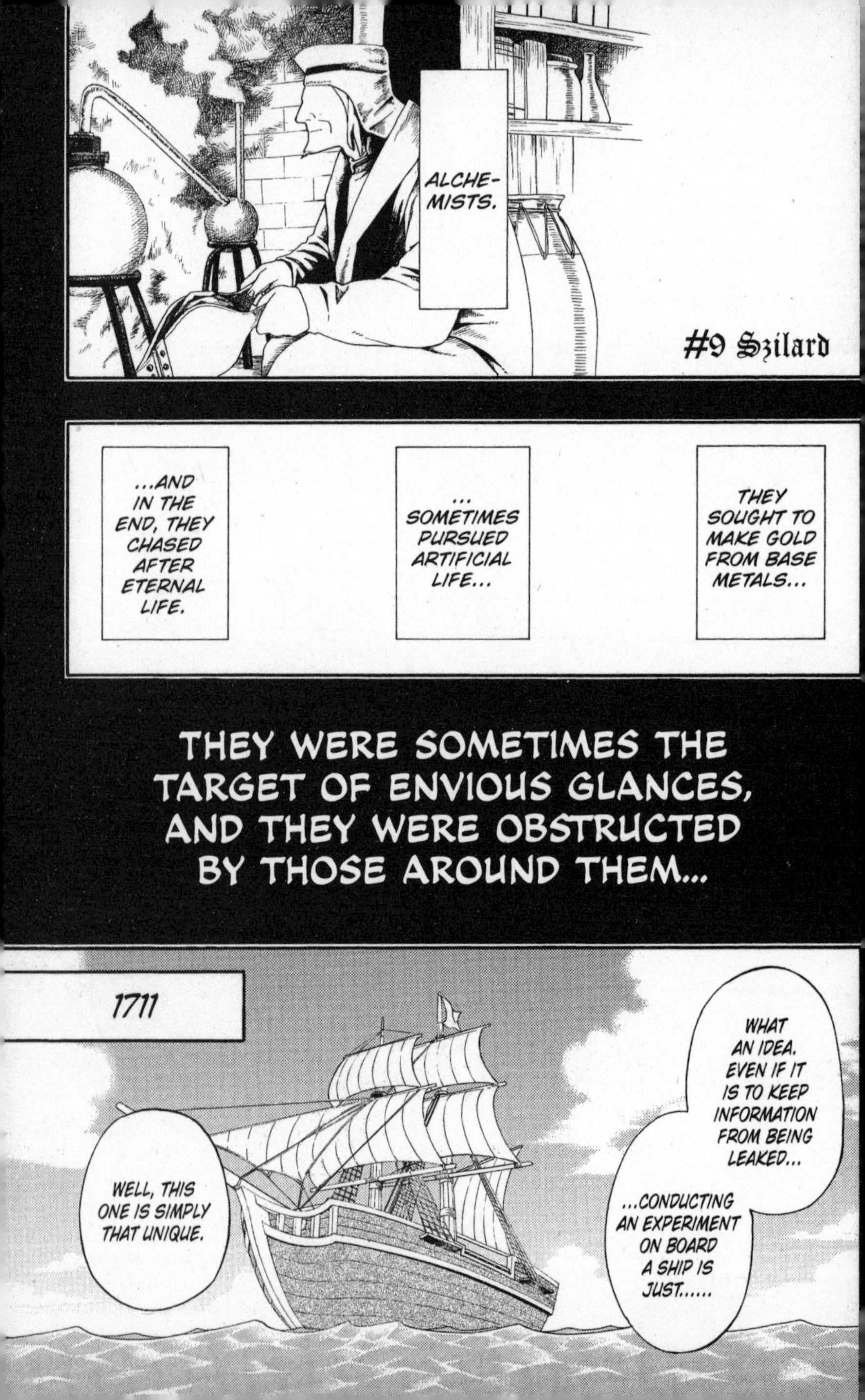

#9 Szilard
ALCHEMISTS.
THEY SOUGHT TO MAKE GOLD FROM BASE METALS...
...SOMETIMES PURSUED ARTIFICIAL LIFE...
...AND IN THE END, THEY CHASED AFTER ETERNAL LIFE.
THEY WERE SOMETIMES THE TARGET OF ENVIOUS GLANCES, AND THEY WERE OBSTRUCTED BY THOSE AROUND THEM...
1711
WHAT AN IDEA. EVEN IF IT IS TO KEEP INFORMATION FROM BEING LEAKED...
...CONDUCTING AN EXPERIMENT ON BOARD A SHIP IS JUST......
WELL, THIS ONE IS SIMPLY THAT UNIQUE.

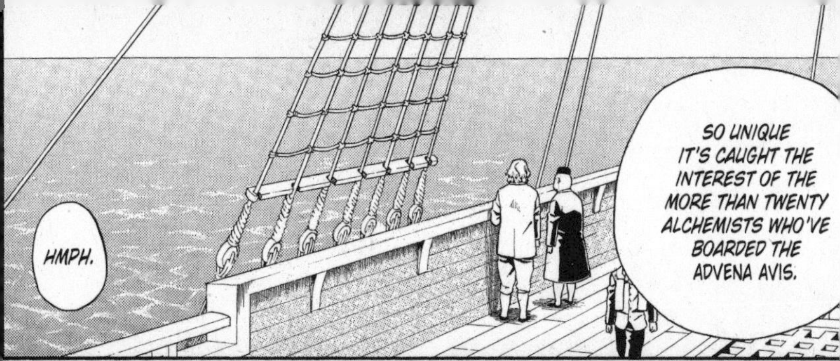
SO UNIQUE IT'S CAUGHT THE INTEREST OF THE MORE THAN TWENTY ALCHEMISTS WHO'VE BOARDED THE ADVENA AVIS.
HMPH.

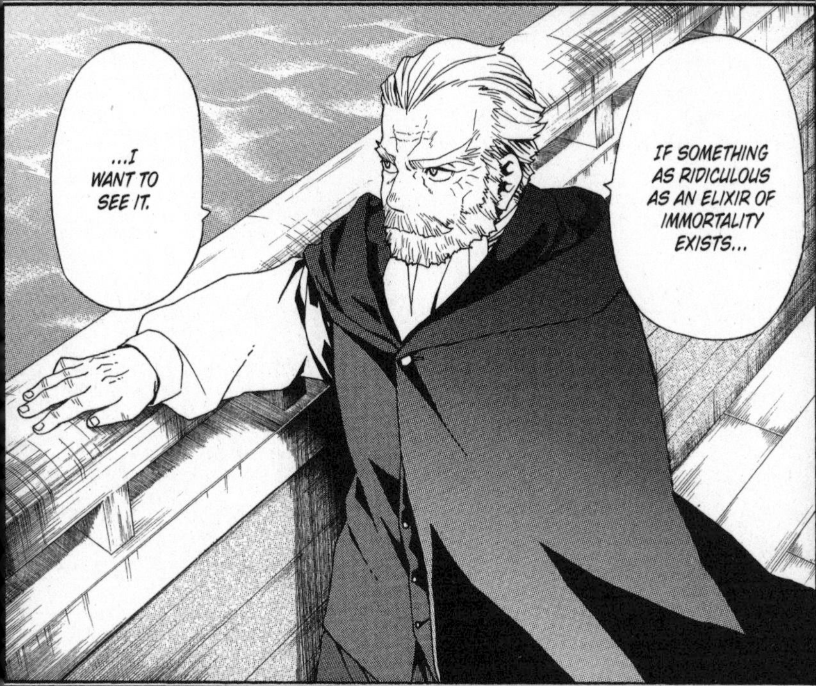
IF SOMETHING AS RIDICULOUS AS AN ELIXIR OF IMMORTALITY EXISTS...
...I WANT TO SEE IT.

#9 Szilard

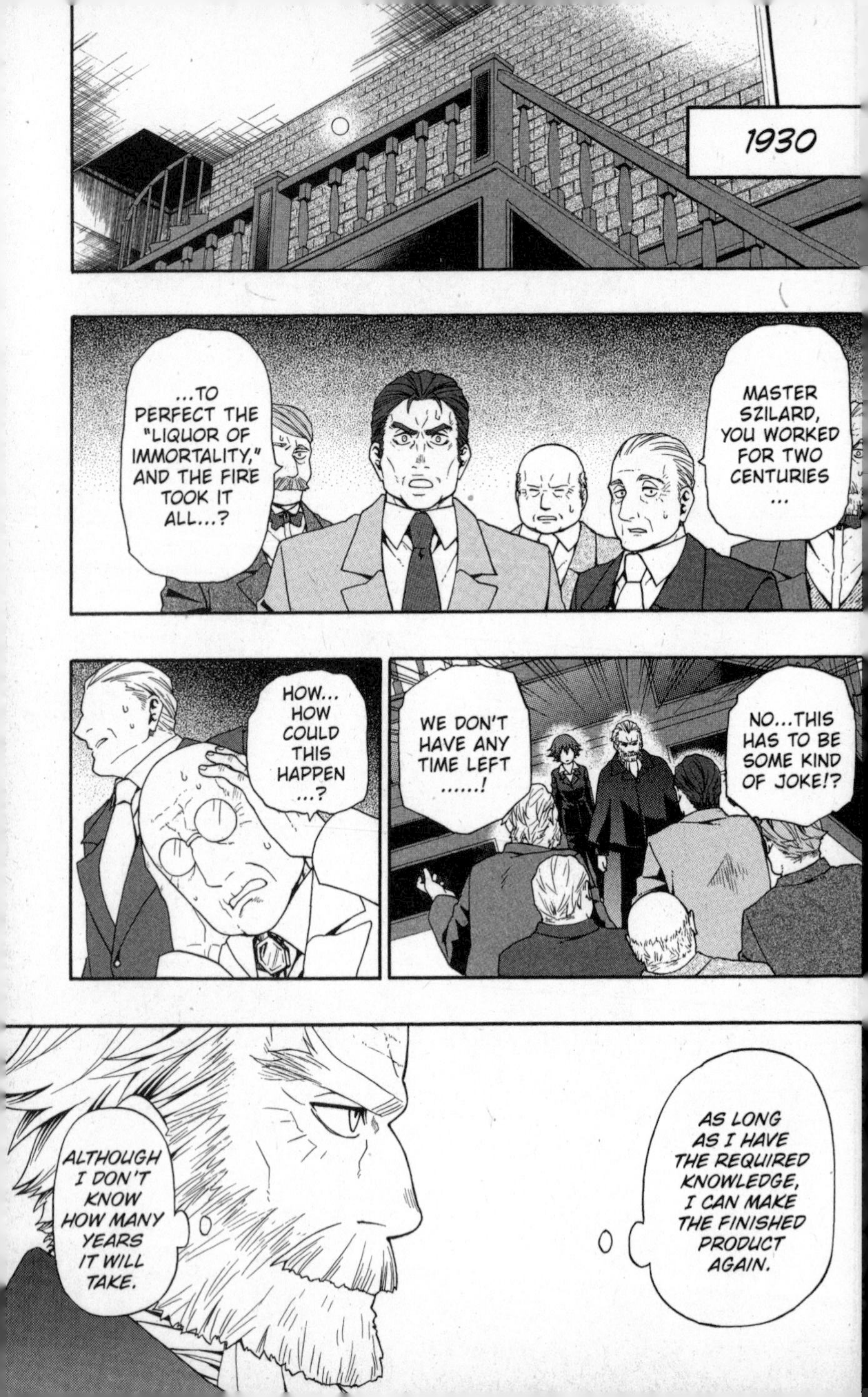
1930
MASTER SZILARD, YOU WORKED FOR TWO CENTURIES...
...TO PERFECT THE "LIQUOR OF IMMORTALITY," AND THE FIRE TOOK IT ALL...?
NO...THIS HAS TO BE SOME KIND OF JOKE!?
WE DON'T HAVE ANY TIME LEFT......!
HOW... HOW COULD THIS HAPPEN...?
AS LONG AS I HAVE THE REQUIRED KNOWLEDGE, I CAN MAKE THE FINISHED PRODUCT AGAIN.
ALTHOUGH I DON'T KNOW HOW MANY YEARS IT WILL TAKE.

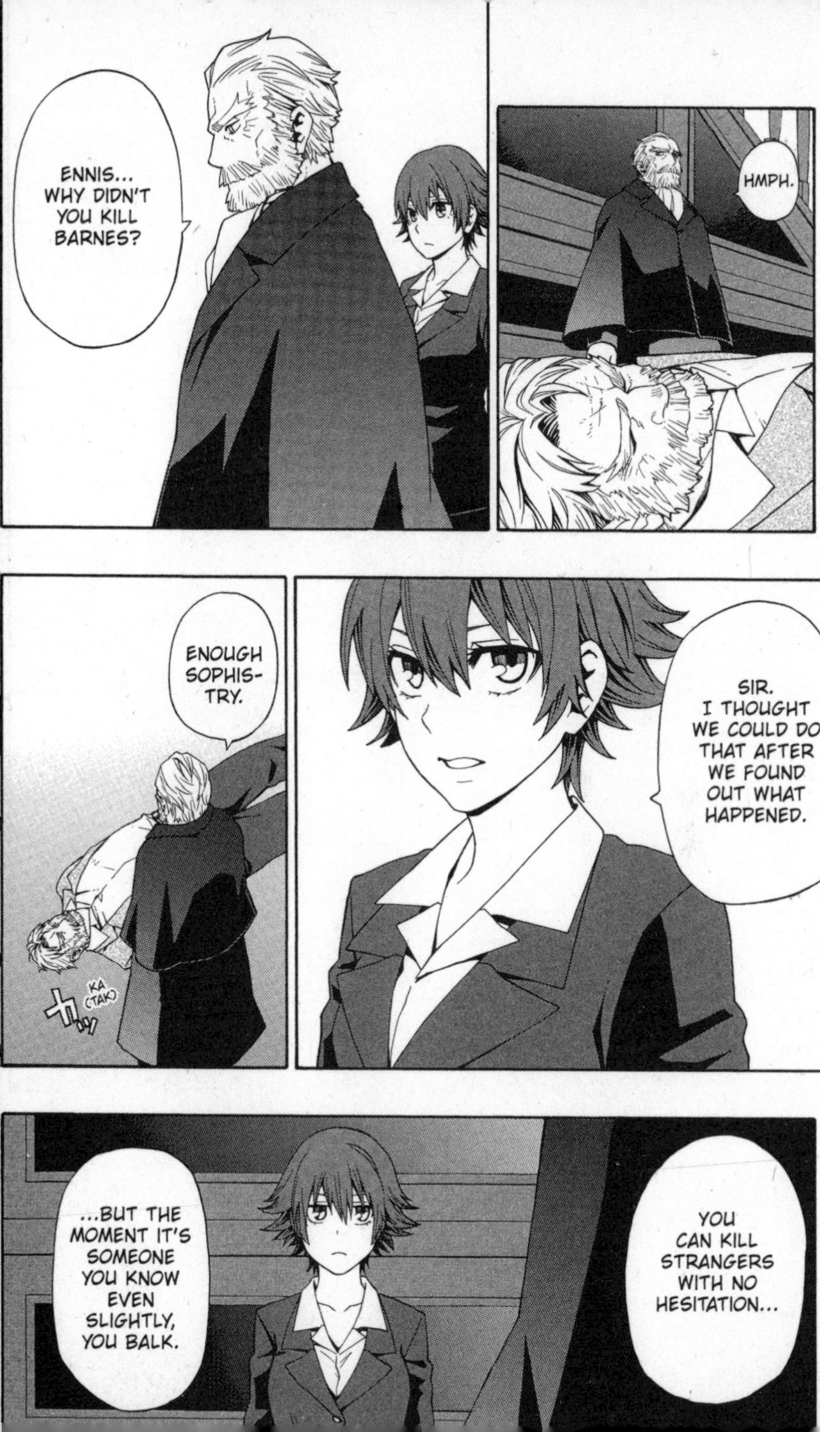
HMPH.
ENNIS... WHY DIDN'T YOU KILL BARNES?
SIR. I THOUGHT WE COULD DO THAT AFTER WE FOUND OUT WHAT HAPPENED.
ENOUGH SOPHISTRY.
KA (TAK)
YOU CAN KILL STRANGERS WITH NO HESITATION...
...BUT THE MOMENT IT'S SOMEONE YOU KNOW EVEN SLIGHTLY, YOU BALK.

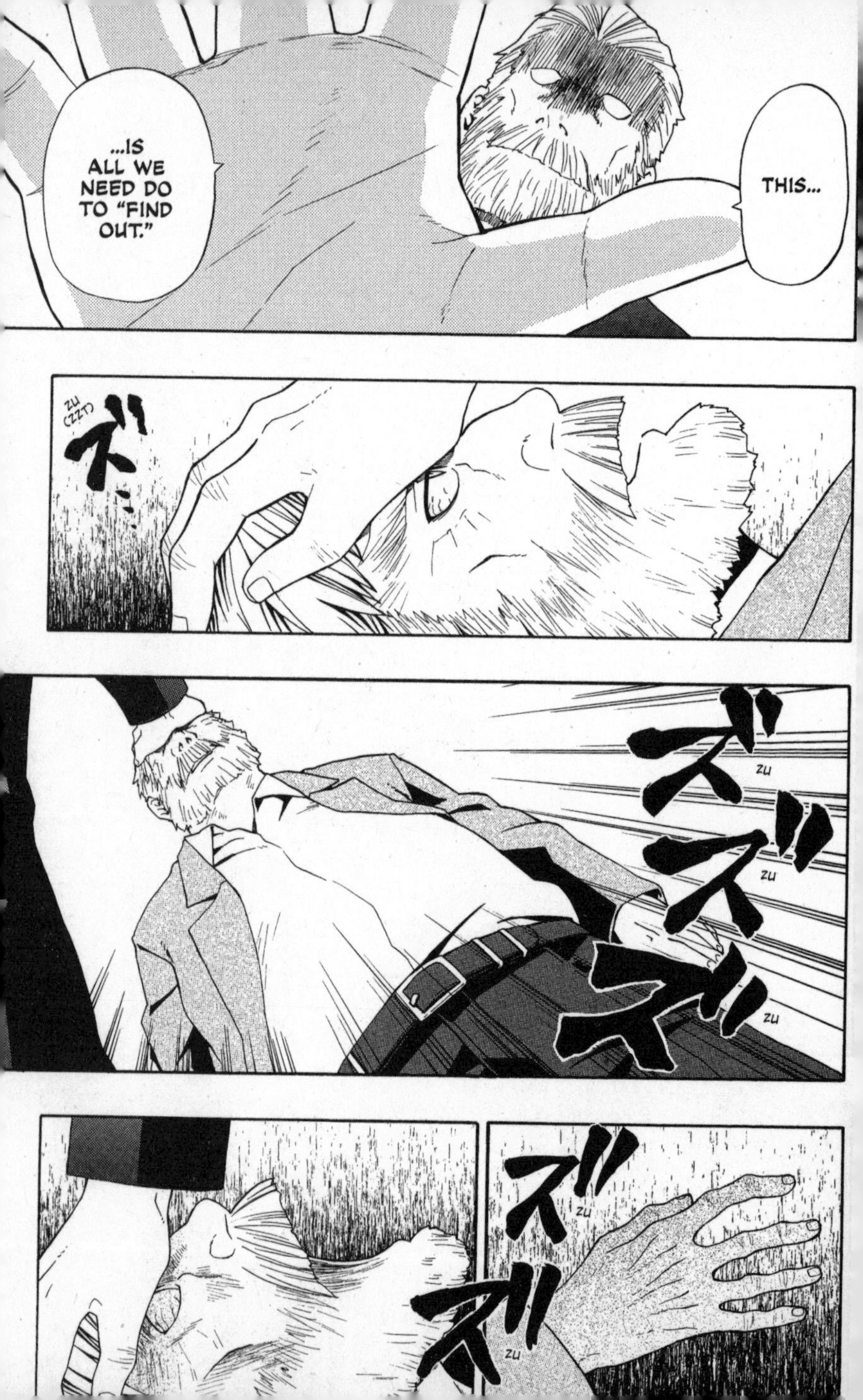
THIS...
...IS ALL WE NEED DO TO "FIND OUT."
ズ
ZU (ZZZT)
ズズズ
ZU
ZU
ZU
ズズ
ZU
ZU

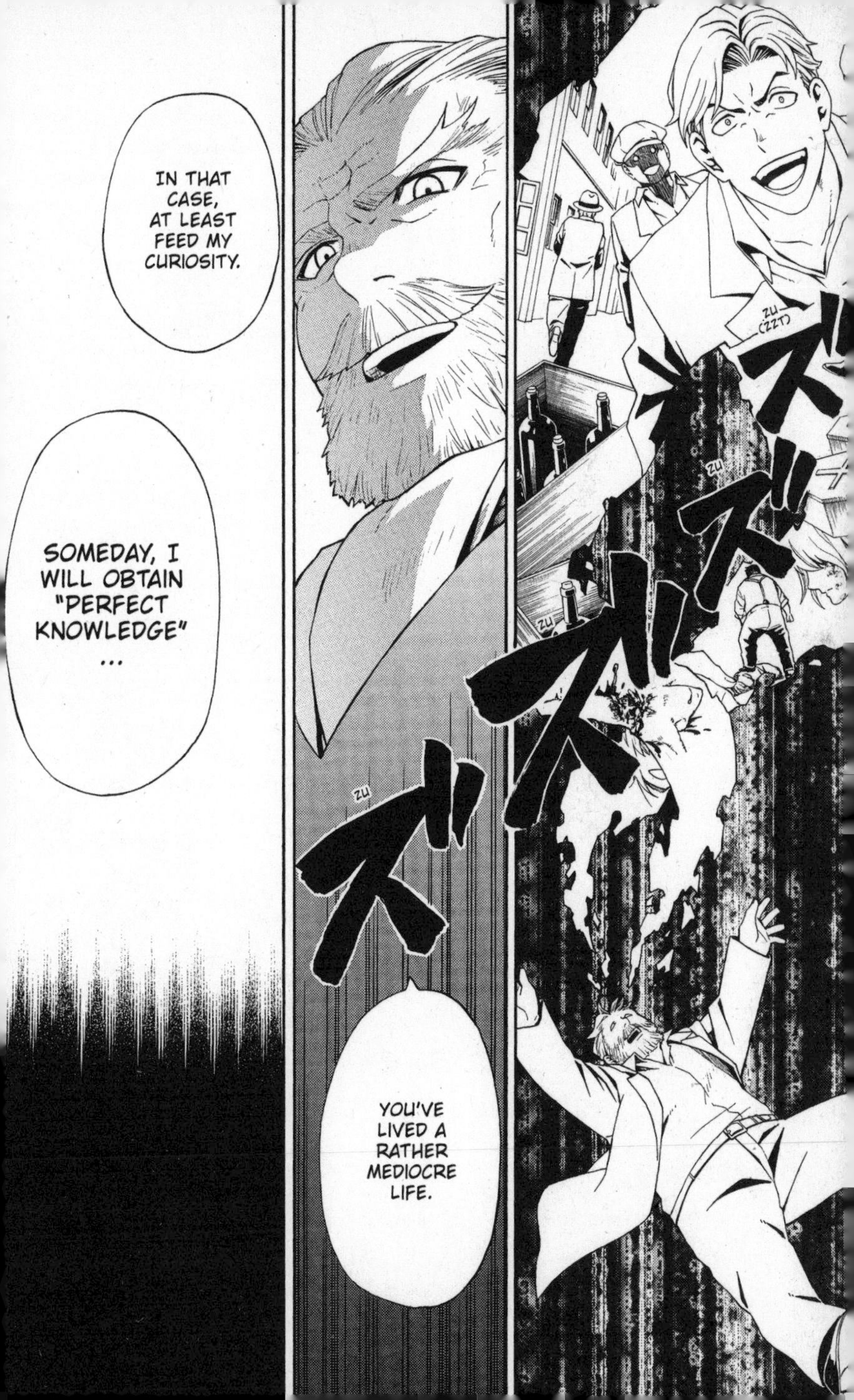
ZU (ZZZT)
ZU
ZU
ZU
YOU'VE LIVED A RATHER MEDIOCRE LIFE.
IN THAT CASE, AT LEAST FEED MY CURIOSITY.
SOMEDAY, I WILL OBTAIN "PERFECT KNOWLEDGE"...

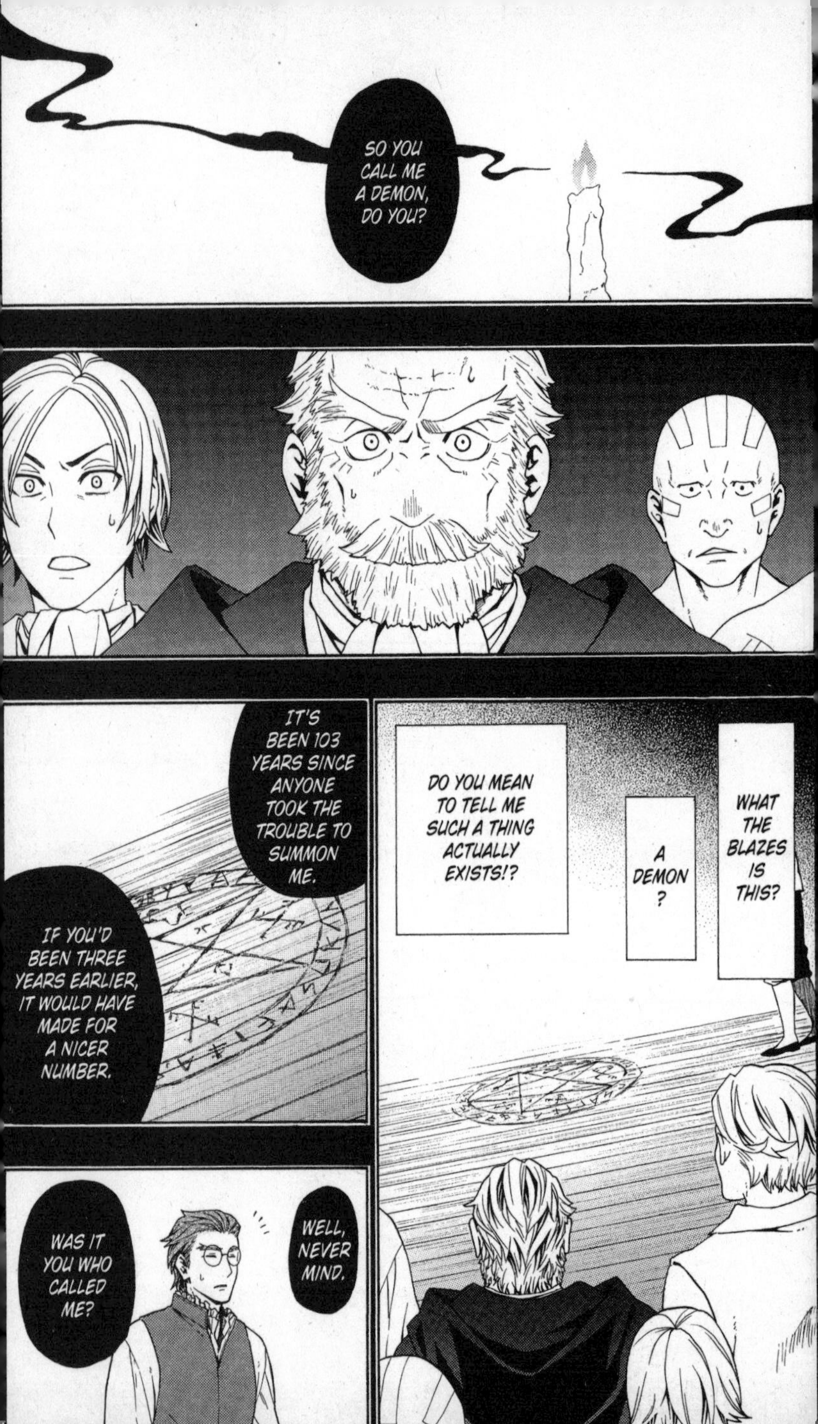
SO YOU CALL ME A DEMON, DO YOU?
WHAT THE BLAZES IS THIS?
A DEMON?
DO YOU MEAN TO TELL ME SUCH A THING ACTUALLY EXISTS!?
IT'S BEEN 103 YEARS SINCE ANYONE TOOK THE TROUBLE TO SUMMON ME.
IF YOU'D BEEN THREE YEARS EARLIER, IT WOULD HAVE MADE FOR A NICER NUMBER.
WELL, NEVER MIND.
WAS IT YOU WHO CALLED ME?

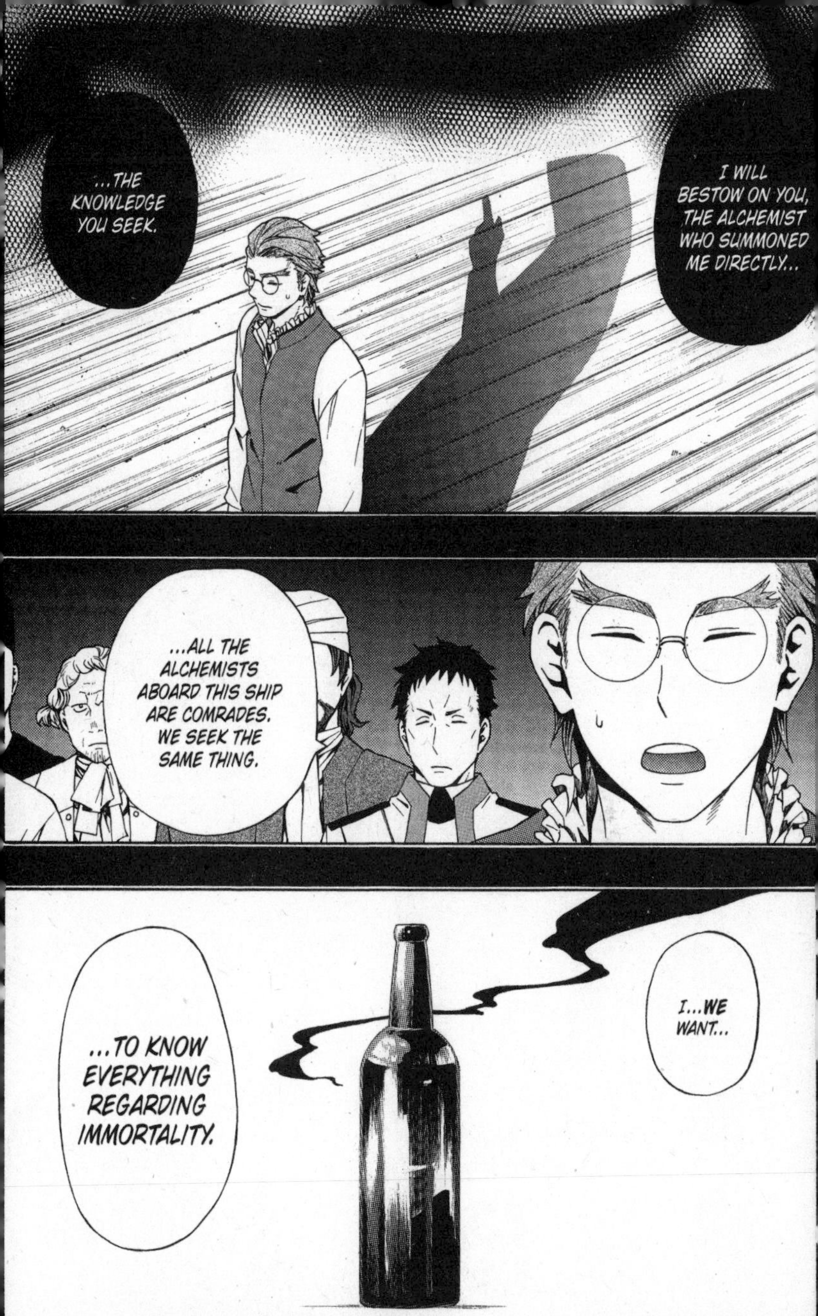
I WILL BESTOW ON YOU, THE ALCHEMIST WHO SUMMONED ME DIRECTLY...
...THE KNOWLEDGE YOU SEEK.
...ALL THE ALCHEMISTS ABOARD THIS SHIP ARE COMRADES. WE SEEK THE SAME THING.
I...WE WANT...
...TO KNOW EVERYTHING REGARDING IMMORTALITY.

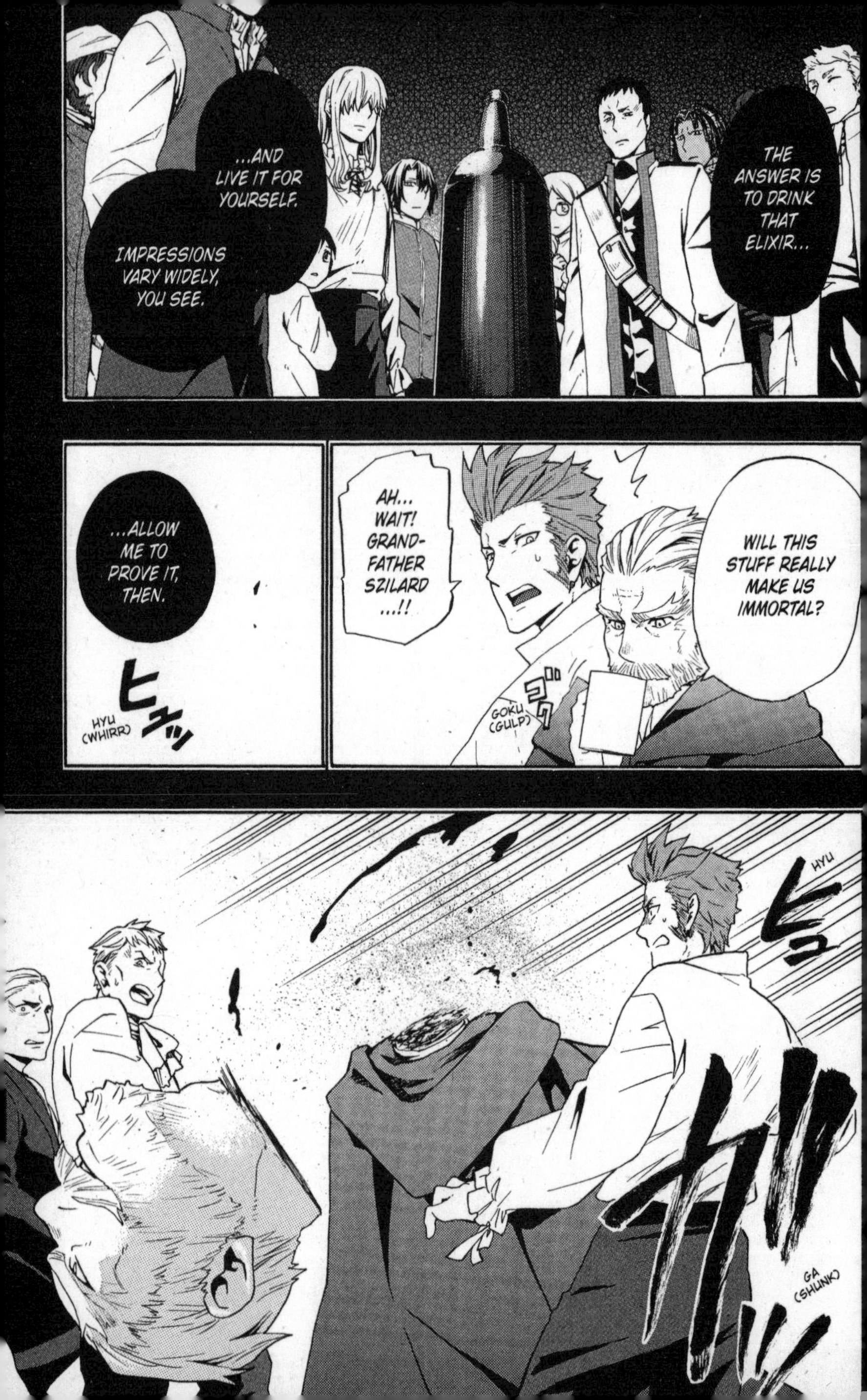
THE ANSWER IS TO DRINK THAT ELIXIR...
...AND LIVE IT FOR YOURSELF.
IMPRESSIONS VARY WIDELY, YOU SEE.
WILL THIS STUFF REALLY MAKE US IMMORTAL?
AH... WAIT! GRAND-FATHER SZILARD ...!!
GOKU (GULP)
...ALLOW ME TO PROVE IT, THEN.
HYU (WHIRR)
HYU
GA (SHUNK)

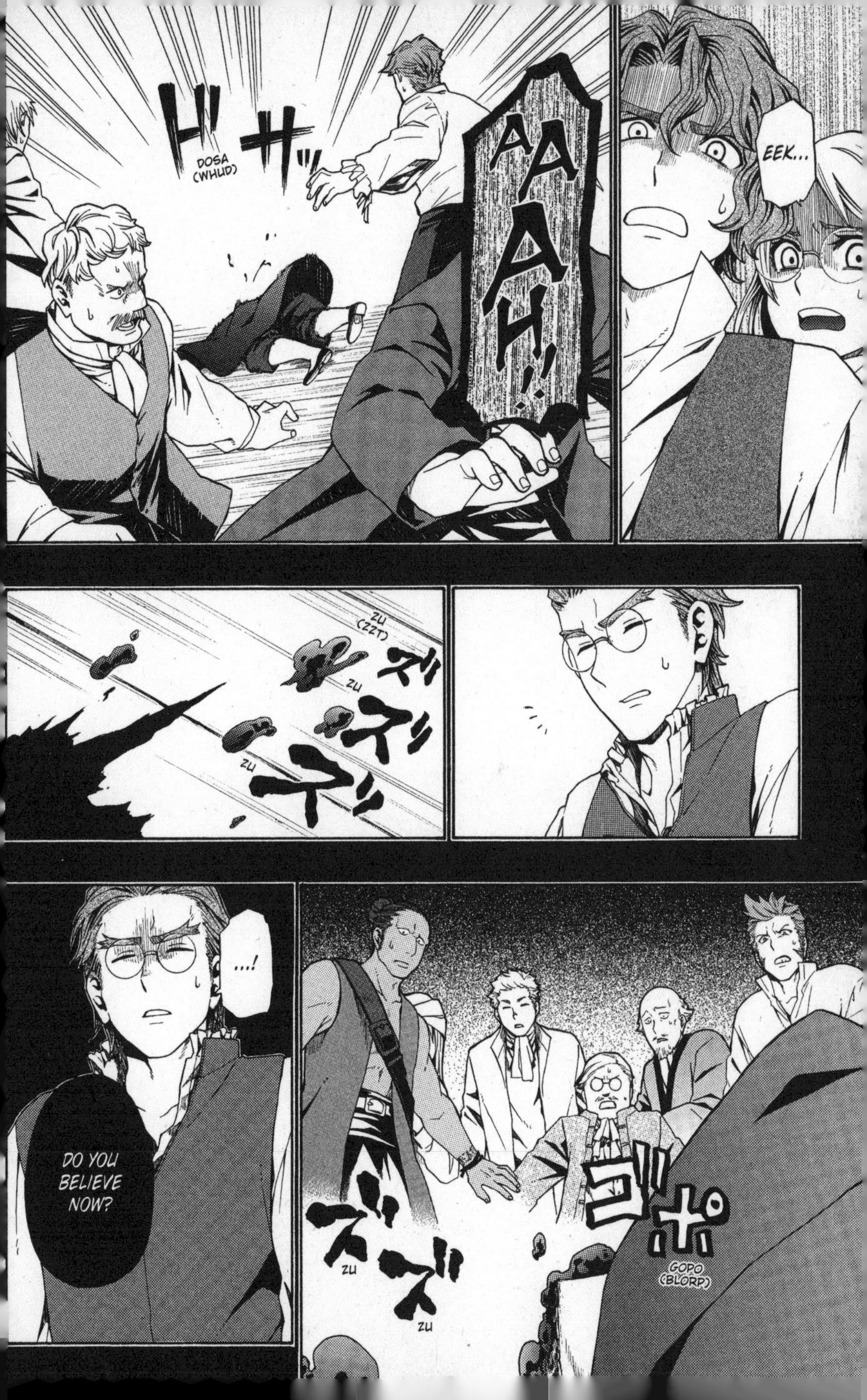
EEK...
AAAH!!
DOSA (WHUD)
ZU (ZZT)
ZU
ZU
GOPO (BLORP)
ZU
ZU
...!
DO YOU BELIEVE NOW?

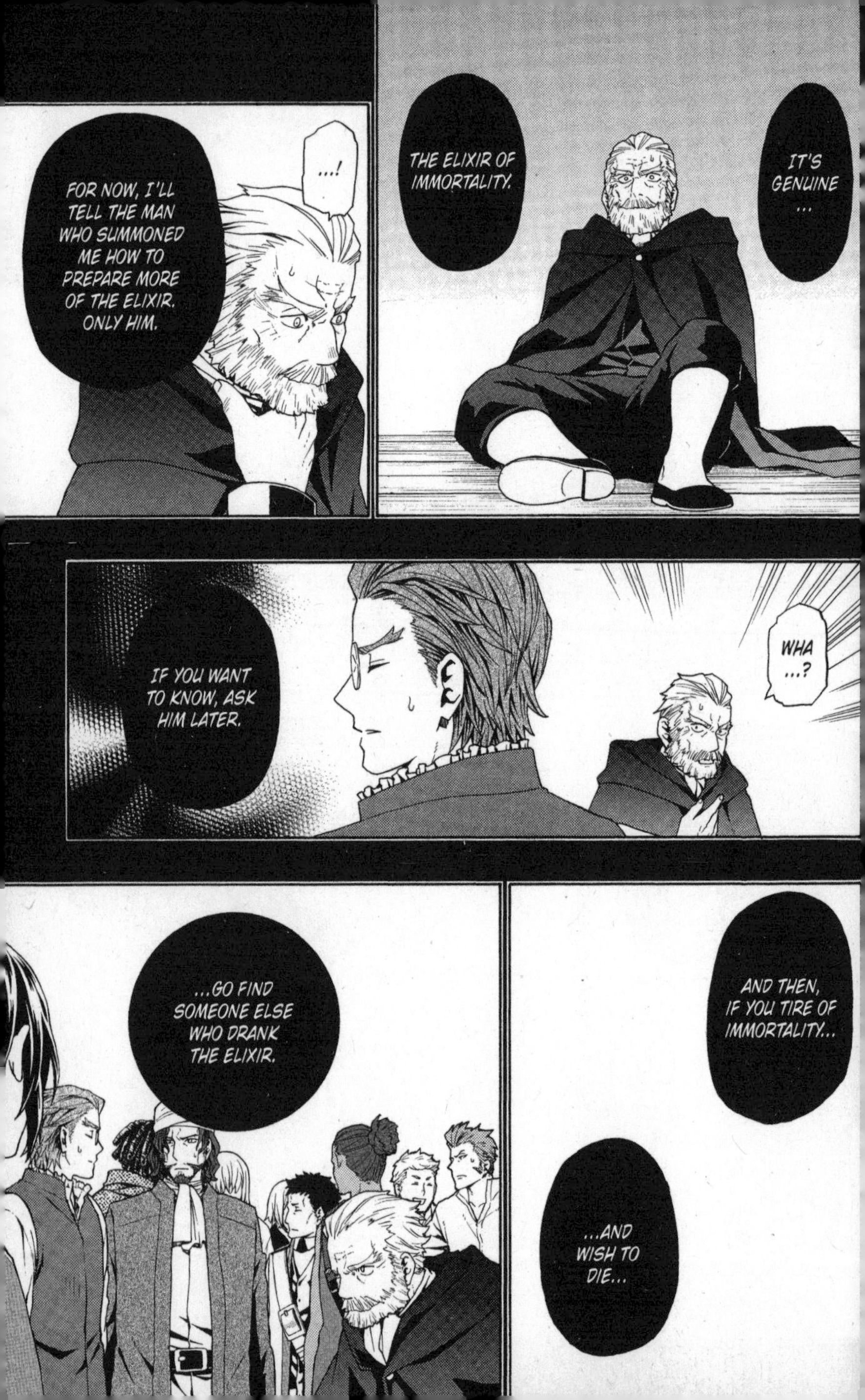
IT'S GENUINE...
THE ELIXIR OF IMMORTALITY.
...!
FOR NOW, I'LL TELL THE MAN WHO SUMMONED ME HOW TO PREPARE MORE OF THE ELIXIR. ONLY HIM.
WHA...?
IF YOU WANT TO KNOW, ASK HIM LATER.
AND THEN, IF YOU TIRE OF IMMORTALITY...
...AND WISH TO DIE...
...GO FIND SOMEONE ELSE WHO DRANK THE ELIXIR.

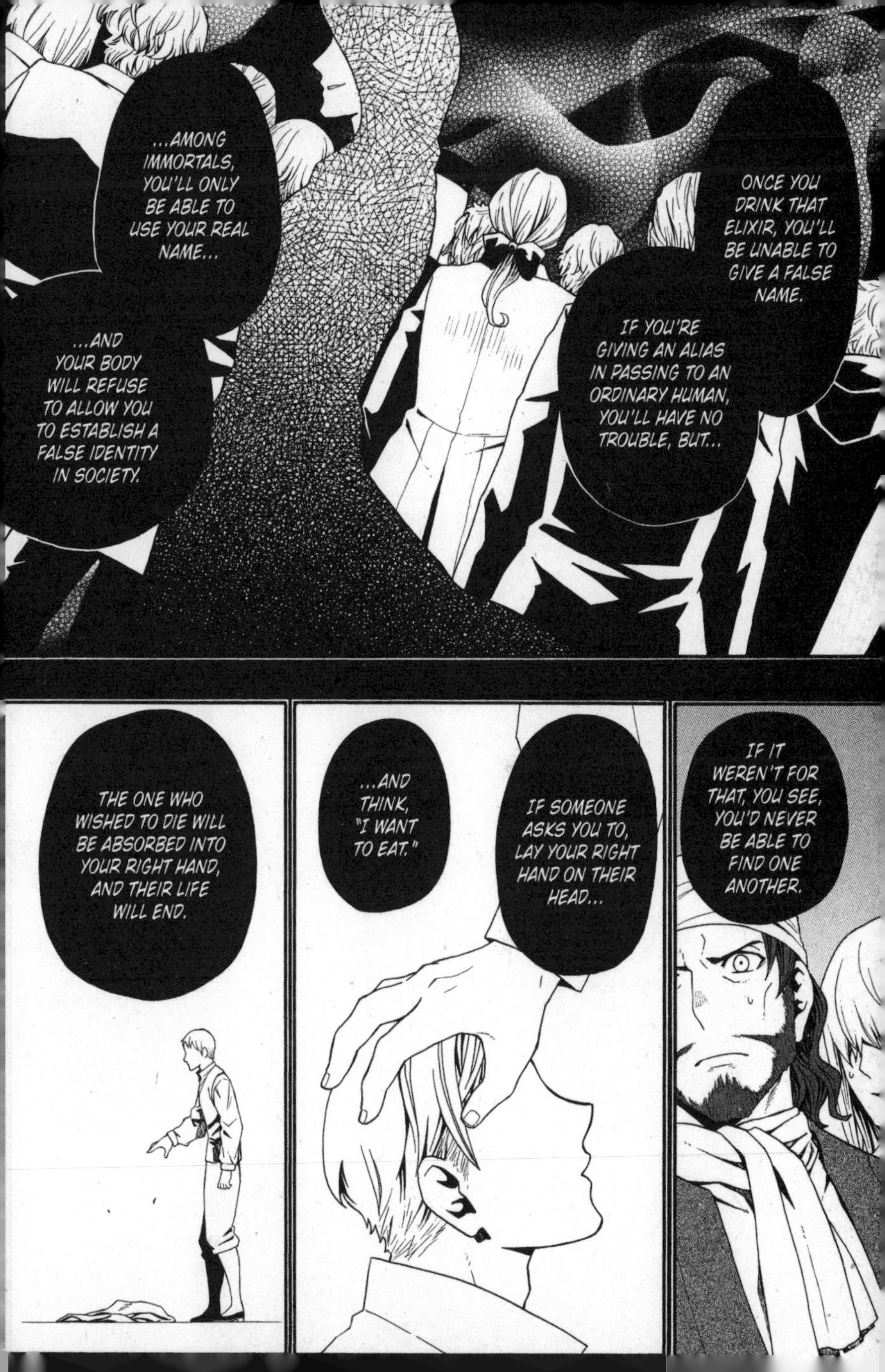
ONCE YOU DRINK THAT ELIXIR, YOU'LL BE UNABLE TO GIVE A FALSE NAME.
IF YOU'RE GIVING AN ALIAS IN PASSING TO AN ORDINARY HUMAN, YOU'LL HAVE NO TROUBLE, BUT...
...AMONG IMMORTALS, YOU'LL ONLY BE ABLE TO USE YOUR REAL NAME...
...AND YOUR BODY WILL REFUSE TO ALLOW YOU TO ESTABLISH A FALSE IDENTITY IN SOCIETY.
IF IT WEREN'T FOR THAT, YOU SEE, YOU'D NEVER BE ABLE TO FIND ONE ANOTHER.
IF SOMEONE ASKS YOU TO, LAY YOUR RIGHT HAND ON THEIR HEAD...
...AND THINK, "I WANT TO EAT."
THE ONE WHO WISHED TO DIE WILL BE ABSORBED INTO YOUR RIGHT HAND, AND THEIR LIFE WILL END.

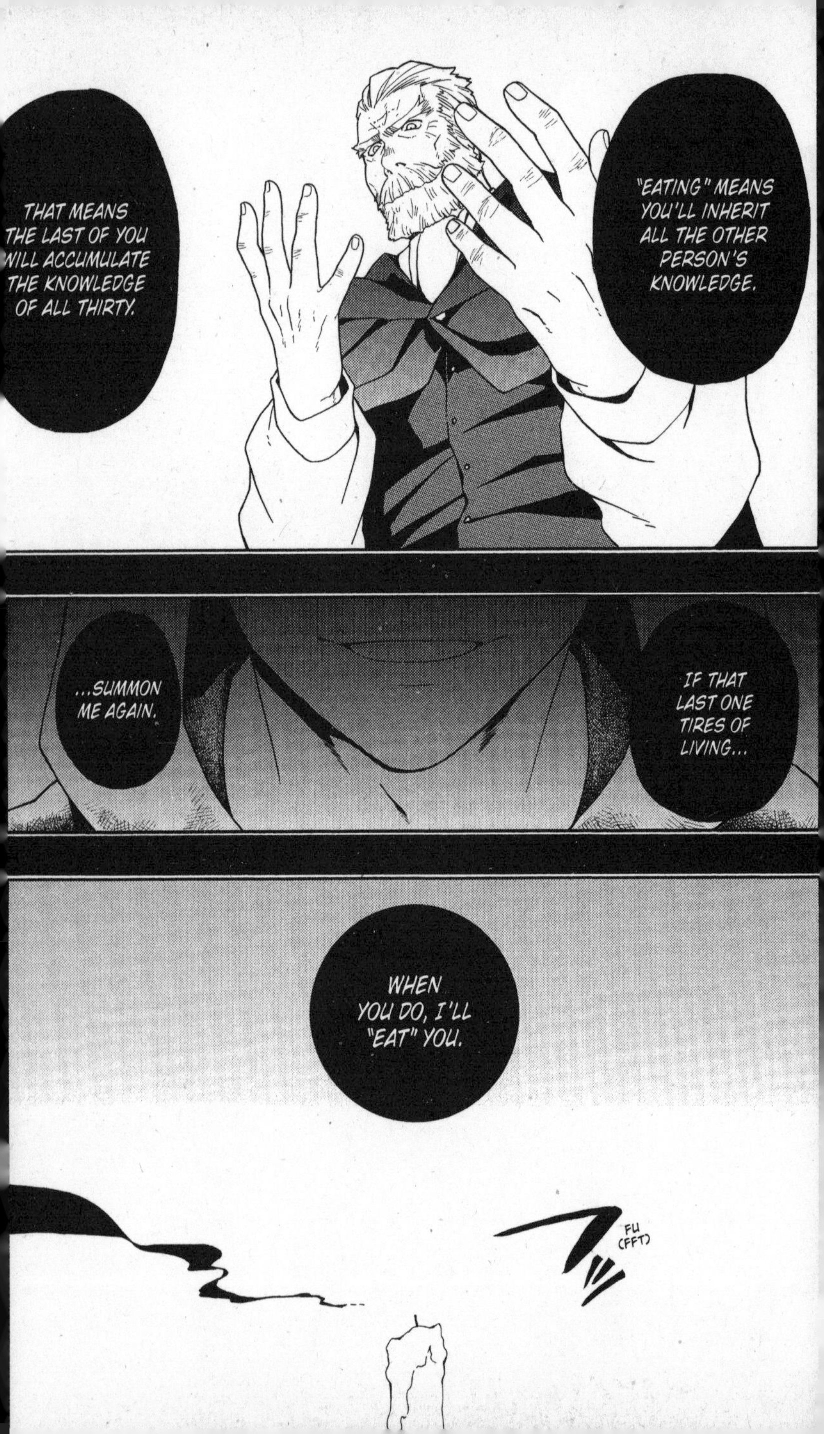
"EATING" MEANS YOU'LL INHERIT ALL THE OTHER PERSON'S KNOWLEDGE.
THAT MEANS THE LAST OF YOU WILL ACCUMULATE THE KNOWLEDGE OF ALL THIRTY.
IF THAT LAST ONE TIRES OF LIVING...
...SUMMON ME AGAIN.
WHEN YOU DO, I'LL "EAT" YOU.
FU (FFT)

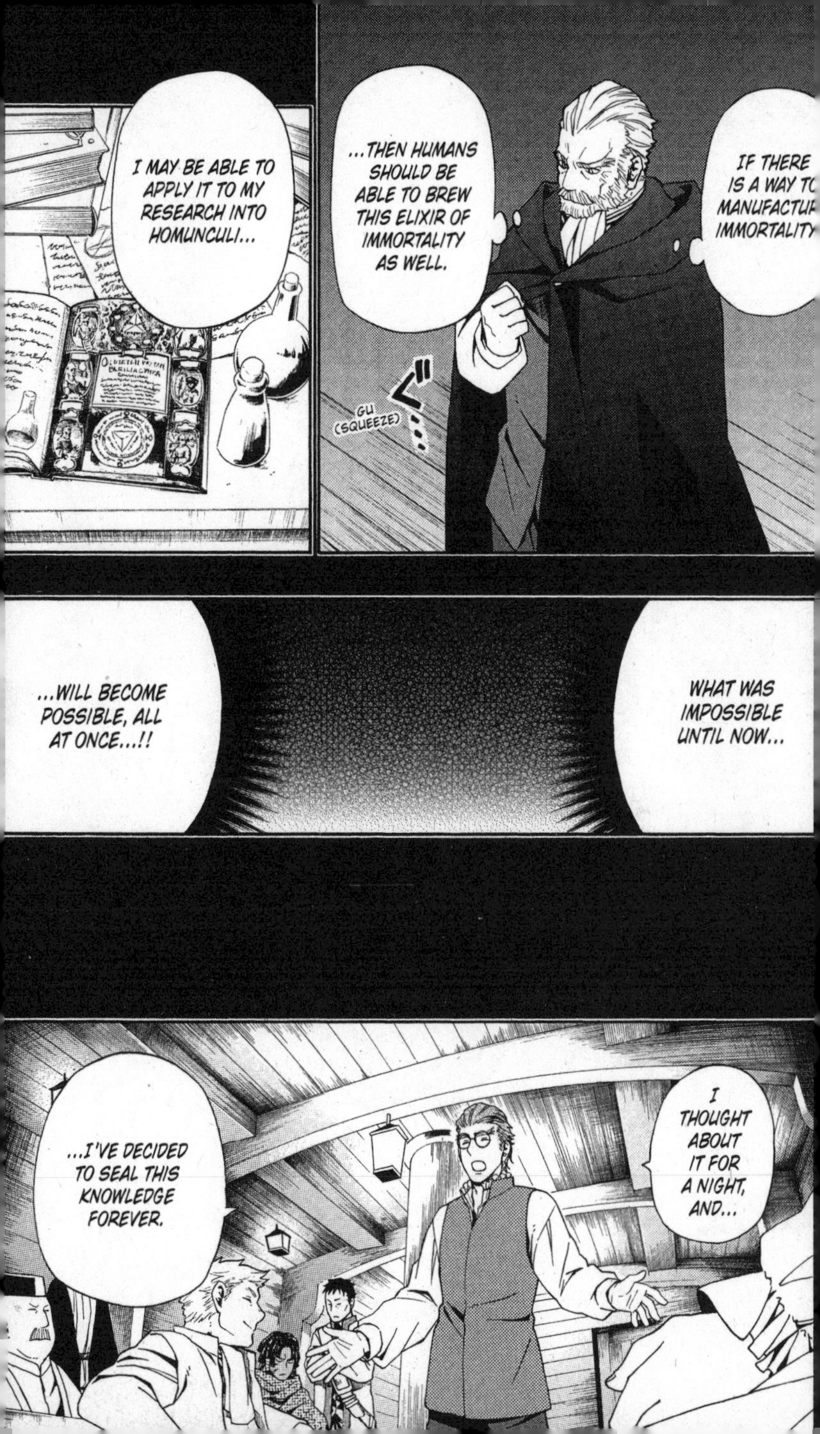
IF THERE IS A WAY TO MANUFACTUR IMMORTALITY
...THEN HUMANS SHOULD BE ABLE TO BREW THIS ELIXIR OF IMMORTALITY AS WELL.
GU (SQUEEZE)
I MAY BE ABLE TO APPLY IT TO MY RESEARCH INTO HOMUNCULI...
WHAT WAS IMPOSSIBLE UNTIL NOW...
...WILL BECOME POSSIBLE, ALL AT ONCE...!!
I THOUGHT ABOUT IT FOR A NIGHT, AND...
...I'VE DECIDED TO SEAL THIS KNOWLEDGE FOREVER.

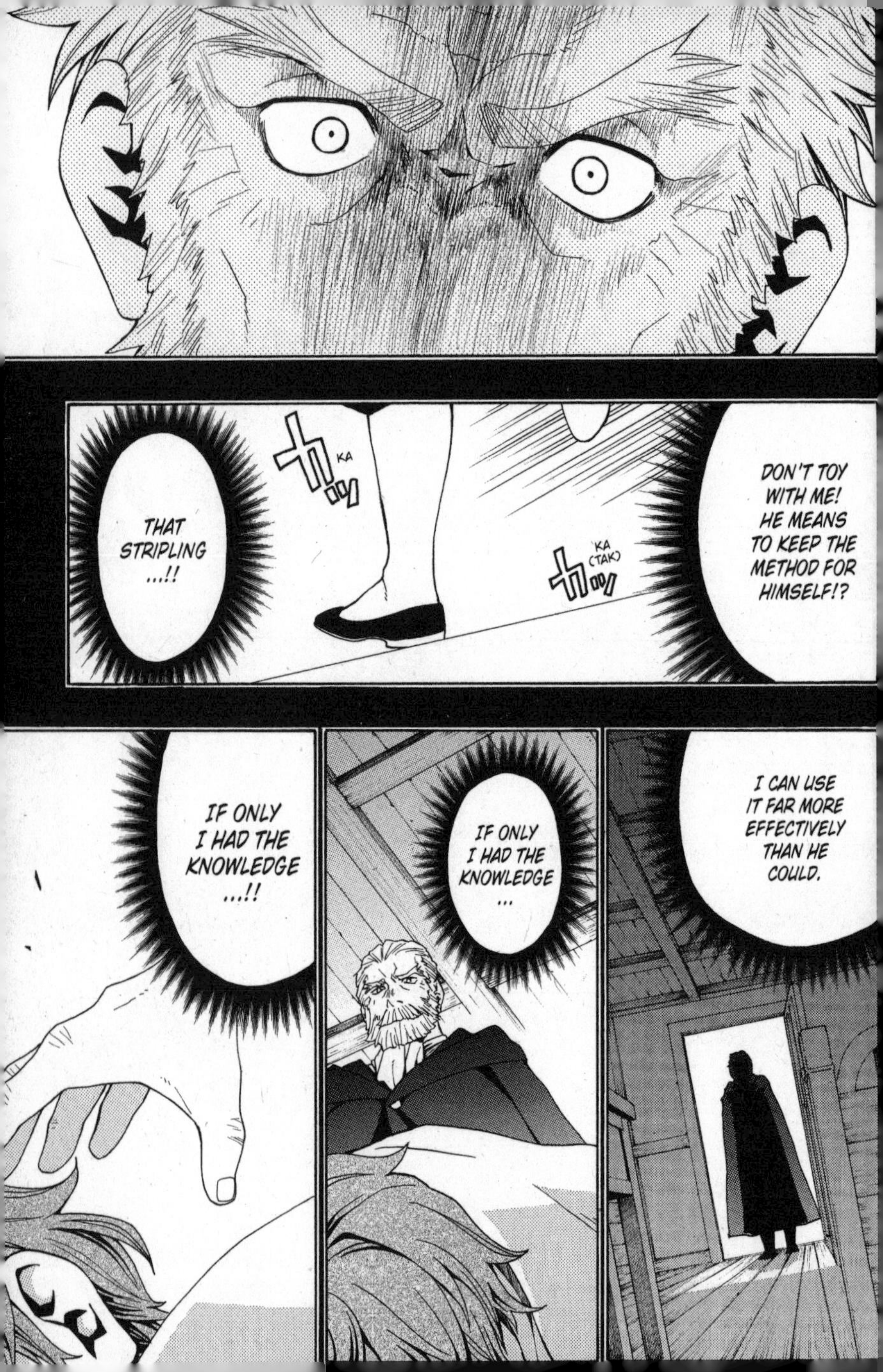
DON'T TOY WITH ME! HE MEANS TO KEEP THE METHOD FOR HIMSELF!?
KA (TAK)
KA
THAT STRIPLING ...!!
I CAN USE IT FAR MORE EFFECTIVELY THAN HE COULD.
IF ONLY I HAD THE KNOWLEDGE ...
IF ONLY I HAD THE KNOWLEDGE ...!!

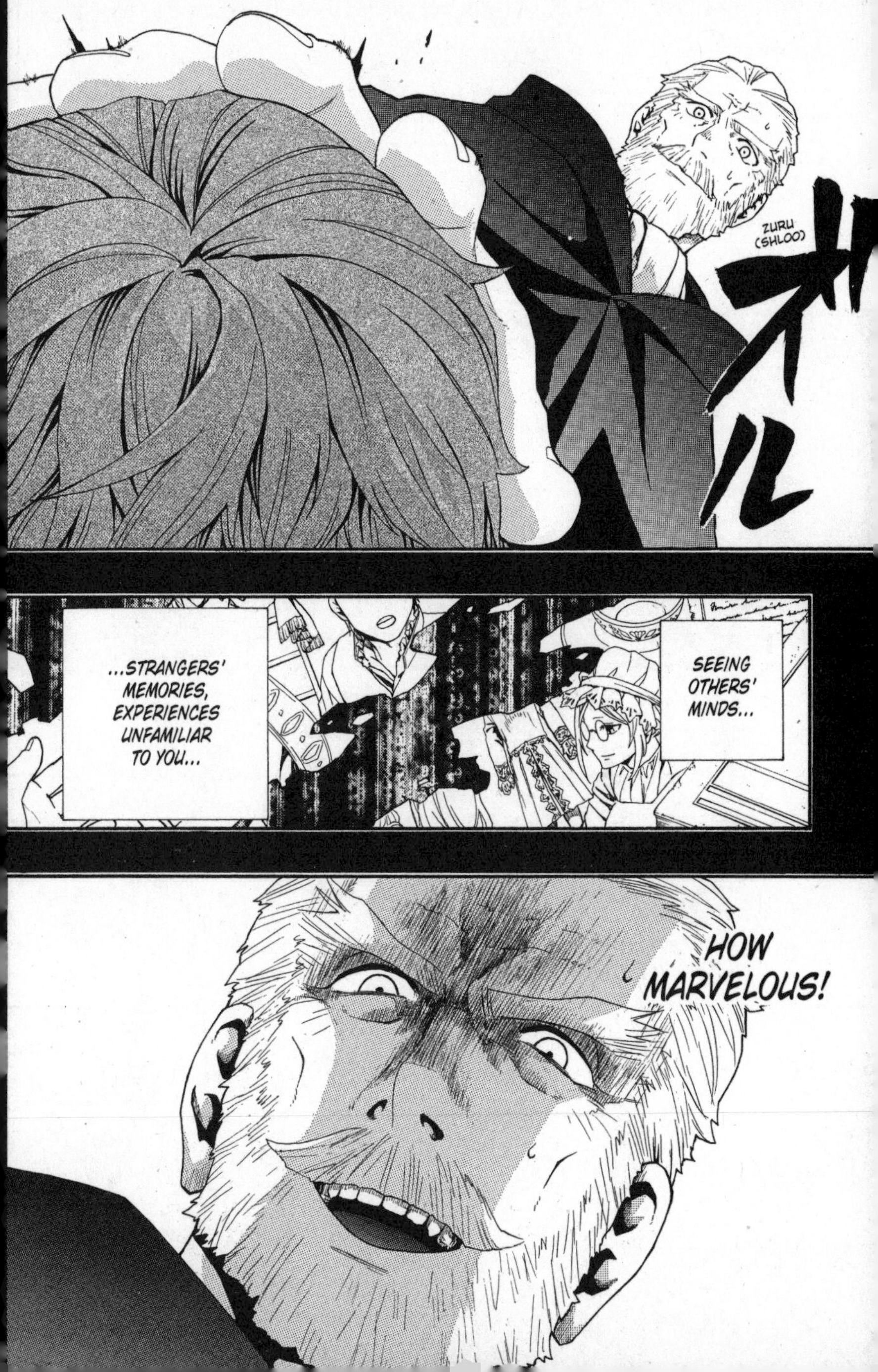
ZURU (SHLOO)
SEEING OTHERS' MINDS...
...STRANGERS' MEMORIES, EXPERIENCES UNFAMILIAR TO YOU...
HOW MARVELOUS!

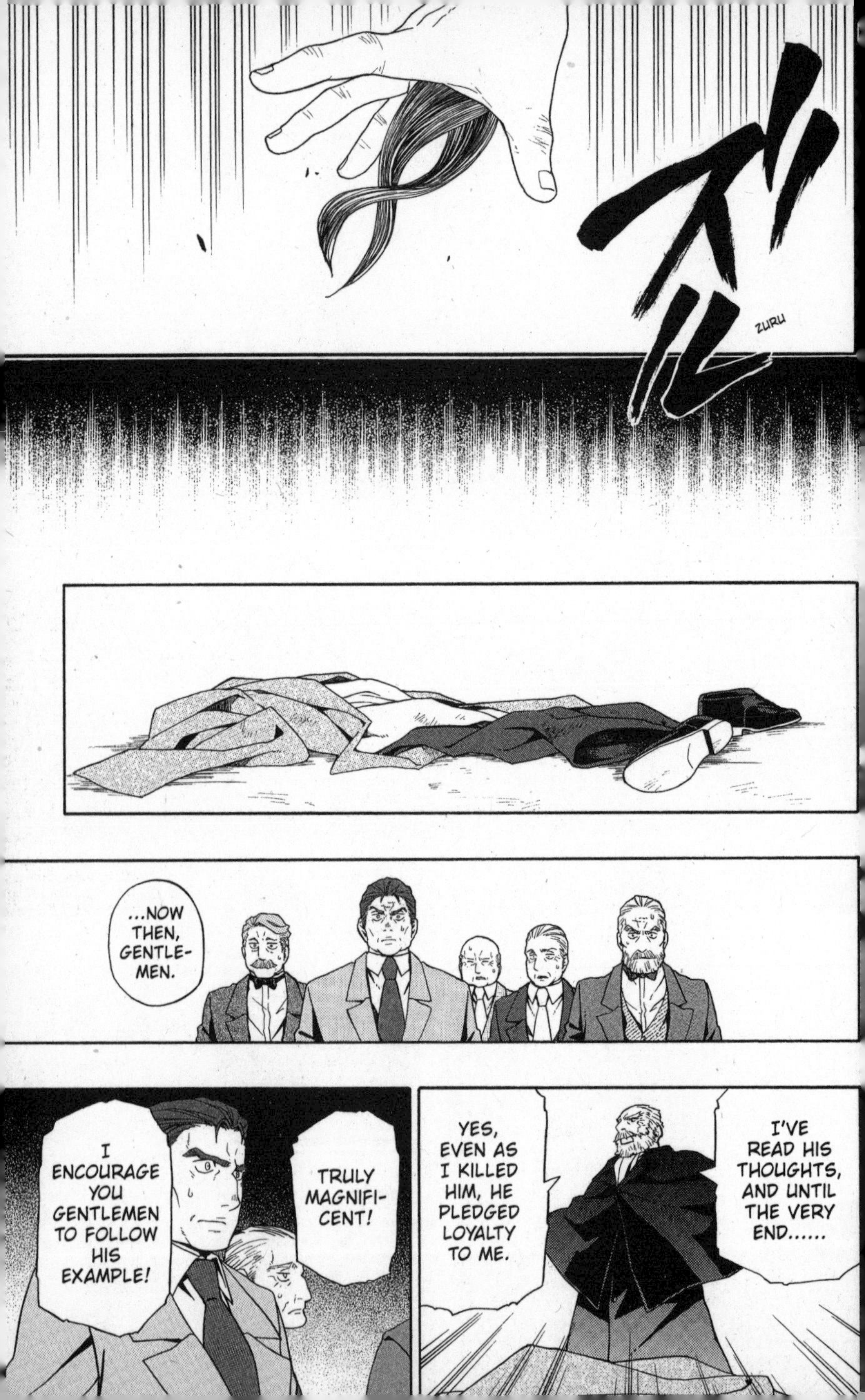

ズル
ZURU
...NOW THEN, GENTLEMEN.
I'VE READ HIS THOUGHTS, AND UNTIL THE VERY END......
YES, EVEN AS I KILLED HIM, HE PLEDGED LOYALTY TO ME.
TRULY MAGNIFICENT!
I ENCOURAGE YOU GENTLEMEN TO FOLLOW HIS EXAMPLE!

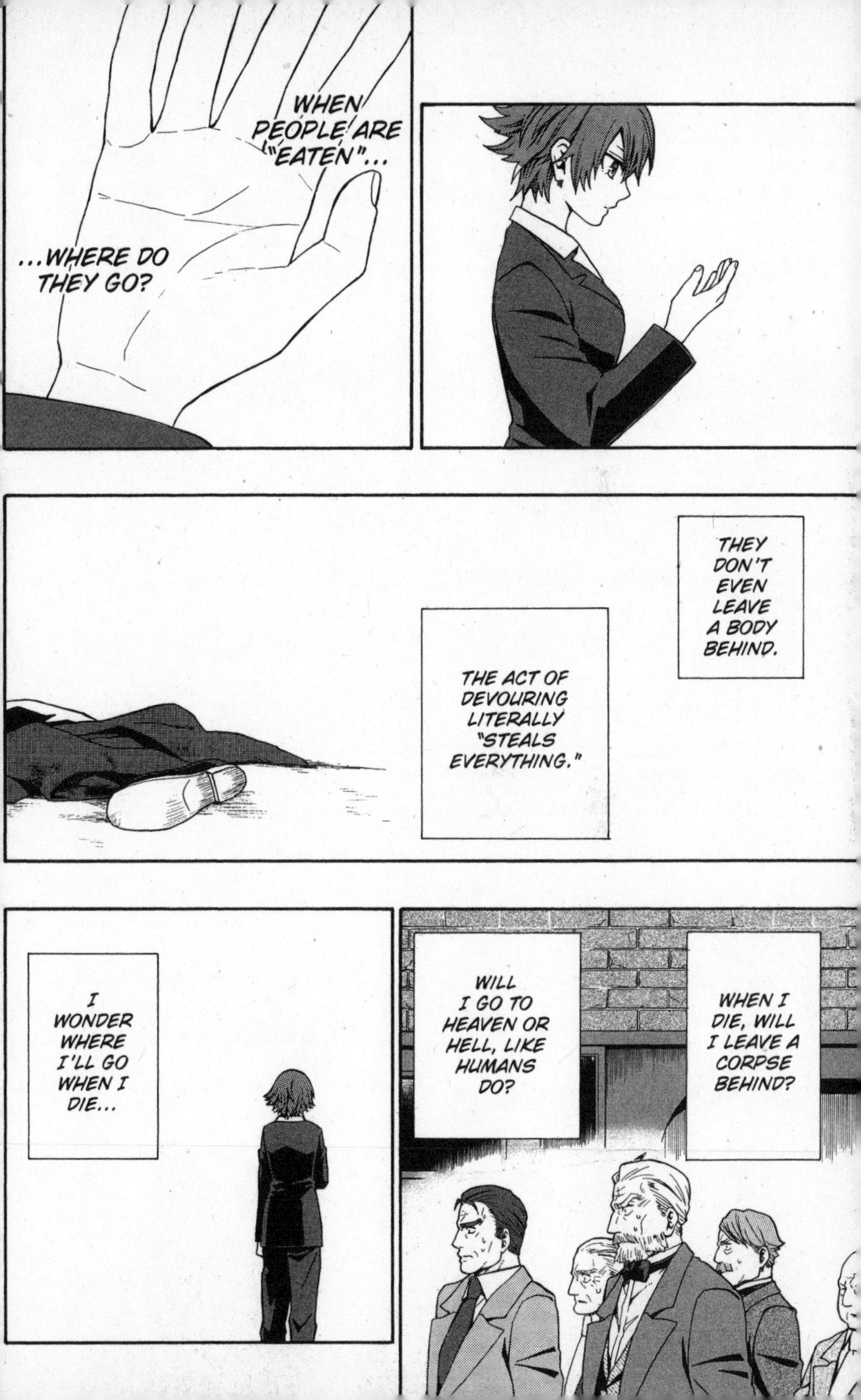
WHEN PEOPLE ARE "EATEN"...
...WHERE DO THEY GO?
THEY DON'T EVEN LEAVE A BODY BEHIND.
THE ACT OF DEVOURING LITERALLY "STEALS EVERYTHING."
WHEN I DIE, WILL I LEAVE A CORPSE BEHIND?
WILL I GO TO HEAVEN OR HELL, LIKE HUMANS DO?
I WONDER WHERE I'LL GO WHEN I DIE...

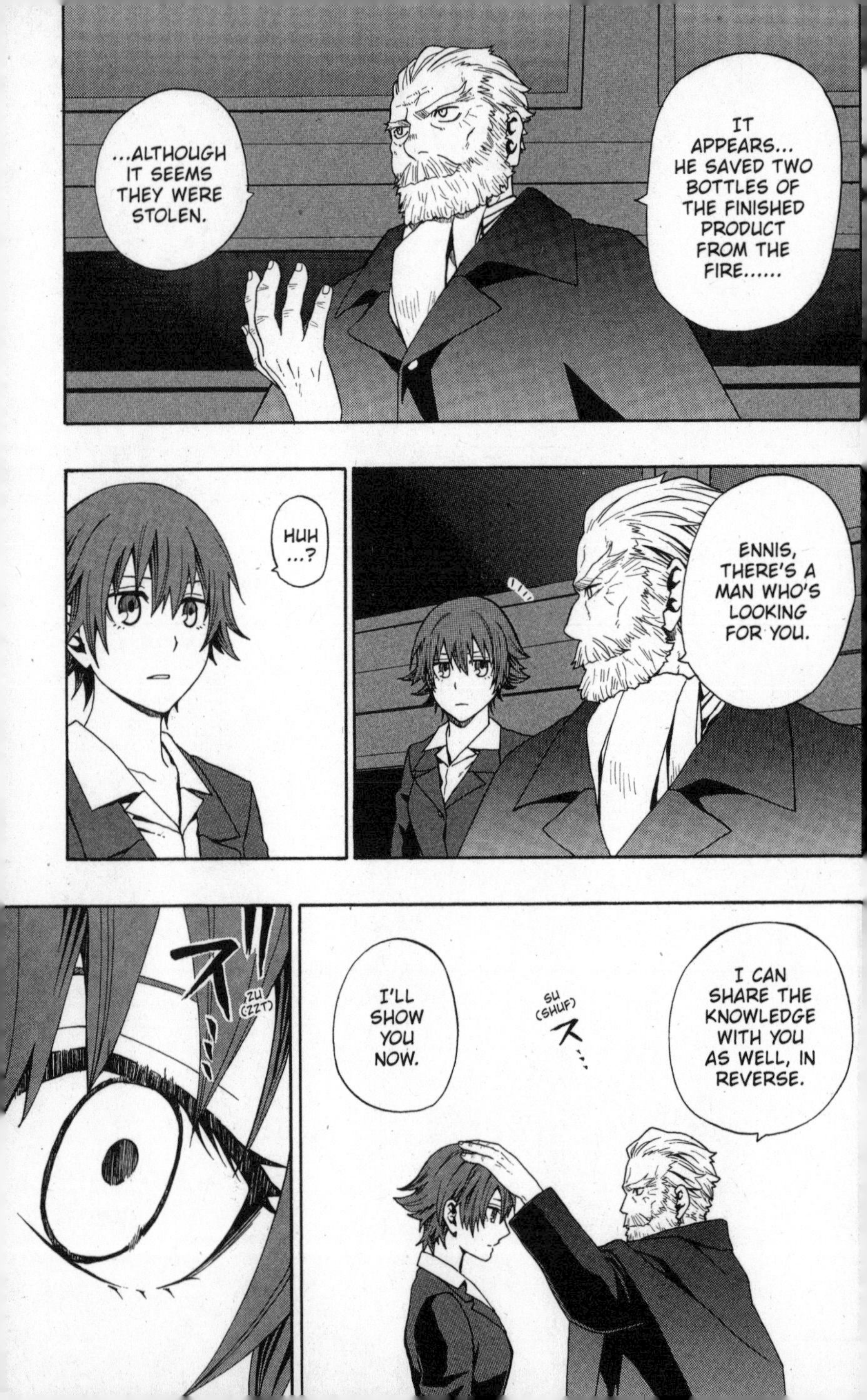

IT APPEARS... HE SAVED TWO BOTTLES OF THE FINISHED PRODUCT FROM THE FIRE......
...ALTHOUGH IT SEEMS THEY WERE STOLEN.
ENNIS, THERE'S A MAN WHO'S LOOKING FOR YOU.
HUH ...?
I CAN SHARE THE KNOWLEDGE WITH YOU AS WELL, IN REVERSE.
SU (SHUF)
I'LL SHOW YOU NOW.
ZU (ZZT)

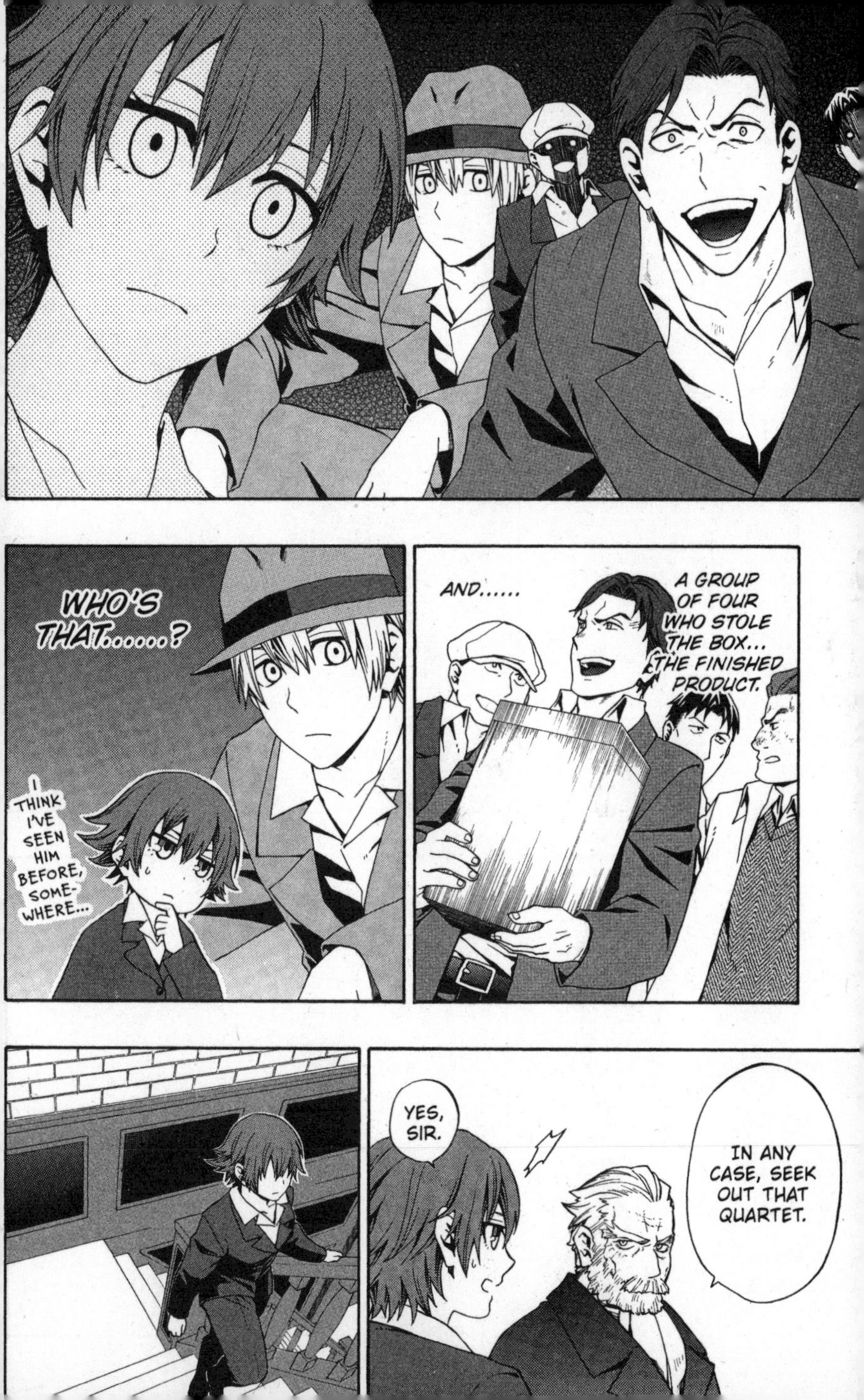
AND......
A GROUP OF FOUR WHO STOLE THE BOX... THE FINISHED PRODUCT.
WHO'S THAT......?
I THINK I'VE SEEN HIM BEFORE, SOME-WHERE...
IN ANY CASE, SEEK OUT THAT QUARTET.
YES, SIR.

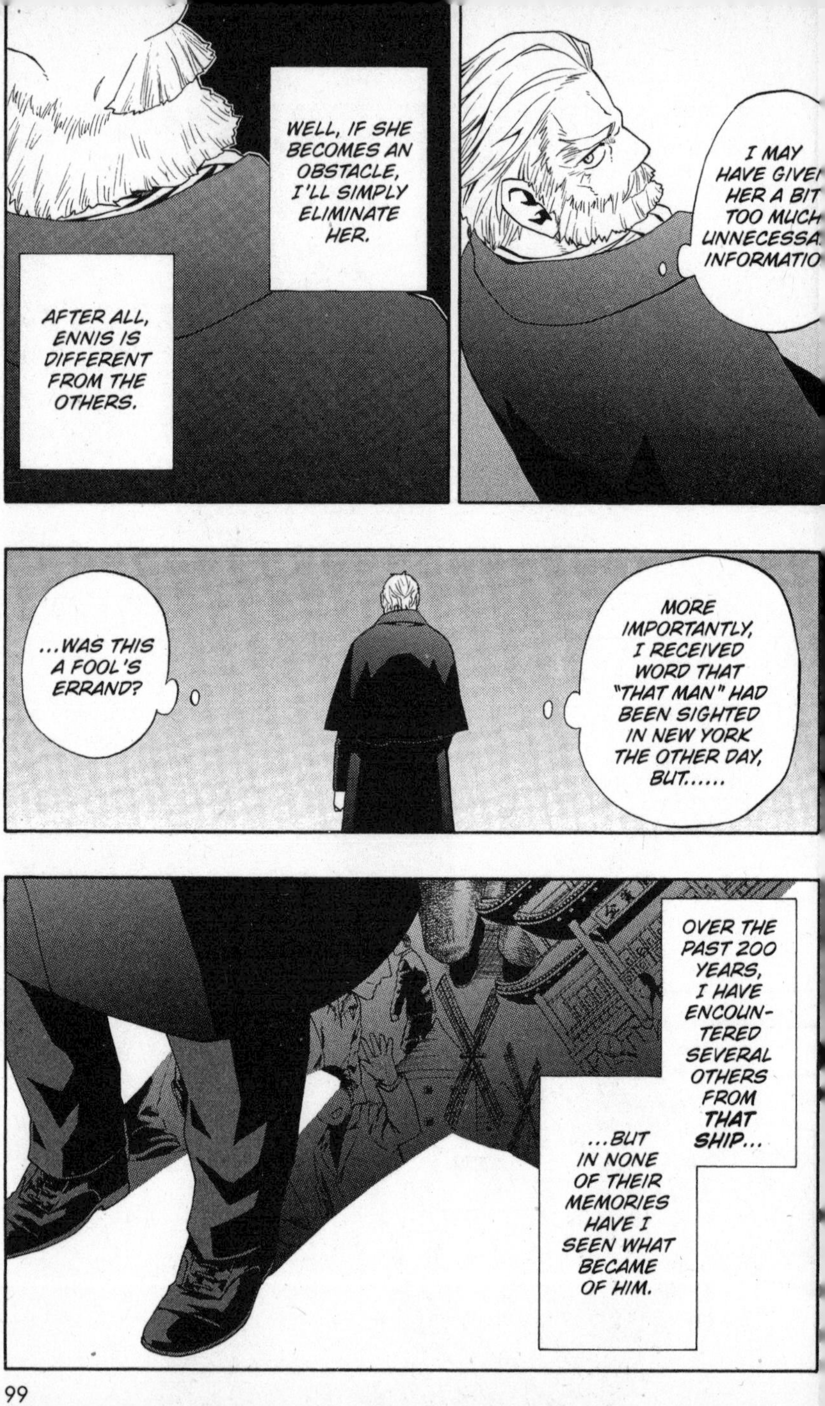
I MAY HAVE GIVEN HER A BIT TOO MUCH UNNECESSA INFORMATIO
WELL, IF SHE BECOMES AN OBSTACLE, I'LL SIMPLY ELIMINATE HER.
AFTER ALL, ENNIS IS DIFFERENT FROM THE OTHERS.
MORE IMPORTANTLY, I RECEIVED WORD THAT "THAT MAN" HAD BEEN SIGHTED IN NEW YORK THE OTHER DAY, BUT......
...WAS THIS A FOOL'S ERRAND?
OVER THE PAST 200 YEARS, I HAVE ENCOUN-TERED SEVERAL OTHERS FROM THAT SHIP...
...BUT IN NONE OF THEIR MEMORIES HAVE I SEEN WHAT BECAME OF HIM.

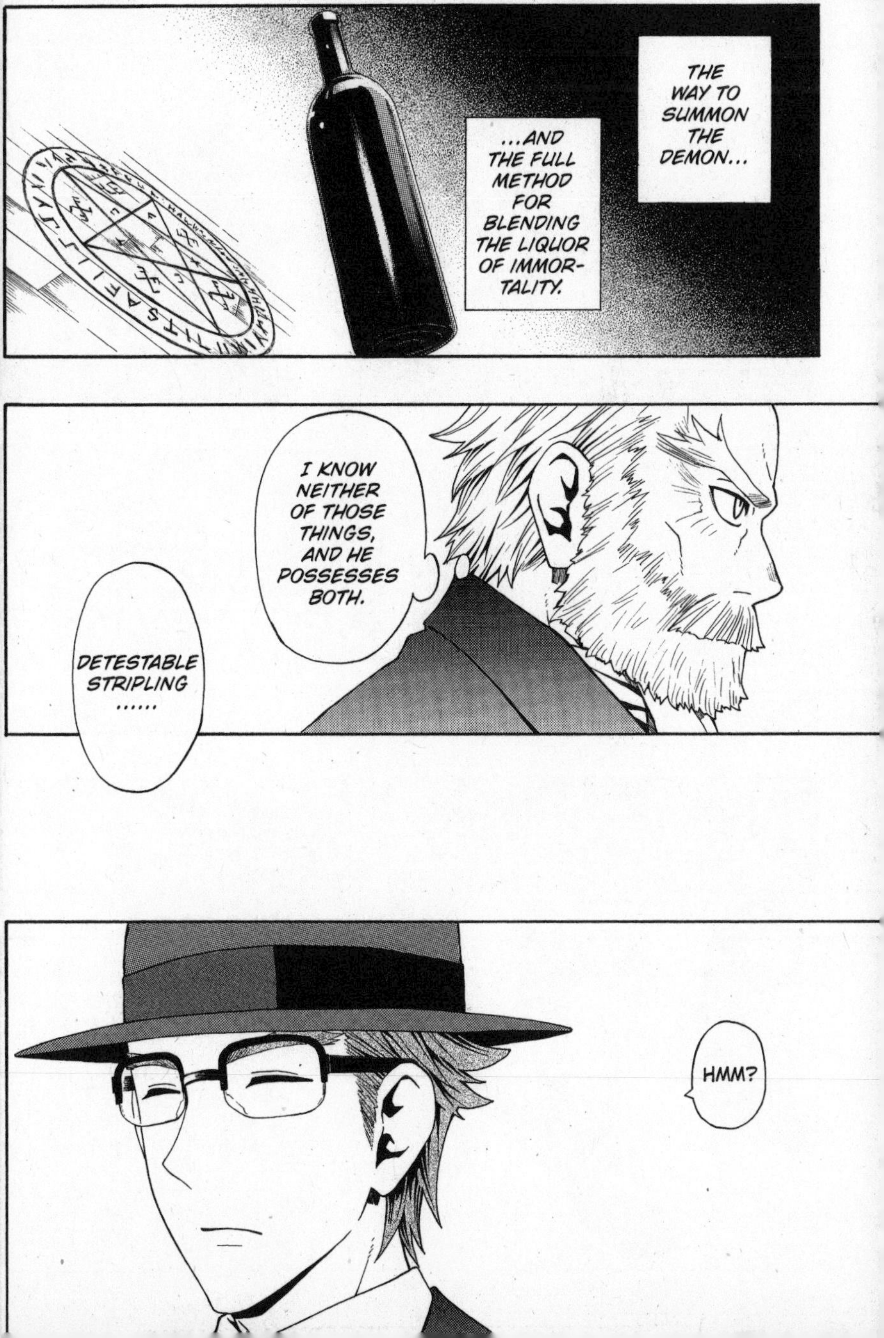
THE WAY TO SUMMON THE DEMON...
...AND THE FULL METHOD FOR BLENDING THE LIQUOR OF IMMOR-TALITY.
I KNOW NEITHER OF THOSE THINGS, AND HE POSSESSES BOTH.
DETESTABLE STRIPLING ......
HMM?

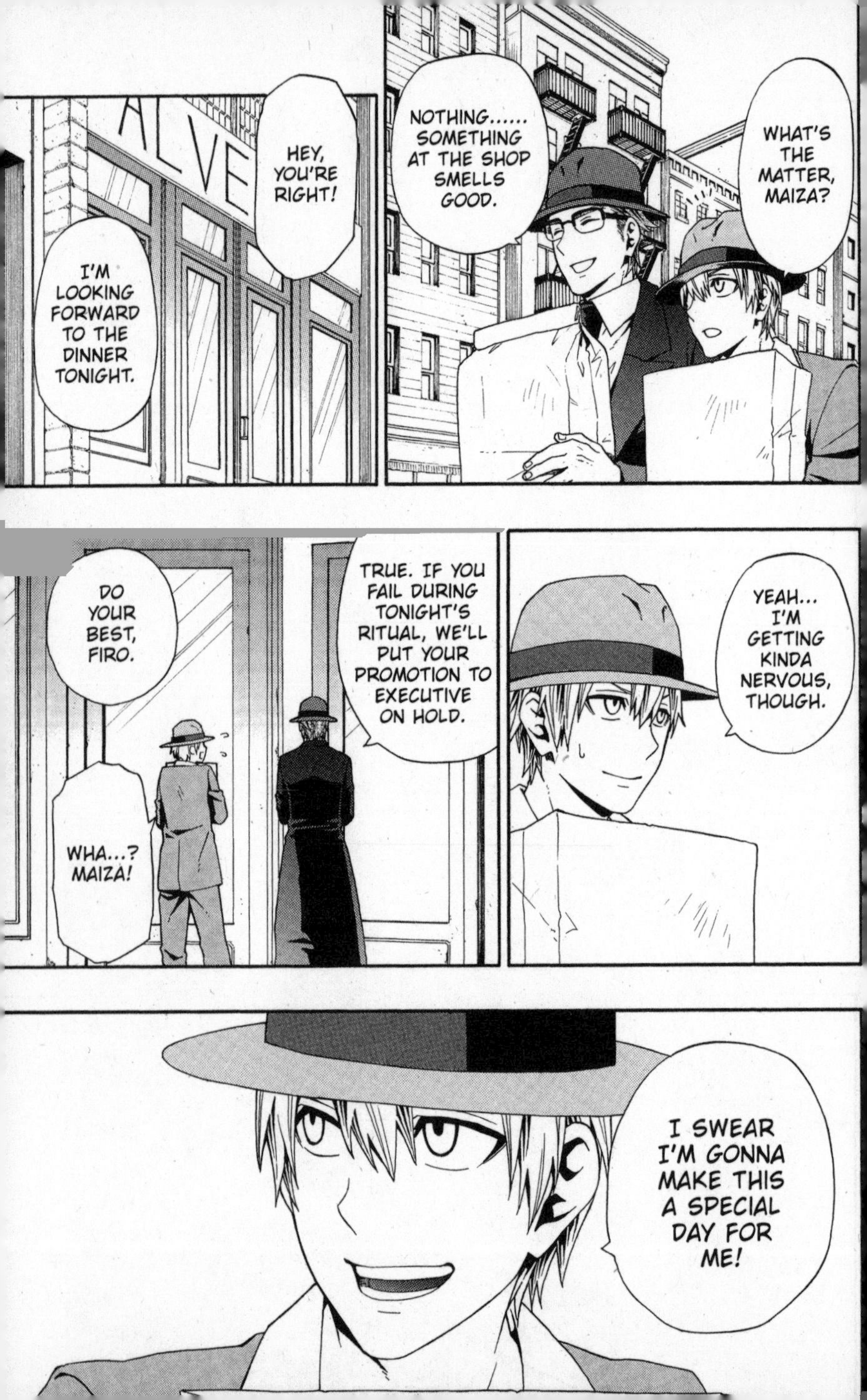
WHAT'S THE MATTER, MAIZA?
NOTHING...... SOMETHING AT THE SHOP SMELLS GOOD.
ALVE
HEY, YOU'RE RIGHT!
I'M LOOKING FORWARD TO THE DINNER TONIGHT.
YEAH... I'M GETTING KINDA NERVOUS, THOUGH.
TRUE. IF YOU FAIL DURING TONIGHT'S RITUAL, WE'LL PUT YOUR PROMOTION TO EXECUTIVE ON HOLD.
DO YOUR BEST, FIRO.
WHA...? MAIZA!
I SWEAR I'M GONNA MAKE THIS A SPECIAL DAY FOR ME!

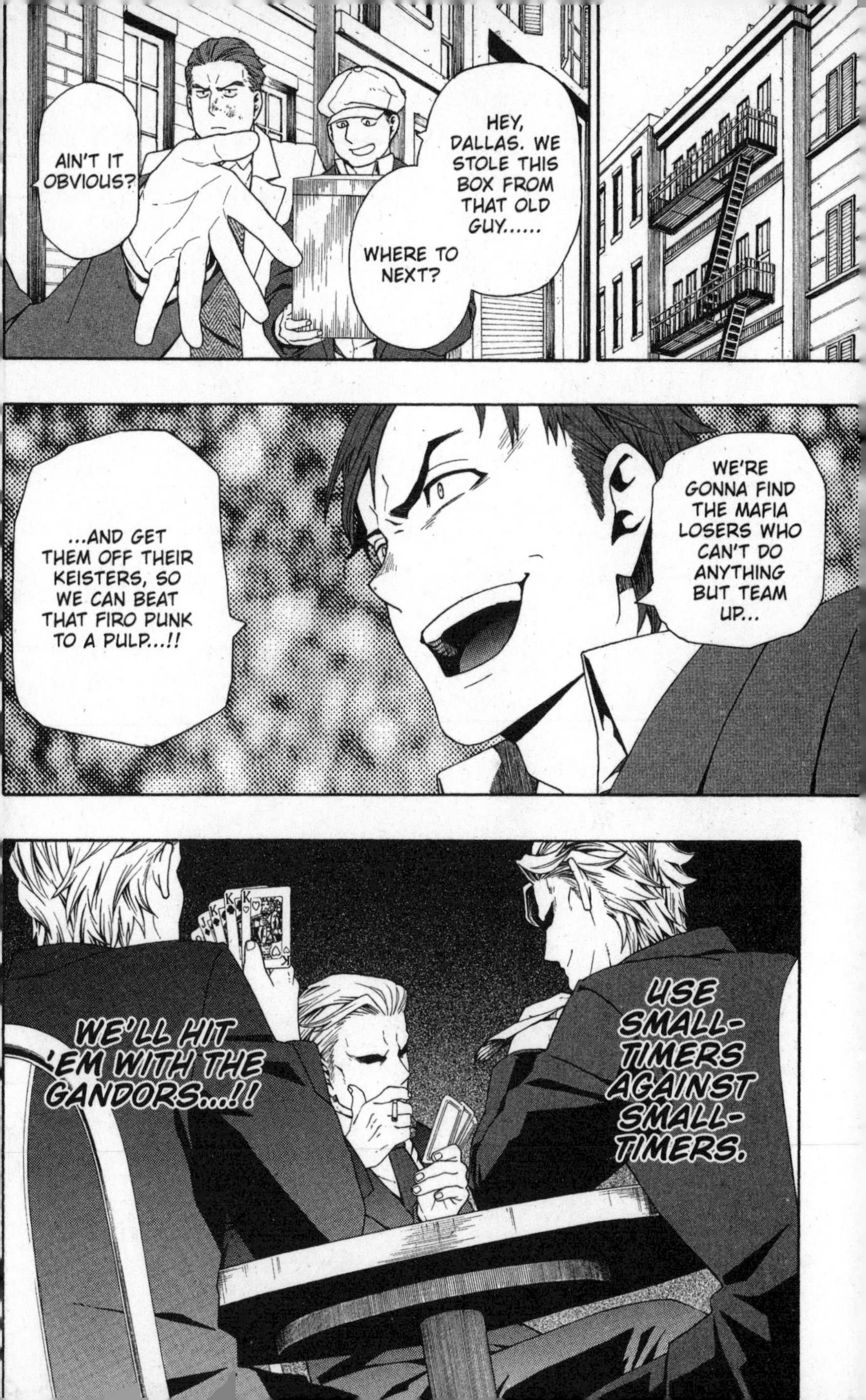
HEY, DALLAS. WE STOLE THIS BOX FROM THAT OLD GUY......
WHERE TO NEXT?
AIN'T IT OBVIOUS?
WE'RE GONNA FIND THE MAFIA LOSERS WHO CAN'T DO ANYTHING BUT TEAM UP...
...AND GET THEM OFF THEIR KEISTERS, SO WE CAN BEAT THAT FIRO PUNK TO A PULP...!!
USE SMALL-TIMERS AGAINST SMALL-TIMERS.
WE'LL HIT 'EM WITH THE GANDORS...!!

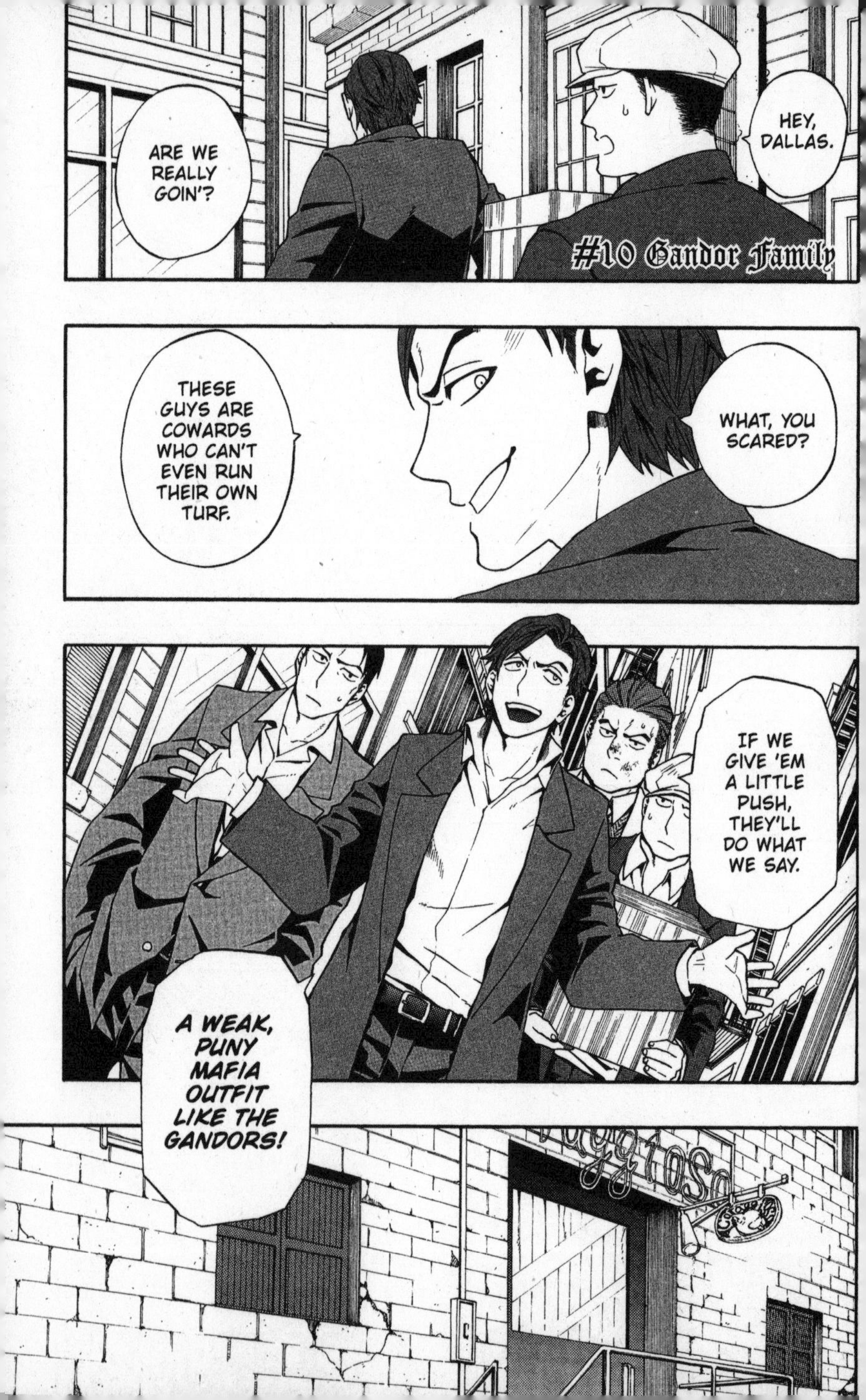
HEY, DALLAS.
ARE WE REALLY GOIN'?
#10 Gandor Family
WHAT, YOU SCARED?
THESE GUYS ARE COWARDS WHO CAN'T EVEN RUN THEIR OWN TURF.
IF WE GIVE 'EM A LITTLE PUSH, THEY'LL DO WHAT WE SAY.
A WEAK, PUNY MAFIA OUTFIT LIKE THE GANDORS!

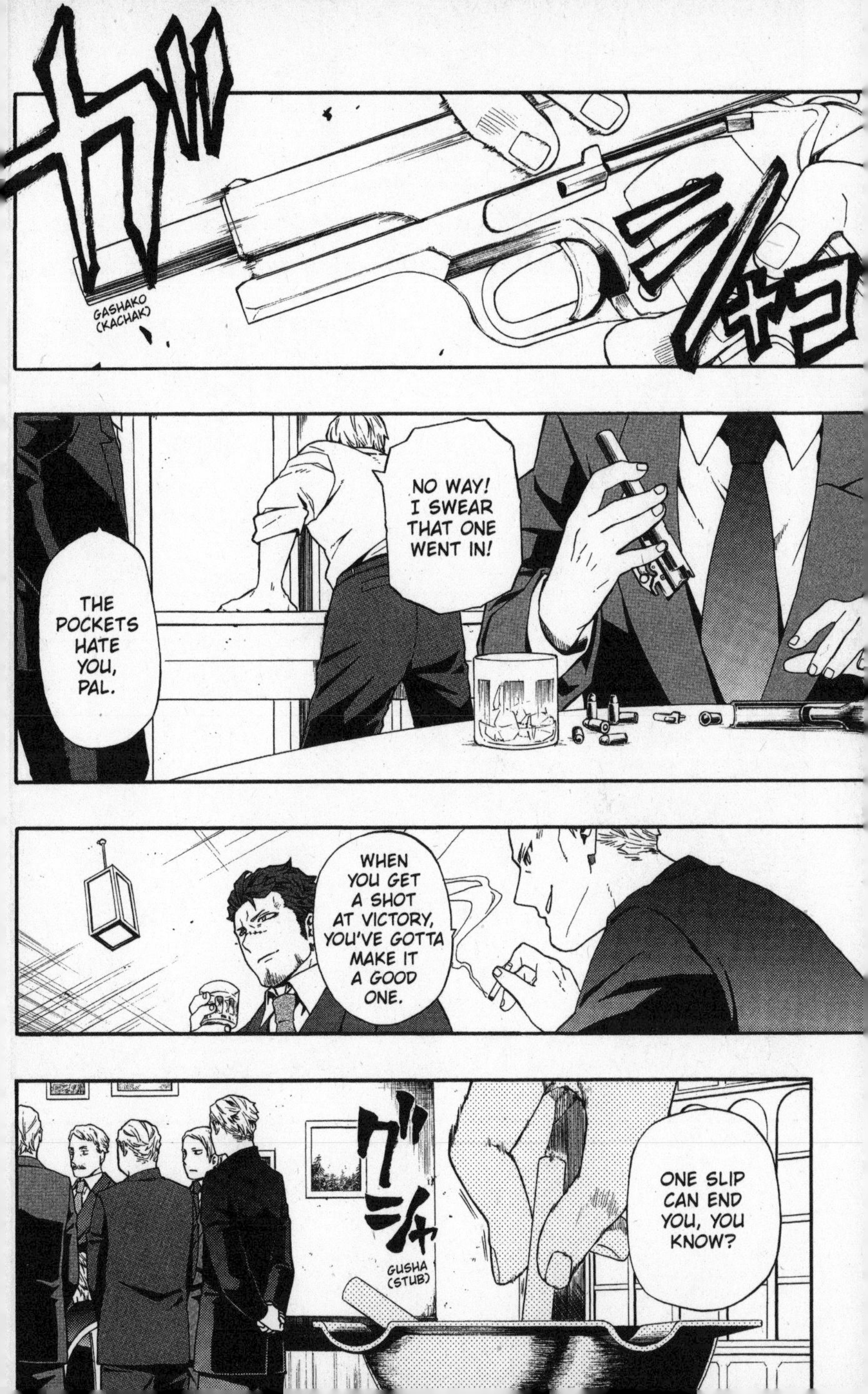
GASHAKO (KACHAK)
NO WAY! I SWEAR THAT ONE WENT IN!
THE POCKETS HATE YOU, PAL.
WHEN YOU GET A SHOT AT VICTORY, YOU'VE GOTTA MAKE IT A GOOD ONE.
ONE SLIP CAN END YOU, YOU KNOW?
GUSHA (STUB)

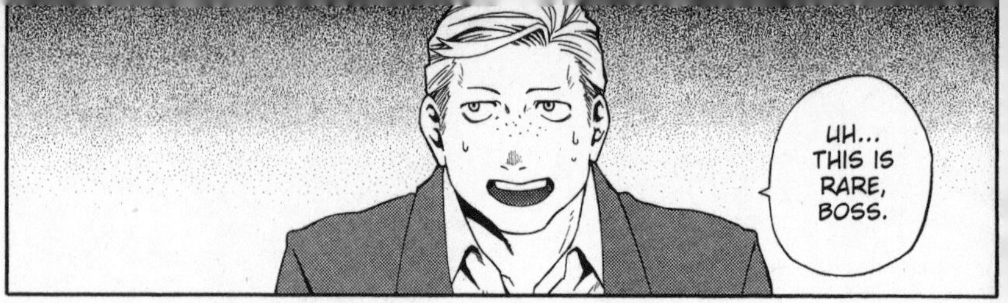
UH... THIS IS RARE, BOSS.

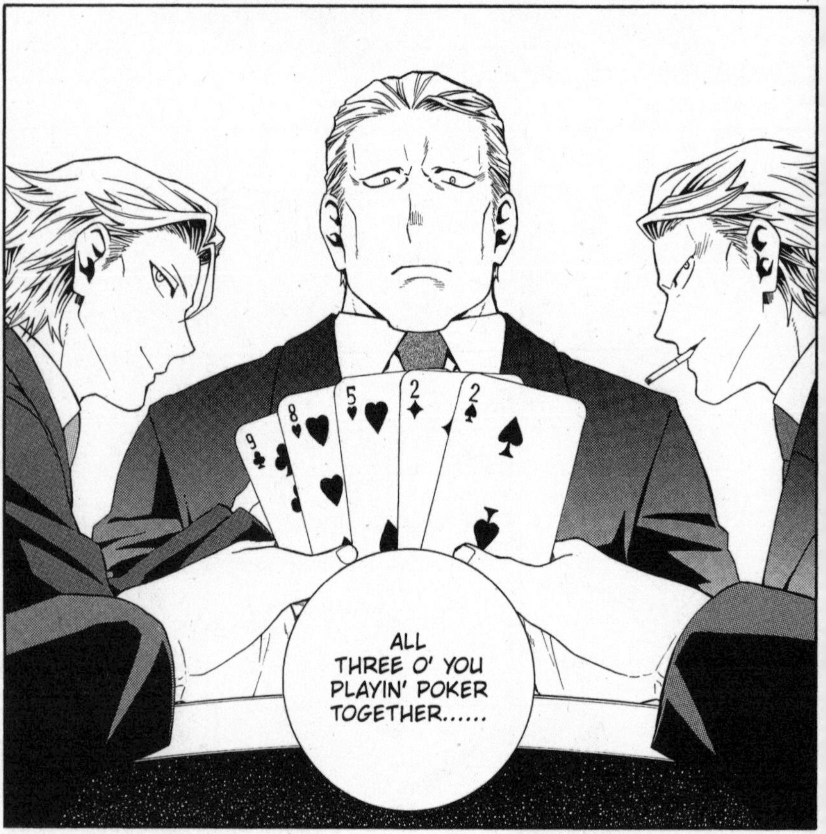
ALL THREE O' YOU PLAYIN' POKER TOGETHER......

#10 Gandor Family

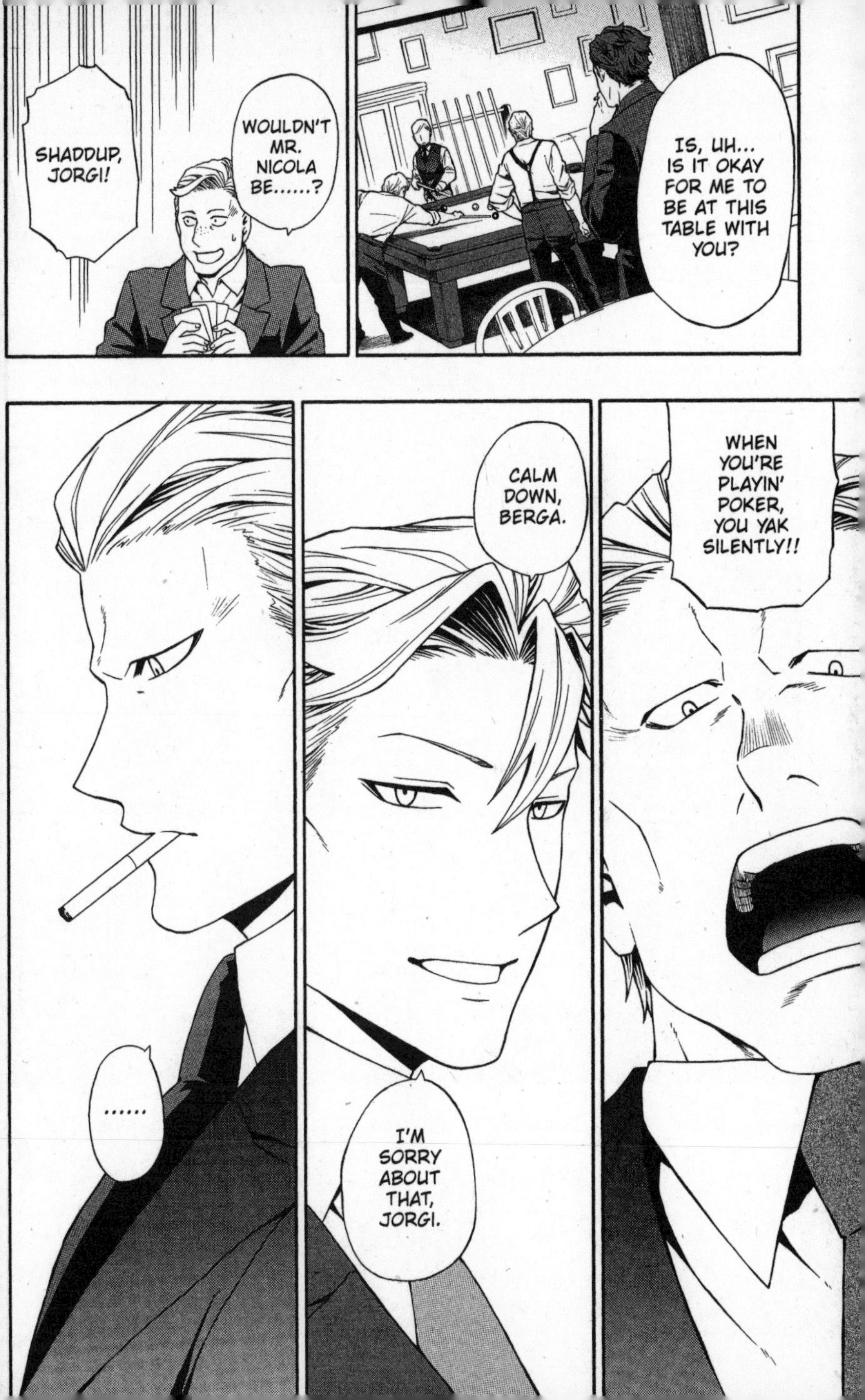
IS, UH... IS IT OKAY FOR ME TO BE AT THIS TABLE WITH YOU?
WOULDN'T MR. NICOLA BE......?
SHADDUP, JORGI!
WHEN YOU'RE PLAYIN' POKER, YOU YAK SILENTLY!!
CALM DOWN, BERGA.
I'M SORRY ABOUT THAT, JORGI.
......

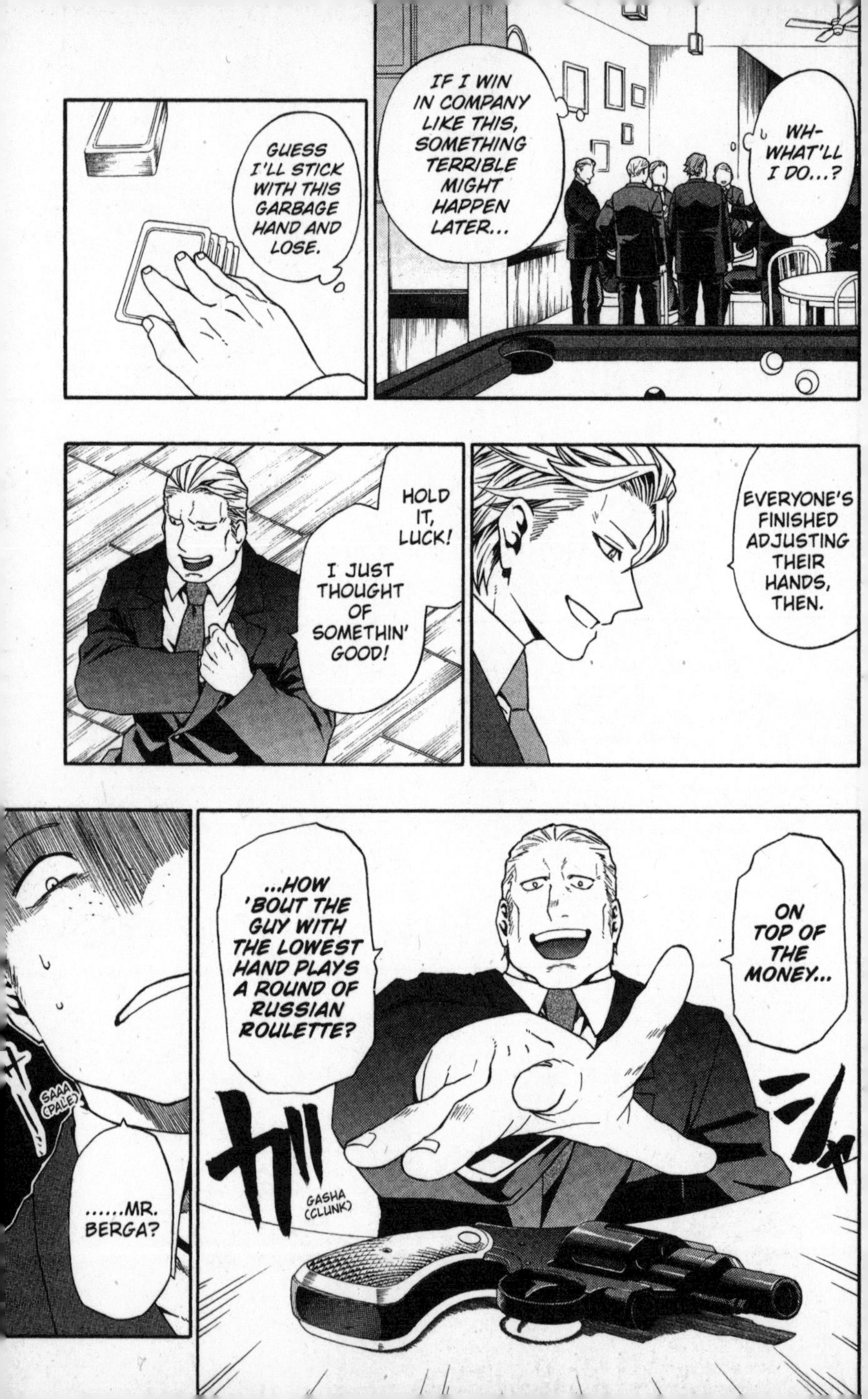
WH-WHAT'LL I DO...?
IF I WIN IN COMPANY LIKE THIS, SOMETHING TERRIBLE MIGHT HAPPEN LATER...
GUESS I'LL STICK WITH THIS GARBAGE HAND AND LOSE.
EVERYONE'S FINISHED ADJUSTING THEIR HANDS, THEN.
HOLD IT, LUCK!
I JUST THOUGHT OF SOMETHIN' GOOD!
ON TOP OF THE MONEY...
...HOW 'BOUT THE GUY WITH THE LOWEST HAND PLAYS A ROUND OF RUSSIAN ROULETTE?
GASHA (CLUNK)
SAAA (PALE)
......MR. BERGA?

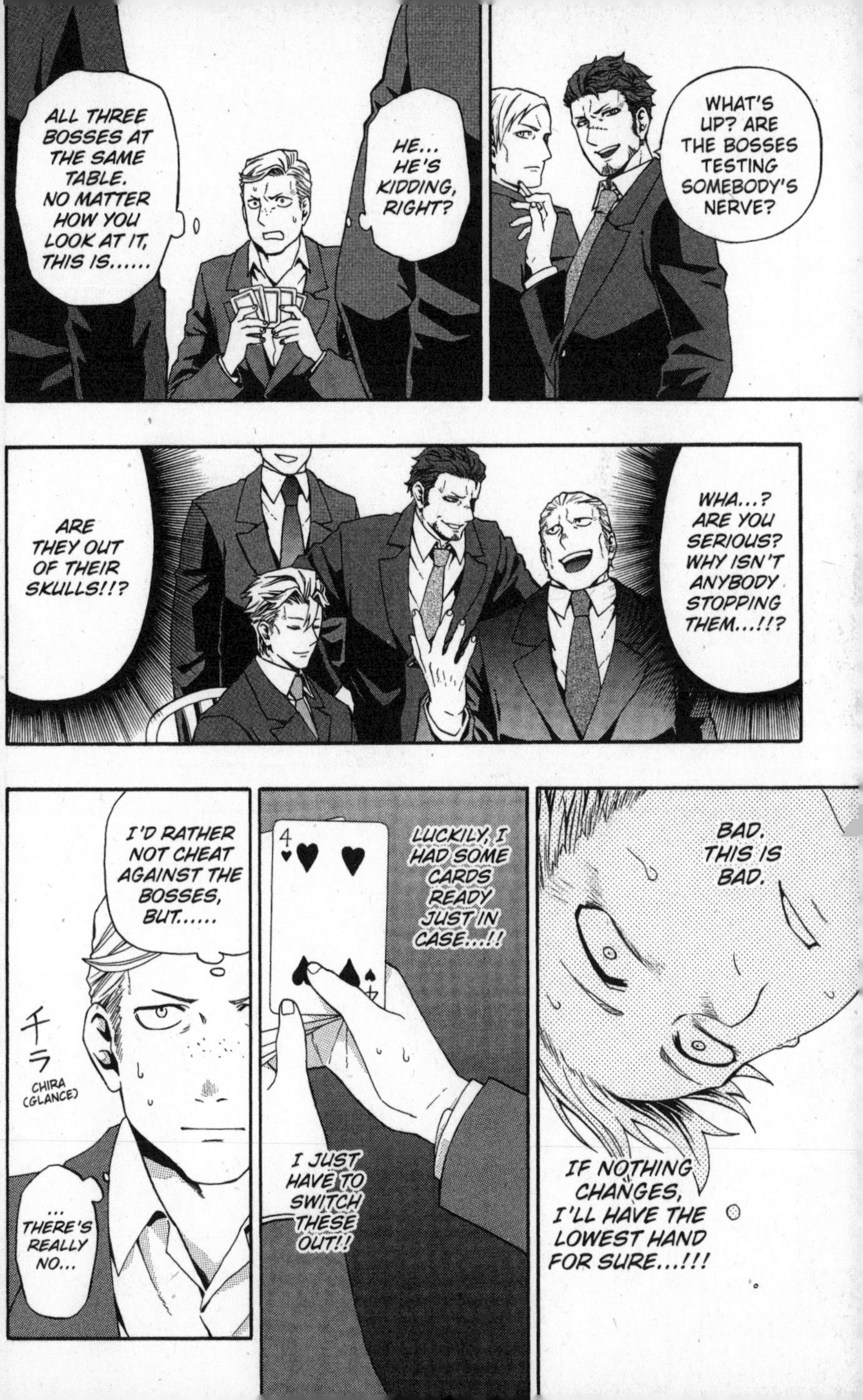
WHAT'S UP? ARE THE BOSSES TESTING SOMEBODY'S NERVE?
HE... HE'S KIDDING, RIGHT?
ALL THREE BOSSES AT THE SAME TABLE. NO MATTER HOW YOU LOOK AT IT, THIS IS......
WHA...? ARE YOU SERIOUS? WHY ISN'T ANYBODY STOPPING THEM...!!?
ARE THEY OUT OF THEIR SKULLS!!?
BAD. THIS IS BAD.
IF NOTHING CHANGES, I'LL HAVE THE LOWEST HAND FOR SURE...!!!
LUCKILY, I HAD SOME CARDS READY JUST IN CASE...!!
I JUST HAVE TO SWITCH THESE OUT!!
I'D RATHER NOT CHEAT AGAINST THE BOSSES, BUT......
チラ
CHIRA (GLANCE)
...THERE'S REALLY NO...

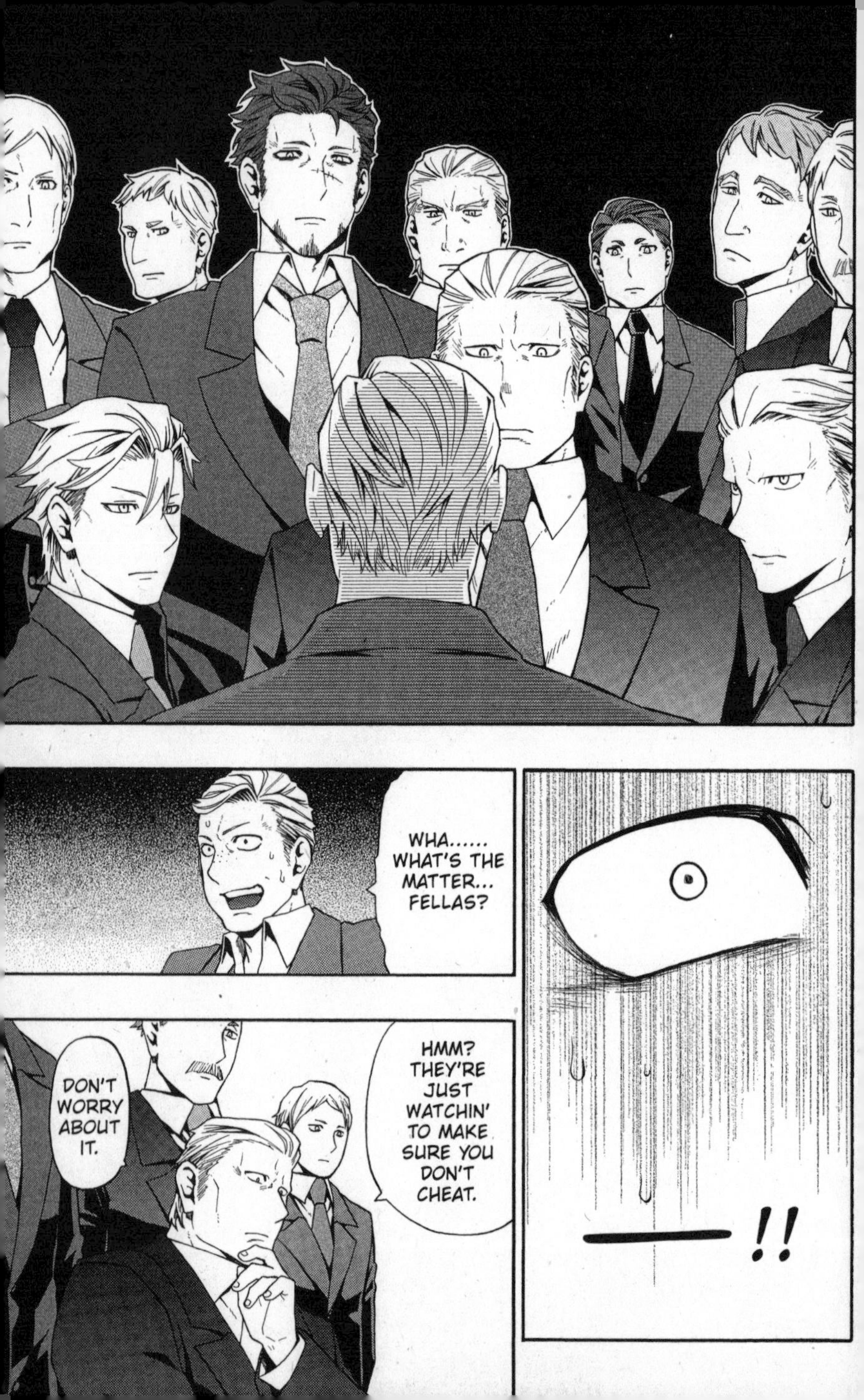
——!!
WHA...... WHAT'S THE MATTER... FELLAS?
HMM? THEY'RE JUST WATCHIN' TO MAKE SURE YOU DON'T CHEAT.
DON'T WORRY ABOUT IT.

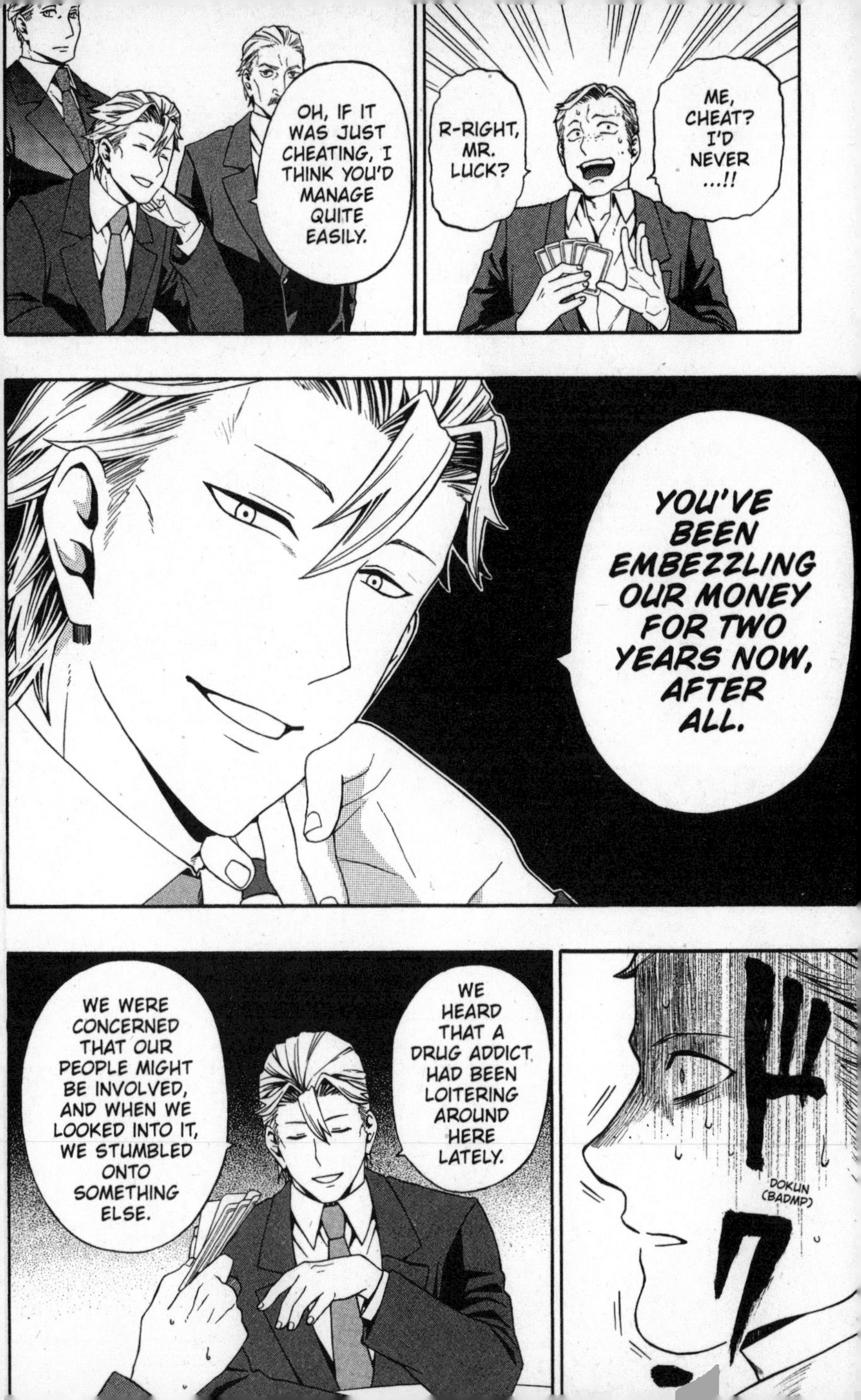
ME, CHEAT? I'D NEVER ...!!
R-RIGHT, MR. LUCK?
OH, IF IT WAS JUST CHEATING, I THINK YOU'D MANAGE QUITE EASILY.
YOU'VE BEEN EMBEZZLING OUR MONEY FOR TWO YEARS NOW, AFTER ALL.
DOKUN (BADMP)
WE HEARD THAT A DRUG ADDICT HAD BEEN LOITERING AROUND HERE LATELY.
WE WERE CONCERNED THAT OUR PEOPLE MIGHT BE INVOLVED, AND WHEN WE LOOKED INTO IT, WE STUMBLED ONTO SOMETHING ELSE.

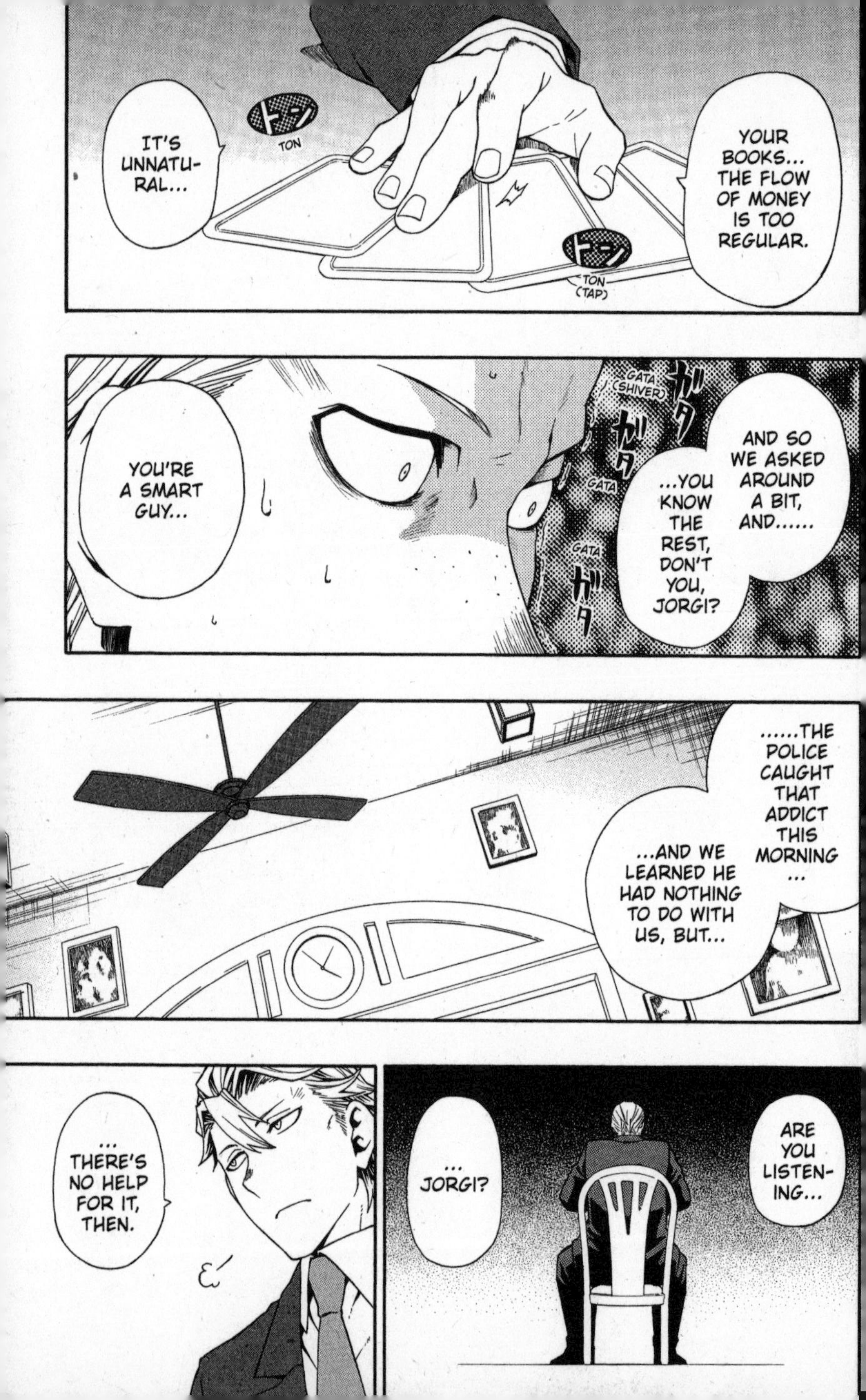
YOUR BOOKS... THE FLOW OF MONEY IS TOO REGULAR.
TON (TAP)
TON
IT'S UNNATU-RAL...
AND SO WE ASKED AROUND A BIT, AND......
...YOU KNOW THE REST, DON'T YOU, JORGI?
GATA (SHIVER)
GATA
GATA
YOU'RE A SMART GUY...
......THE POLICE CAUGHT THAT ADDICT THIS MORNING...
...AND WE LEARNED HE HAD NOTHING TO DO WITH US, BUT...
ARE YOU LISTEN-ING...
... JORGI?
... THERE'S NO HELP FOR IT, THEN.

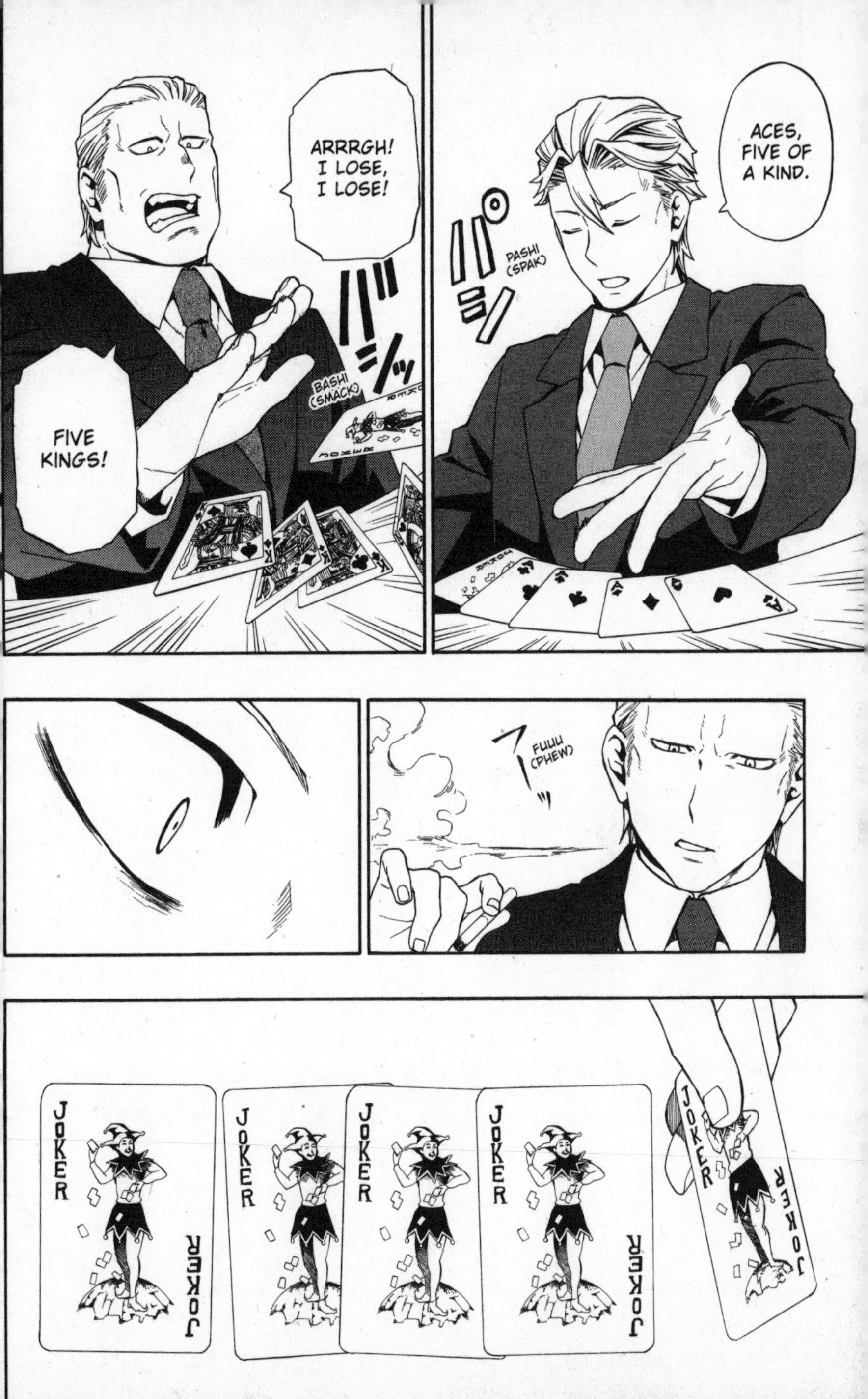
ACES, FIVE OF A KIND.
PASHI (SPAK)
ARRRGH! I LOSE, I LOSE!
BASHI (SMACK)
FIVE KINGS!
FUUU (PHEW)

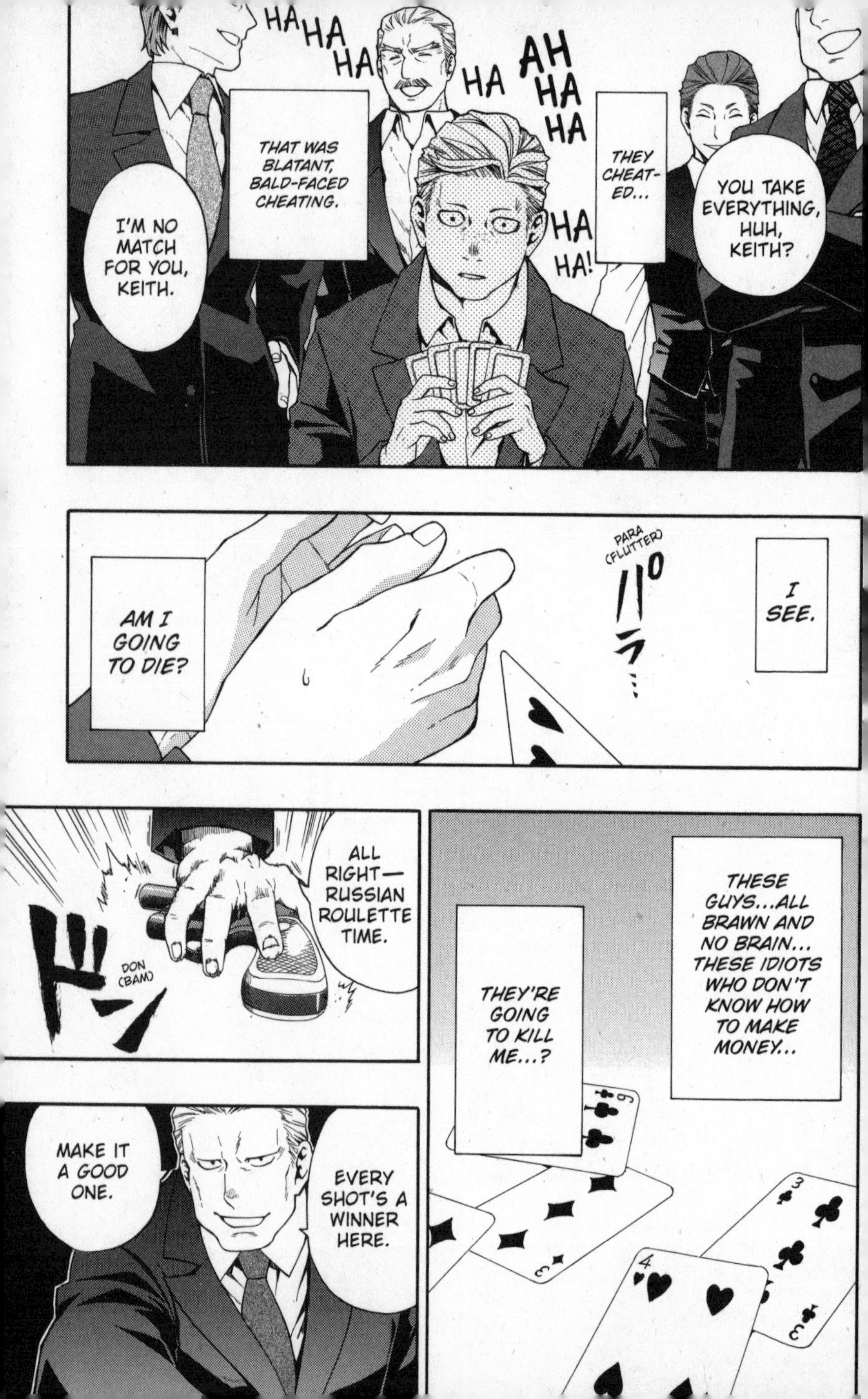
YOU TAKE EVERYTHING, HUH, KEITH?
THEY CHEATED...
HA HA!
AH HA HA HA
HA
THAT WAS BLATANT, BALD-FACED CHEATING.
HA HA HA
I'M NO MATCH FOR YOU, KEITH.
I SEE.
PARA (FLUTTER)
AM I GOING TO DIE?
THESE GUYS...ALL BRAWN AND NO BRAIN... THESE IDIOTS WHO DON'T KNOW HOW TO MAKE MONEY...
THEY'RE GOING TO KILL ME...?
ALL RIGHT— RUSSIAN ROULETTE TIME.
DON (BAM)
EVERY SHOT'S A WINNER HERE.
MAKE IT A GOOD ONE.

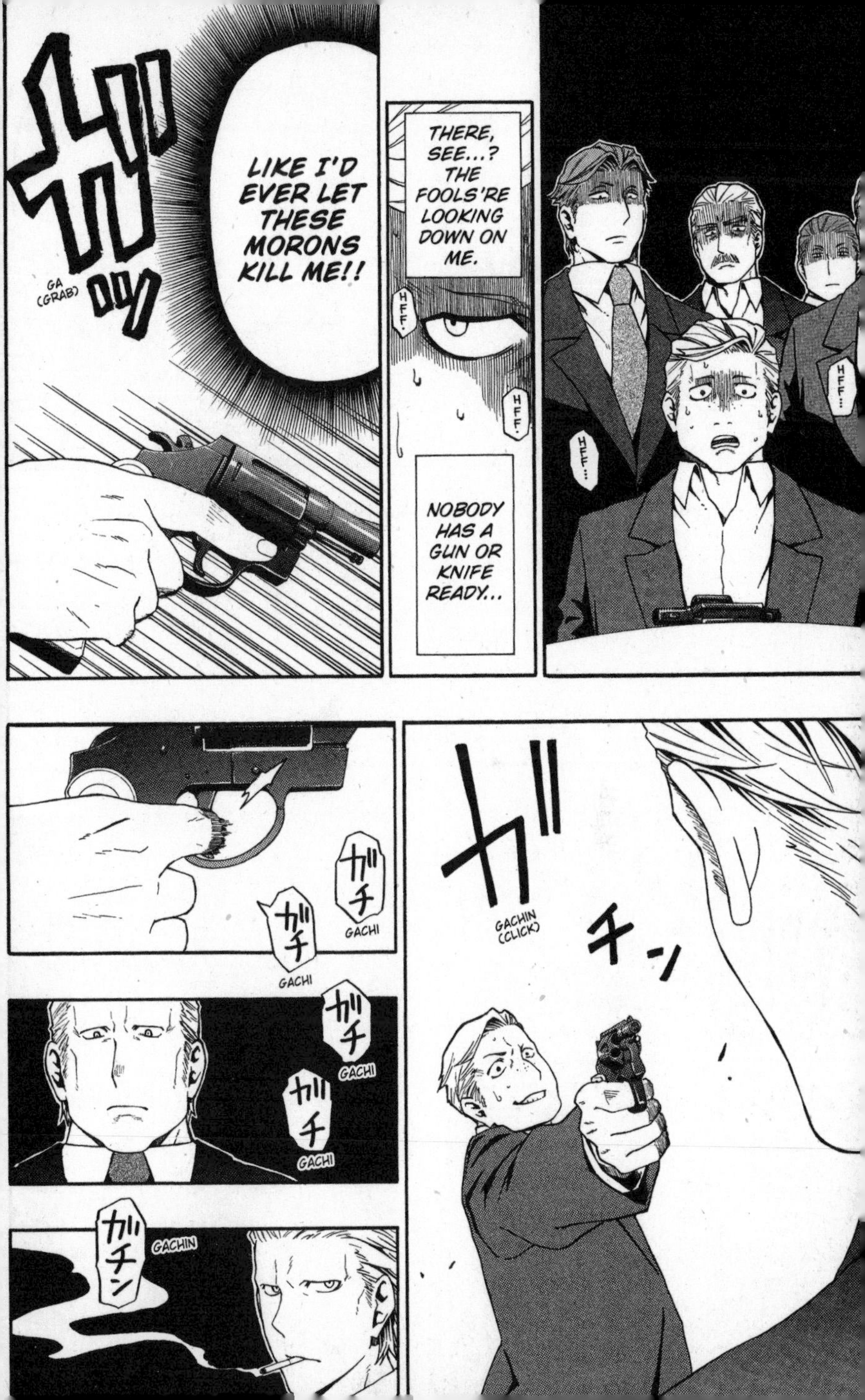
HFF...
HFF...
THERE, SEE...? THE FOOLS'RE LOOKING DOWN ON ME.
HFF.
HFF.
NOBODY HAS A GUN OR KNIFE READY...
LIKE I'D EVER LET THESE MORONS KILL ME!!
GA (GRAB)
ガチン
GACHIN (CLICK)
ガチ
GACHI
ガチ
GACHI
ガチ
GACHI
ガチ
GACHI
ガチン
GACHIN

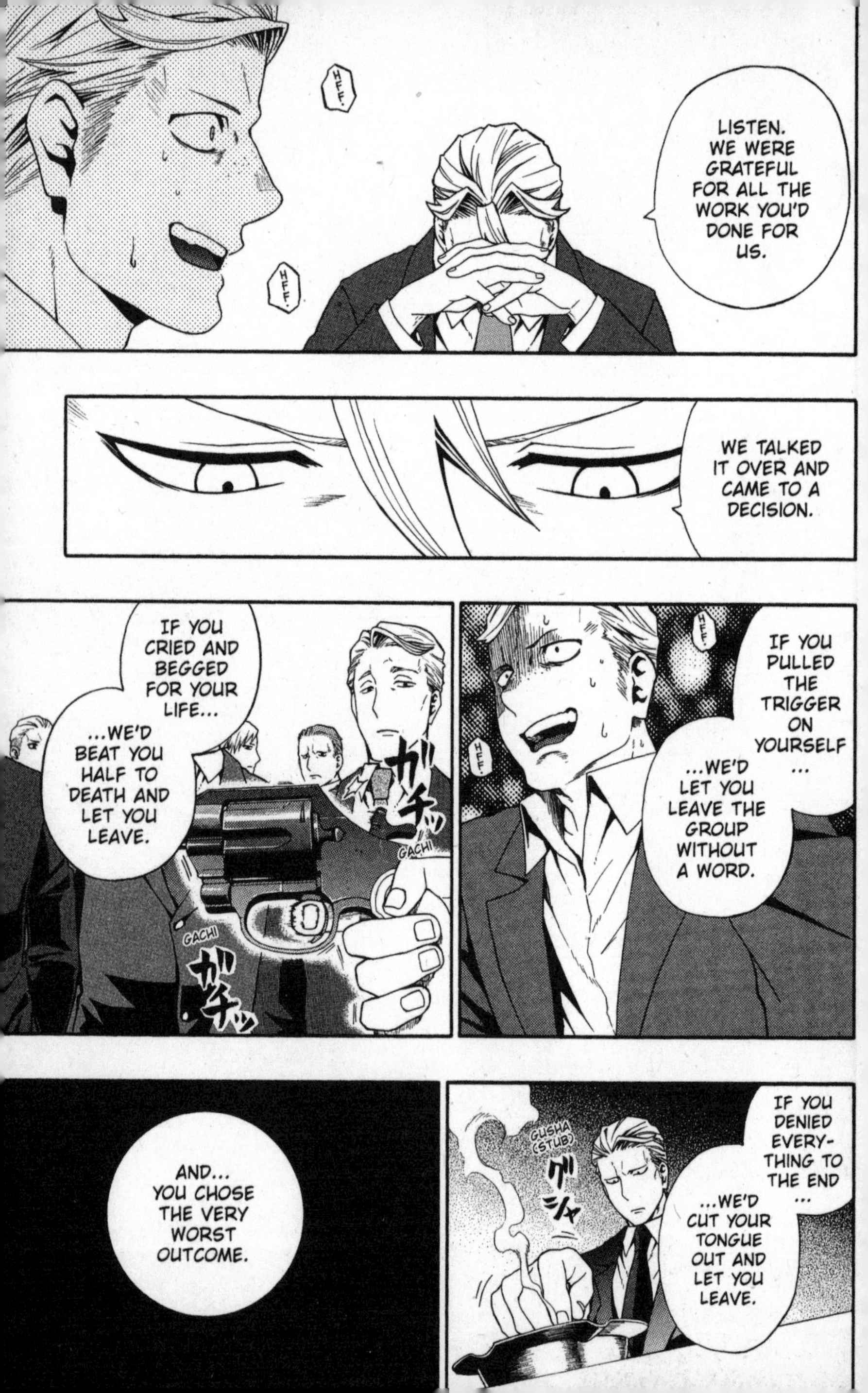
LISTEN. WE WERE GRATEFUL FOR ALL THE WORK YOU'D DONE FOR US.
HFF.
HFF.
WE TALKED IT OVER AND CAME TO A DECISION.
HFF.
IF YOU PULLED THE TRIGGER ON YOURSELF...
HFF.
...WE'D LET YOU LEAVE THE GROUP WITHOUT A WORD.
IF YOU CRIED AND BEGGED FOR YOUR LIFE...
...WE'D BEAT YOU HALF TO DEATH AND LET YOU LEAVE.
ガチッ
GACHI
GACHI
ガチッ
IF YOU DENIED EVERY-THING TO THE END...
GUSHA (STUB)
グシャ
...WE'D CUT YOUR TONGUE OUT AND LET YOU LEAVE.
AND... YOU CHOSE THE VERY WORST OUTCOME.

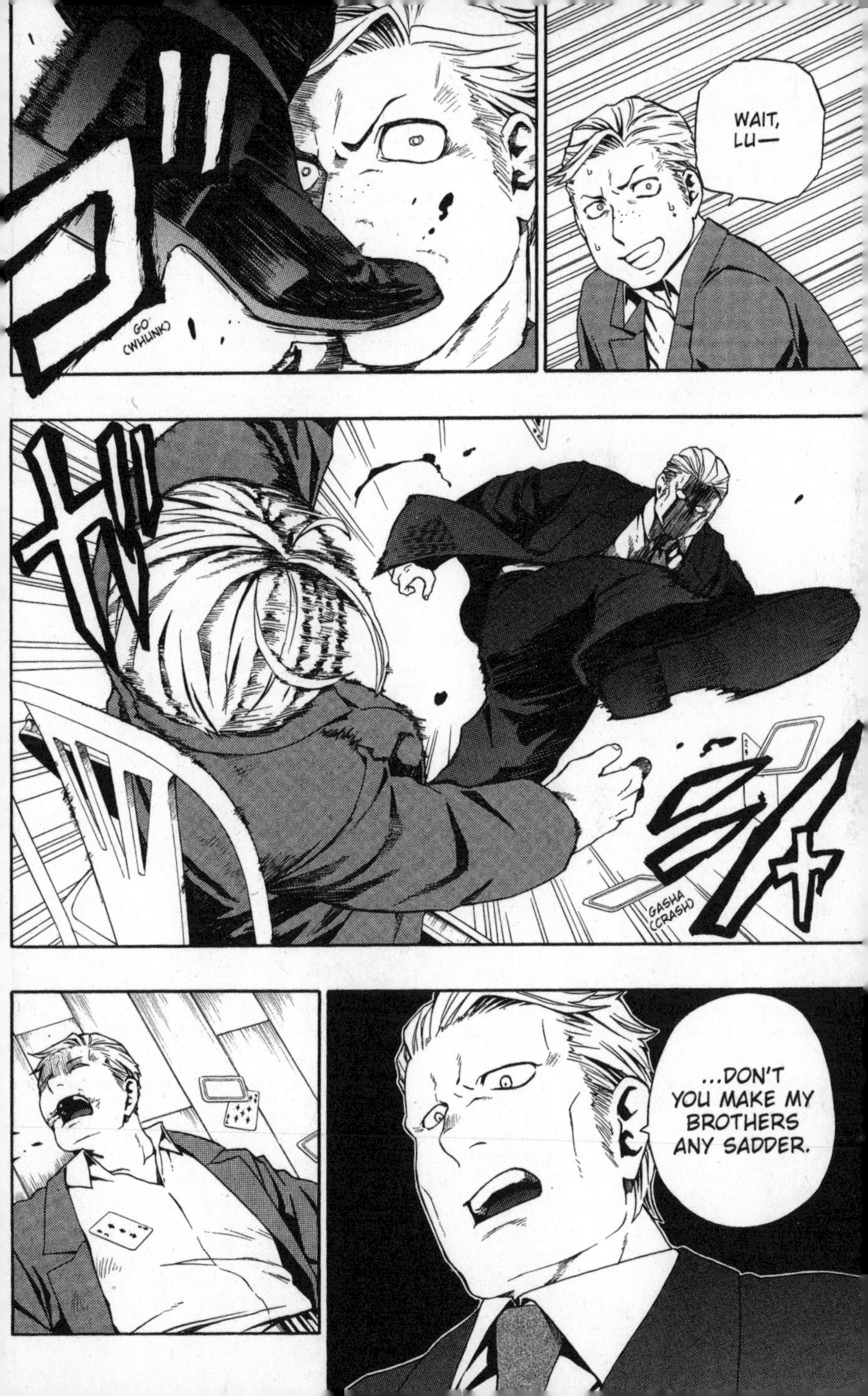
WAIT, LU—
GO (WHUNK)
GASHA (CRASH)
...DON'T YOU MAKE MY BROTHERS ANY SADDER.

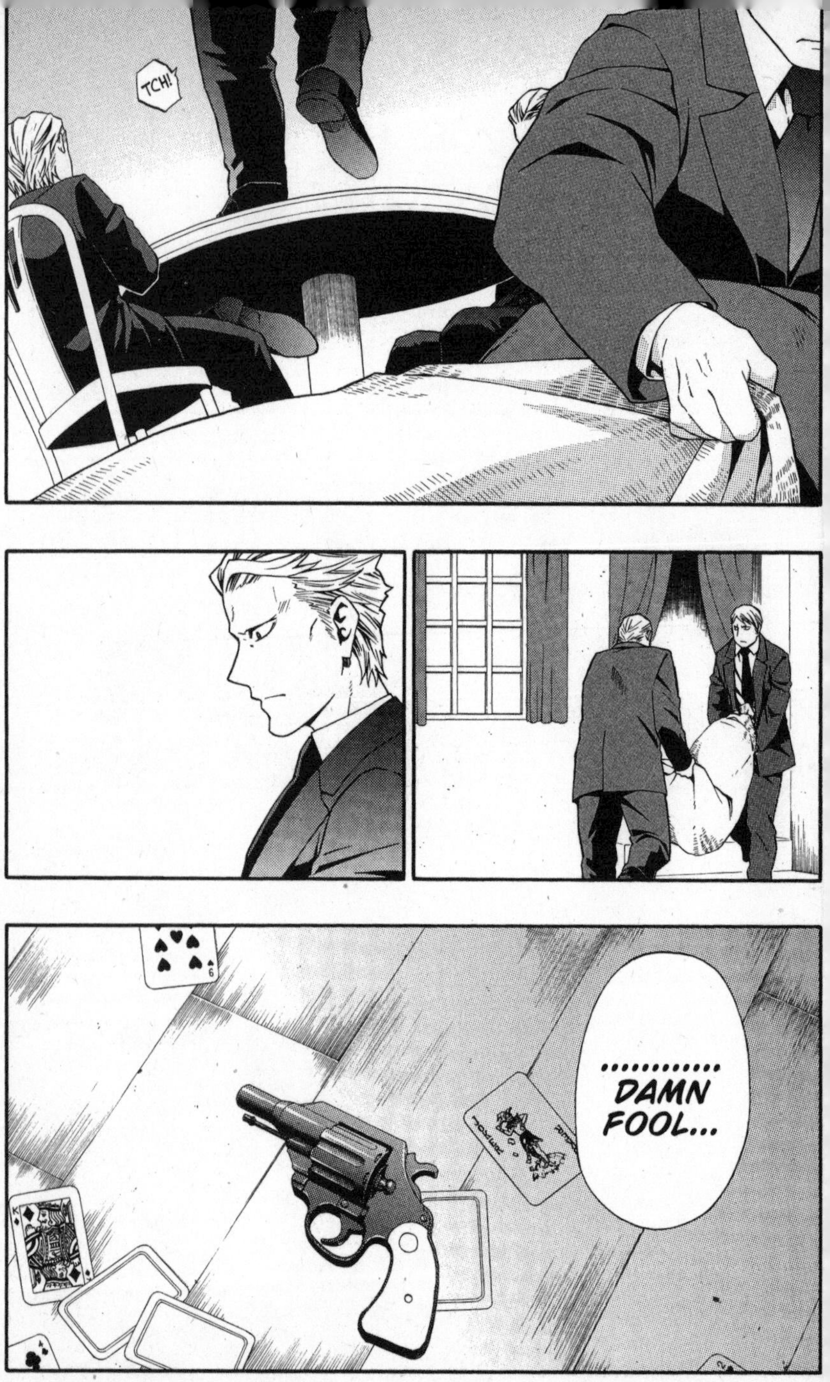
TCH!
.... DAMN FOOL...

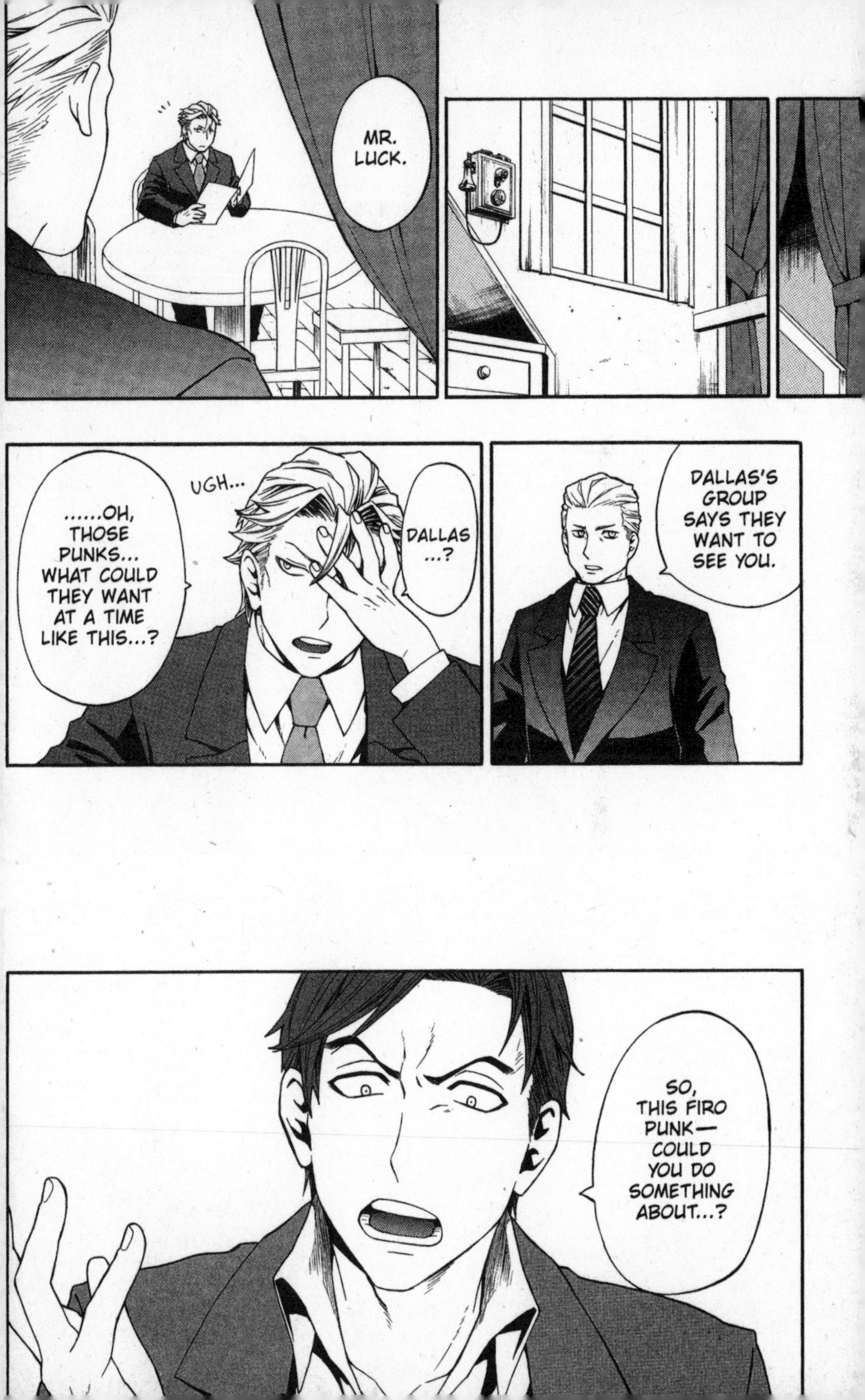
MR. LUCK.
DALLAS'S GROUP SAYS THEY WANT TO SEE YOU.
DALLAS ...?
UGH...
......OH, THOSE PUNKS... WHAT COULD THEY WANT AT A TIME LIKE THIS...?
SO, THIS FIRO PUNK—COULD YOU DO SOMETHING ABOUT...?

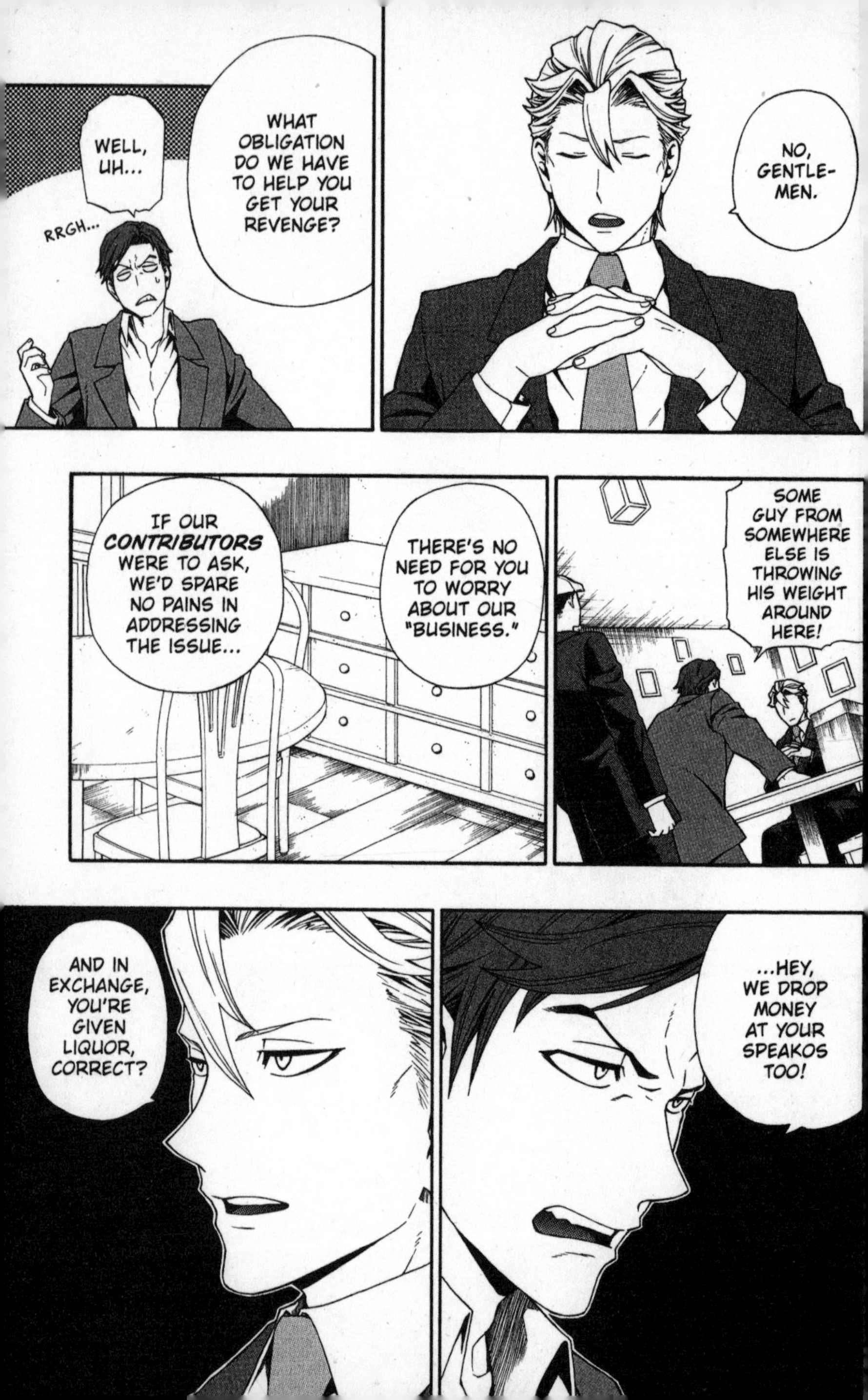
NO, GENTLE-MEN.
WHAT OBLIGATION DO WE HAVE TO HELP YOU GET YOUR REVENGE?
WELL, UH...
RRGH...
SOME GUY FROM SOMEWHERE ELSE IS THROWING HIS WEIGHT AROUND HERE!
THERE'S NO NEED FOR YOU TO WORRY ABOUT OUR "BUSINESS."
IF OUR **CONTRIBUTORS** WERE TO ASK, WE'D SPARE NO PAINS IN ADDRESSING THE ISSUE...
...HEY, WE DROP MONEY AT YOUR SPEAKOS TOO!
AND IN EXCHANGE, YOU'RE GIVEN LIQUOR, CORRECT?

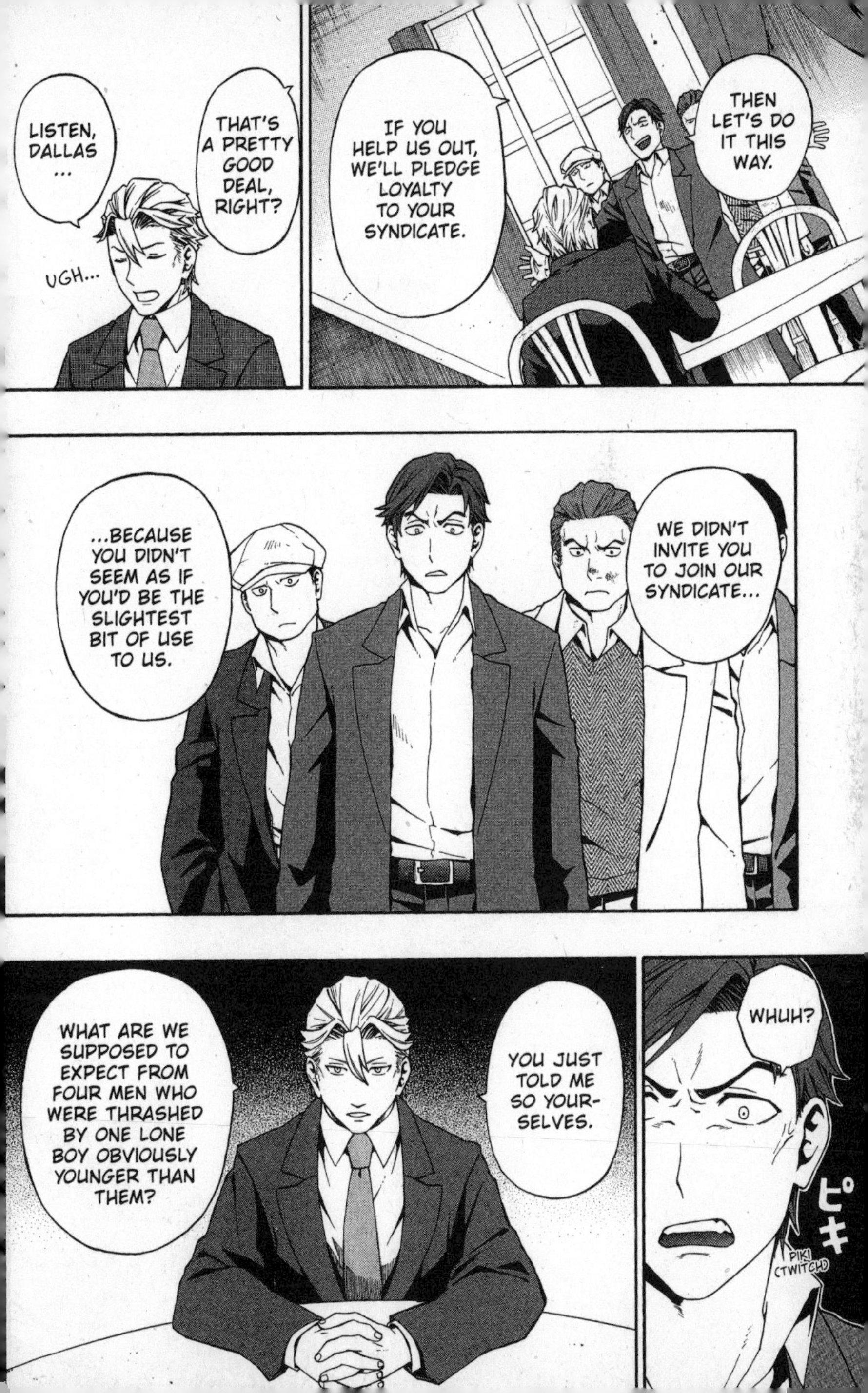
THEN LET'S DO IT THIS WAY.
IF YOU HELP US OUT, WE'LL PLEDGE LOYALTY TO YOUR SYNDICATE.
THAT'S A PRETTY GOOD DEAL, RIGHT?
LISTEN, DALLAS ...
UGH...
WE DIDN'T INVITE YOU TO JOIN OUR SYNDICATE...
...BECAUSE YOU DIDN'T SEEM AS IF YOU'D BE THE SLIGHTEST BIT OF USE TO US.
WHUH?
ピキ
PIKI (TWITCH)
YOU JUST TOLD ME SO YOUR-SELVES.
WHAT ARE WE SUPPOSED TO EXPECT FROM FOUR MEN WHO WERE THRASHED BY ONE LONE BOY OBVIOUSLY YOUNGER THAN THEM?

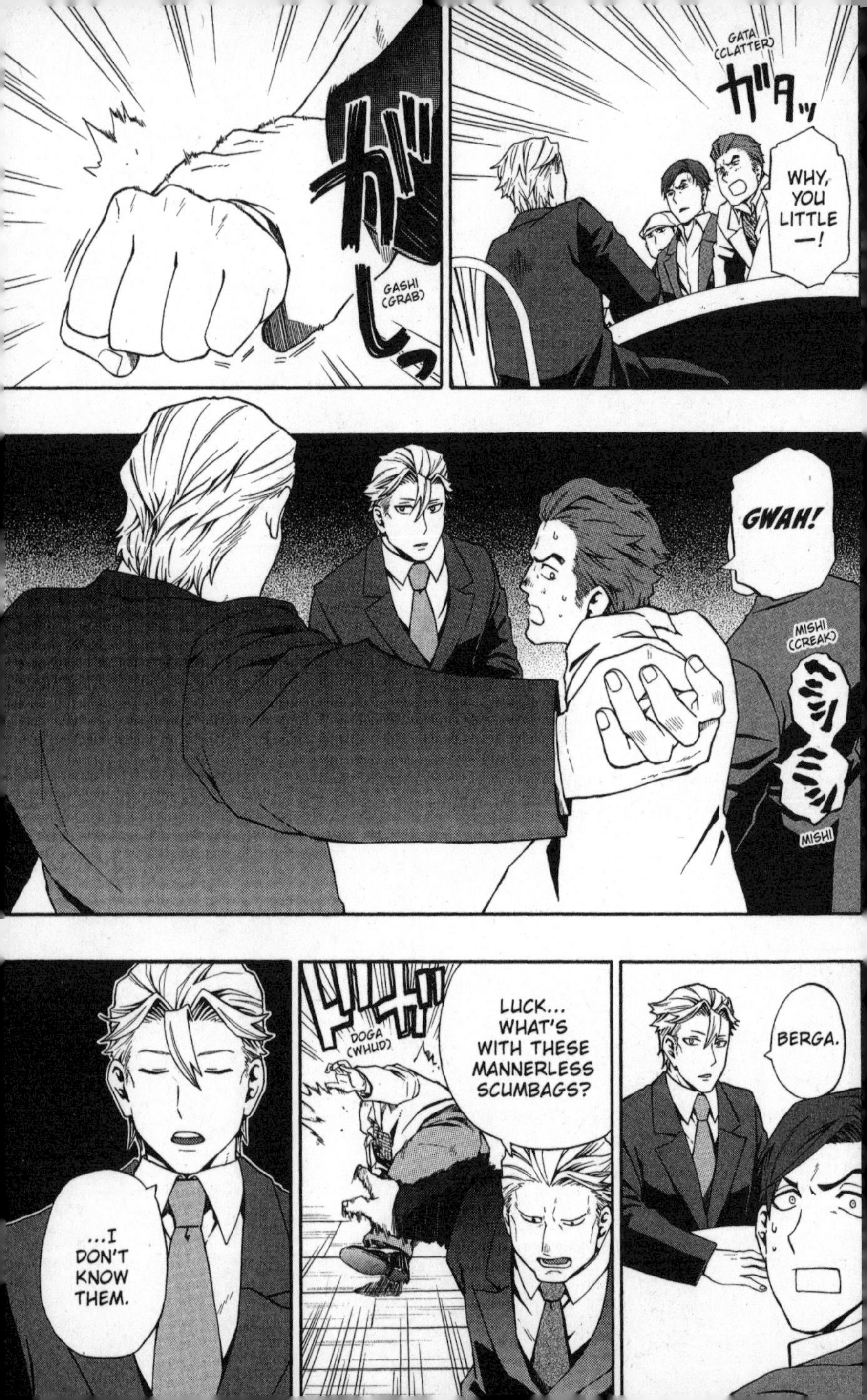
GATA (CLATTER)
WHY, YOU LITTLE—!
GASHI (GRAB)
GWAH!
MISHI (CREAK)
MISHI
BERGA.
LUCK... WHAT'S WITH THESE MANNERLESS SCUMBAGS?
DOGA (WHUD)
...I DON'T KNOW THEM.

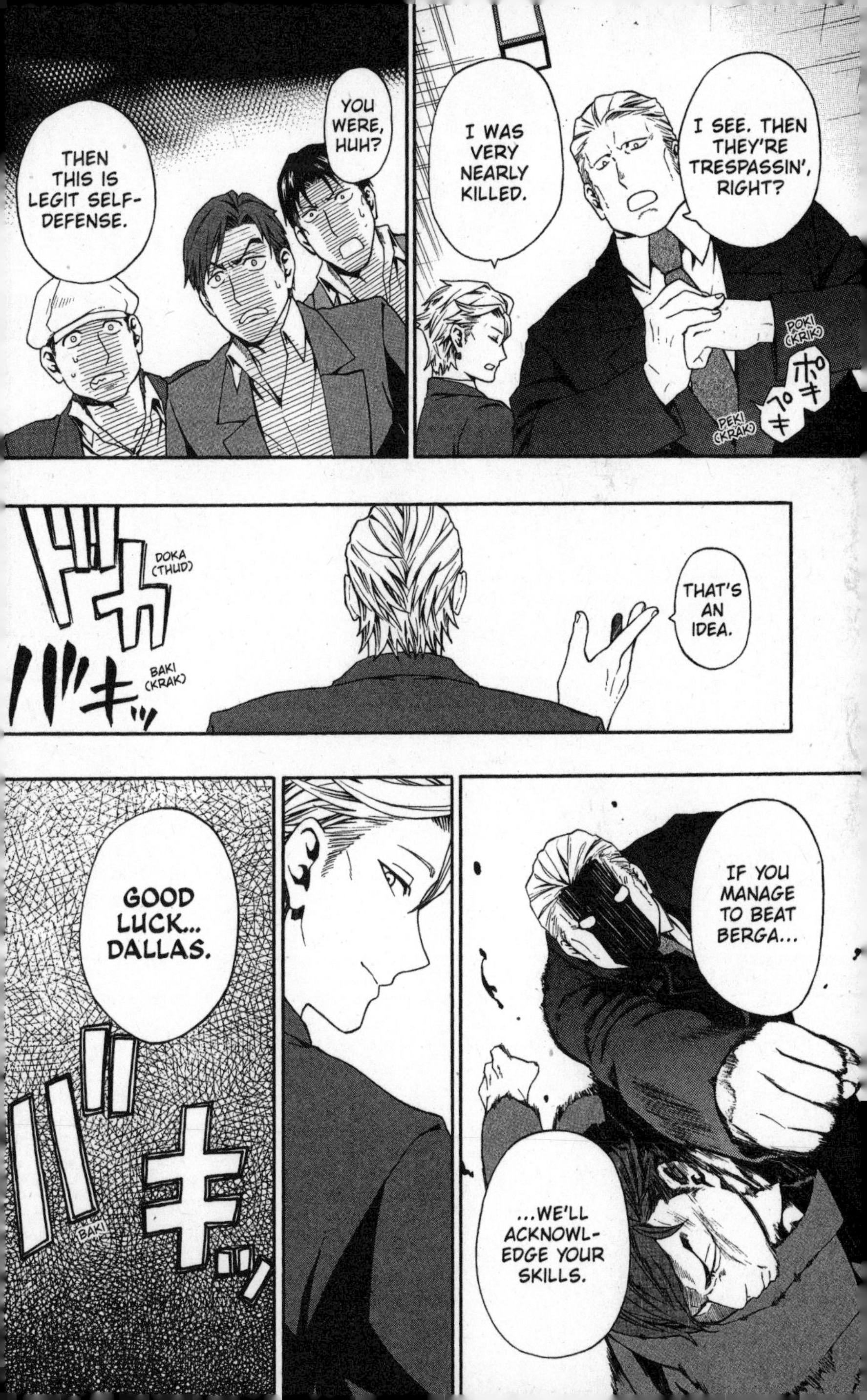
I SEE. THEN THEY'RE TRESPASSIN', RIGHT?
I WAS VERY NEARLY KILLED.
ポキ
POKI (KRIK)
ペキ
PEKI (KRAK)
YOU WERE, HUH?
THEN THIS IS LEGIT SELF-DEFENSE.
THAT'S AN IDEA.
ドカ
DOKA (THUD)
バキッ
BAKI (KRAK)
IF YOU MANAGE TO BEAT BERGA...
...WE'LL ACKNOWL-EDGE YOUR SKILLS.
GOOD LUCK... DALLAS.
バキッ
BAKI

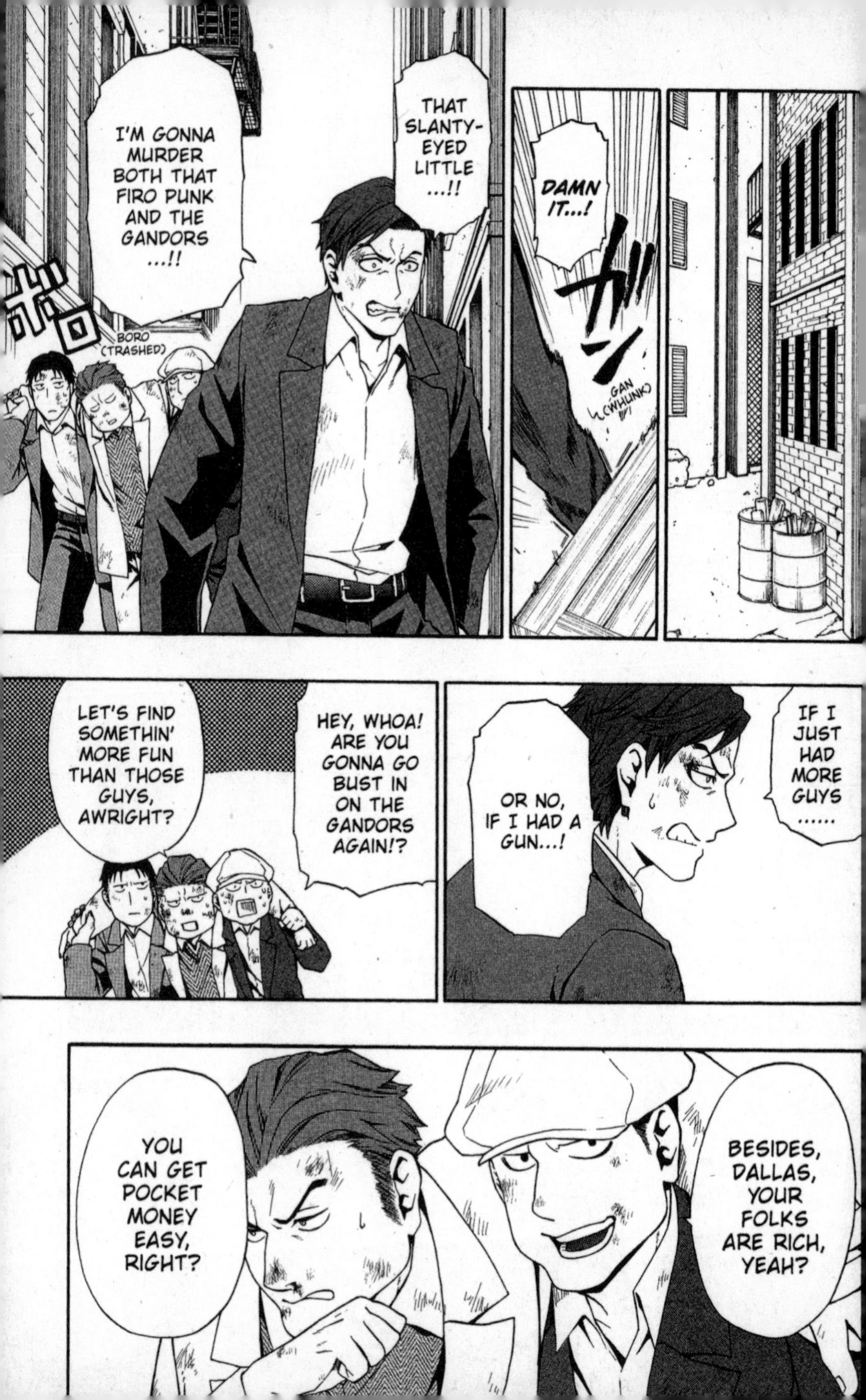
DAMN IT...!
GAN (WHUNK)
THAT SLANTY-EYED LITTLE ...!!
I'M GONNA MURDER BOTH THAT FIRO PUNK AND THE GANDORS ...!!
BORO (TRASHED)
IF I JUST HAD MORE GUYS ......
OR NO, IF I HAD A GUN...!
HEY, WHOA! ARE YOU GONNA GO BUST IN ON THE GANDORS AGAIN!?
LET'S FIND SOMETHIN' MORE FUN THAN THOSE GUYS, AWRIGHT?
BESIDES, DALLAS, YOUR FOLKS ARE RICH, YEAH?
YOU CAN GET POCKET MONEY EASY, RIGHT?

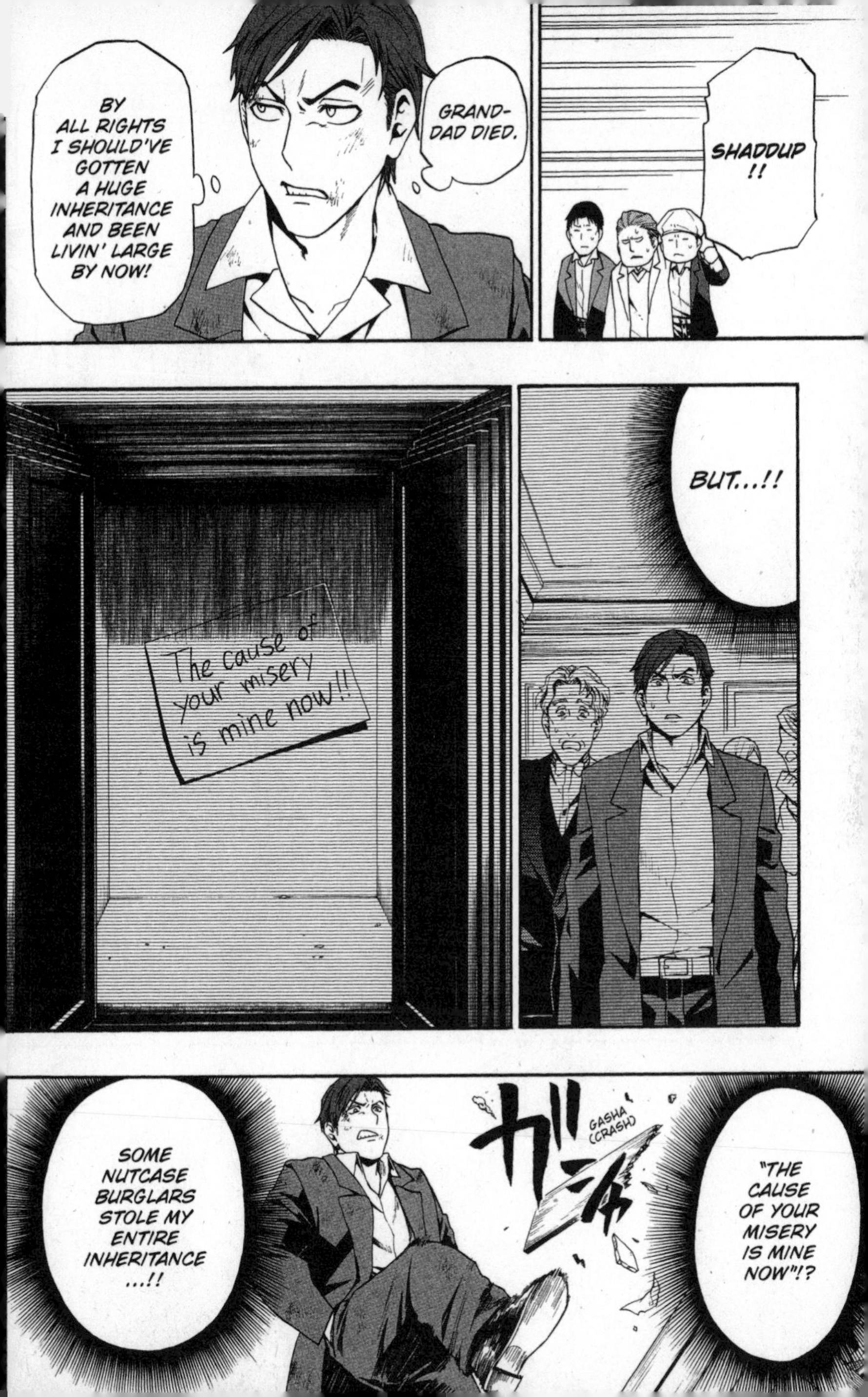
SHADDUP!!
GRAND-DAD DIED.
BY ALL RIGHTS I SHOULD'VE GOTTEN A HUGE INHERITANCE AND BEEN LIVIN' LARGE BY NOW!
BUT...!!
The cause of your misery is mine now!!
"THE CAUSE OF YOUR MISERY IS MINE NOW"!?
GASHA (CRASH)
SOME NUTCASE BURGLARS STOLE MY ENTIRE INHERITANCE ...!!

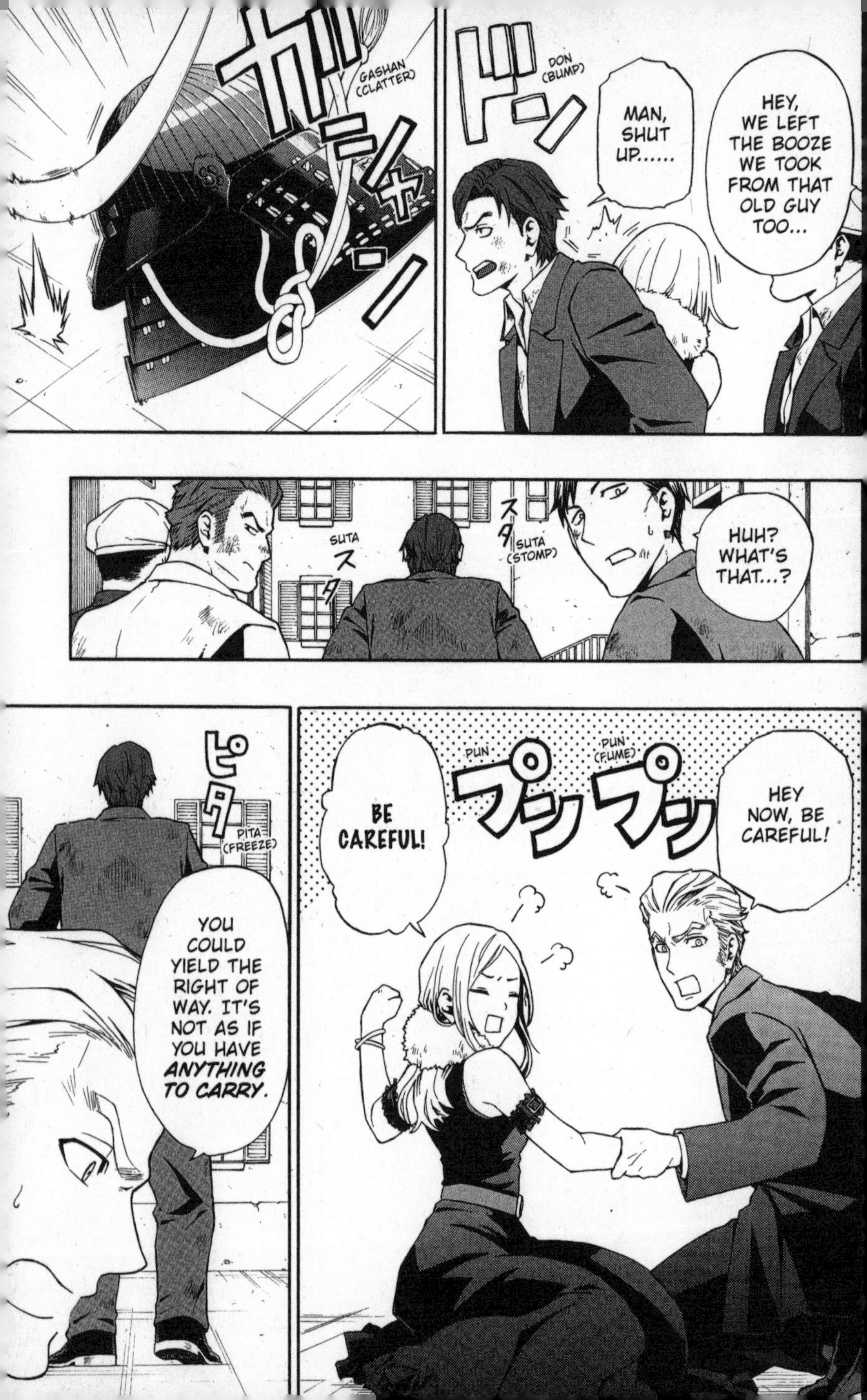
HEY, WE LEFT THE BOOZE WE TOOK FROM THAT OLD GUY TOO...
MAN, SHUT UP......
DON (BUMP)
GASHAN (CLATTER)
HUH? WHAT'S THAT...?
SUTA (STOMP)
SUTA
HEY NOW, BE CAREFUL!
PUN (FUME)
PUN
BE CAREFUL!
PITA (FREEZE)
YOU COULD YIELD THE RIGHT OF WAY. IT'S NOT AS IF YOU HAVE *ANYTHING TO CARRY*.

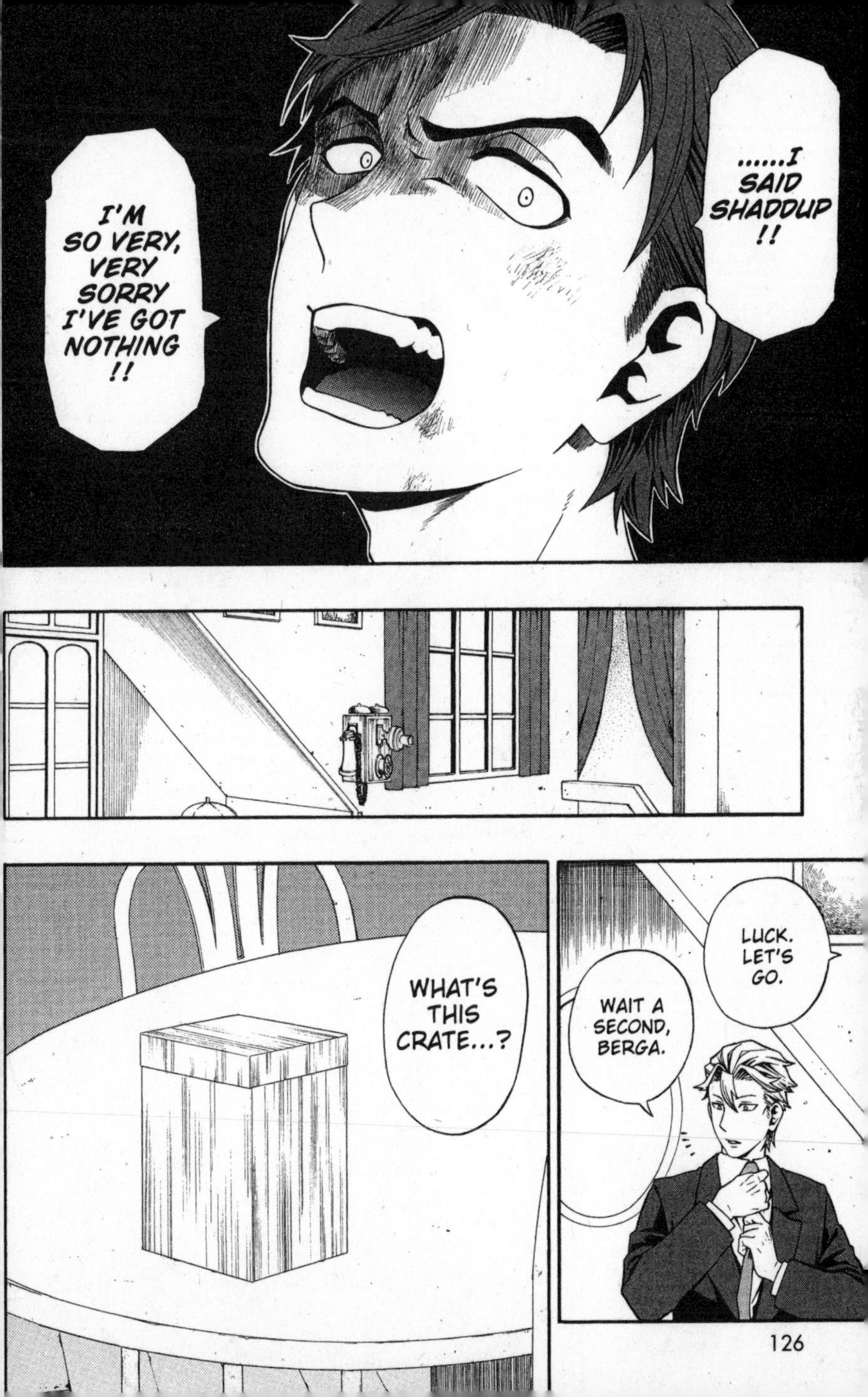
......I SAID SHADDUP!!
I'M SO VERY, VERY SORRY I'VE GOT NOTHING!!
LUCK. LET'S GO.
WAIT A SECOND, BERGA.
WHAT'S THIS CRATE...?

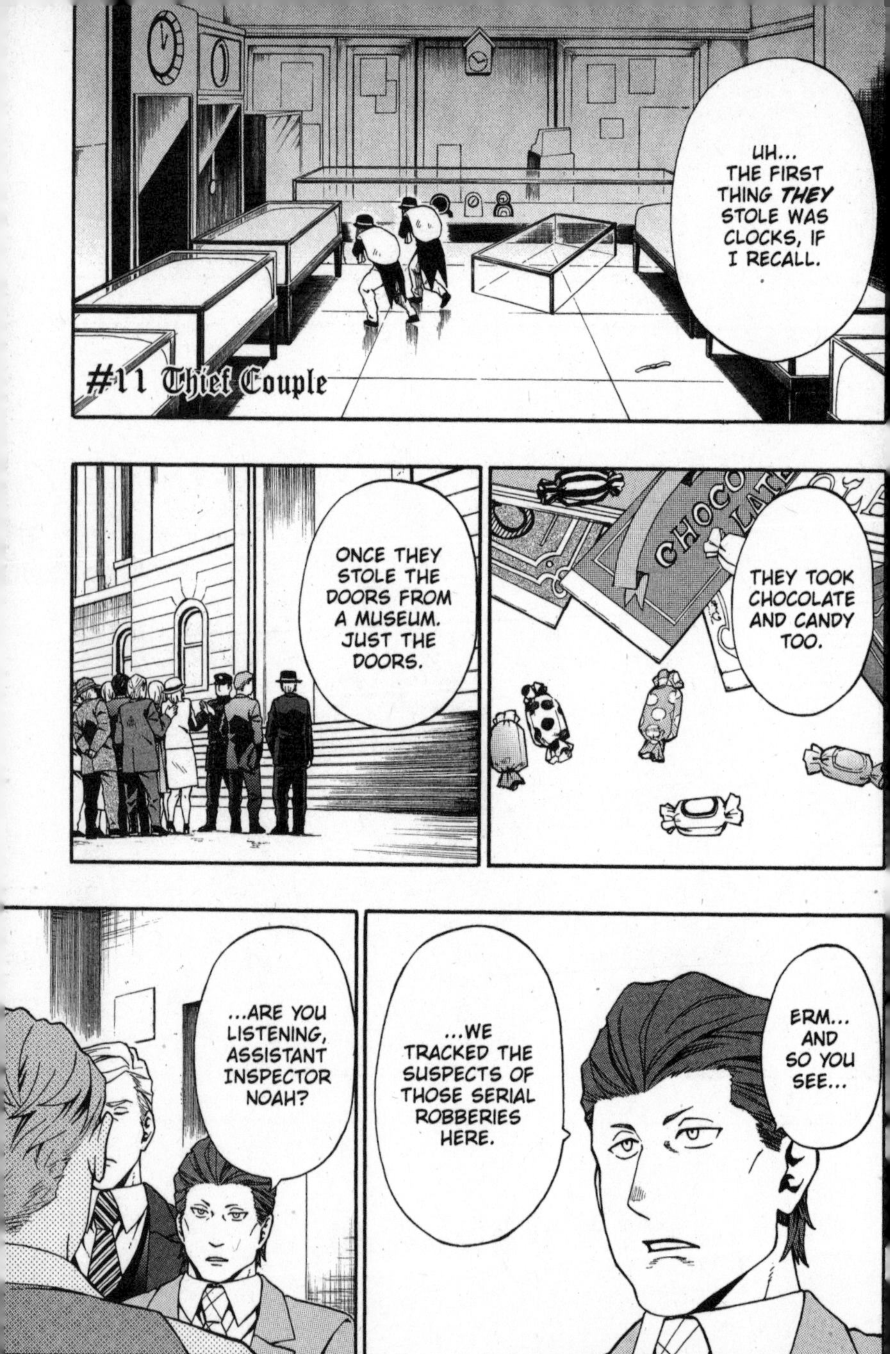
#11 Thief Couple
UH... THE FIRST THING *THEY* STOLE WAS CLOCKS, IF I RECALL.
THEY TOOK CHOCOLATE AND CANDY TOO.
ONCE THEY STOLE THE DOORS FROM A MUSEUM. JUST THE DOORS.
ERM... AND SO YOU SEE...
...WE TRACKED THE SUSPECTS OF THOSE SERIAL ROBBERIES HERE.
...ARE YOU LISTENING, ASSISTANT INSPECTOR NOAH?

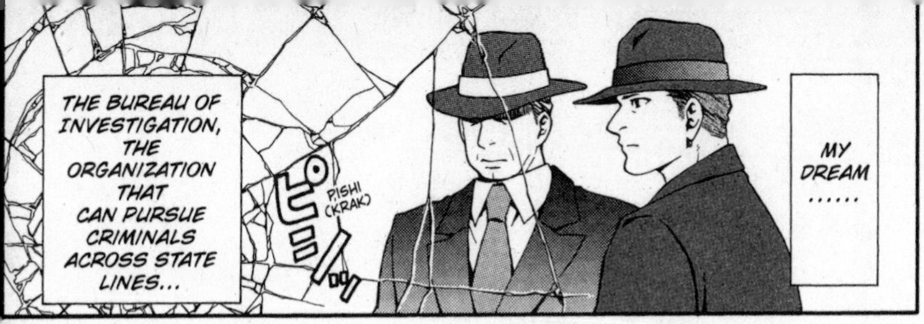
MY DREAM ......
THE BUREAU OF INVESTIGATION, THE ORGANIZATION THAT CAN PURSUE CRIMINALS ACROSS STATE LINES...
PISHI (KRAK)

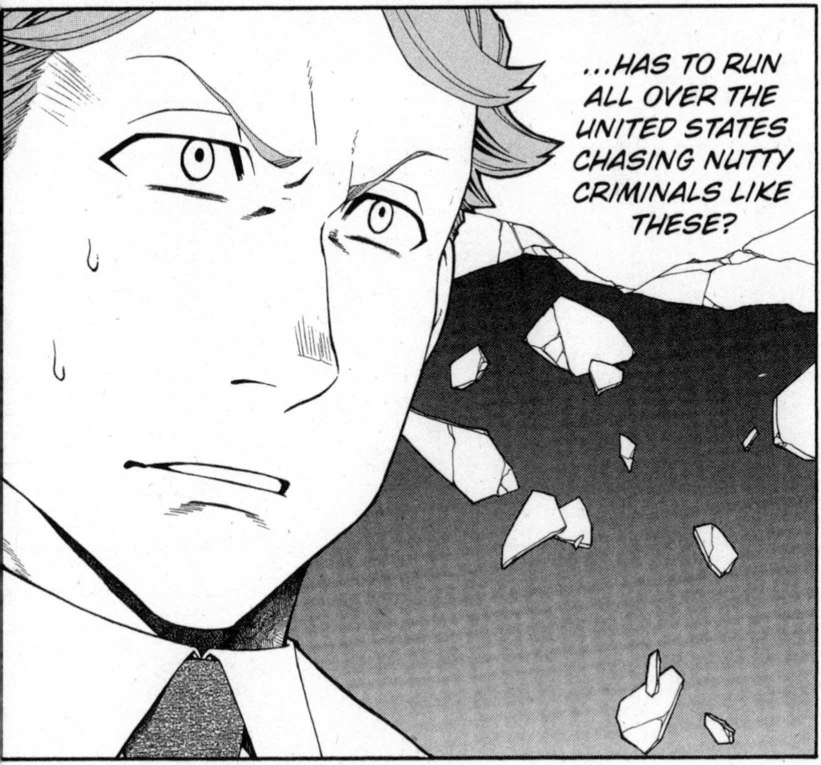
...HAS TO RUN ALL OVER THE UNITED STATES CHASING NUTTY CRIMINALS LIKE THESE?

#11 Thief Couple

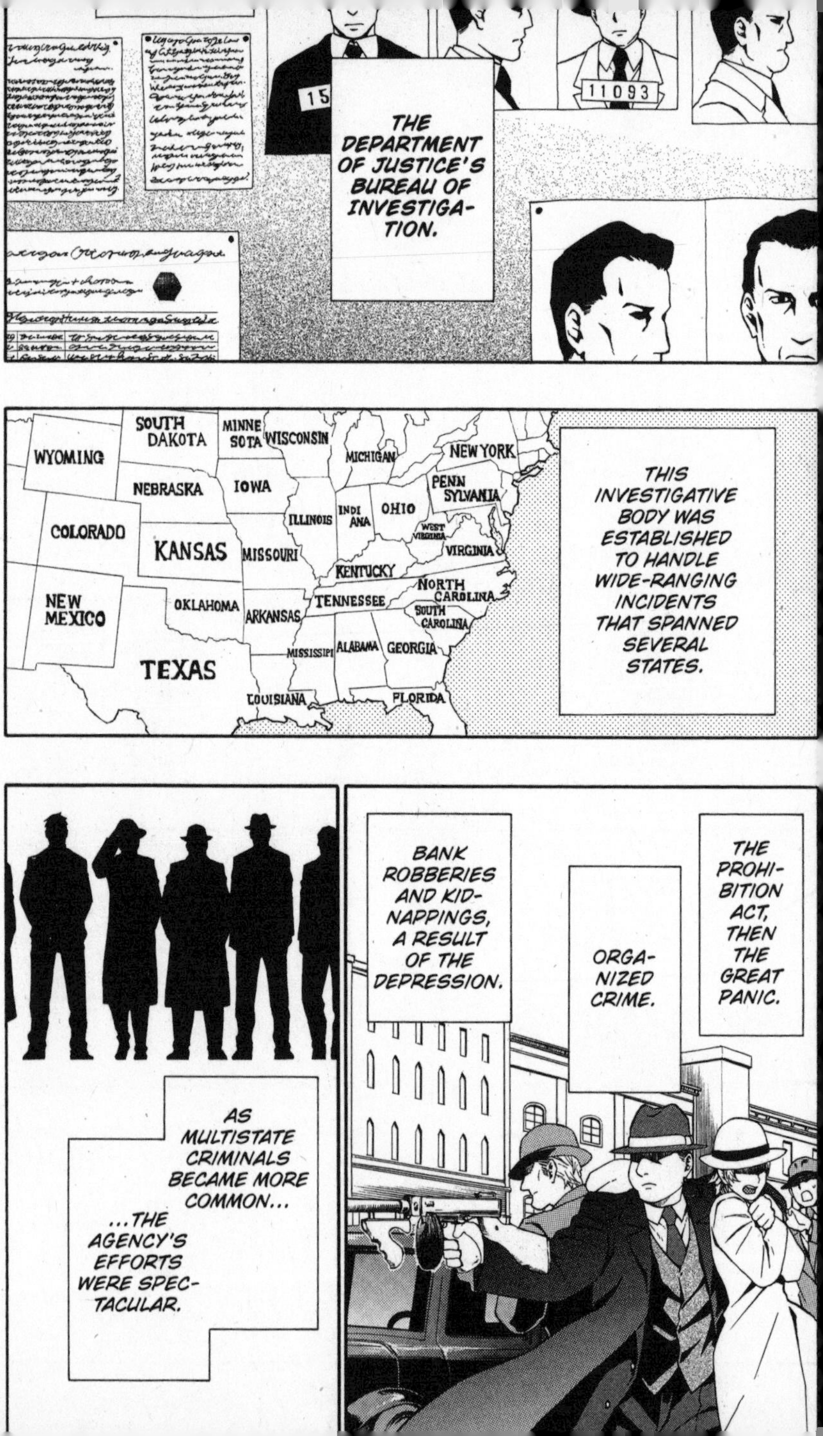
11093
15
THE DEPARTMENT OF JUSTICE'S BUREAU OF INVESTIGA-TION.
THIS INVESTIGATIVE BODY WAS ESTABLISHED TO HANDLE WIDE-RANGING INCIDENTS THAT SPANNED SEVERAL STATES.
SOUTH DAKOTA
MINNE SOTA
WISCONSIN
MICHIGAN
NEW YORK
WYOMING
NEBRASKA
IOWA
PENN SYLVANIA
INDI ANA
OHIO
ILLINOIS
COLORADO
KANSAS
MISSOURI
WEST VIRGINIA
VIRGINIA
KENTUCKY
NORTH CAROLINA
NEW MEXICO
OKLAHOMA
TENNESSEE
ARKANSAS
SOUTH CAROLINA
MISSISSIPI
ALABAMA
GEORGIA
TEXAS
LOUISIANA
FLORIDA
THE PROHI-BITION ACT, THEN THE GREAT PANIC.
ORGA-NIZED CRIME.
BANK ROBBERIES AND KID-NAPPINGS, A RESULT OF THE DEPRESSION.
AS MULTISTATE CRIMINALS BECAME MORE COMMON...
...THE AGENCY'S EFFORTS WERE SPEC-TACULAR.

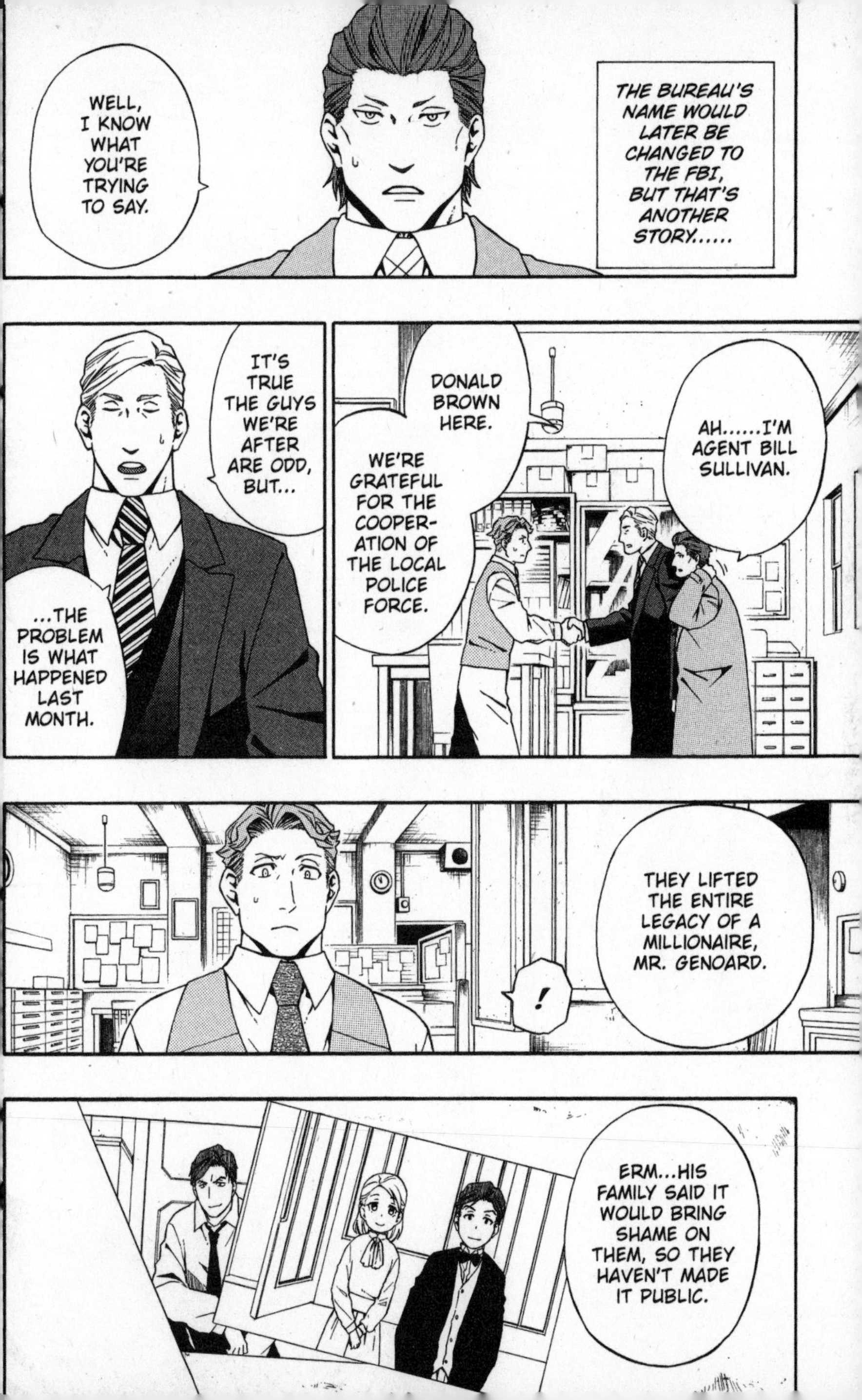
THE BUREAU'S NAME WOULD LATER BE CHANGED TO THE FBI, BUT THAT'S ANOTHER STORY......
WELL, I KNOW WHAT YOU'RE TRYING TO SAY.
AH......I'M AGENT BILL SULLIVAN.
DONALD BROWN HERE.
WE'RE GRATEFUL FOR THE COOPER-ATION OF THE LOCAL POLICE FORCE.
IT'S TRUE THE GUYS WE'RE AFTER ARE ODD, BUT...
...THE PROBLEM IS WHAT HAPPENED LAST MONTH.
THEY LIFTED THE ENTIRE LEGACY OF A MILLIONAIRE, MR. GENOARD.
!
ERM...HIS FAMILY SAID IT WOULD BRING SHAME ON THEM, SO THEY HAVEN'T MADE IT PUBLIC.

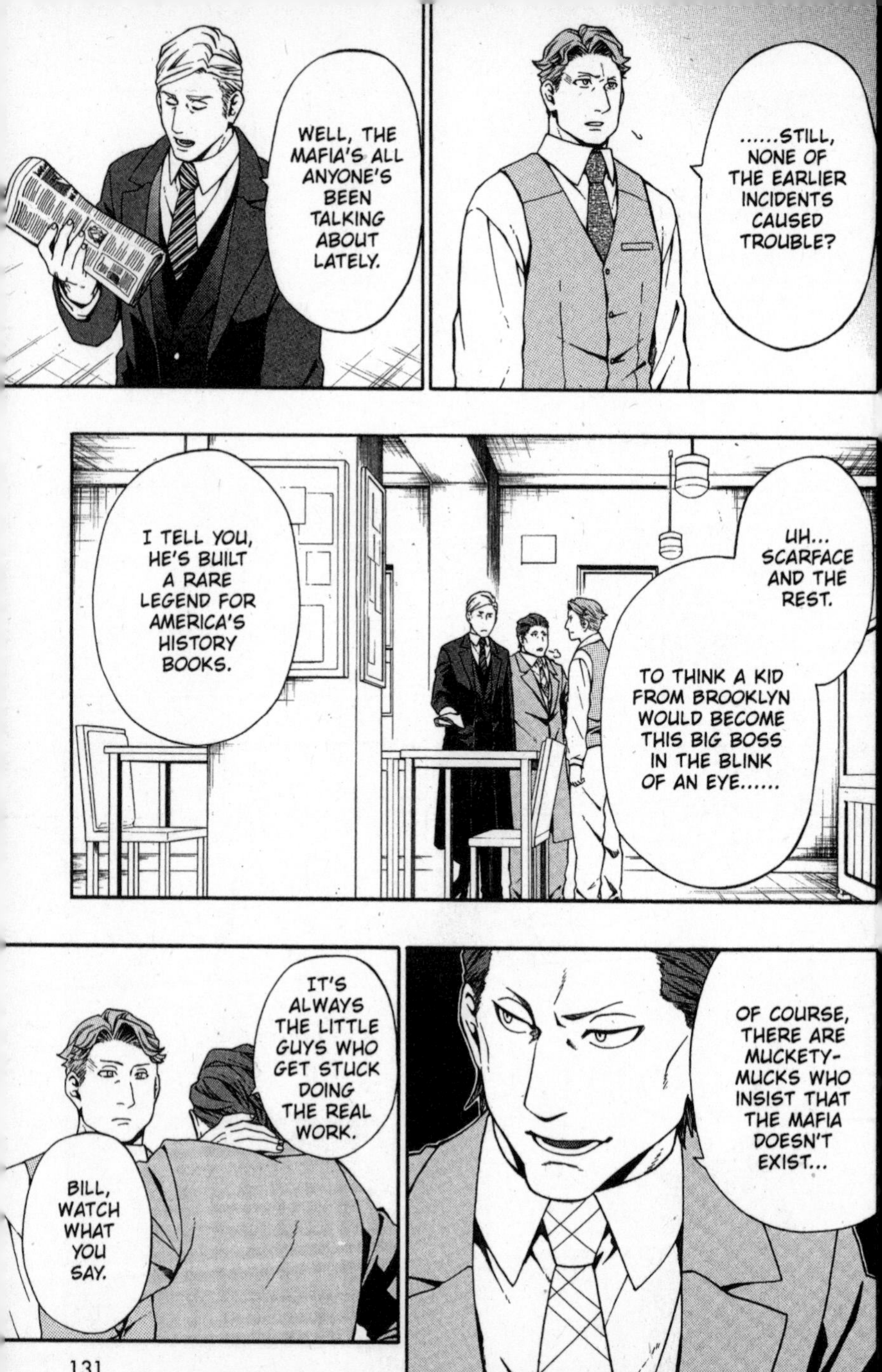
......STILL, NONE OF THE EARLIER INCIDENTS CAUSED TROUBLE?
WELL, THE MAFIA'S ALL ANYONE'S BEEN TALKING ABOUT LATELY.
UH... SCARFACE AND THE REST.
TO THINK A KID FROM BROOKLYN WOULD BECOME THIS BIG BOSS IN THE BLINK OF AN EYE......
I TELL YOU, HE'S BUILT A RARE LEGEND FOR AMERICA'S HISTORY BOOKS.
OF COURSE, THERE ARE MUCKETY-MUCKS WHO INSIST THAT THE MAFIA DOESN'T EXIST...
IT'S ALWAYS THE LITTLE GUYS WHO GET STUCK DOING THE REAL WORK.
BILL, WATCH WHAT YOU SAY.

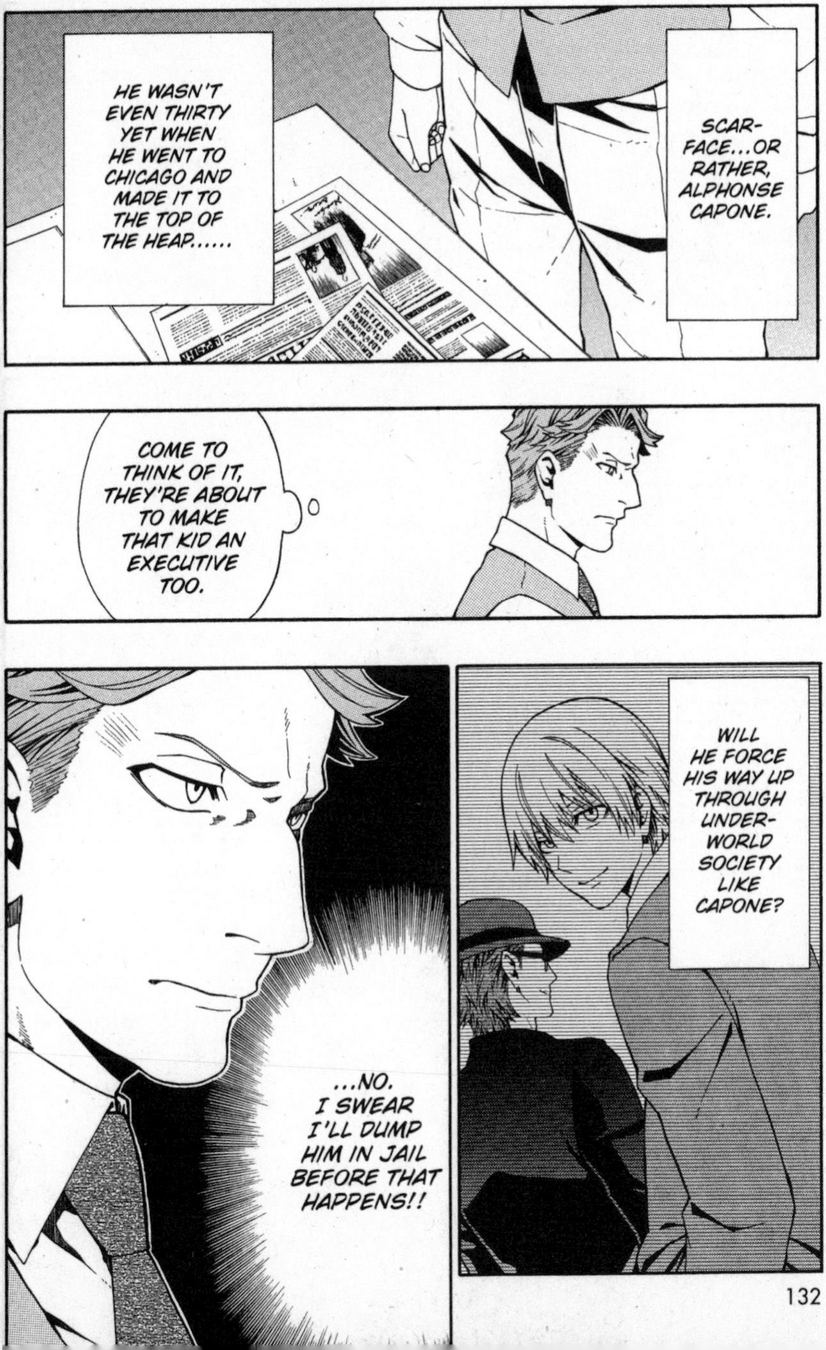
SCAR-FACE...OR RATHER, ALPHONSE CAPONE.
HE WASN'T EVEN THIRTY YET WHEN HE WENT TO CHICAGO AND MADE IT TO THE TOP OF THE HEAP......
COME TO THINK OF IT, THEY'RE ABOUT TO MAKE THAT KID AN EXECUTIVE TOO.
WILL HE FORCE HIS WAY UP THROUGH UNDER-WORLD SOCIETY LIKE CAPONE?
...NO. I SWEAR I'LL DUMP HIM IN JAIL BEFORE THAT HAPPENS!!

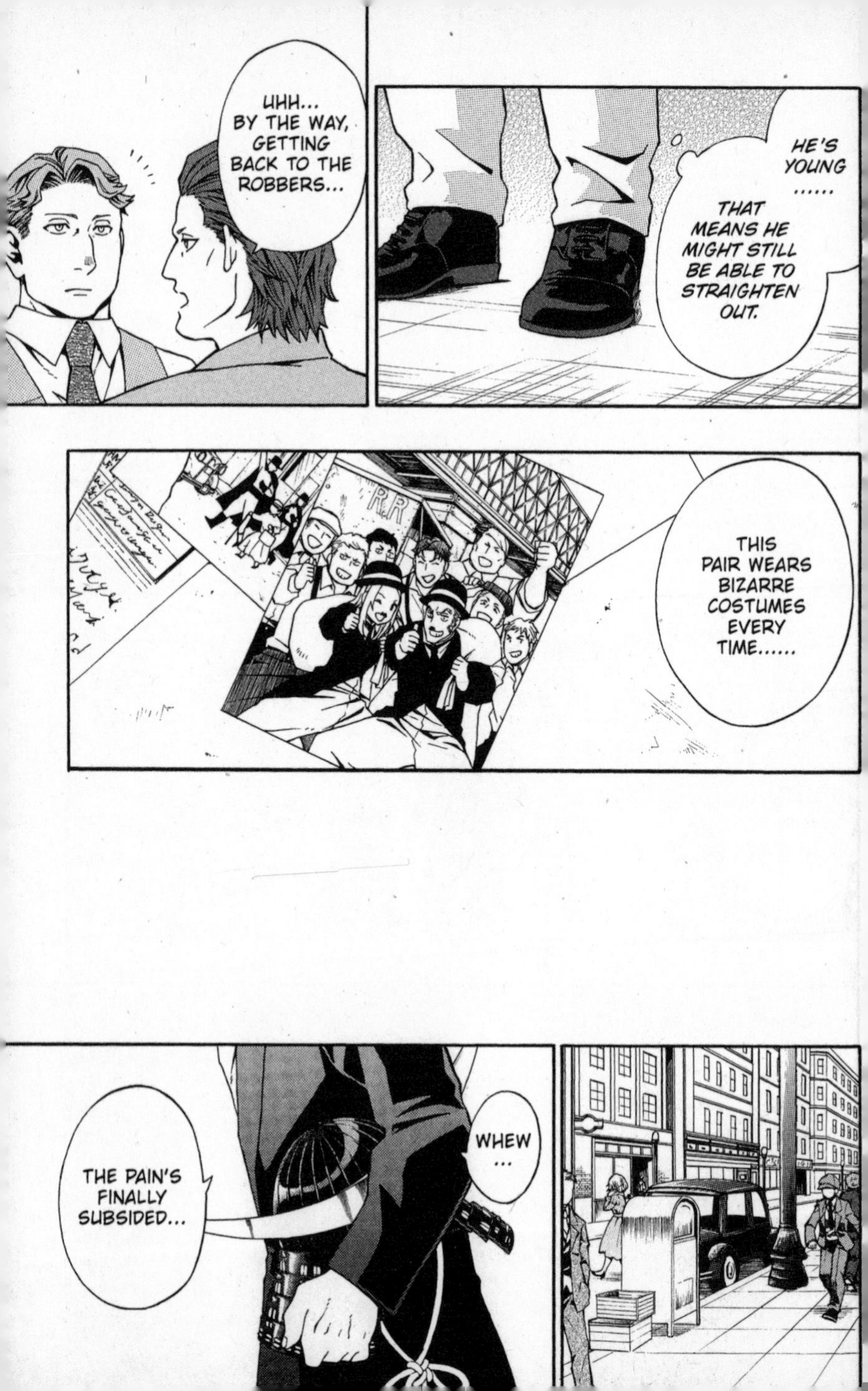
HE'S YOUNG ......
THAT MEANS HE MIGHT STILL BE ABLE TO STRAIGHTEN OUT.
UHH... BY THE WAY, GETTING BACK TO THE ROBBERS...
THIS PAIR WEARS BIZARRE COSTUMES EVERY TIME......
WHEW ...
THE PAIN'S FINALLY SUBSIDED...

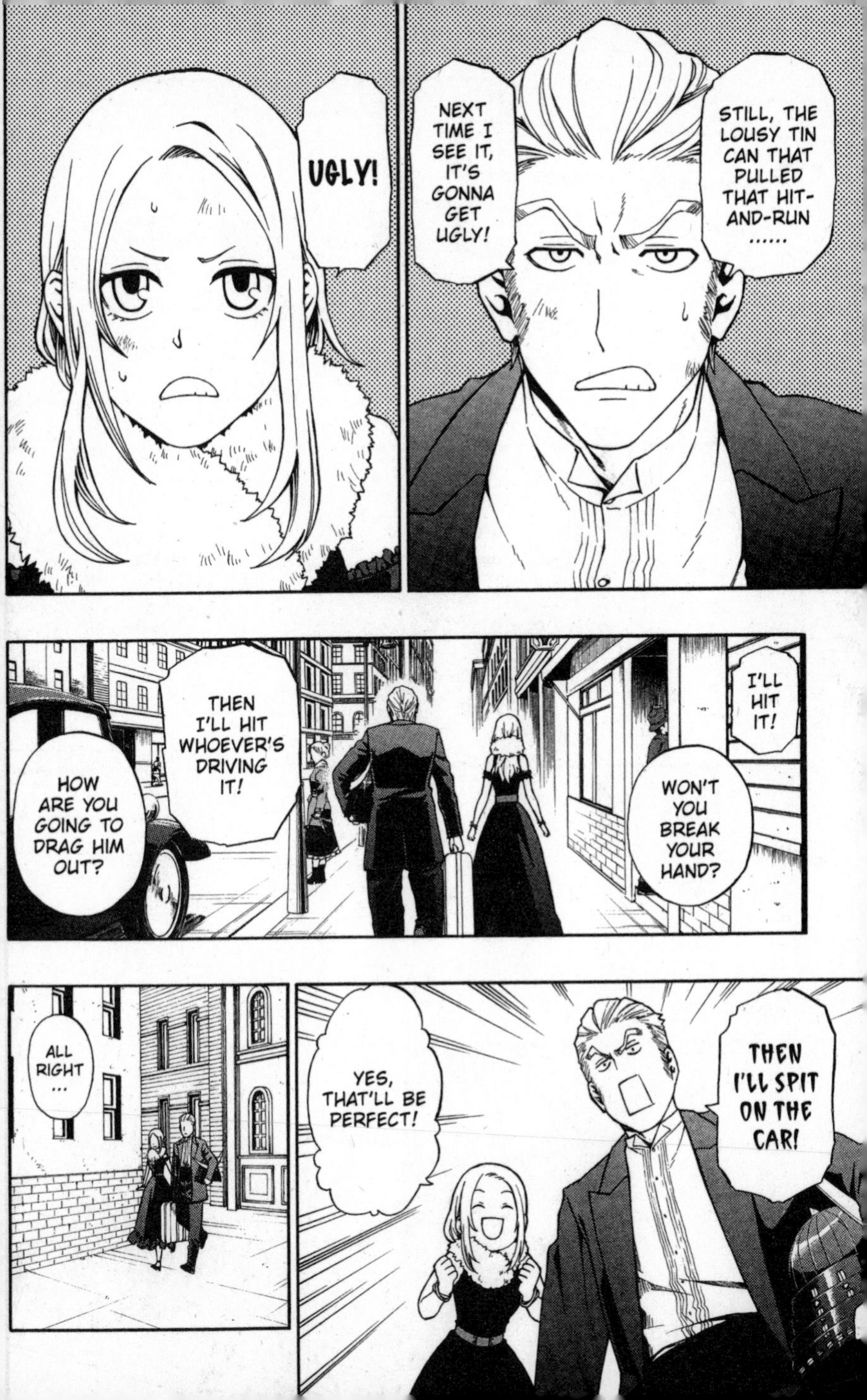
STILL, THE LOUSY TIN CAN THAT PULLED THAT HIT-AND-RUN ......
NEXT TIME I SEE IT, IT'S GONNA GET UGLY!
UGLY!
I'LL HIT IT!
WON'T YOU BREAK YOUR HAND?
THEN I'LL HIT WHOEVER'S DRIVING IT!
HOW ARE YOU GOING TO DRAG HIM OUT?
THEN I'LL SPIT ON THE CAR!
YES, THAT'LL BE PERFECT!
ALL RIGHT ...

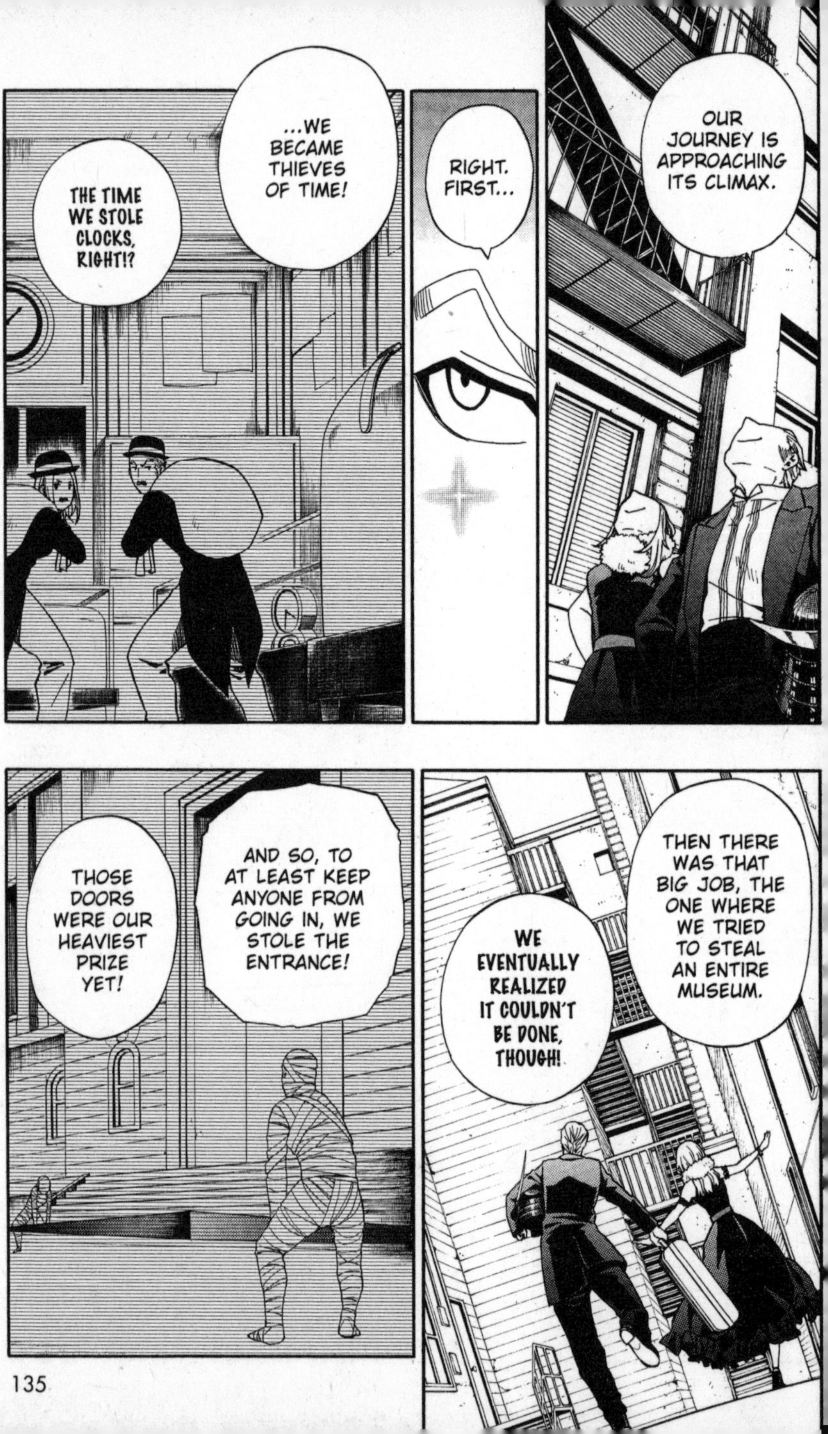
OUR JOURNEY IS APPROACHING ITS CLIMAX.
RIGHT. FIRST...
...WE BECAME THIEVES OF TIME!
THE TIME WE STOLE CLOCKS, RIGHT!?
THEN THERE WAS THAT BIG JOB, THE ONE WHERE WE TRIED TO STEAL AN ENTIRE MUSEUM.
WE EVENTUALLY REALIZED IT COULDN'T BE DONE, THOUGH!
AND SO, TO AT LEAST KEEP ANYONE FROM GOING IN, WE STOLE THE ENTRANCE!
THOSE DOORS WERE OUR HEAVIEST PRIZE YET!

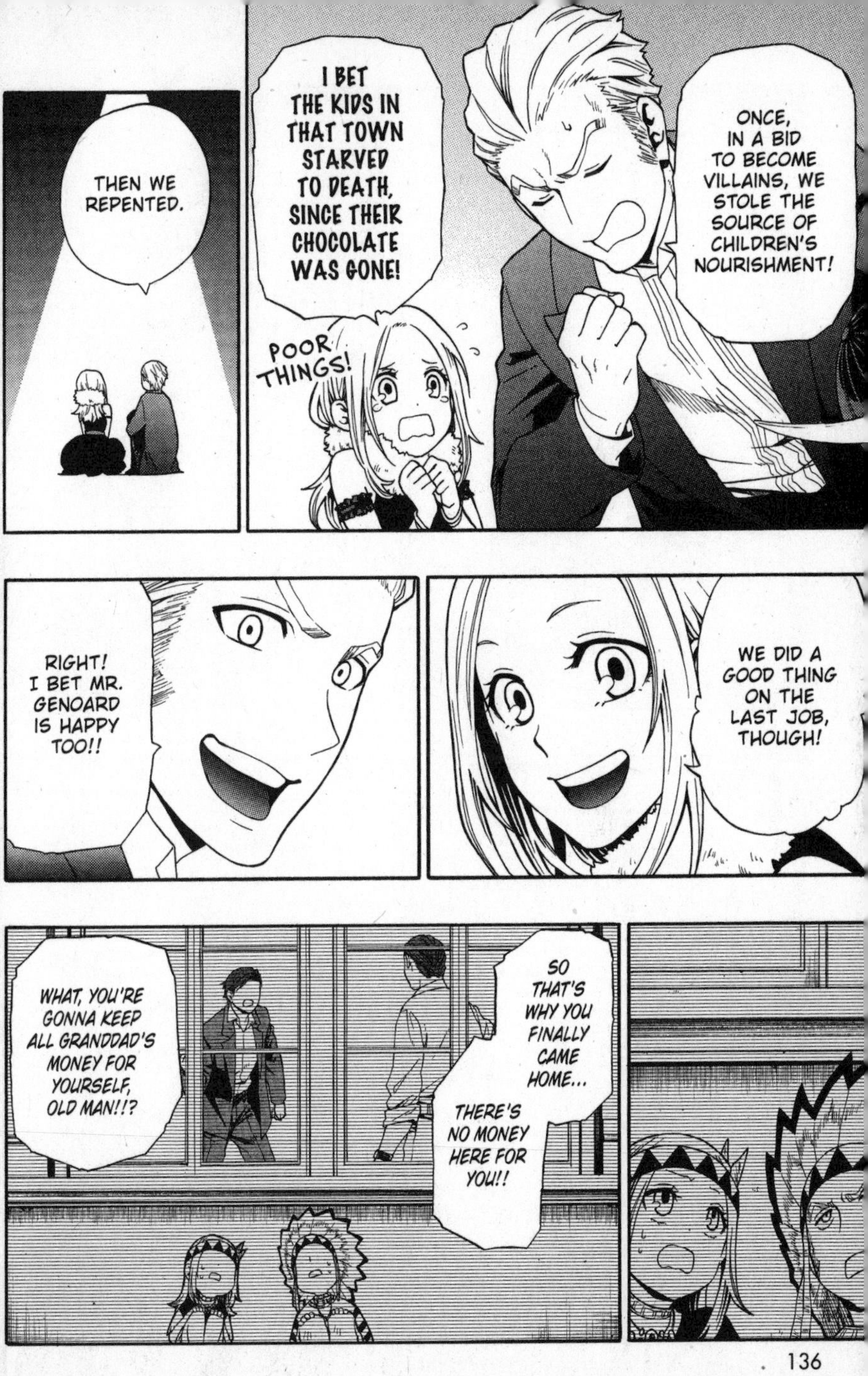
ONCE, IN A BID TO BECOME VILLAINS, WE STOLE THE SOURCE OF CHILDREN'S NOURISHMENT!
I BET THE KIDS IN THAT TOWN STARVED TO DEATH, SINCE THEIR CHOCOLATE WAS GONE!
POOR THINGS!
THEN WE REPENTED.
WE DID A GOOD THING ON THE LAST JOB, THOUGH!
RIGHT! I BET MR. GENOARD IS HAPPY TOO!!
SO THAT'S WHY YOU FINALLY CAME HOME...
THERE'S NO MONEY HERE FOR YOU!!
WHAT, YOU'RE GONNA KEEP ALL GRANDDAD'S MONEY FOR YOURSELF, OLD MAN!!?

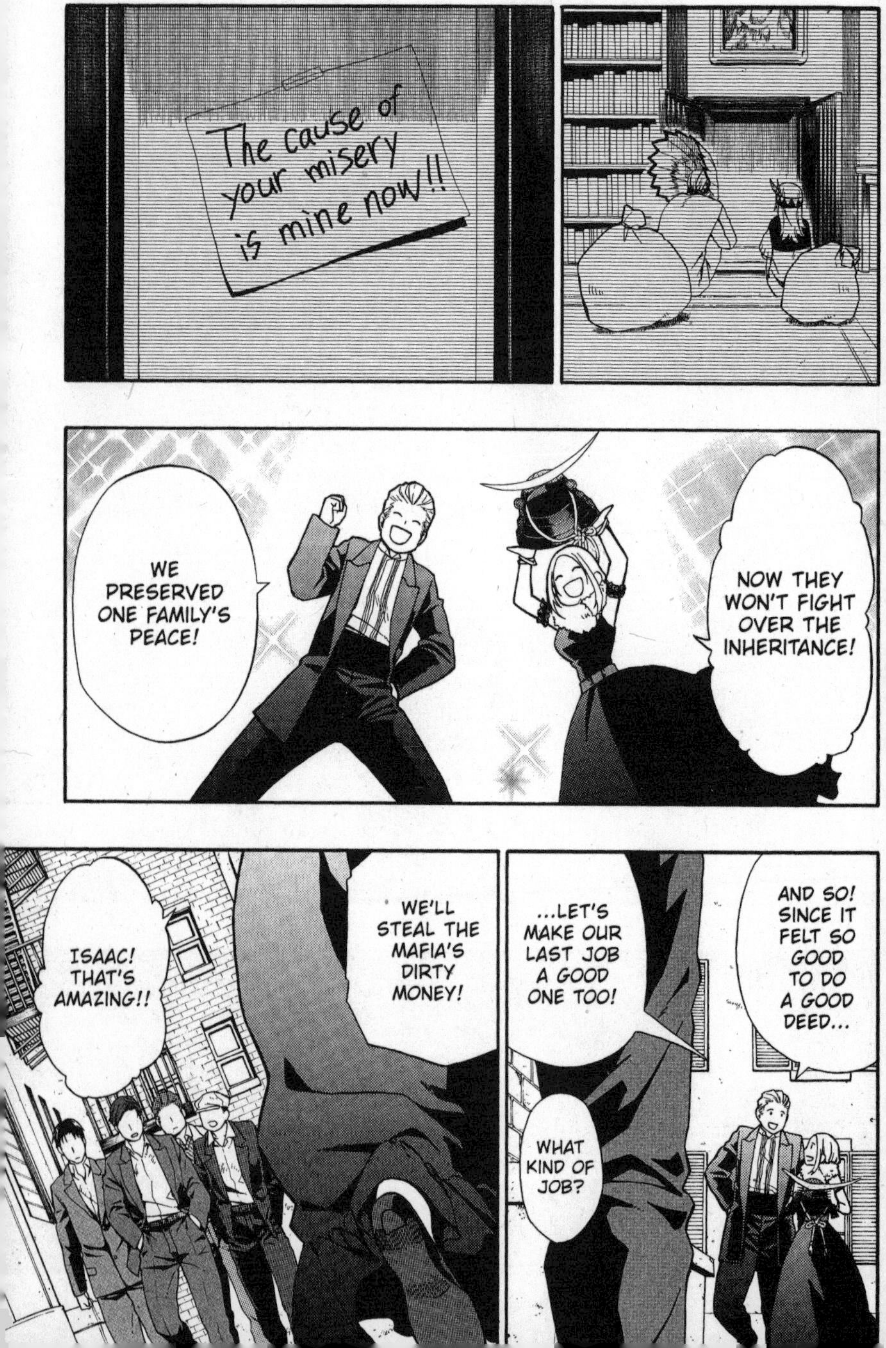
The cause of your misery is mine now!!
NOW THEY WON'T FIGHT OVER THE INHERITANCE!
WE PRESERVED ONE FAMILY'S PEACE!
AND SO! SINCE IT FELT SO GOOD TO DO A GOOD DEED...
...LET'S MAKE OUR LAST JOB A GOOD ONE TOO!
WHAT KIND OF JOB?
WE'LL STEAL THE MAFIA'S DIRTY MONEY!
ISAAC! THAT'S AMAZING!!

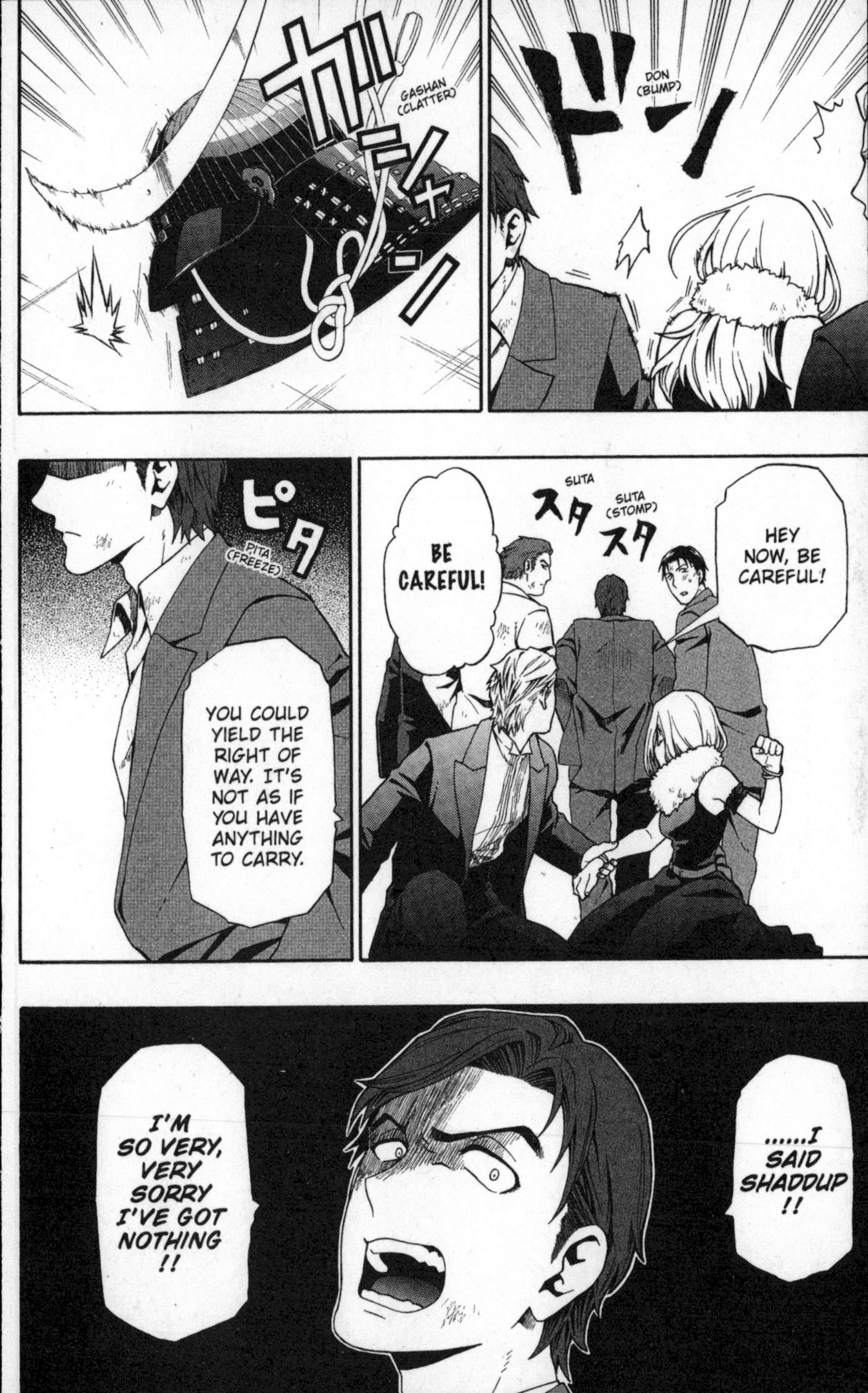
ドーン
DON (BUMP)
ガシャーン
GASHAN (CLATTER)
HEY NOW, BE CAREFUL!
スタ
SUTA
スタ
SUTA (STOMP)
BE CAREFUL!
ピタ
PITA (FREEZE)
YOU COULD YIELD THE RIGHT OF WAY. IT'S NOT AS IF YOU HAVE ANYTHING TO CARRY.
......I SAID SHADDUP !!
I'M SO VERY, VERY SORRY I'VE GOT NOTHING !!

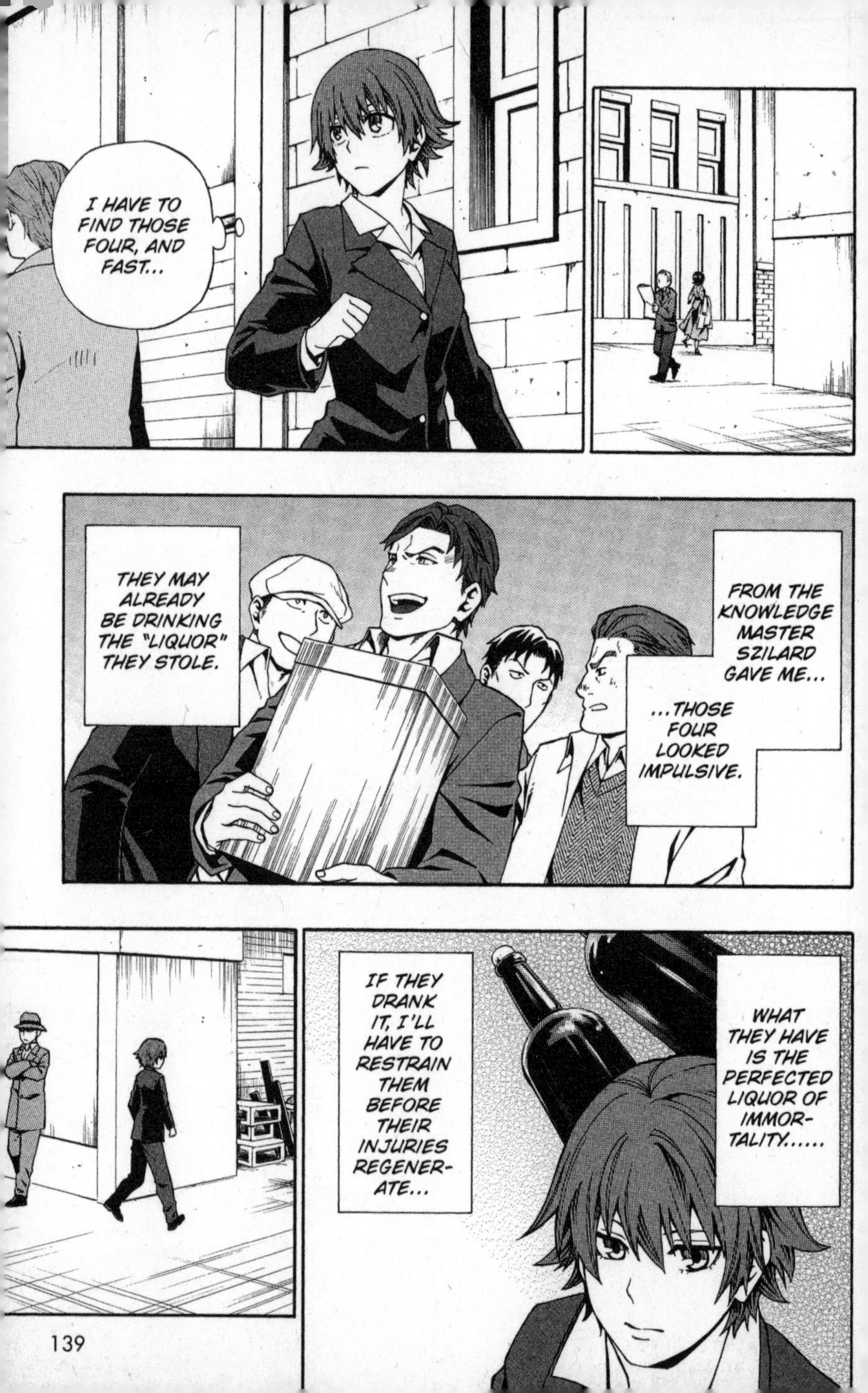
I HAVE TO FIND THOSE FOUR, AND FAST...
FROM THE KNOWLEDGE MASTER SZILARD GAVE ME...
...THOSE FOUR LOOKED IMPULSIVE.
THEY MAY ALREADY BE DRINKING THE "LIQUOR" THEY STOLE.
WHAT THEY HAVE IS THE PERFECTED LIQUOR OF IMMORTALITY......
IF THEY DRANK IT, I'LL HAVE TO RESTRAIN THEM BEFORE THEIR INJURIES REGENERATE...

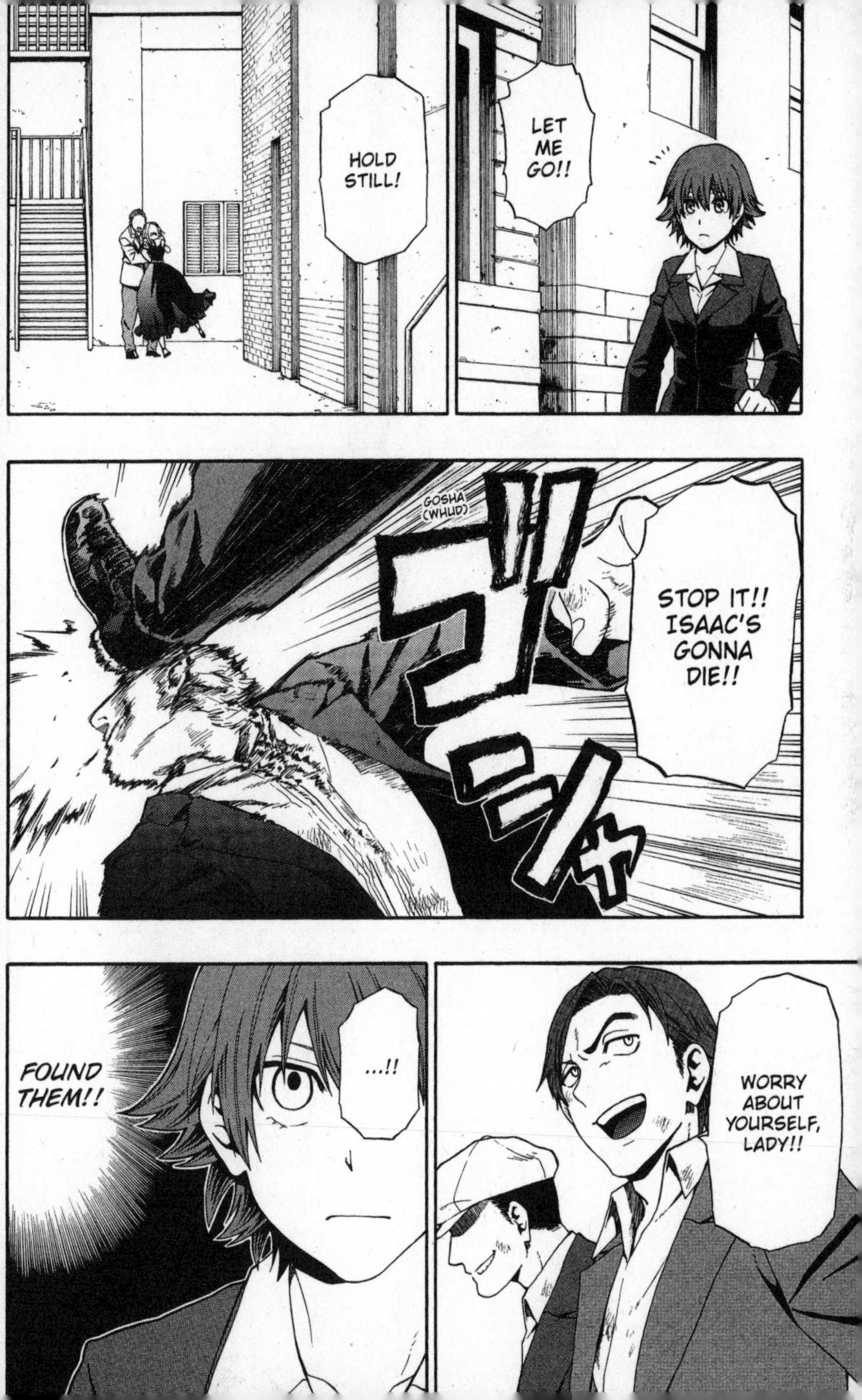
LET ME GO!!
HOLD STILL!
STOP IT!! ISAAC'S GONNA DIE!!
GOSHA (WHUD)
WORRY ABOUT YOURSELF, LADY!!
...!!
FOUND THEM!!

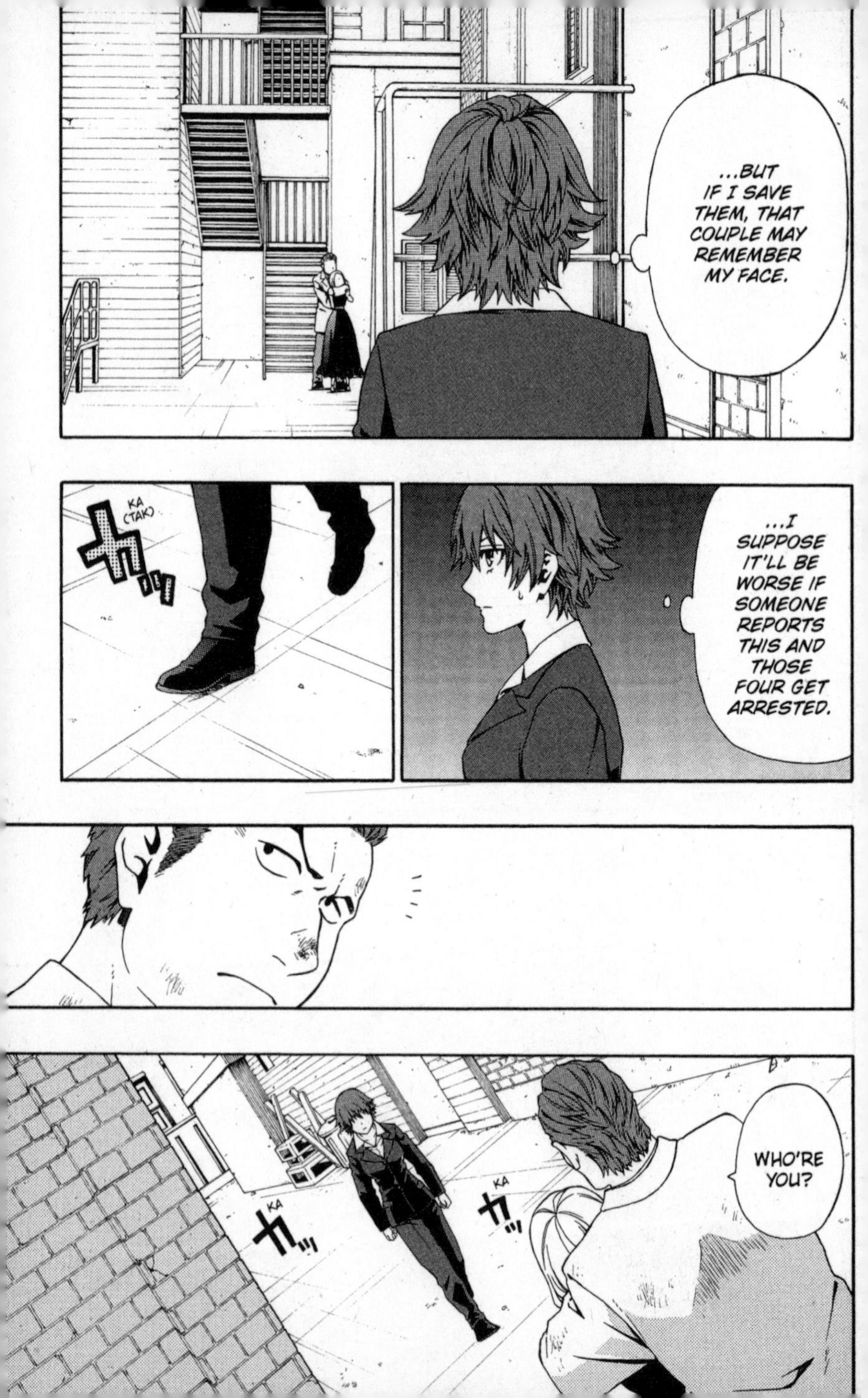
...BUT IF I SAVE THEM, THAT COUPLE MAY REMEMBER MY FACE.
...I SUPPOSE IT'LL BE WORSE IF SOMEONE REPORTS THIS AND THOSE FOUR GET ARRESTED.
KA (TAK)
WHO'RE YOU?
KA
KA

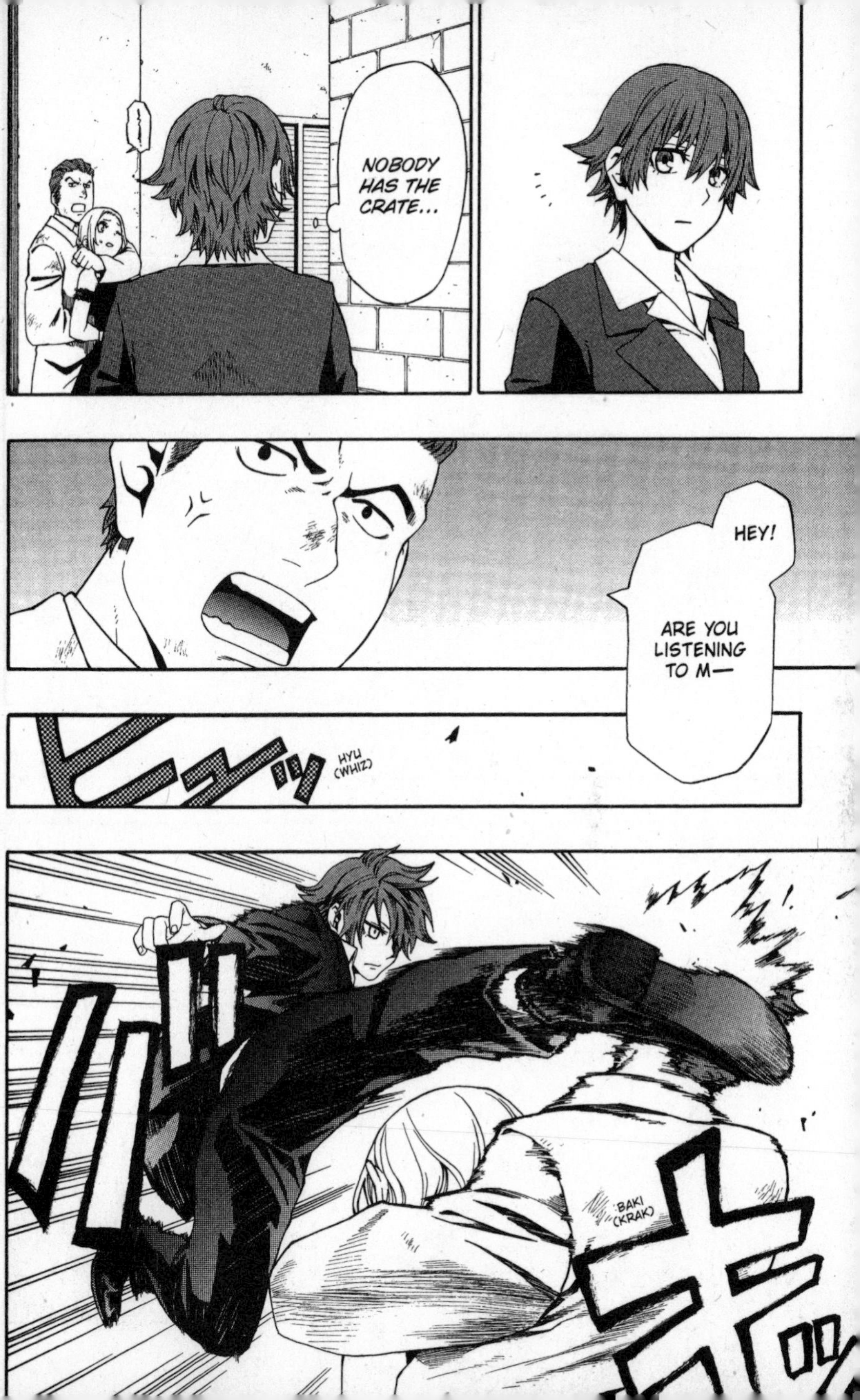
NOBODY HAS THE CRATE...
HEY!
ARE YOU LISTENING TO M—
HYU (WHIZ)
BAKI (KRAK)

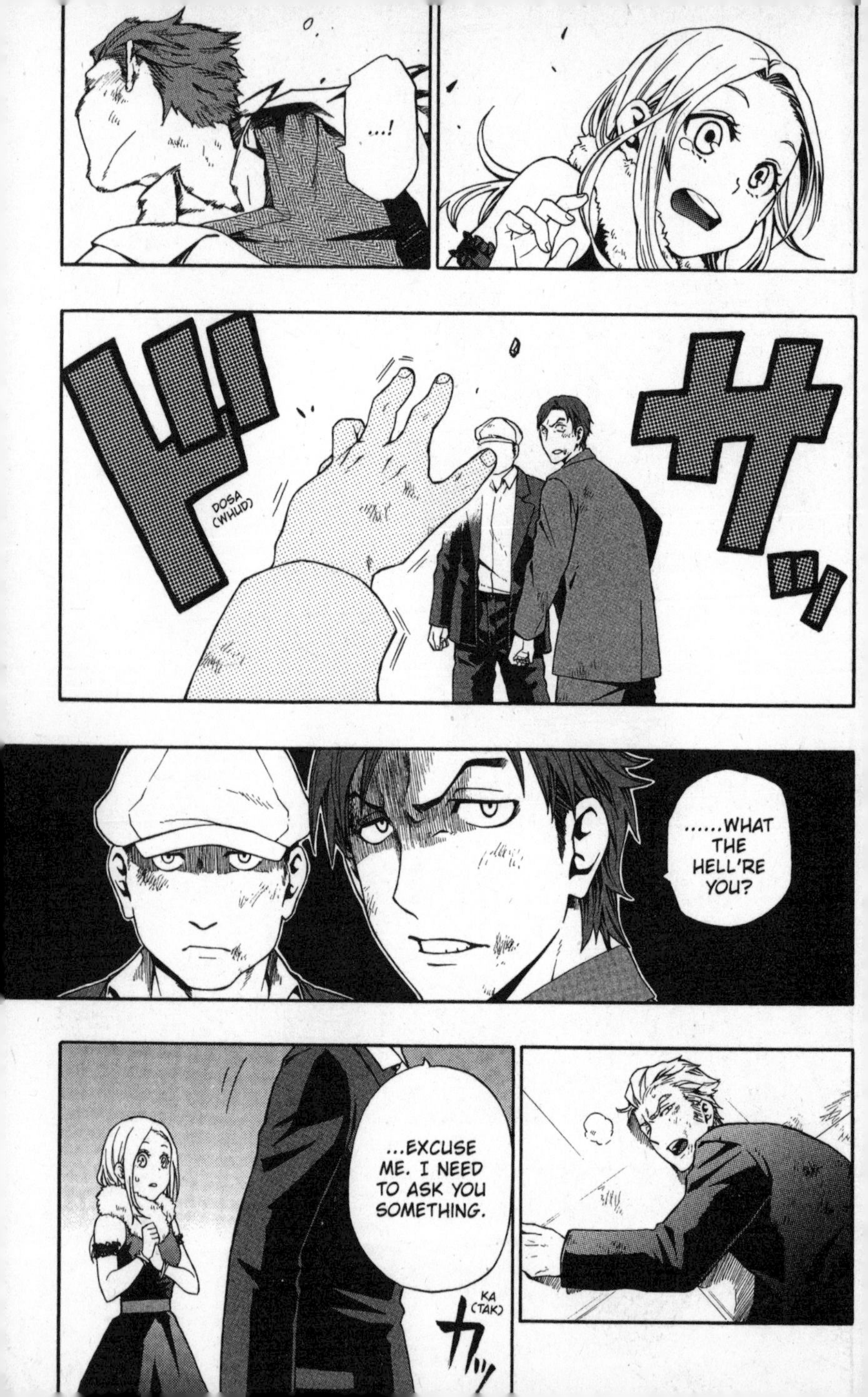
...!
DOSA (WHUD)
......WHAT THE HELL'RE YOU?
...EXCUSE ME. I NEED TO ASK YOU SOMETHING.
KA (TAK)

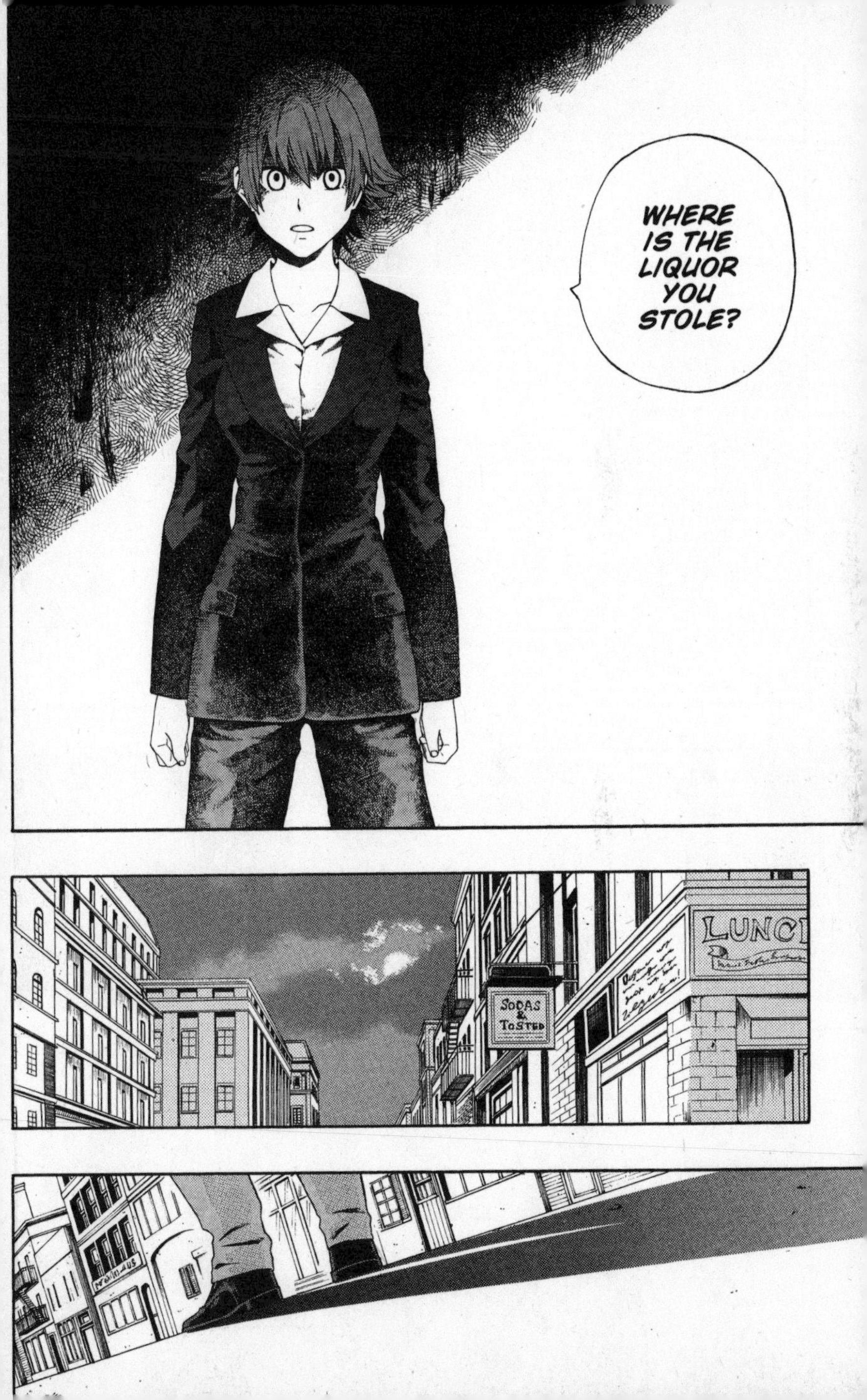
WHERE IS THE LIQUOR YOU STOLE?

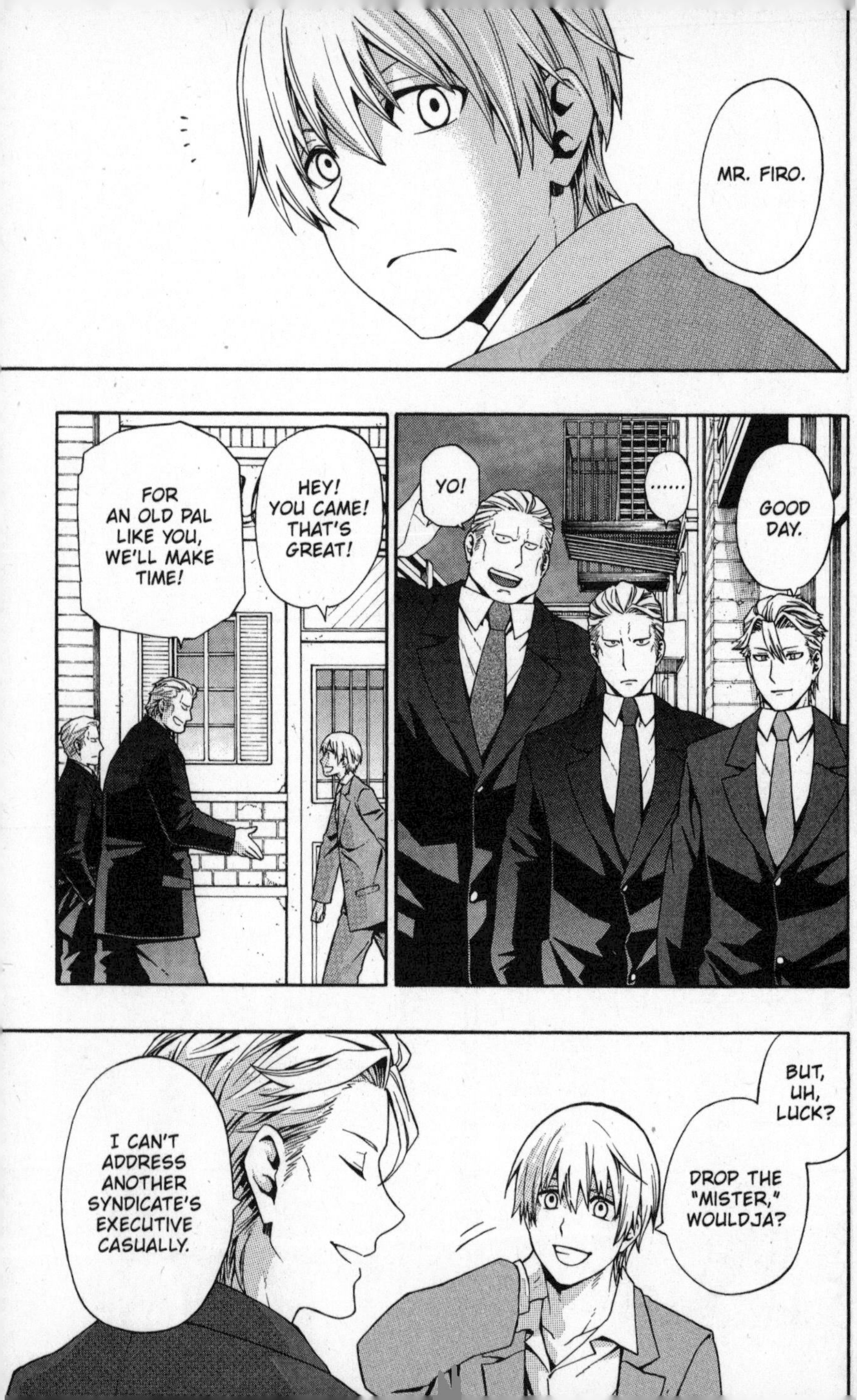
MR. FIRO.
GOOD DAY.
......
YO!
HEY! YOU CAME! THAT'S GREAT!
FOR AN OLD PAL LIKE YOU, WE'LL MAKE TIME!
BUT, UH, LUCK?
DROP THE "MISTER," WOULDJA?
I CAN'T ADDRESS ANOTHER SYNDICATE'S EXECUTIVE CASUALLY.

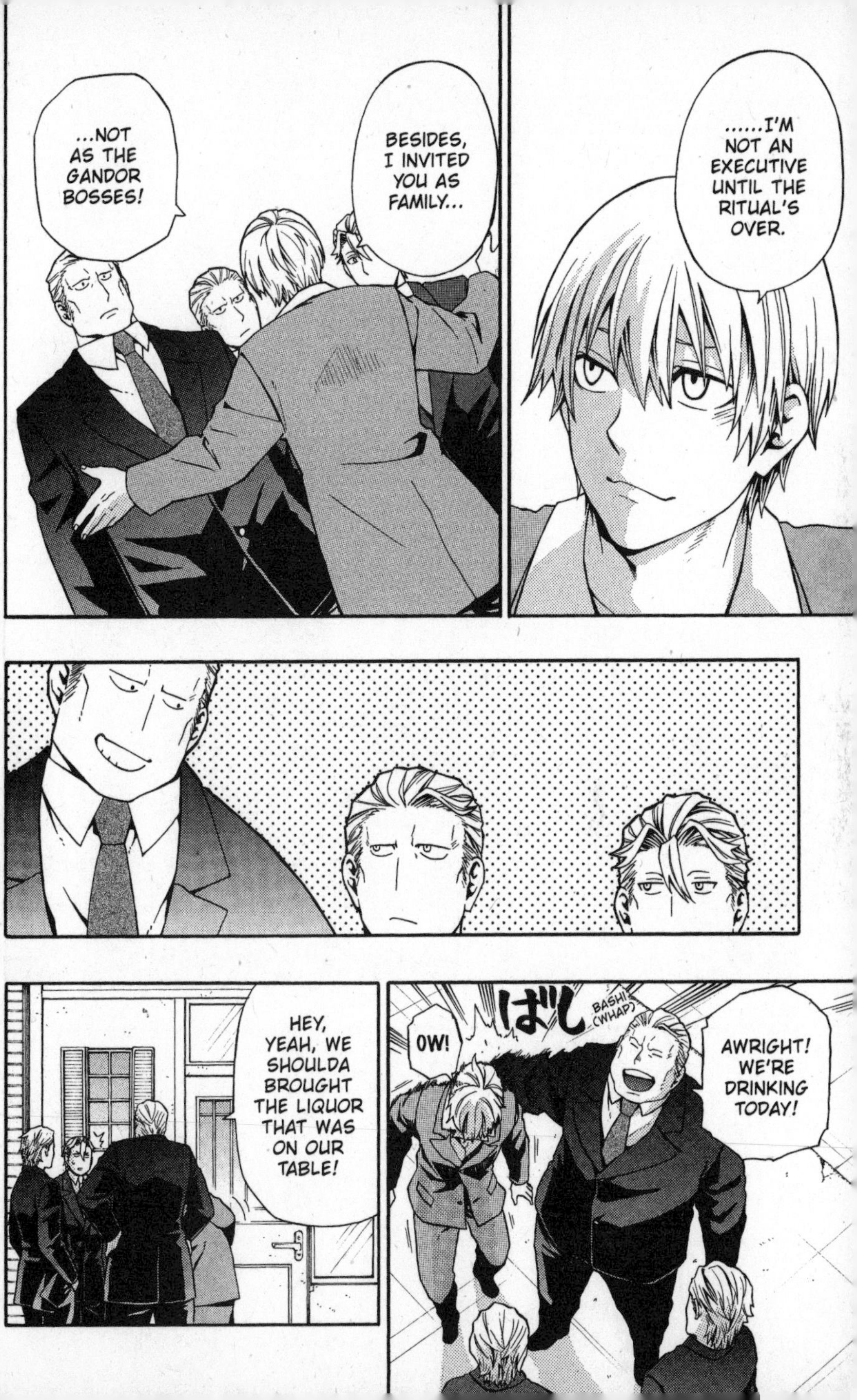
......I'M NOT AN EXECUTIVE UNTIL THE RITUAL'S OVER.
BESIDES, I INVITED YOU AS FAMILY...
...NOT AS THE GANDOR BOSSES!
AWRIGHT! WE'RE DRINKING TODAY!
ばし
BASH! (WHAP)
OW!
HEY, YEAH, WE SHOULDA BROUGHT THE LIQUOR THAT WAS ON OUR TABLE!

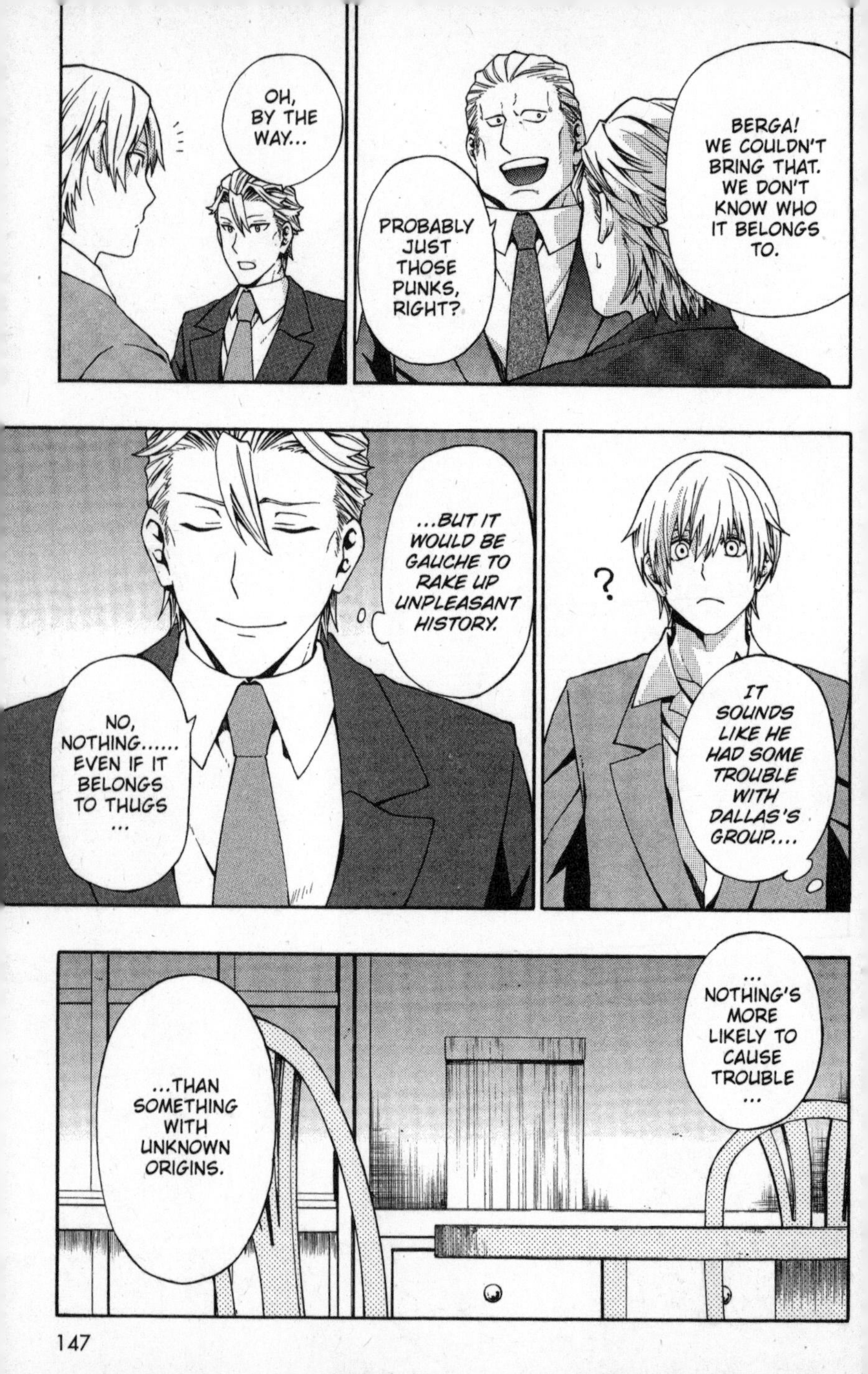
BERGA! WE COULDN'T BRING THAT. WE DON'T KNOW WHO IT BELONGS TO.
PROBABLY JUST THOSE PUNKS, RIGHT?
OH, BY THE WAY...
?
IT SOUNDS LIKE HE HAD SOME TROUBLE WITH DALLAS'S GROUP....
...BUT IT WOULD BE GAUCHE TO RAKE UP UNPLEASANT HISTORY.
NO, NOTHING...... EVEN IF IT BELONGS TO THUGS ...
... NOTHING'S MORE LIKELY TO CAUSE TROUBLE ...
...THAN SOMETHING WITH UNKNOWN ORIGINS.

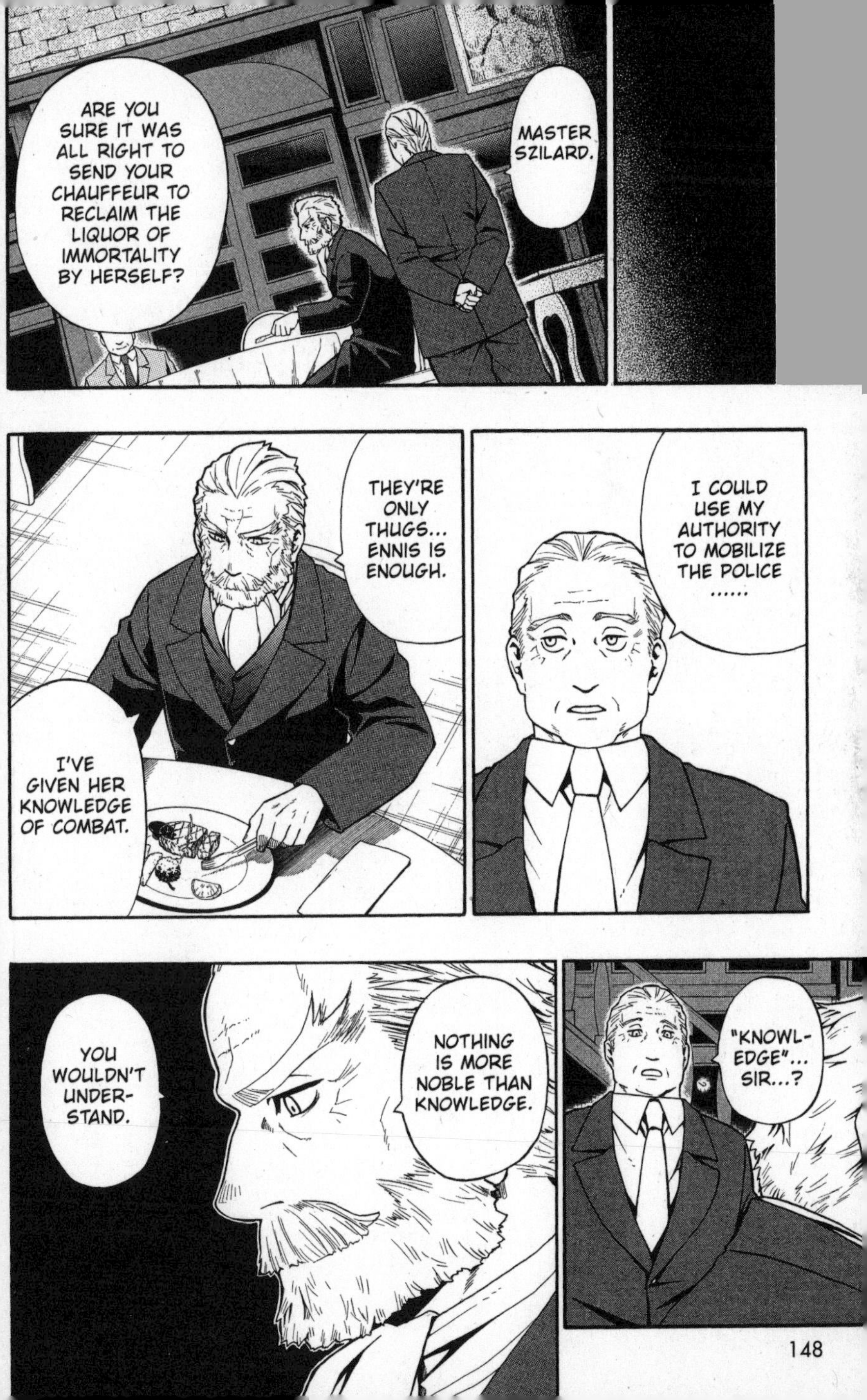
MASTER SZILARD.
ARE YOU SURE IT WAS ALL RIGHT TO SEND YOUR CHAUFFEUR TO RECLAIM THE LIQUOR OF IMMORTALITY BY HERSELF?
I COULD USE MY AUTHORITY TO MOBILIZE THE POLICE ......
THEY'RE ONLY THUGS... ENNIS IS ENOUGH.
I'VE GIVEN HER KNOWLEDGE OF COMBAT.
"KNOWL-EDGE"... SIR...?
NOTHING IS MORE NOBLE THAN KNOWLEDGE.
YOU WOULDN'T UNDER-STAND.

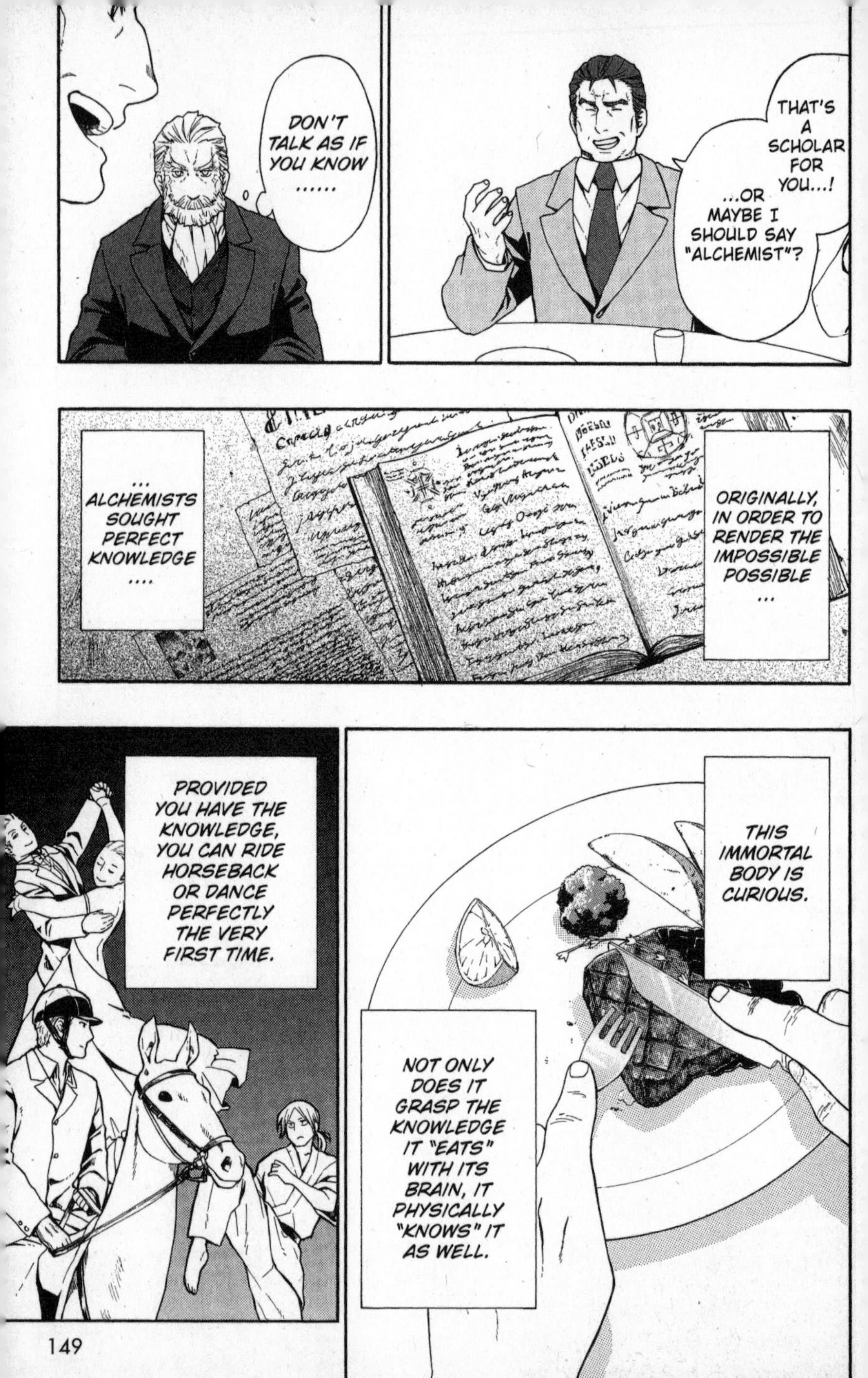
THAT'S A SCHOLAR FOR YOU...!
...OR MAYBE I SHOULD SAY "ALCHEMIST"?
DON'T TALK AS IF YOU KNOW ......
ORIGINALLY, IN ORDER TO RENDER THE IMPOSSIBLE POSSIBLE ...
... ALCHEMISTS SOUGHT PERFECT KNOWLEDGE ....
THIS IMMORTAL BODY IS CURIOUS.
NOT ONLY DOES IT GRASP THE KNOWLEDGE IT "EATS" WITH ITS BRAIN, IT PHYSICALLY "KNOWS" IT AS WELL.
PROVIDED YOU HAVE THE KNOWLEDGE, YOU CAN RIDE HORSEBACK OR DANCE PERFECTLY THE VERY FIRST TIME.

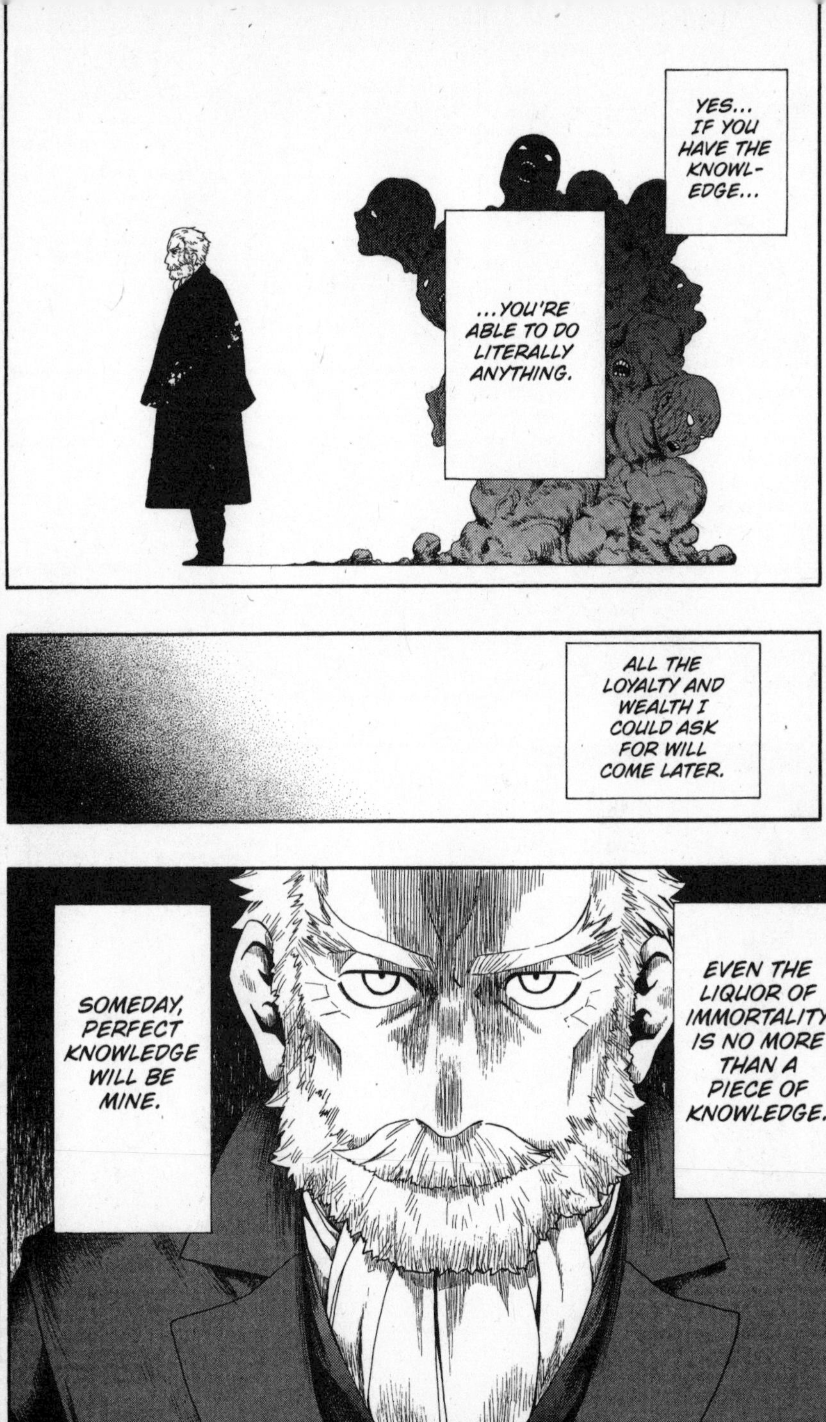
YES... IF YOU HAVE THE KNOWL-EDGE...
...YOU'RE ABLE TO DO LITERALLY ANYTHING.
ALL THE LOYALTY AND WEALTH I COULD ASK FOR WILL COME LATER.
EVEN THE LIQUOR OF IMMORTALITY IS NO MORE THAN A PIECE OF KNOWLEDGE.
SOMEDAY, PERFECT KNOWLEDGE WILL BE MINE.

#12 Ennis

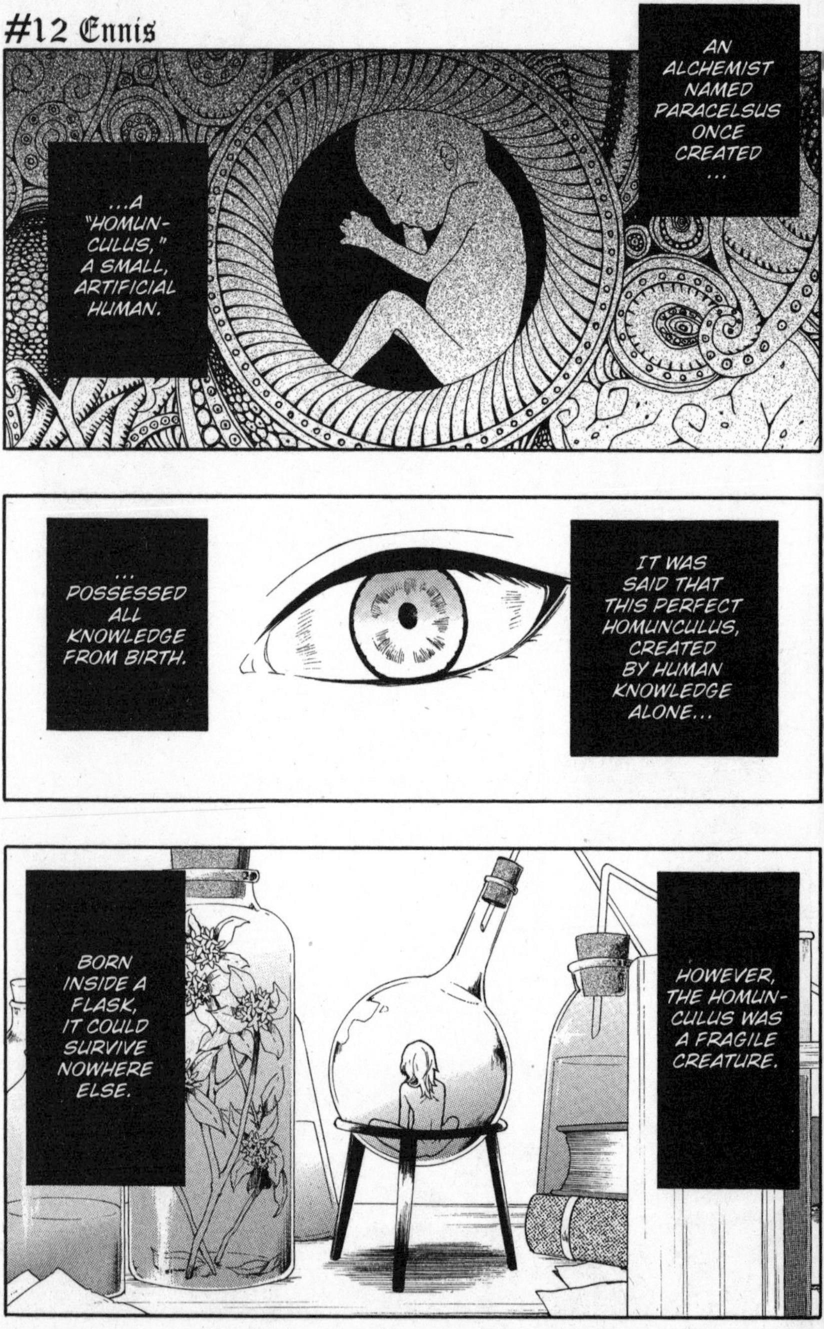
AN ALCHEMIST NAMED PARACELSUS ONCE CREATED ...
...A "HOMUNCULUS," A SMALL, ARTIFICIAL HUMAN.
IT WAS SAID THAT THIS PERFECT HOMUNCULUS, CREATED BY HUMAN KNOWLEDGE ALONE...
... POSSESSED ALL KNOWLEDGE FROM BIRTH.
HOWEVER, THE HOMUNCULUS WAS A FRAGILE CREATURE.
BORN INSIDE A FLASK, IT COULD SURVIVE NOWHERE ELSE.

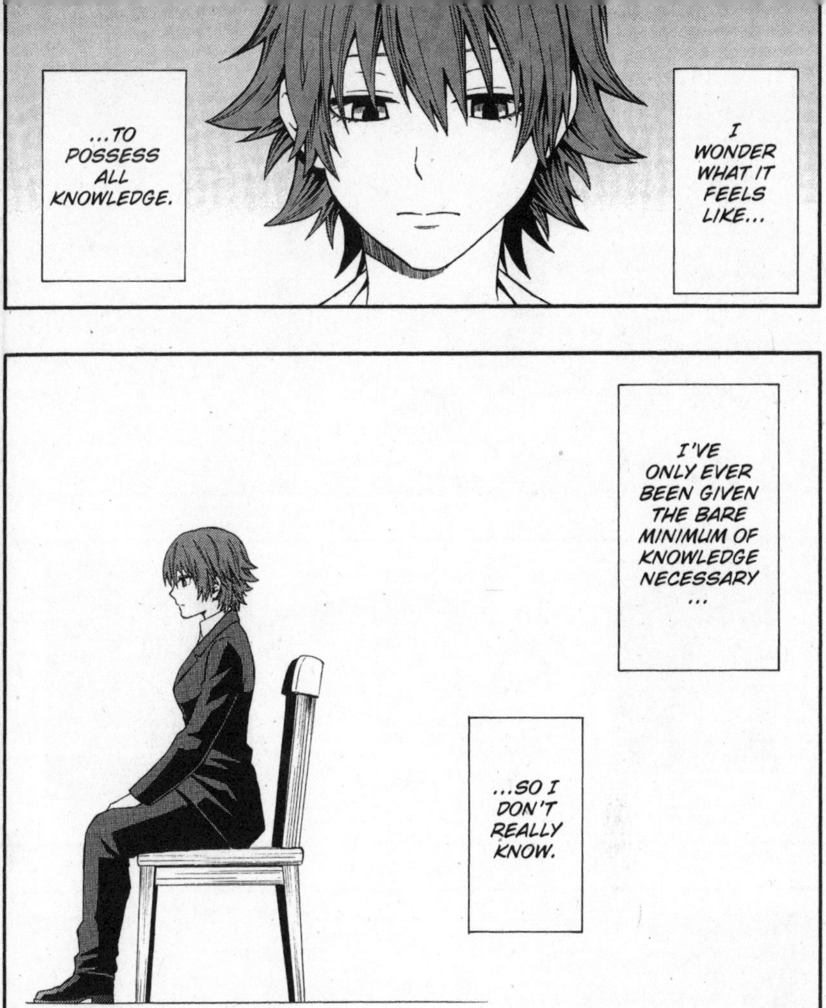
I WONDER WHAT IT FEELS LIKE...
...TO POSSESS ALL KNOWLEDGE.
I'VE ONLY EVER BEEN GIVEN THE BARE MINIMUM OF KNOWLEDGE NECESSARY...
...SO I DON'T REALLY KNOW.

#12 Ennis

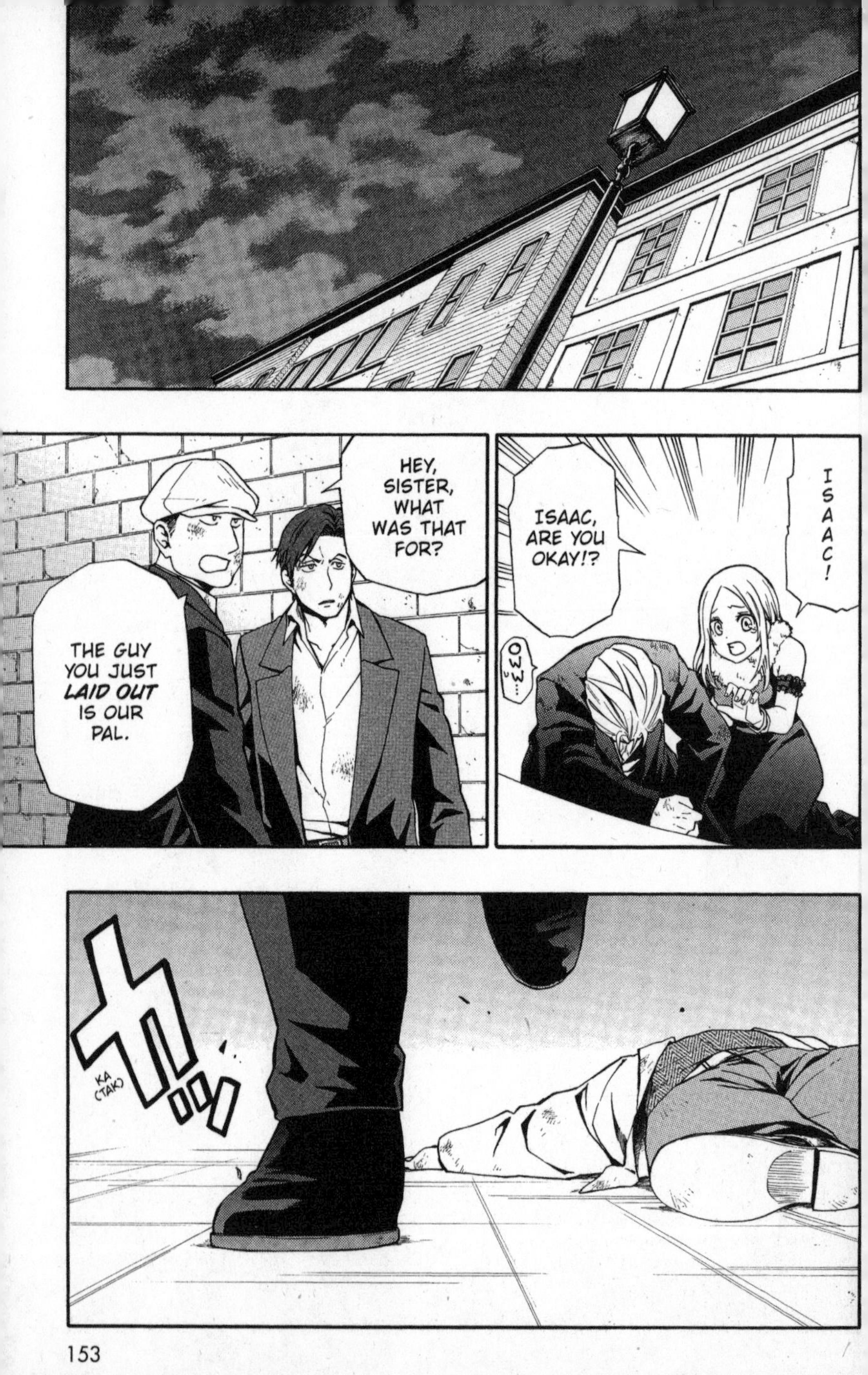
ISAAC!
ISAAC, ARE YOU OKAY!?
OWW...
HEY, SISTER, WHAT WAS THAT FOR?
THE GUY YOU JUST **LAID OUT** IS OUR PAL.
KA (TAK)

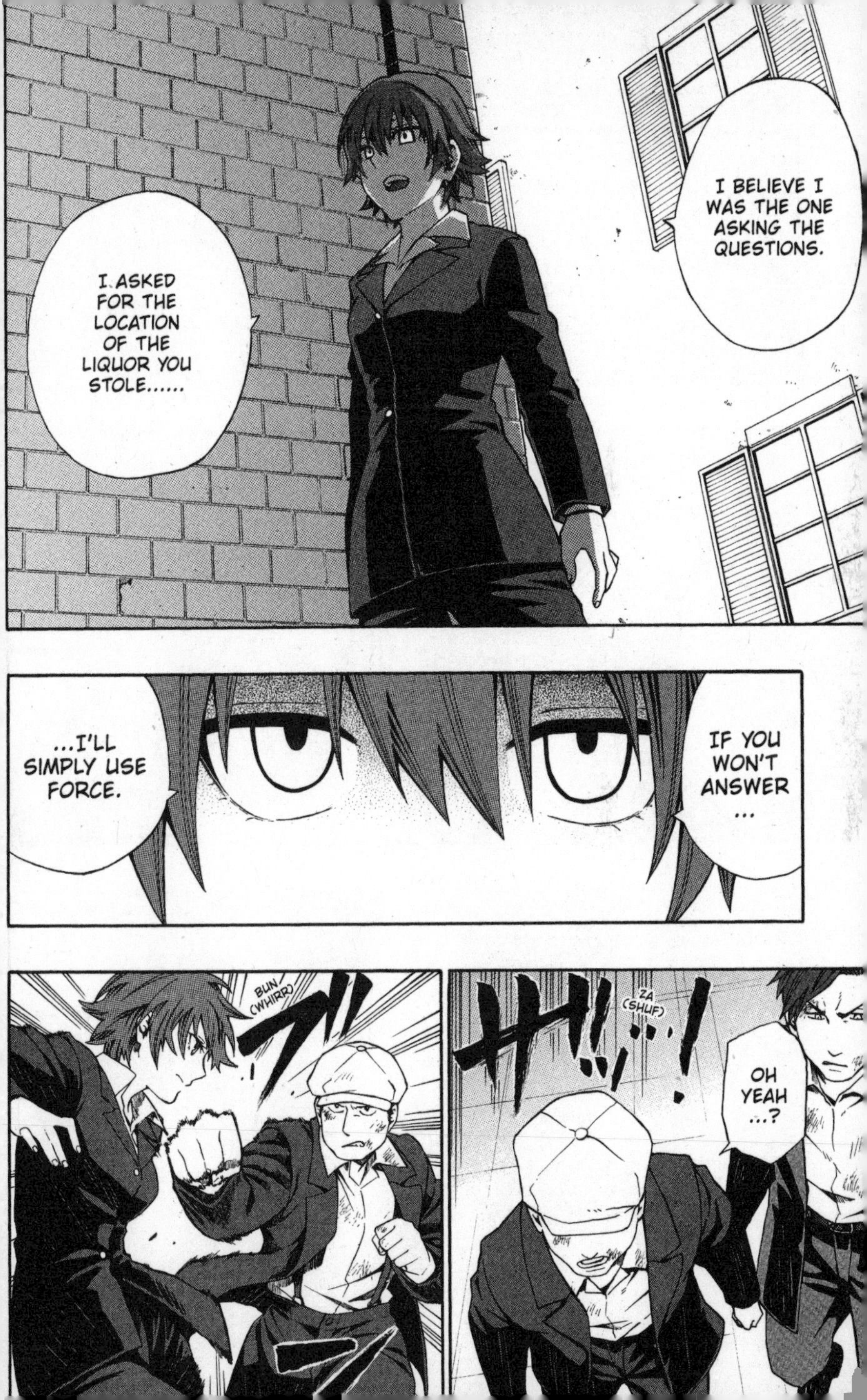
I BELIEVE I WAS THE ONE ASKING THE QUESTIONS.
I ASKED FOR THE LOCATION OF THE LIQUOR YOU STOLE......
IF YOU WON'T ANSWER ...
...I'LL SIMPLY USE FORCE.
ZA (SHUF)
OH YEAH ...?
BUN (WHIRR)

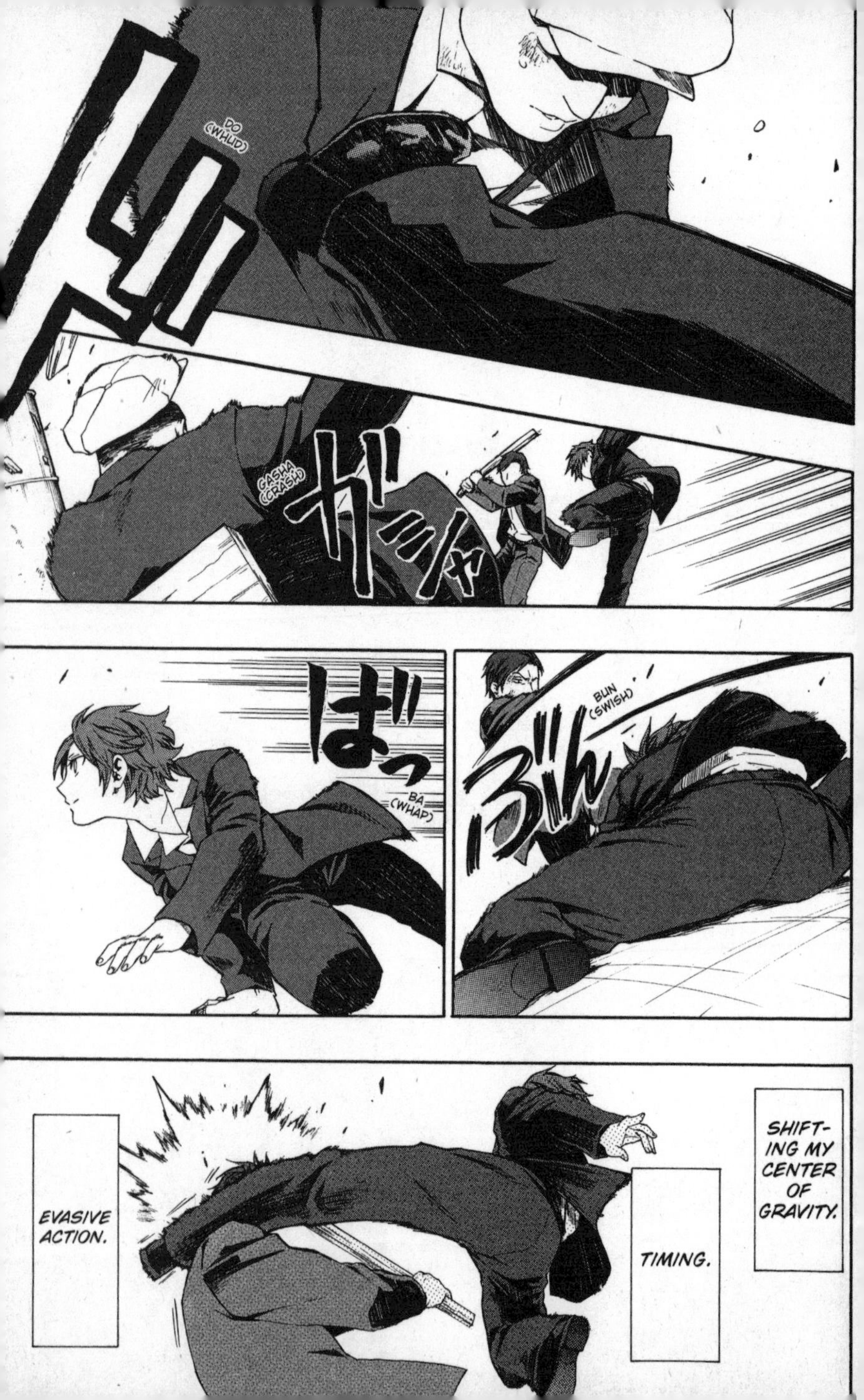
DO (WHUD)
GASHA (CRASH)
ガシャ
BUN (SWISH)
ぶん
ばっ
BA (WHAP)
SHIFTING MY CENTER OF GRAVITY.
TIMING.
EVASIVE ACTION.

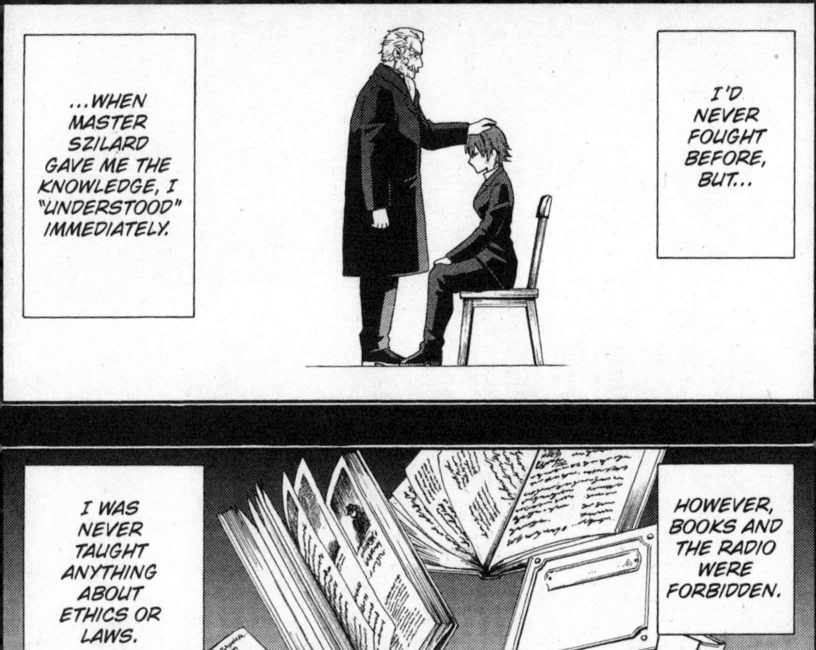

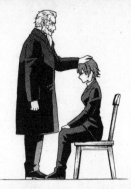

I'D NEVER FOUGHT BEFORE, BUT...
...WHEN MASTER SZILARD GAVE ME THE KNOWLEDGE, I "UNDERSTOOD" IMMEDIATELY.
HOWEVER, BOOKS AND THE RADIO WERE FORBIDDEN.
I WAS NEVER TAUGHT ANYTHING ABOUT ETHICS OR LAWS.
I DIDN'T PARTIC-ULARLY CARE ABOUT THAT.
"AS LONG AS I DO WHAT MASTER SZILARD TELLS ME, I WON'T BE KILLED."

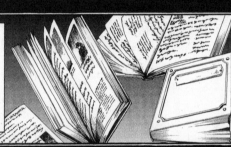

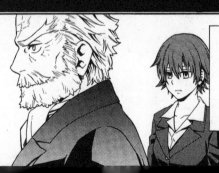

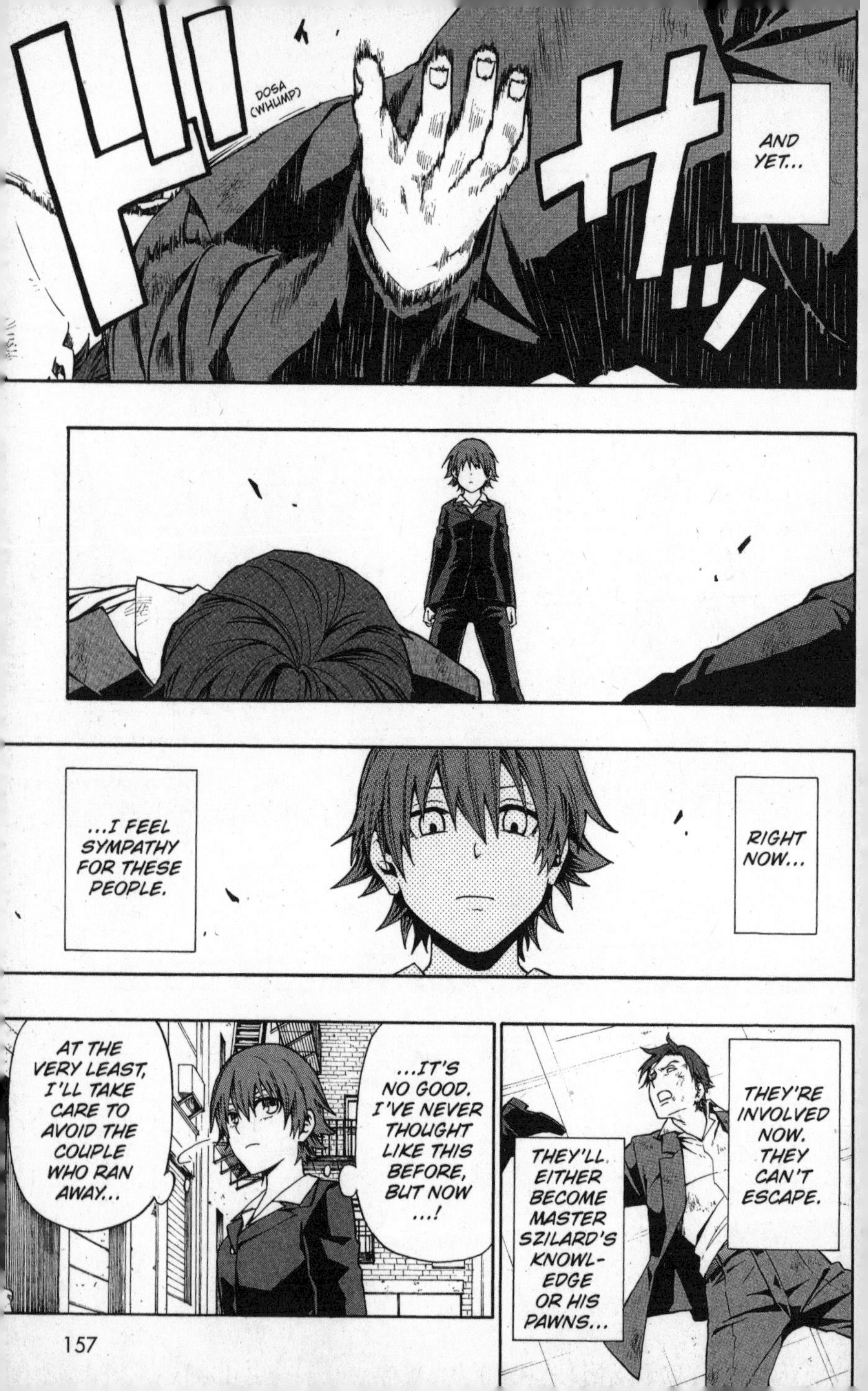
AND YET...
DOSA (WHUMP)
RIGHT NOW...
...I FEEL SYMPATHY FOR THESE PEOPLE.
THEY'RE INVOLVED NOW. THEY CAN'T ESCAPE.
THEY'LL EITHER BECOME MASTER SZILARD'S KNOWL-EDGE OR HIS PAWNS...
...IT'S NO GOOD. I'VE NEVER THOUGHT LIKE THIS BEFORE, BUT NOW ...!
AT THE VERY LEAST, I'LL TAKE CARE TO AVOID THE COUPLE WHO RAN AWAY...

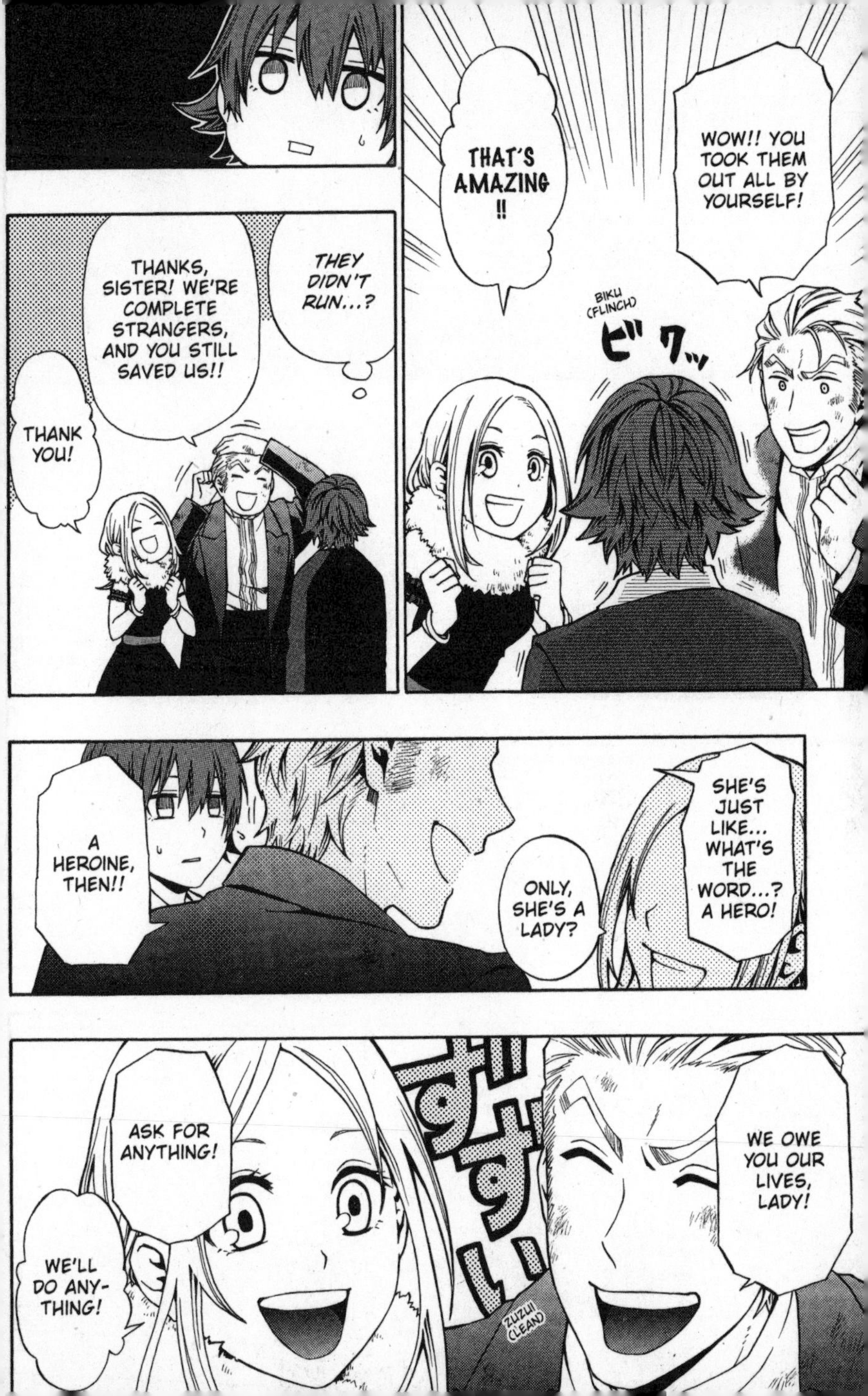
WOW!! YOU TOOK THEM OUT ALL BY YOURSELF!
THAT'S AMAZING!!
BIKU (FLINCH)
ビクッ
THEY DIDN'T RUN...?
THANKS, SISTER! WE'RE COMPLETE STRANGERS, AND YOU STILL SAVED US!!
THANK YOU!
SHE'S JUST LIKE... WHAT'S THE WORD...? A HERO!
ONLY, SHE'S A LADY?
A HEROINE, THEN!!
WE OWE YOU OUR LIVES, LADY!
ずずい
ZUZUI (LEAN)
ASK FOR ANYTHING!
WE'LL DO ANYTHING!

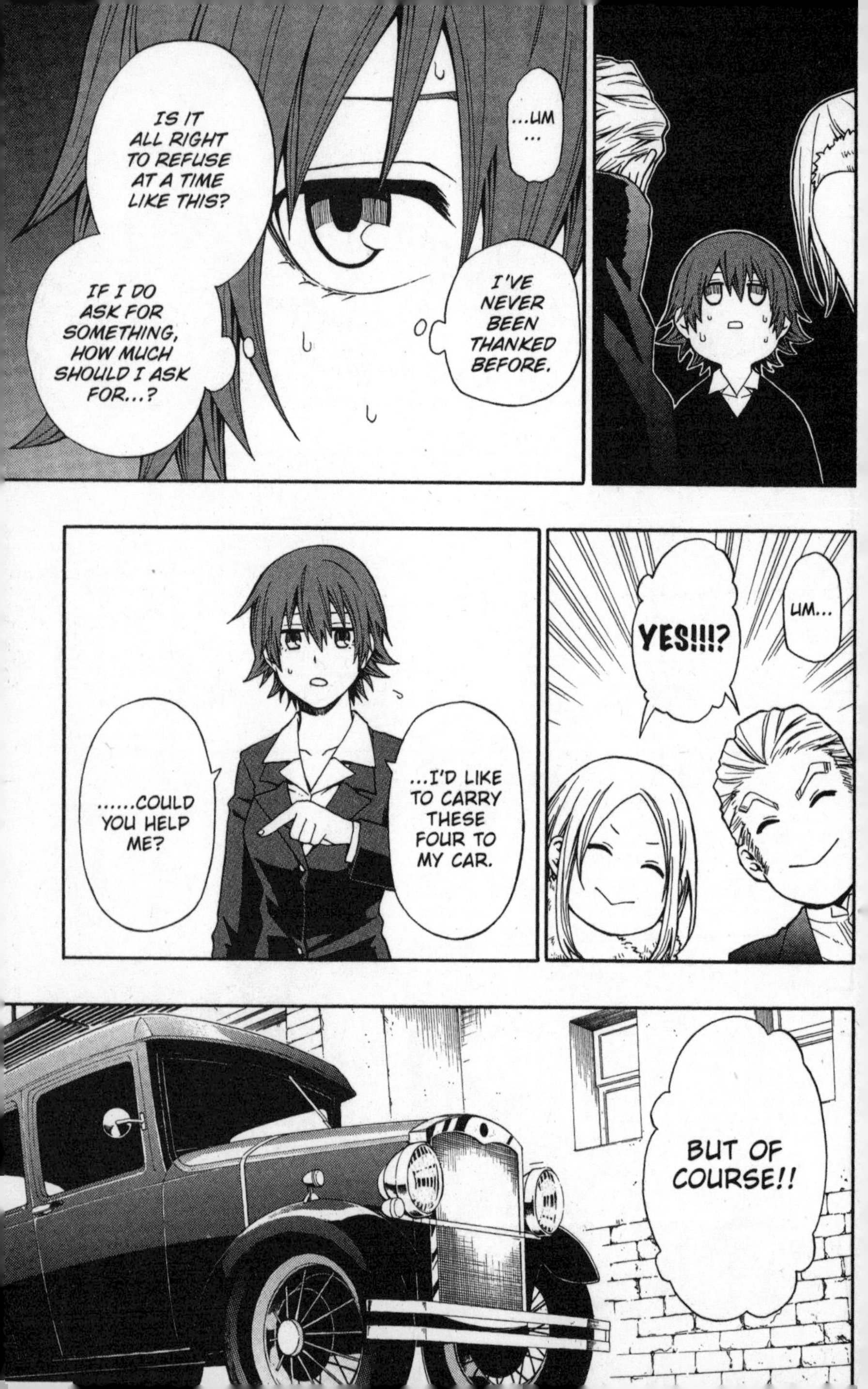
...UM ...
I'VE NEVER BEEN THANKED BEFORE.
IS IT ALL RIGHT TO REFUSE AT A TIME LIKE THIS?
IF I DO ASK FOR SOMETHING, HOW MUCH SHOULD I ASK FOR...?
UM...
YES!!!!?
...I'D LIKE TO CARRY THESE FOUR TO MY CAR.
......COULD YOU HELP ME?
BUT OF COURSE!!

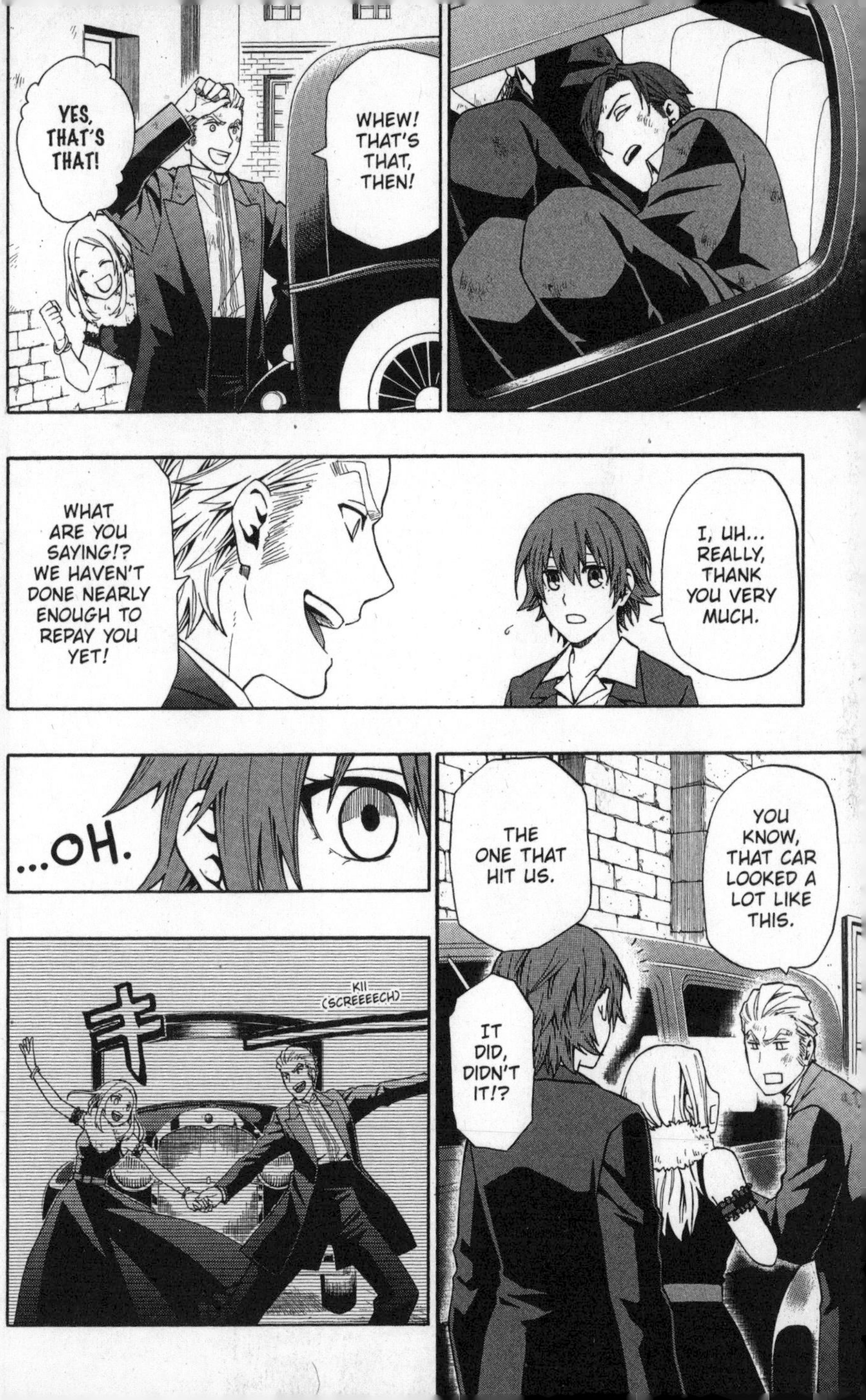
WHEW! THAT'S THAT, THEN!
YES, THAT'S THAT!
I, UH... REALLY, THANK YOU VERY MUCH.
WHAT ARE YOU SAYING!? WE HAVEN'T DONE NEARLY ENOUGH TO REPAY YOU YET!
YOU KNOW, THAT CAR LOOKED A LOT LIKE THIS.
THE ONE THAT HIT US.
IT DID, DIDN'T IT!?
...OH.
キ
KII (SCREEEECH)

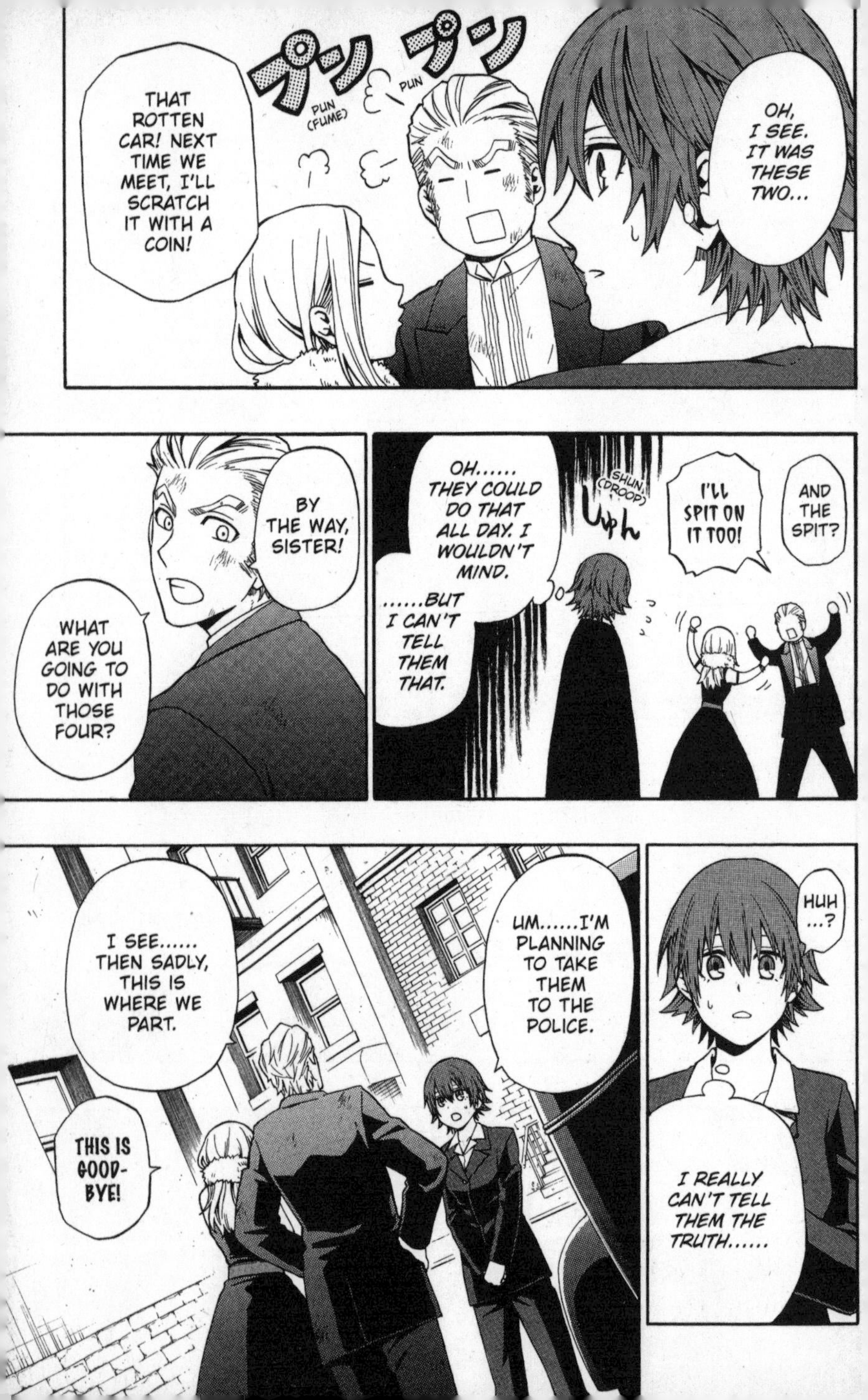
OH, I SEE. IT WAS THESE TWO...
プン プン
PUN
PUN (FUME)
THAT ROTTEN CAR! NEXT TIME WE MEET, I'LL SCRATCH IT WITH A COIN!
AND THE SPIT?
I'LL SPIT ON IT TOO!
SHUN (DROOP)
しゅん
OH...... THEY COULD DO THAT ALL DAY. I WOULDN'T MIND.
......BUT I CAN'T TELL THEM THAT.
BY THE WAY, SISTER!
WHAT ARE YOU GOING TO DO WITH THOSE FOUR?
HUH ...?
I REALLY CAN'T TELL THEM THE TRUTH......
UM......I'M PLANNING TO TAKE THEM TO THE POLICE.
I SEE...... THEN SADLY, THIS IS WHERE WE PART.
THIS IS GOOD-BYE!

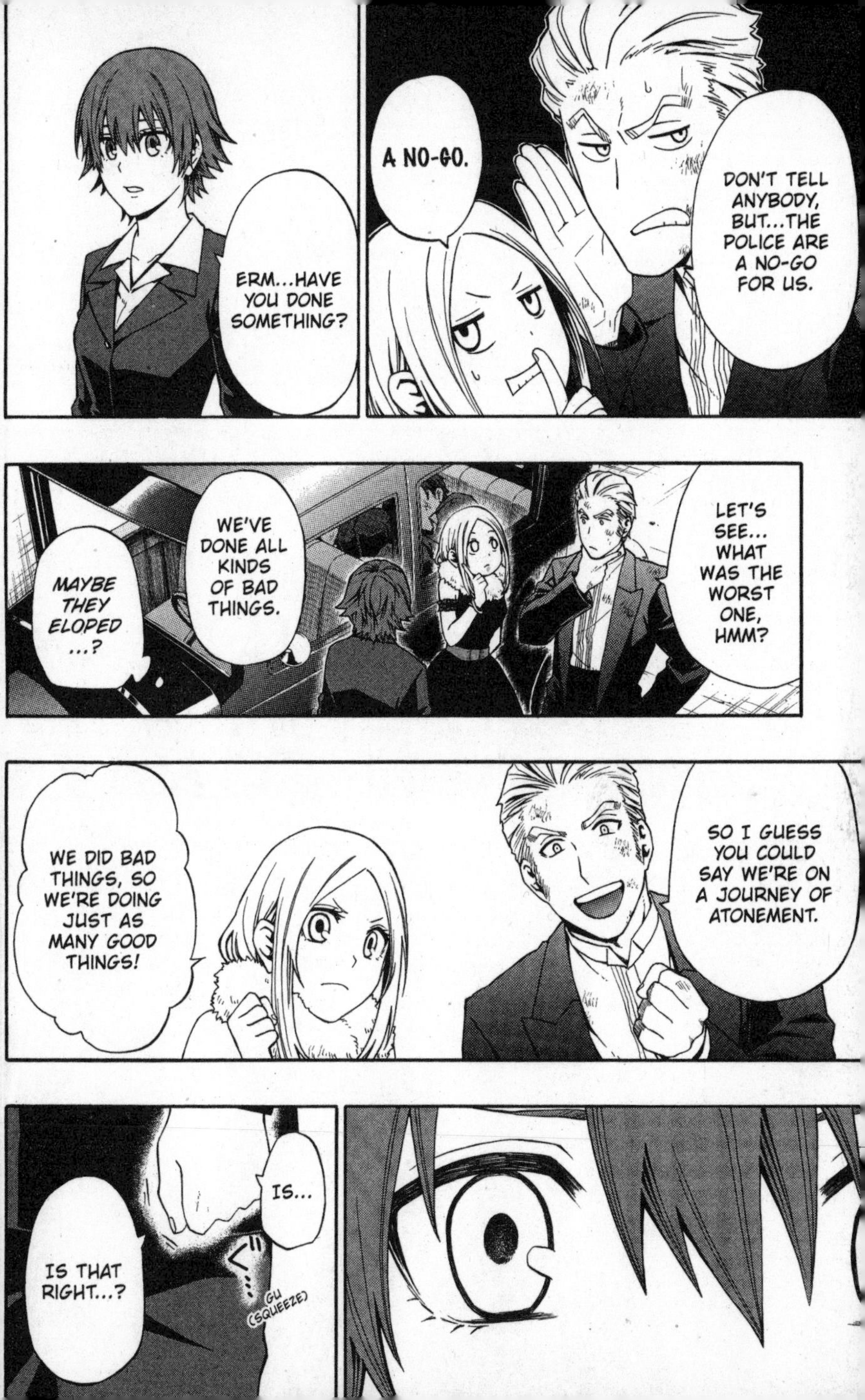
DON'T TELL ANYBODY, BUT...THE POLICE ARE A NO-GO FOR US.
A NO-GO.
ERM...HAVE YOU DONE SOMETHING?
LET'S SEE... WHAT WAS THE WORST ONE, HMM?
WE'VE DONE ALL KINDS OF BAD THINGS.
MAYBE THEY ELOPED...?
SO I GUESS YOU COULD SAY WE'RE ON A JOURNEY OF ATONEMENT.
WE DID BAD THINGS, SO WE'RE DOING JUST AS MANY GOOD THINGS!
IS...
IS THAT RIGHT...?
GU (SQUEEZE)

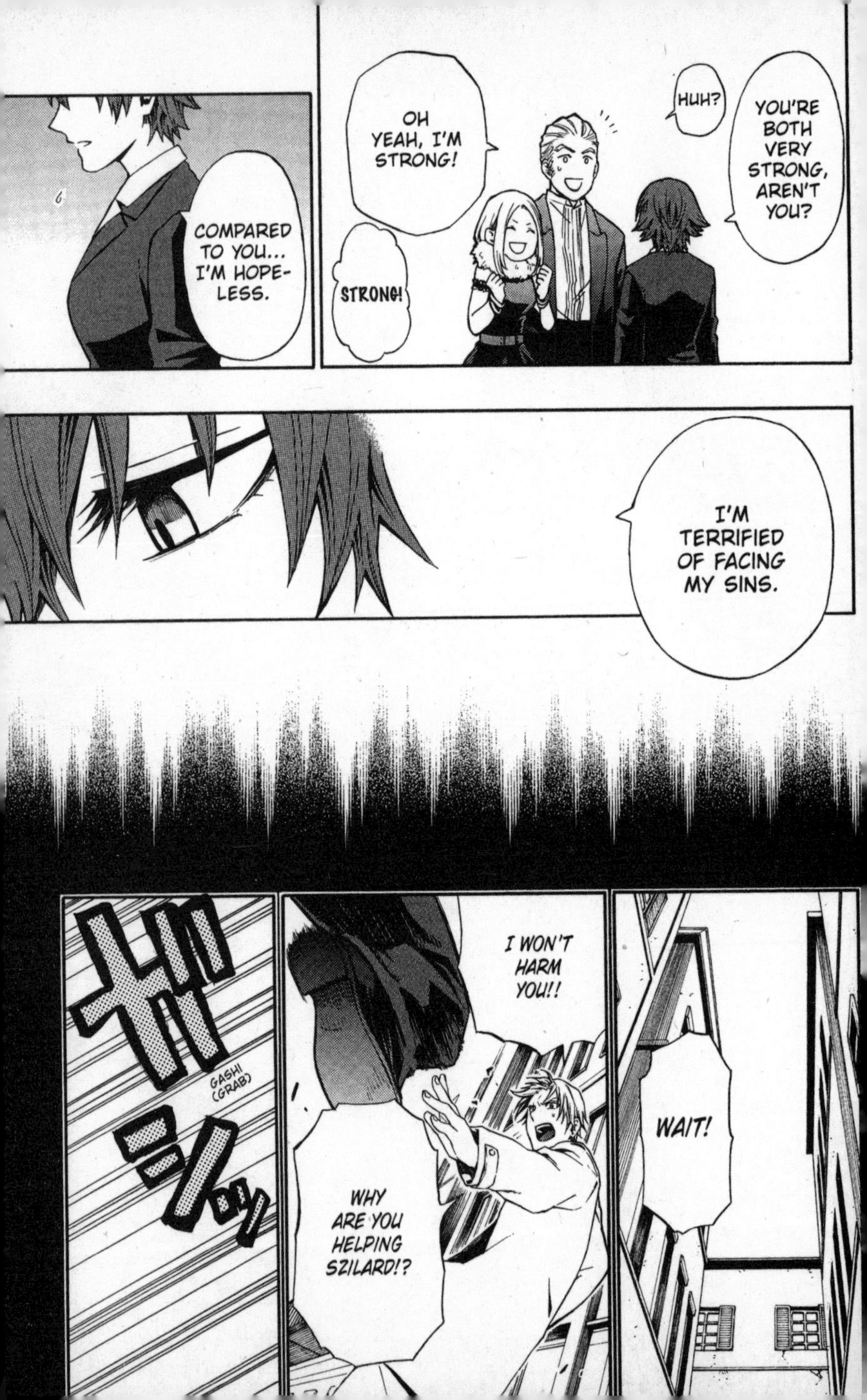
YOU'RE BOTH VERY STRONG, AREN'T YOU?
HUH?
OH YEAH, I'M STRONG!
STRONG!
COMPARED TO YOU... I'M HOPELESS.
I'M TERRIFIED OF FACING MY SINS.
WAIT!
I WON'T HARM YOU!!
WHY ARE YOU HELPING SZILARD!?
GASHI (GRAB)

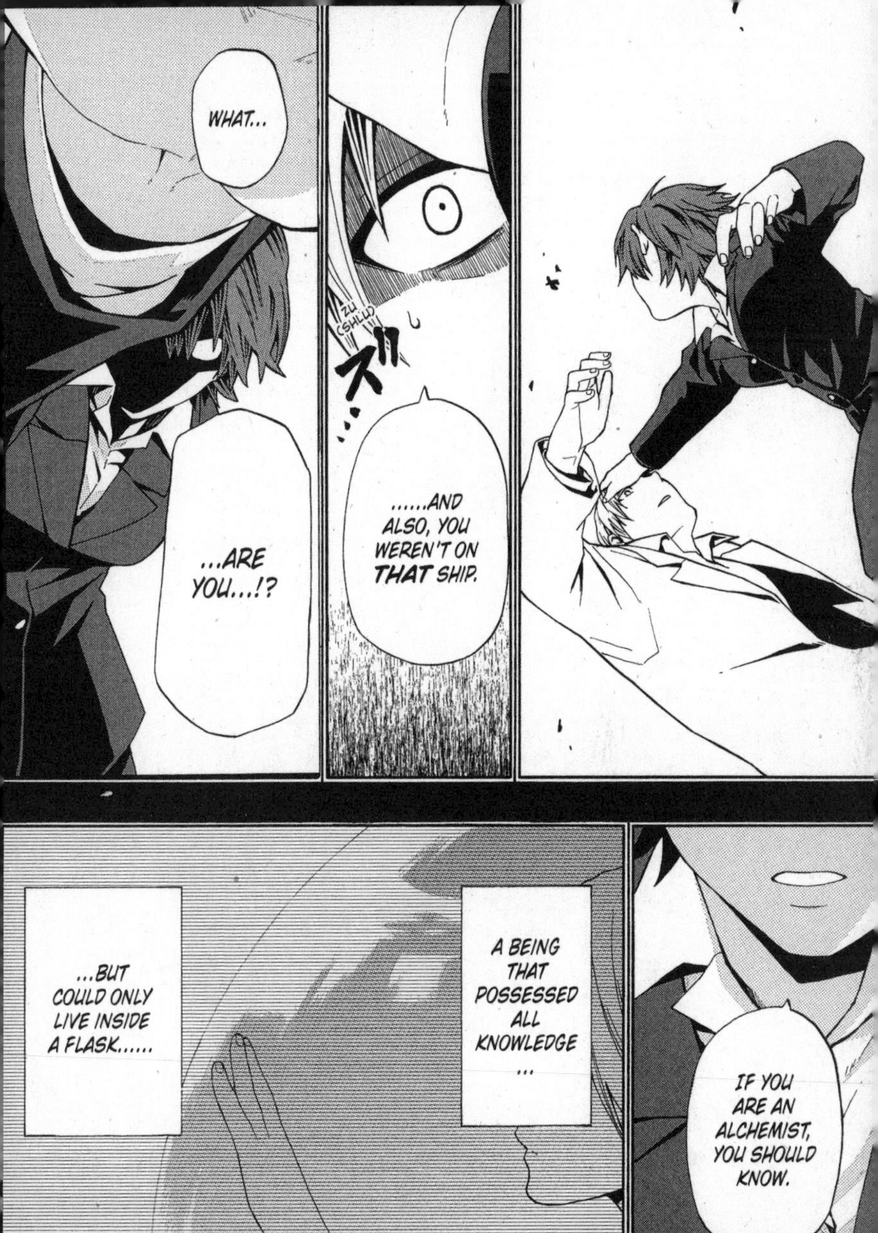
ZU (SHLU)
......AND ALSO, YOU WEREN'T ON THAT SHIP.
WHAT...
...ARE YOU...!?
IF YOU ARE AN ALCHEMIST, YOU SHOULD KNOW.
A BEING THAT POSSESSED ALL KNOWLEDGE ...
...BUT COULD ONLY LIVE INSIDE A FLASK......

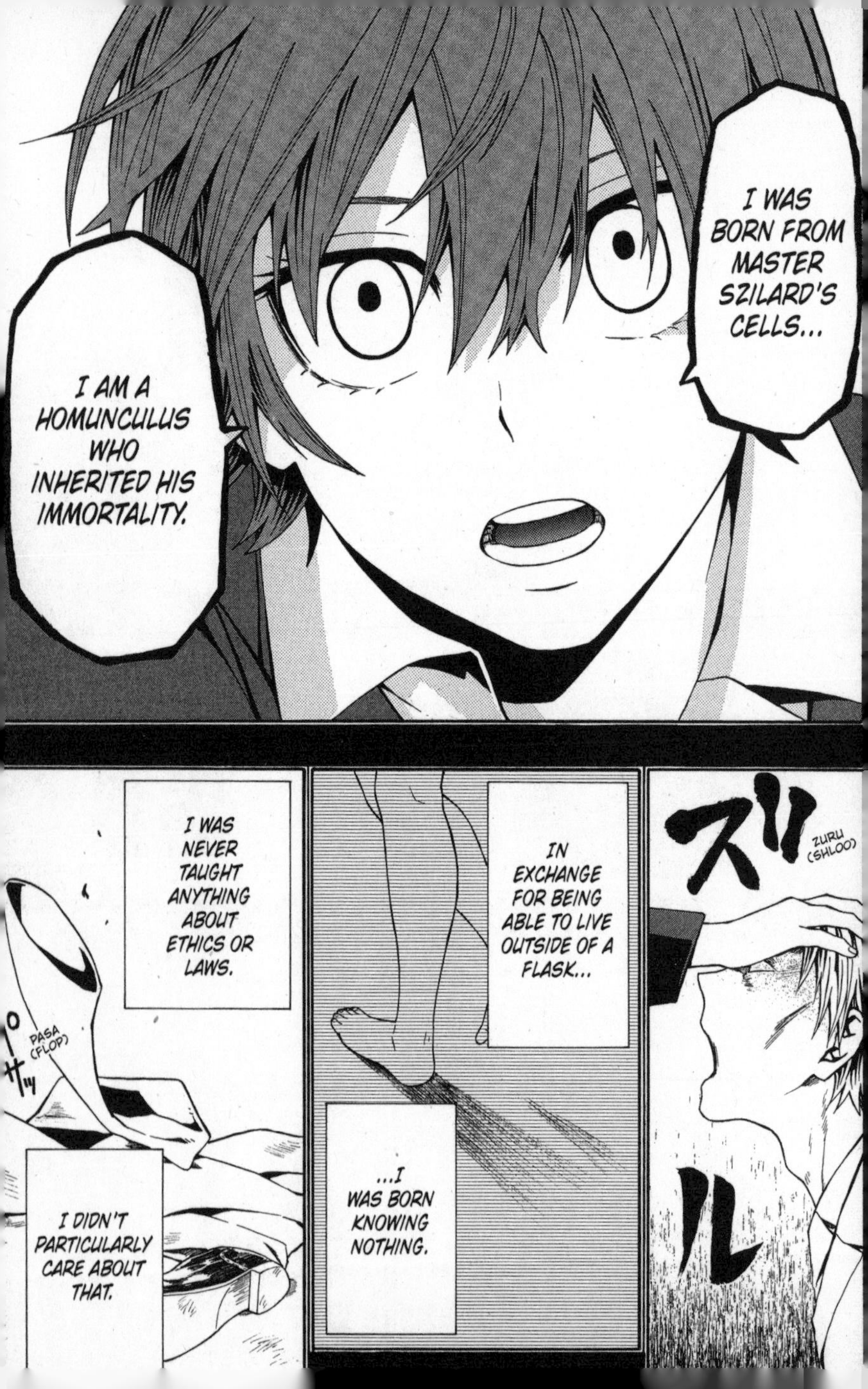
I WAS BORN FROM MASTER SZILARD'S CELLS...
I AM A HOMUNCULUS WHO INHERITED HIS IMMORTALITY.
スル
ZURU (SHLOO)
IN EXCHANGE FOR BEING ABLE TO LIVE OUTSIDE OF A FLASK...
...I WAS BORN KNOWING NOTHING.
I WAS NEVER TAUGHT ANYTHING ABOUT ETHICS OR LAWS.
PASA (FLOP)
I DIDN'T PARTICULARLY CARE ABOUT THAT.

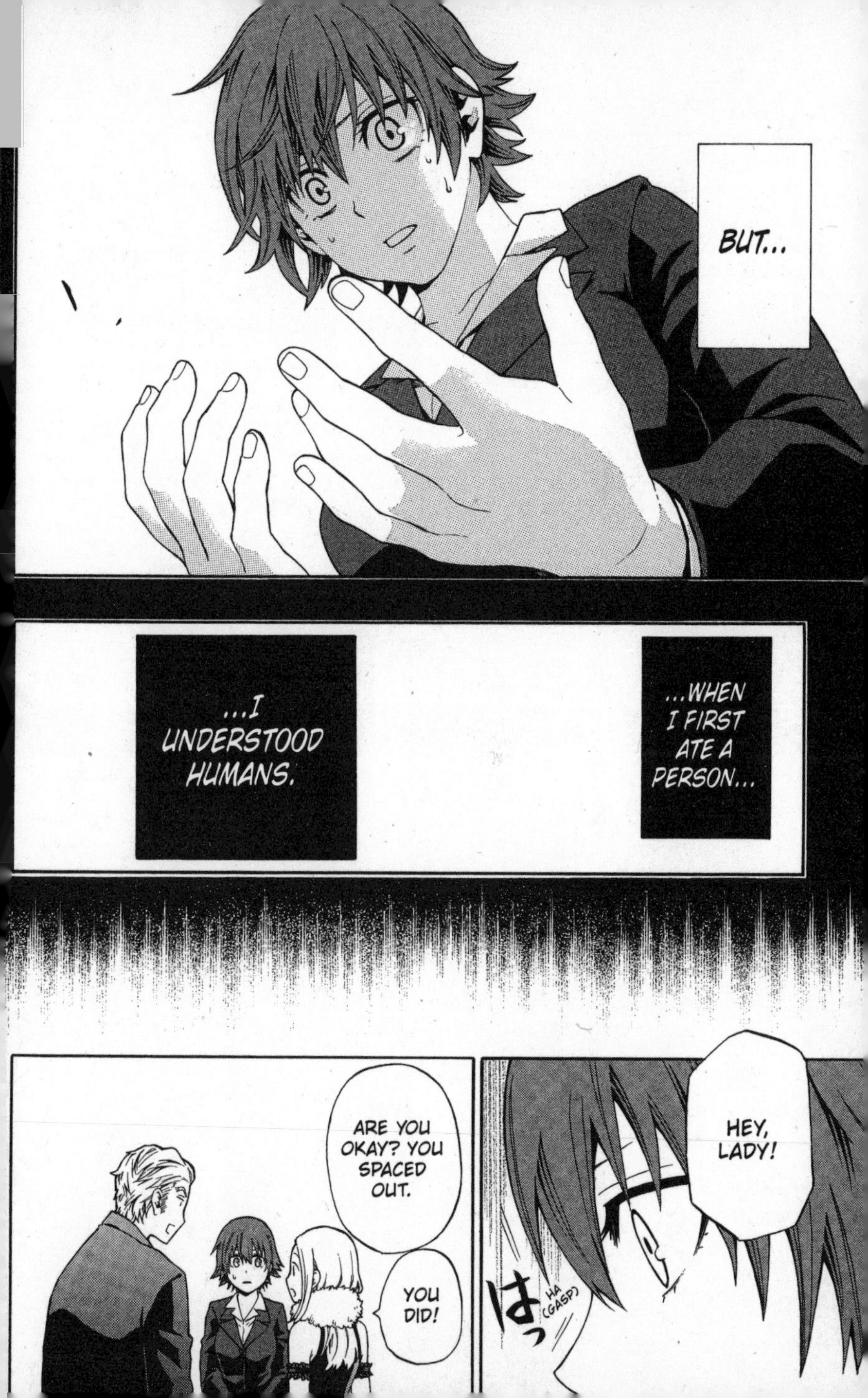
BUT...
...WHEN I FIRST ATE A PERSON...
...I UNDERSTOOD HUMANS.
HEY, LADY!
はっ
HA (GASP)
ARE YOU OKAY? YOU SPACED OUT.
YOU DID!

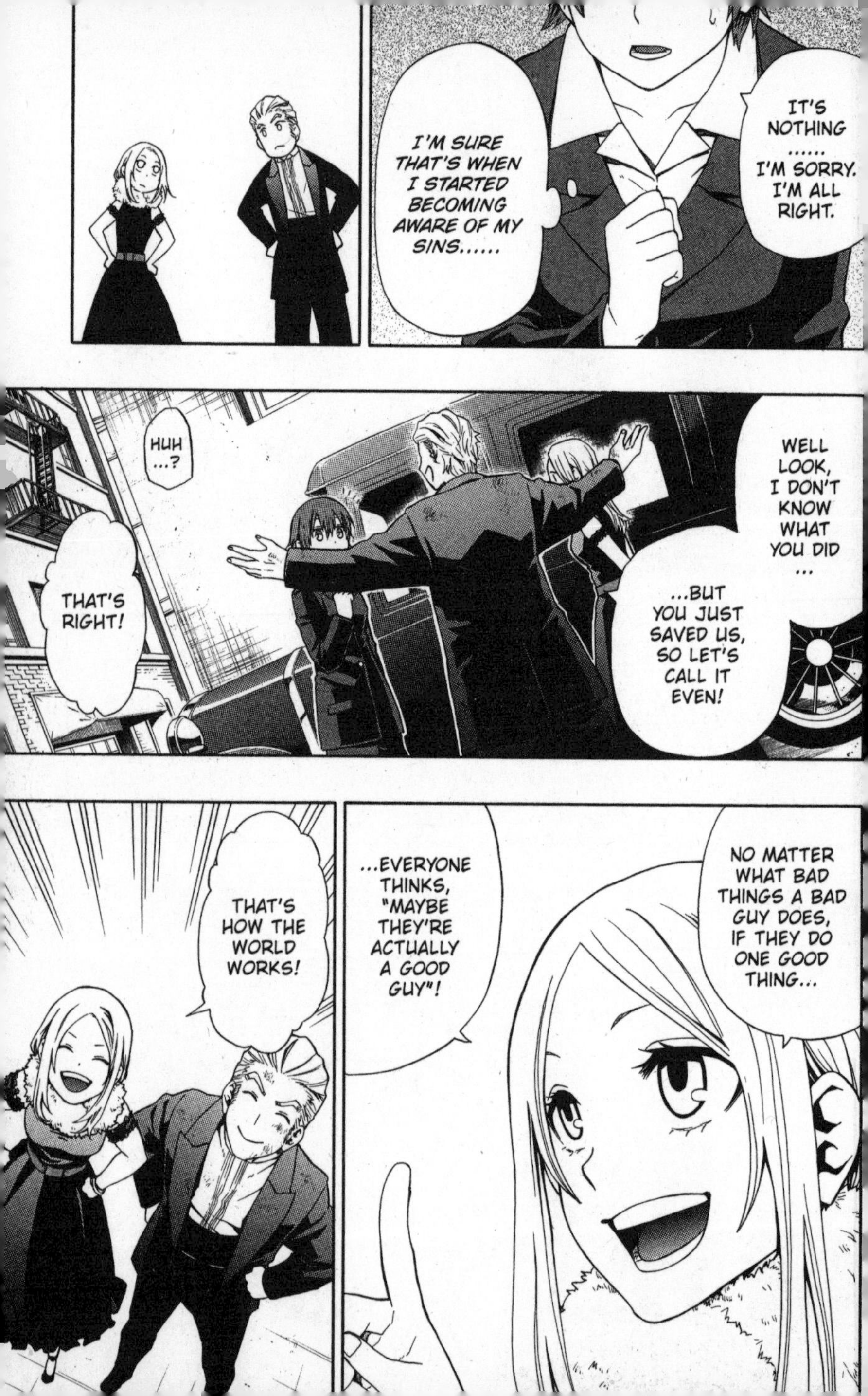
IT'S NOTHING ...... I'M SORRY. I'M ALL RIGHT.
I'M SURE THAT'S WHEN I STARTED BECOMING AWARE OF MY SINS......
WELL LOOK, I DON'T KNOW WHAT YOU DID ...
...BUT YOU JUST SAVED US, SO LET'S CALL IT EVEN!
HUH ...?
THAT'S RIGHT!
NO MATTER WHAT BAD THINGS A BAD GUY DOES, IF THEY DO ONE GOOD THING...
...EVERYONE THINKS, "MAYBE THEY'RE ACTUALLY A GOOD GUY"!
THAT'S HOW THE WORLD WORKS!

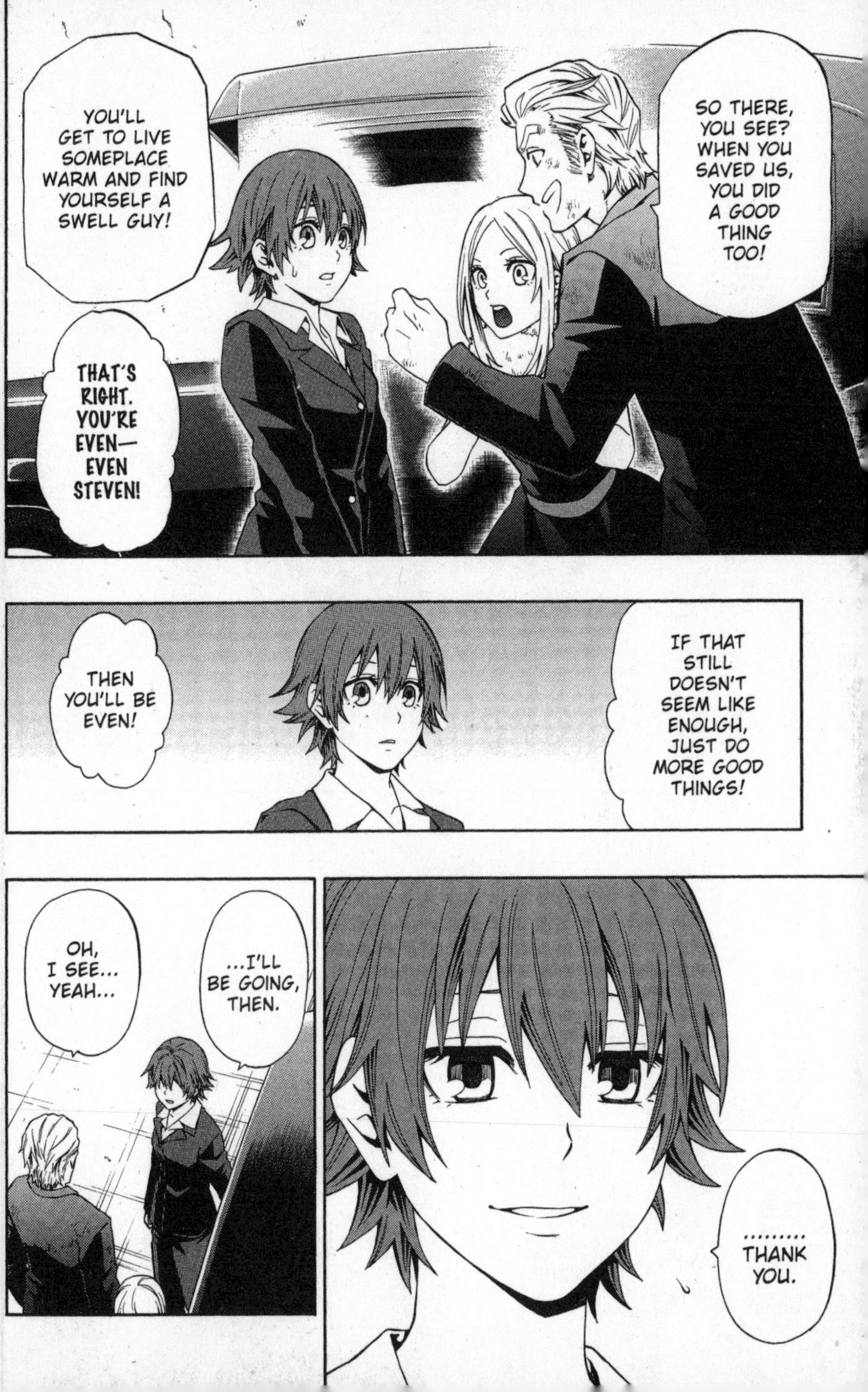
SO THERE, YOU SEE? WHEN YOU SAVED US, YOU DID A GOOD THING TOO!
YOU'LL GET TO LIVE SOMEPLACE WARM AND FIND YOURSELF A SWELL GUY!
THAT'S RIGHT. YOU'RE EVEN— EVEN STEVEN!
IF THAT STILL DOESN'T SEEM LIKE ENOUGH, JUST DO MORE GOOD THINGS!
THEN YOU'LL BE EVEN!
.... THANK YOU.
...I'LL BE GOING, THEN.
OH, I SEE... YEAH...

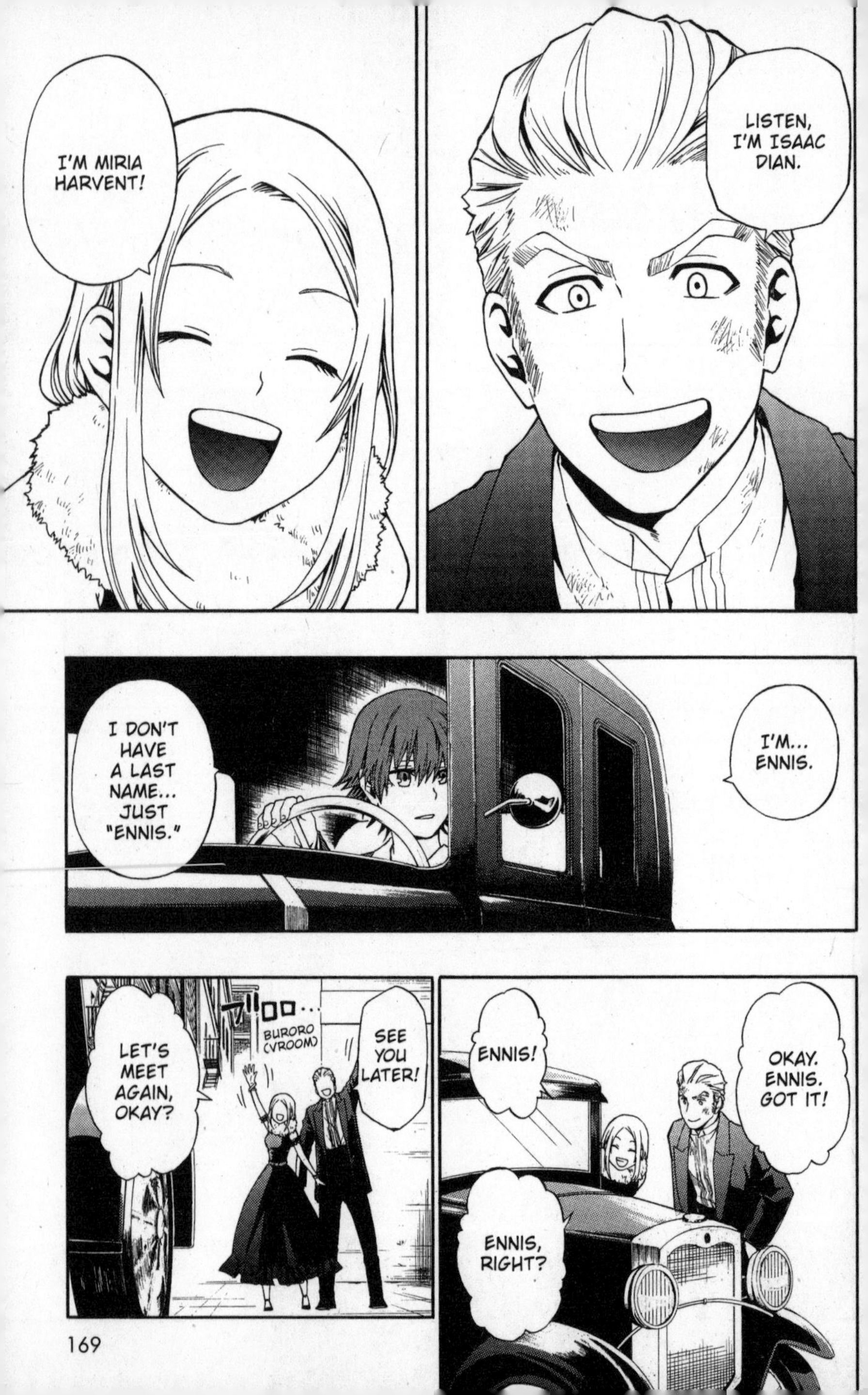
LISTEN, I'M ISAAC DIAN.
I'M MIRIA HARVENT!
I'M... ENNIS.
I DON'T HAVE A LAST NAME... JUST "ENNIS."
OKAY. ENNIS. GOT IT!
ENNIS!
ENNIS, RIGHT?
SEE YOU LATER!
ブロロ…
BURORO (VROOM)
LET'S MEET AGAIN, OKAY?

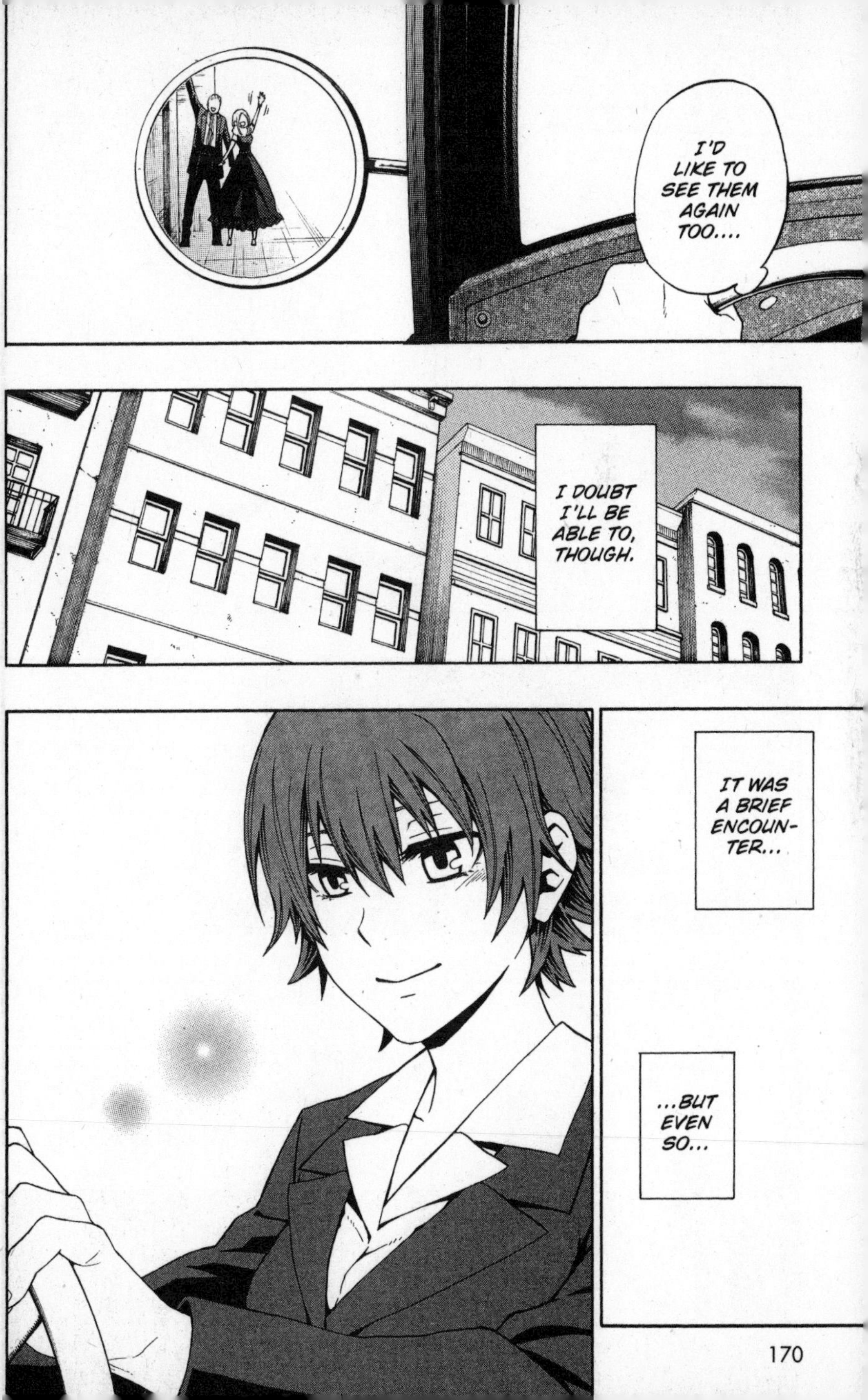
I'D LIKE TO SEE THEM AGAIN TOO....
I DOUBT I'LL BE ABLE TO, THOUGH.
IT WAS A BRIEF ENCOUN-TER...
...BUT EVEN SO...

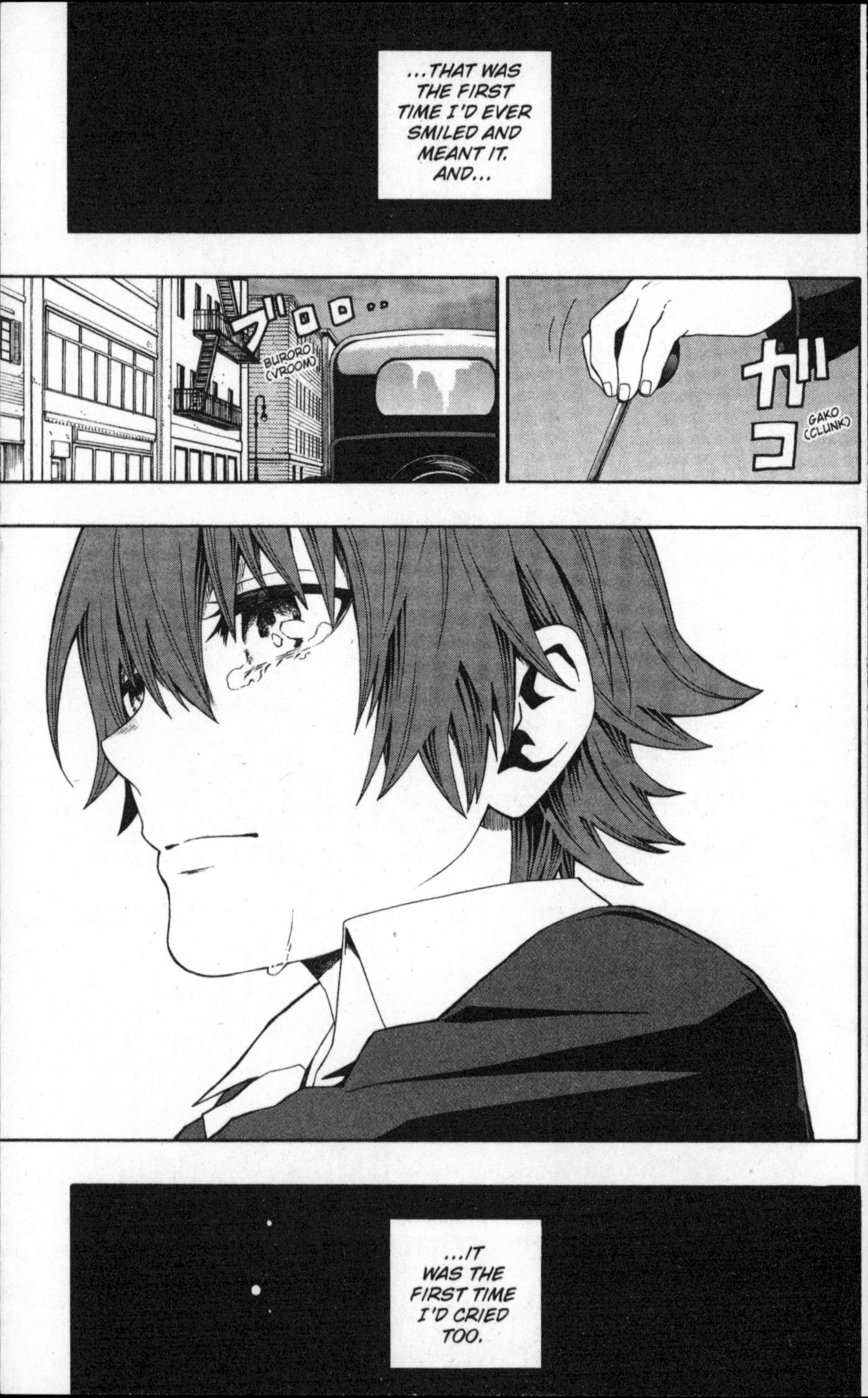
...THAT WAS THE FIRST TIME I'D EVER SMILED AND MEANT IT. AND...
ガコ
GAKO (CLUNK)
ブロロ
BURORO (VROOM)
...IT WAS THE FIRST TIME I'D CRIED TOO.

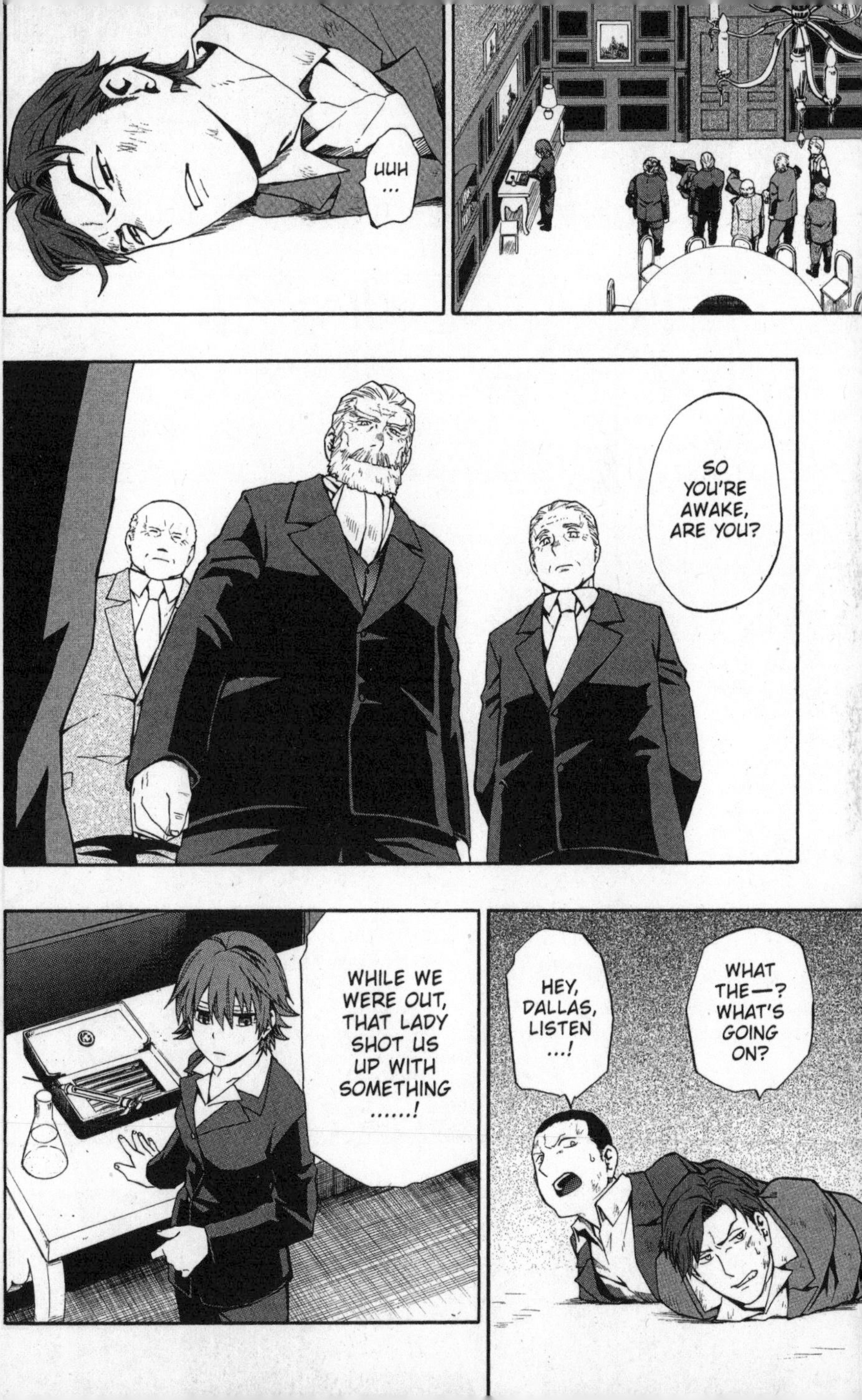
UUH ...
SO YOU'RE AWAKE, ARE YOU?
WHAT THE—? WHAT'S GOING ON?
HEY, DALLAS, LISTEN ...!
WHILE WE WERE OUT, THAT LADY SHOT US UP WITH SOMETHING ......!

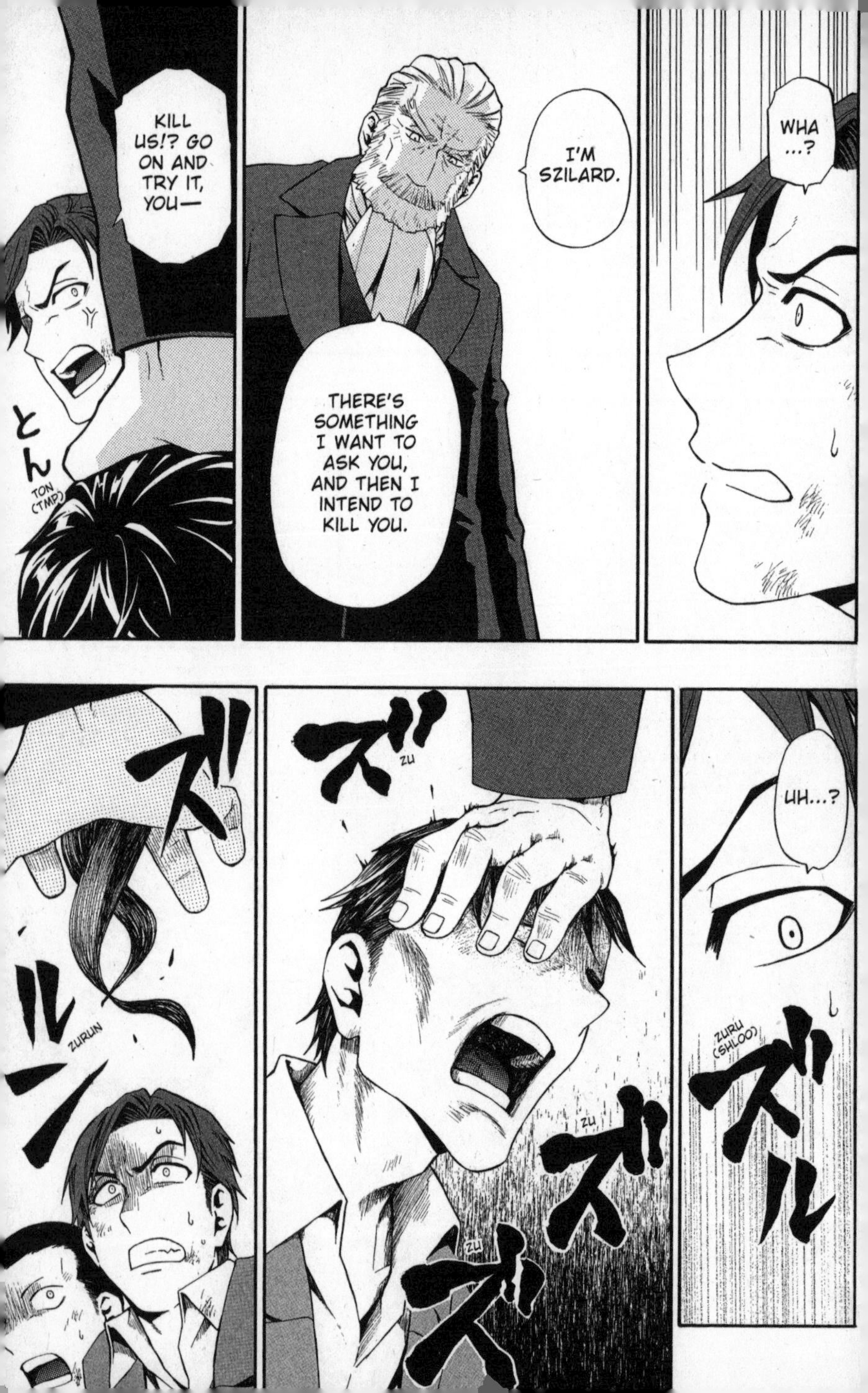
WHA ...?
I'M SZILARD.
THERE'S SOMETHING I WANT TO ASK YOU, AND THEN I INTEND TO KILL YOU.
KILL US!? GO ON AND TRY IT, YOU—
とん
TON (TMP)
UH...?
ズル
ZURU (SHLOO)
ズ
ZU
ズ
ZU
ズ
ZU
ズルン
ZURUN

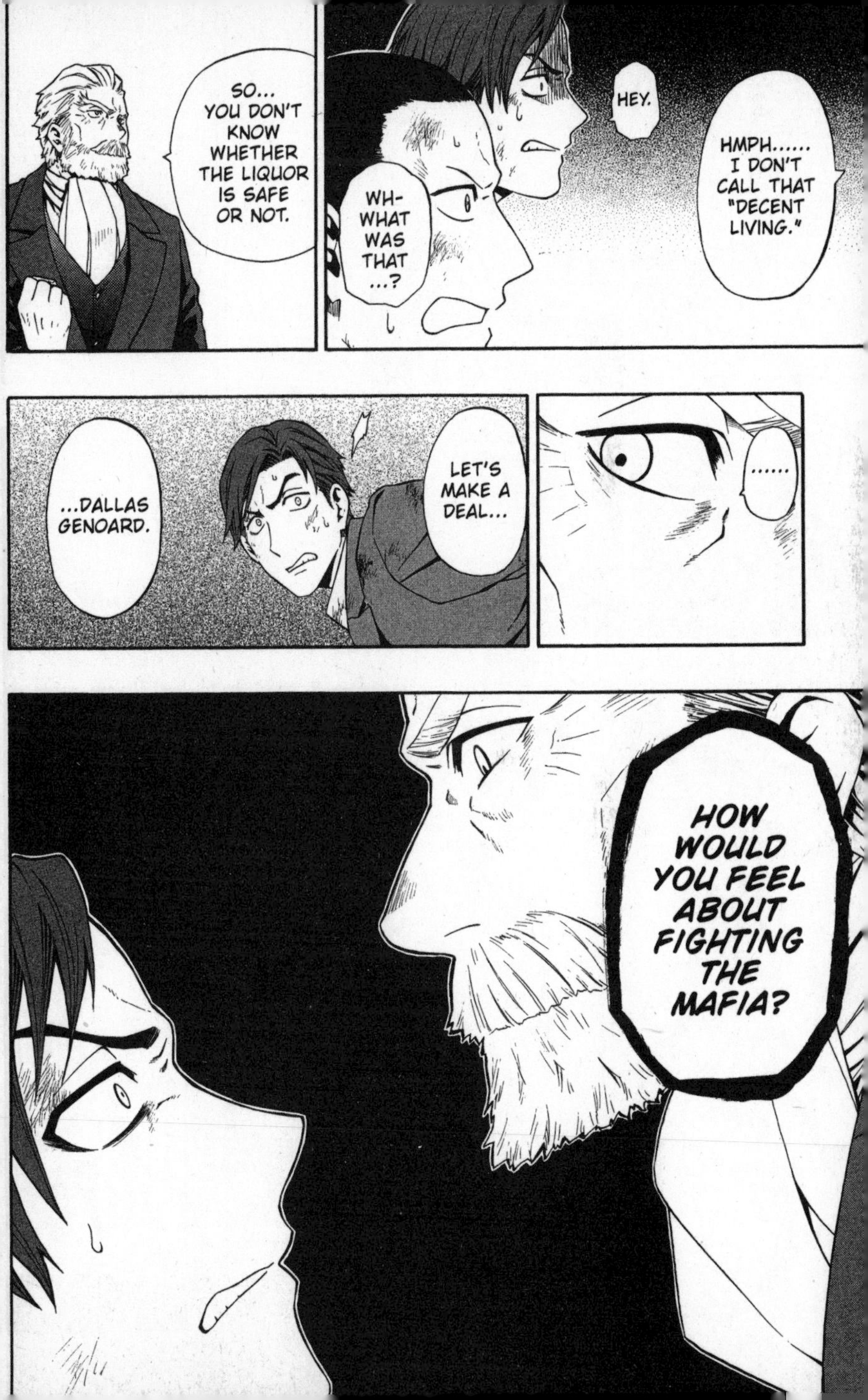
HEY.
HMPH...... I DON'T CALL THAT "DECENT LIVING."
WH- WHAT WAS THAT ...?
SO... YOU DON'T KNOW WHETHER THE LIQUOR IS SAFE OR NOT.
......
LET'S MAKE A DEAL...
...DALLAS GENOARD.
HOW WOULD YOU FEEL ABOUT FIGHTING THE MAFIA?

#13 Tipping Point

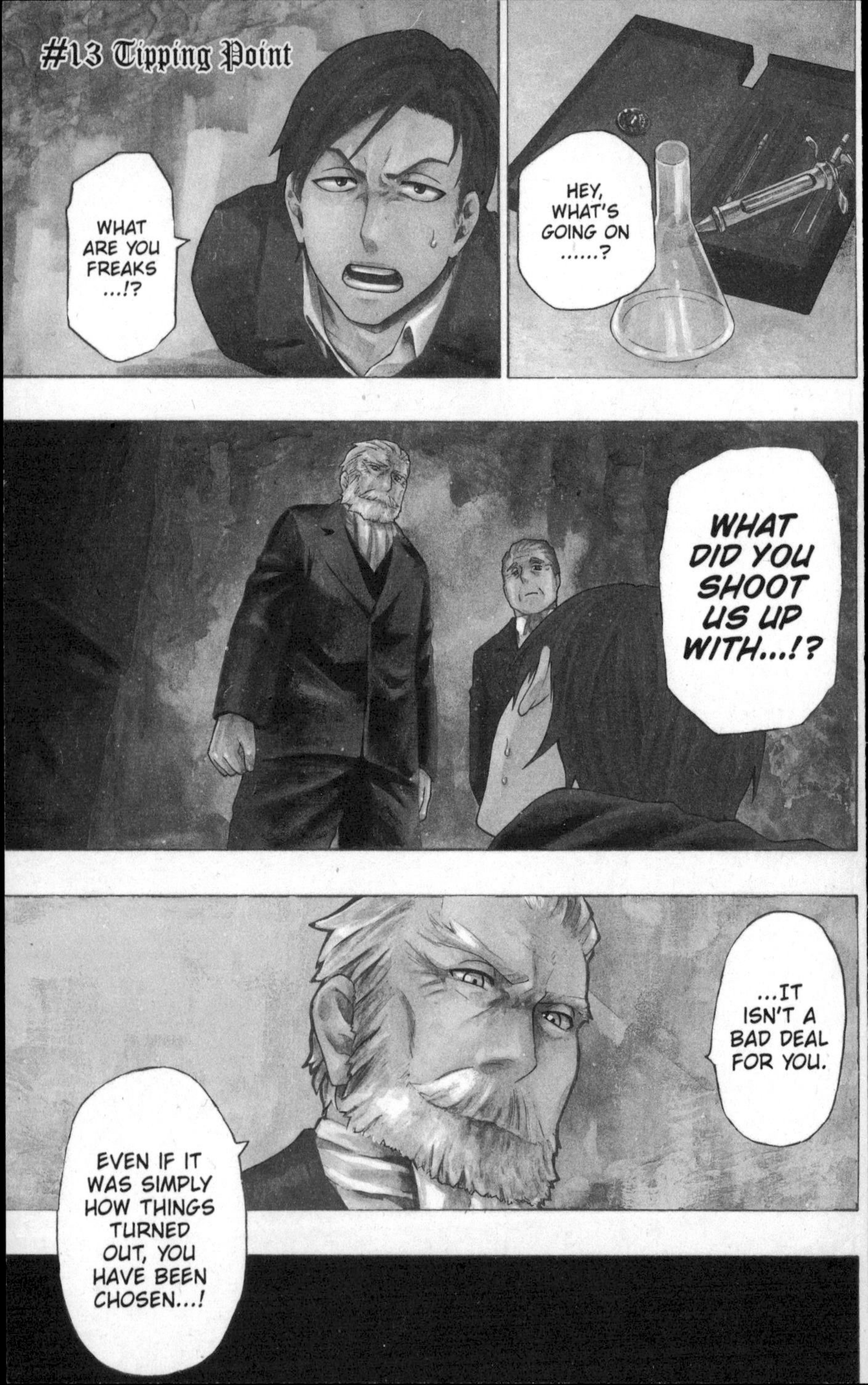
HEY, WHAT'S GOING ON ......?
WHAT ARE YOU FREAKS ...!?
WHAT DID YOU SHOOT US UP WITH...!?
...IT ISN'T A BAD DEAL FOR YOU.
EVEN IF IT WAS SIMPLY HOW THINGS TURNED OUT, YOU HAVE BEEN CHOSEN...!

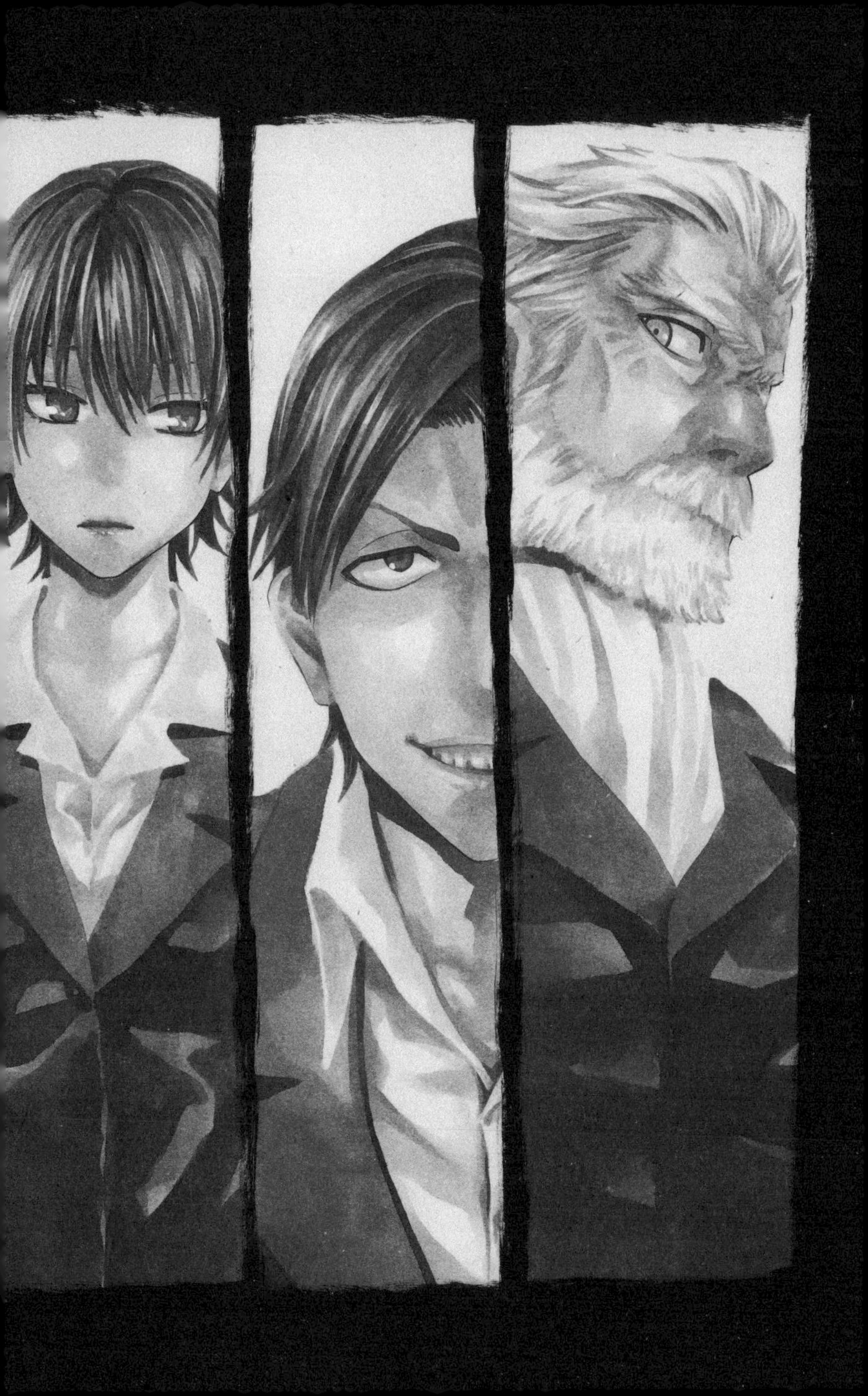

#13 Tipping Point

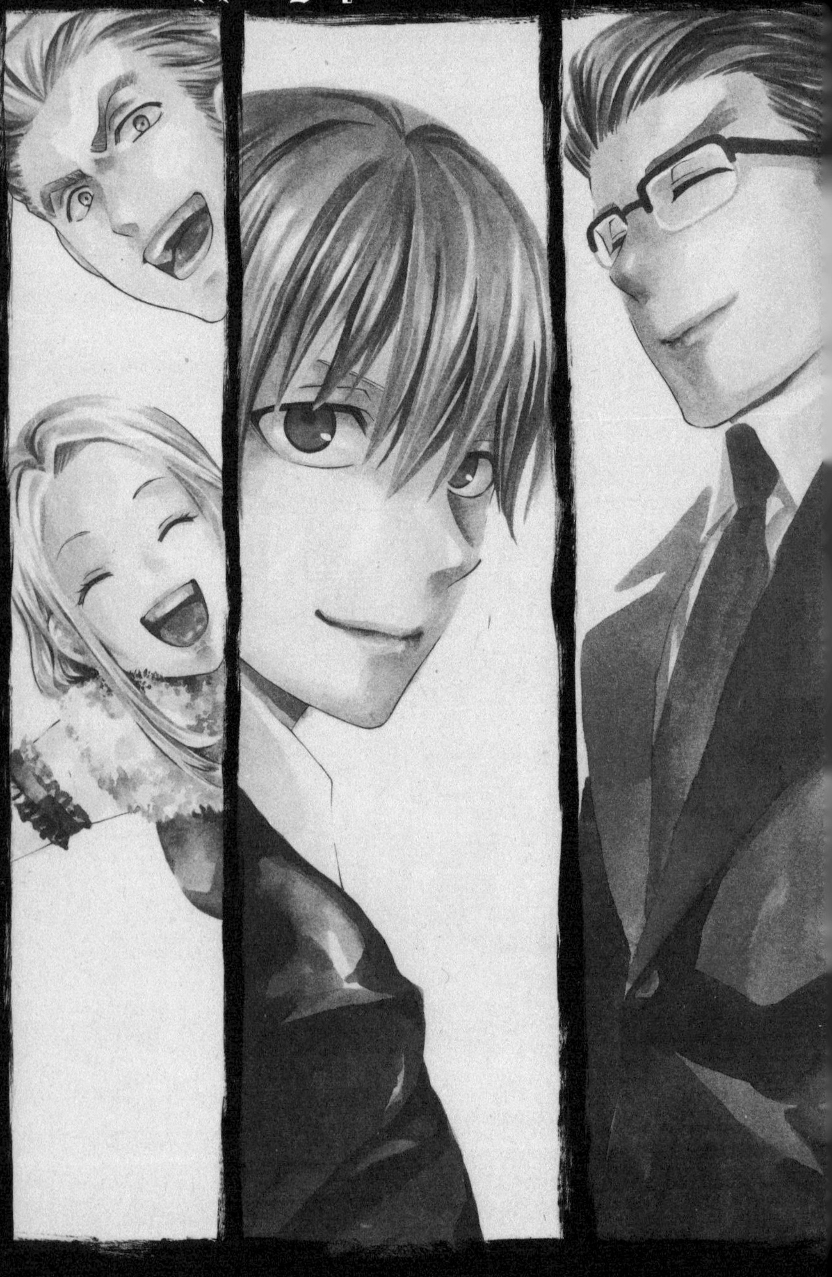

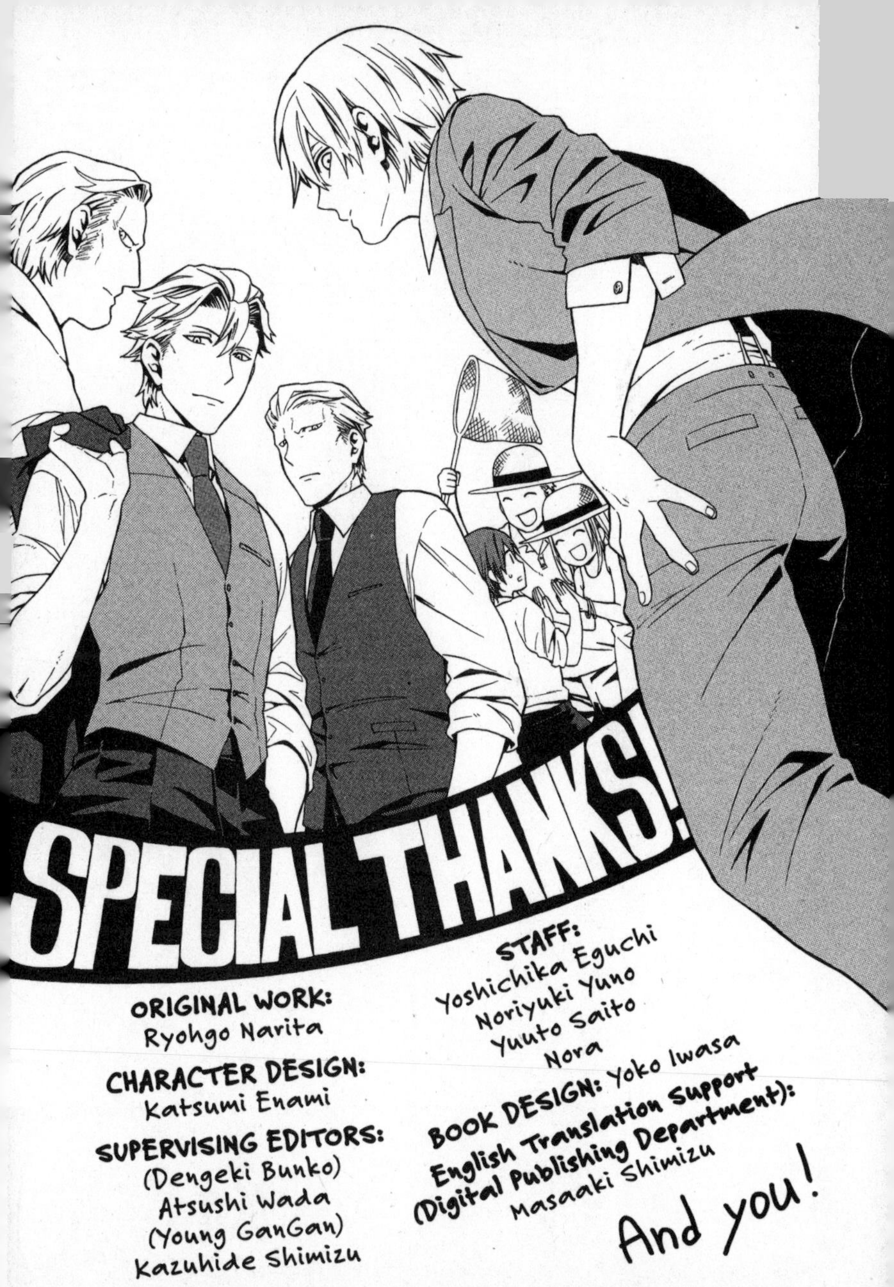
SPECIAL THANKS!

ORIGINAL WORK:
Ryohgo Narita

CHARACTER DESIGN:
Katsumi Enami

SUPERVISING EDITORS:
(Dengeki Bunko)
Atsushi Wada
(Young GanGan)
Kazuhide Shimizu

STAFF:
Yoshichika Eguchi
Noriyuki Yuno
Yuuto Saito
Nora

BOOK DESIGN: Yoko Iwasa

English Translation Support
(Digital Publishing Department):
Masaaki Shimizu

And you!

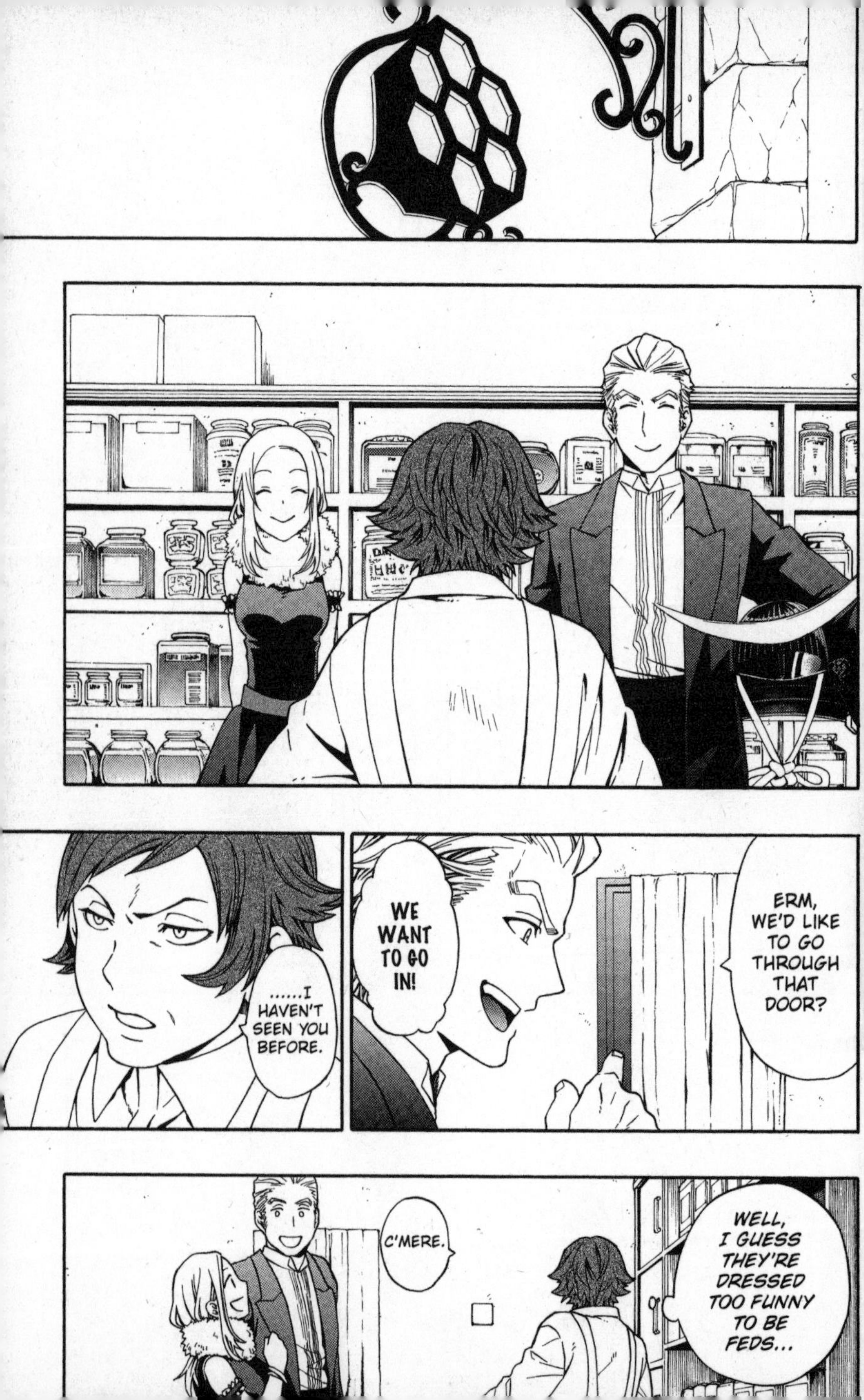
ERM, WE'D LIKE TO GO THROUGH THAT DOOR?
WE WANT TO GO IN!
......I HAVEN'T SEEN YOU BEFORE.
WELL, I GUESS THEY'RE DRESSED TOO FUNNY TO BE FEDS...
C'MERE.

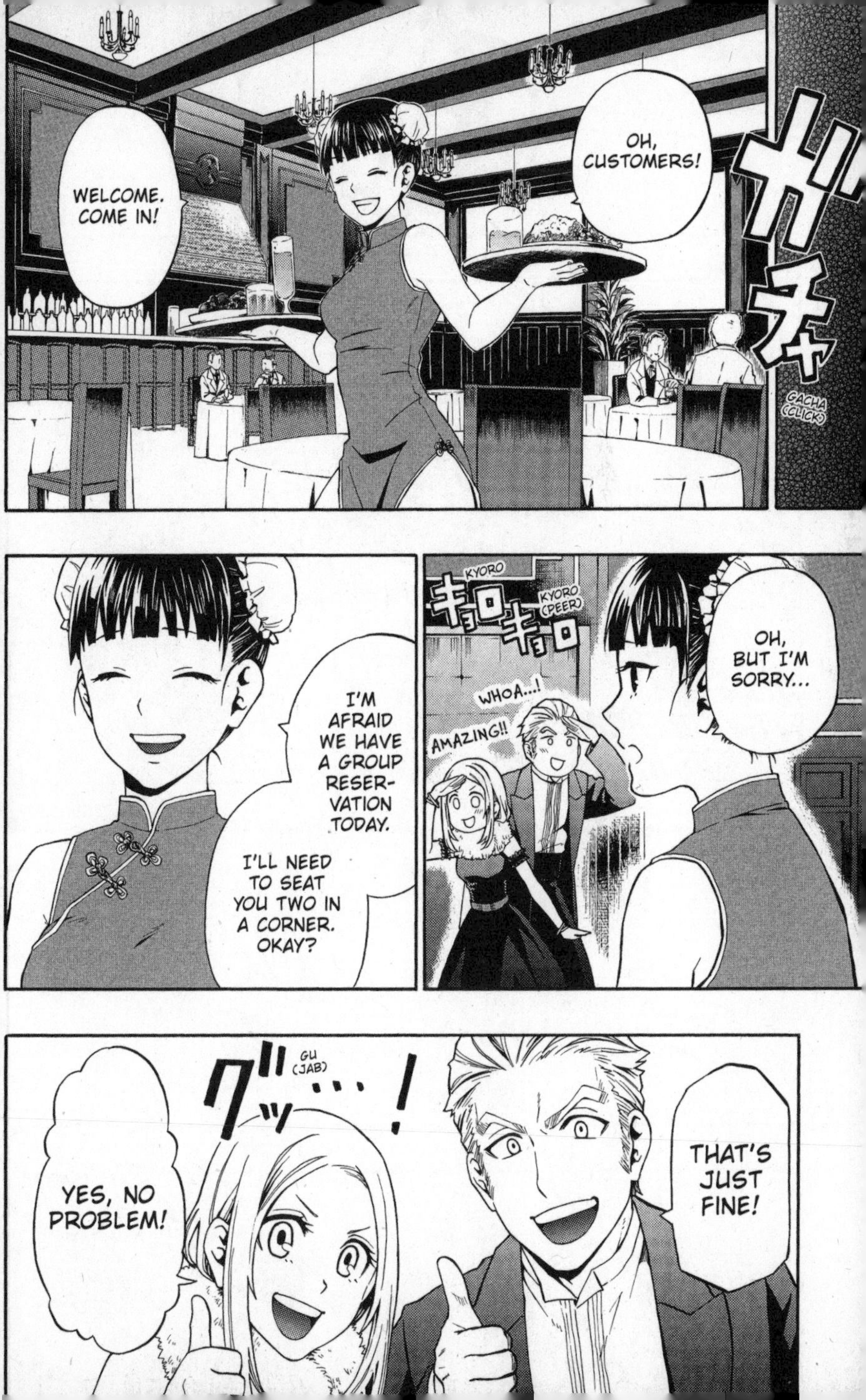
ガチャ
GACHA (CLICK)
OH, CUSTOMERS!
WELCOME. COME IN!
キョロキョロ
KYORO KYORO (PEER)
OH, BUT I'M SORRY...
WHOA...!
AMAZING!!
I'M AFRAID WE HAVE A GROUP RESER-VATION TODAY.
I'LL NEED TO SEAT YOU TWO IN A CORNER. OKAY?
THAT'S JUST FINE!
グッ…！
GU (JAB)
YES, NO PROBLEM!

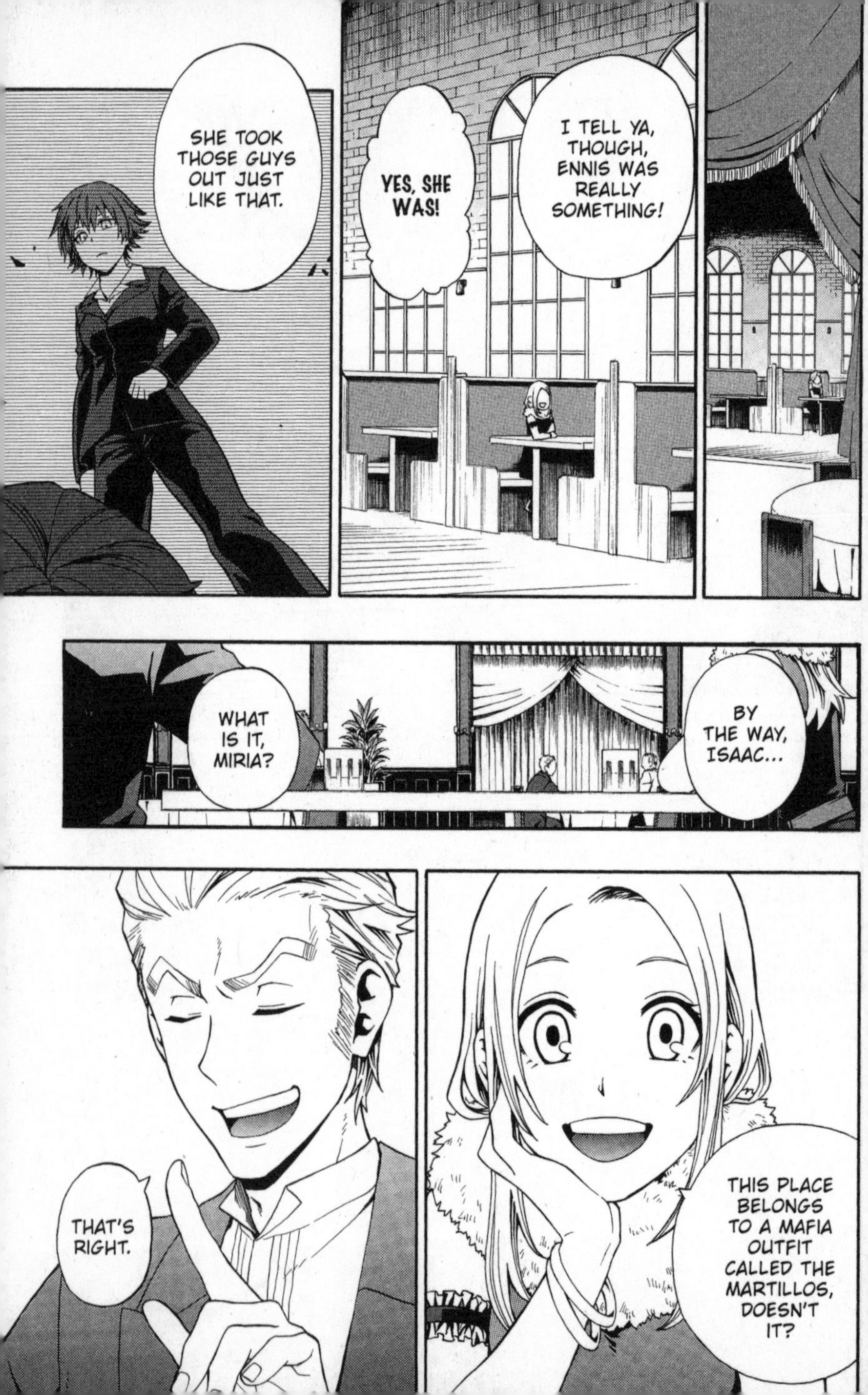
I TELL YA, THOUGH, ENNIS WAS REALLY SOMETHING!
YES, SHE WAS!
SHE TOOK THOSE GUYS OUT JUST LIKE THAT.
BY THE WAY, ISAAC...
WHAT IS IT, MIRIA?
THIS PLACE BELONGS TO A MAFIA OUTFIT CALLED THE MARTILLOS, DOESN'T IT?
THAT'S RIGHT.

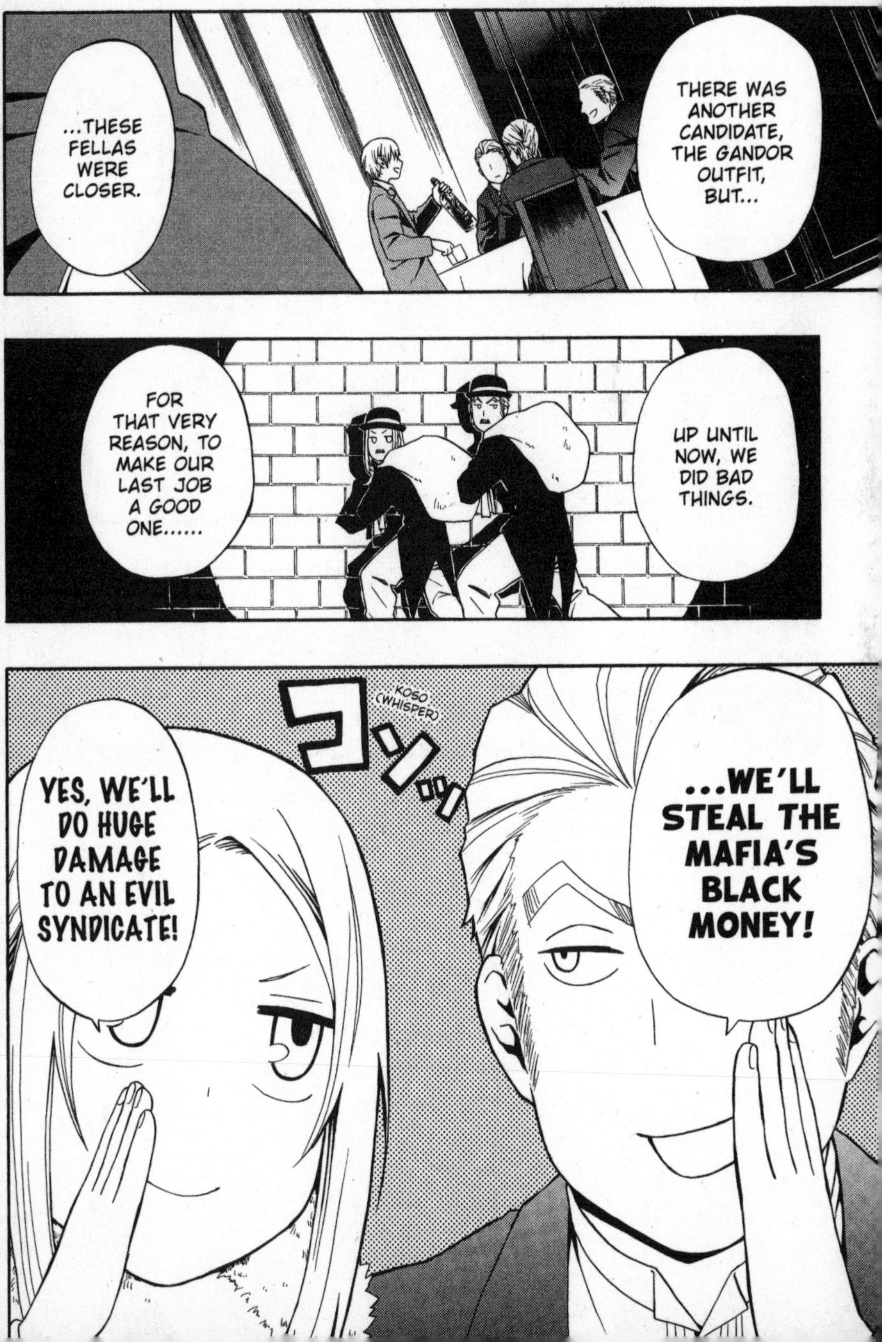
THERE WAS ANOTHER CANDIDATE, THE GANDOR OUTFIT, BUT...
...THESE FELLAS WERE CLOSER.
UP UNTIL NOW, WE DID BAD THINGS.
FOR THAT VERY REASON, TO MAKE OUR LAST JOB A GOOD ONE......
...WE'LL STEAL THE MAFIA'S BLACK MONEY!
KOSO (WHISPER)
コソッ
YES, WE'LL DO HUGE DAMAGE TO AN EVIL SYNDICATE!

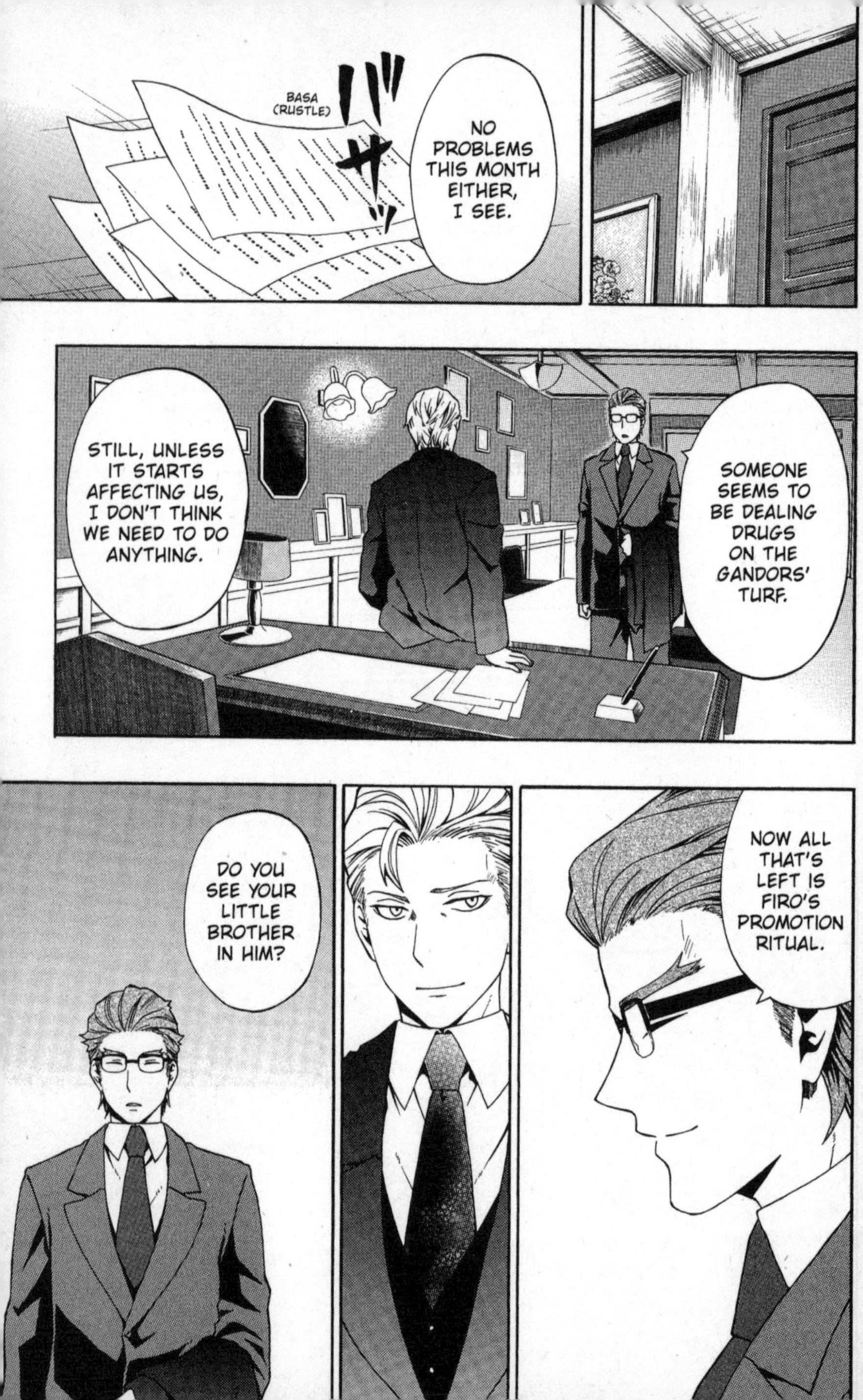
NO PROBLEMS THIS MONTH EITHER, I SEE.
BASA (RUSTLE)
SOMEONE SEEMS TO BE DEALING DRUGS ON THE GANDORS' TURF.
STILL, UNLESS IT STARTS AFFECTING US, I DON'T THINK WE NEED TO DO ANYTHING.
NOW ALL THAT'S LEFT IS FIRO'S PROMOTION RITUAL.
DO YOU SEE YOUR LITTLE BROTHER IN HIM?

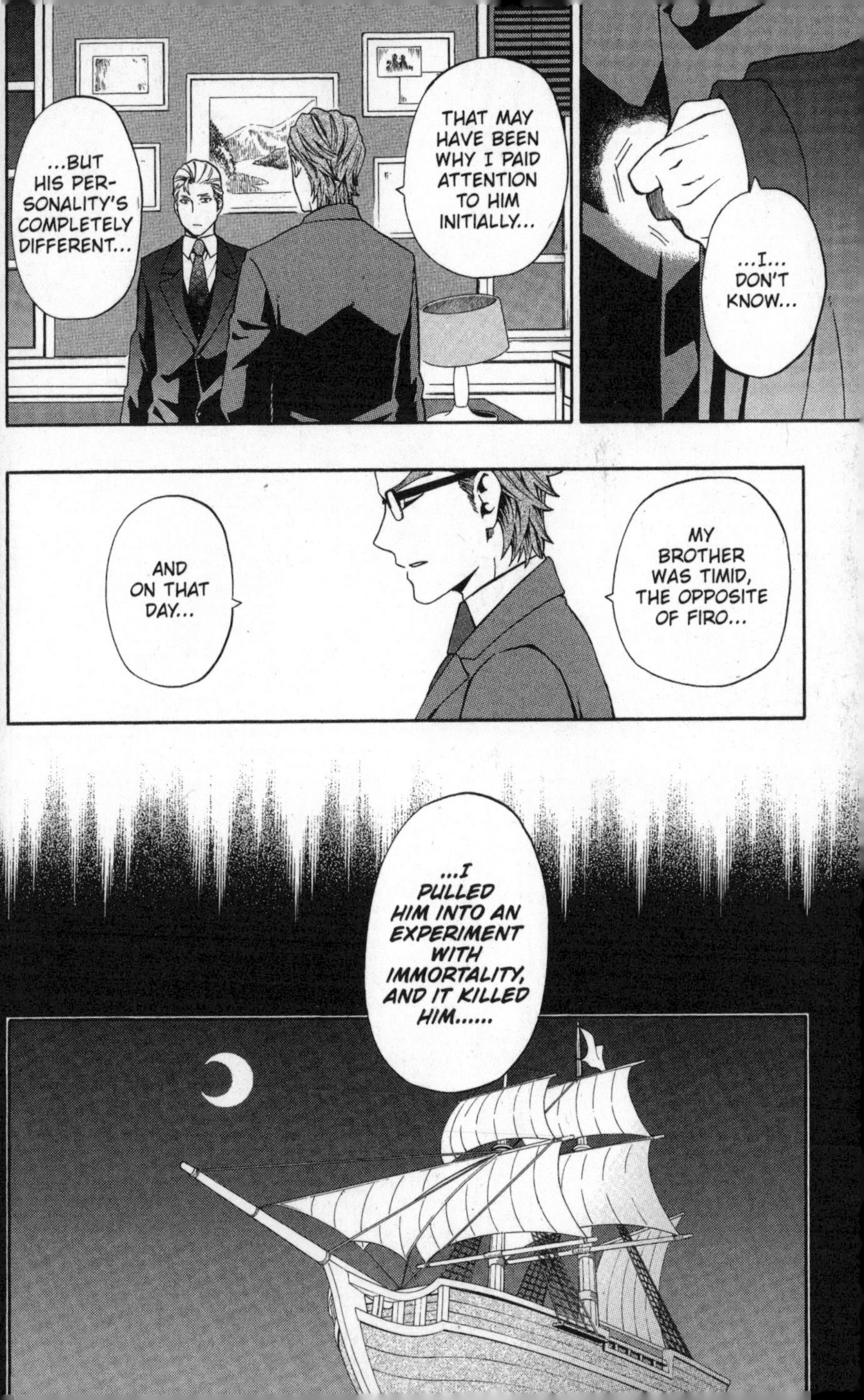
...I... DON'T KNOW...
THAT MAY HAVE BEEN WHY I PAID ATTENTION TO HIM INITIALLY...
...BUT HIS PER-SONALITY'S COMPLETELY DIFFERENT...
MY BROTHER WAS TIMID, THE OPPOSITE OF FIRO...
AND ON THAT DAY...
...I PULLED HIM INTO AN EXPERIMENT WITH IMMORTALITY, AND IT KILLED HIM......

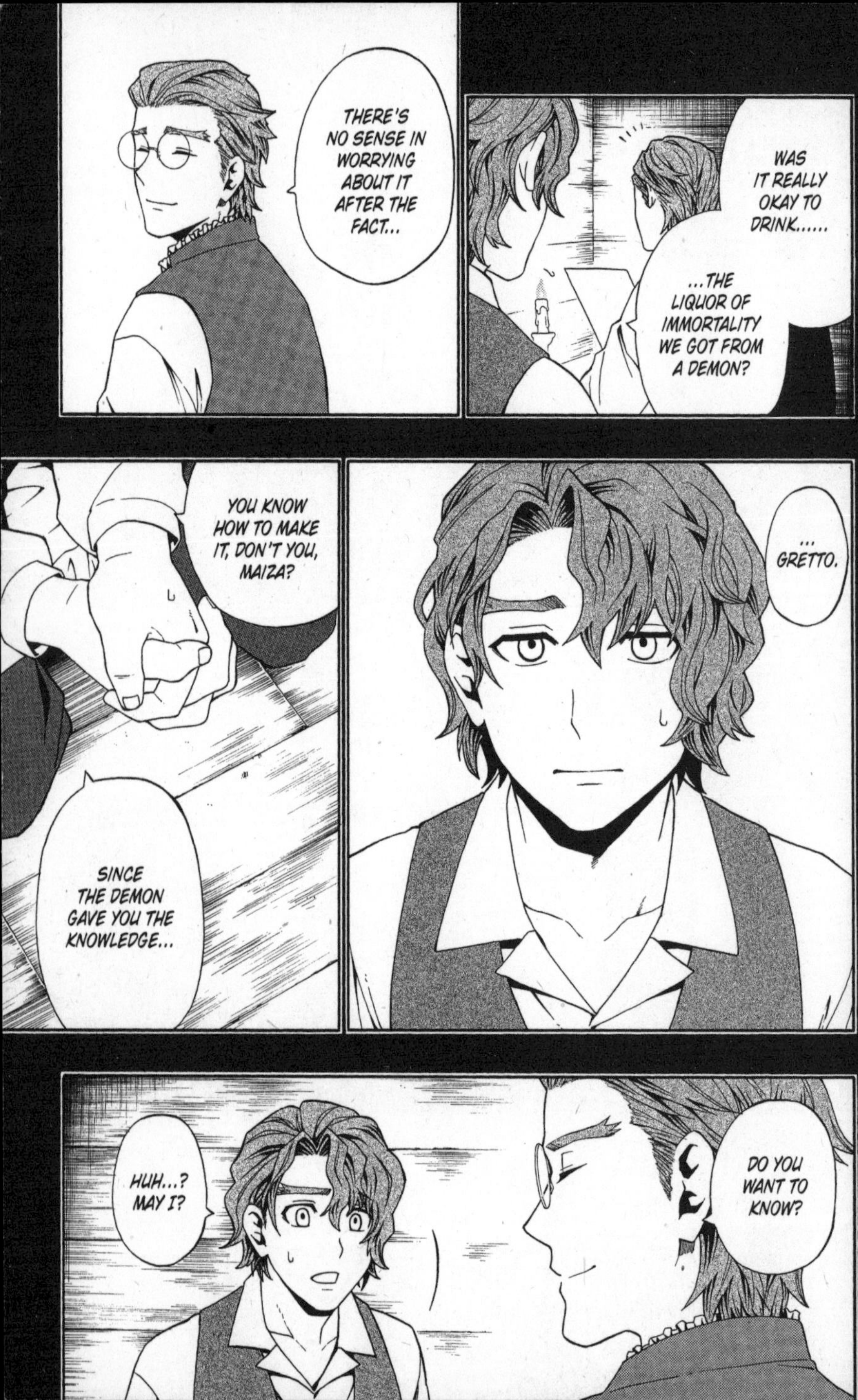
WAS IT REALLY OKAY TO DRINK......
...THE LIQUOR OF IMMORTALITY WE GOT FROM A DEMON?
THERE'S NO SENSE IN WORRYING ABOUT IT AFTER THE FACT...
... GRETTO.
YOU KNOW HOW TO MAKE IT, DON'T YOU, MAIZA?
SINCE THE DEMON GAVE YOU THE KNOWLEDGE...
DO YOU WANT TO KNOW?
HUH...? MAY I?

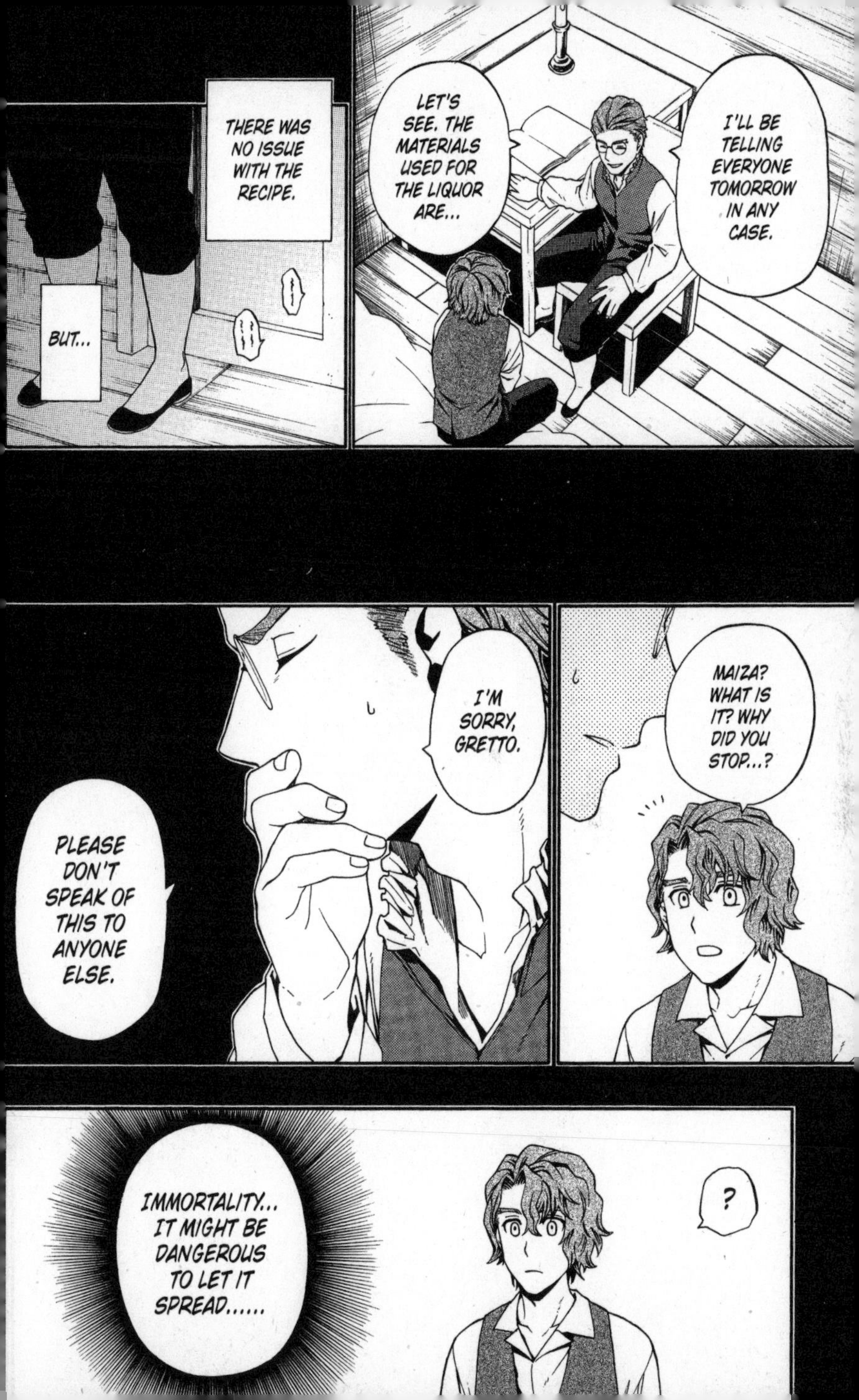

I'LL BE TELLING EVERYONE TOMORROW IN ANY CASE.
LET'S SEE. THE MATERIALS USED FOR THE LIQUOR ARE...
THERE WAS NO ISSUE WITH THE RECIPE.
BUT...
MAIZA? WHAT IS IT? WHY DID YOU STOP...?
I'M SORRY, GRETTO.
PLEASE DON'T SPEAK OF THIS TO ANYONE ELSE.
?
IMMORTALITY... IT MIGHT BE DANGEROUS TO LET IT SPREAD......

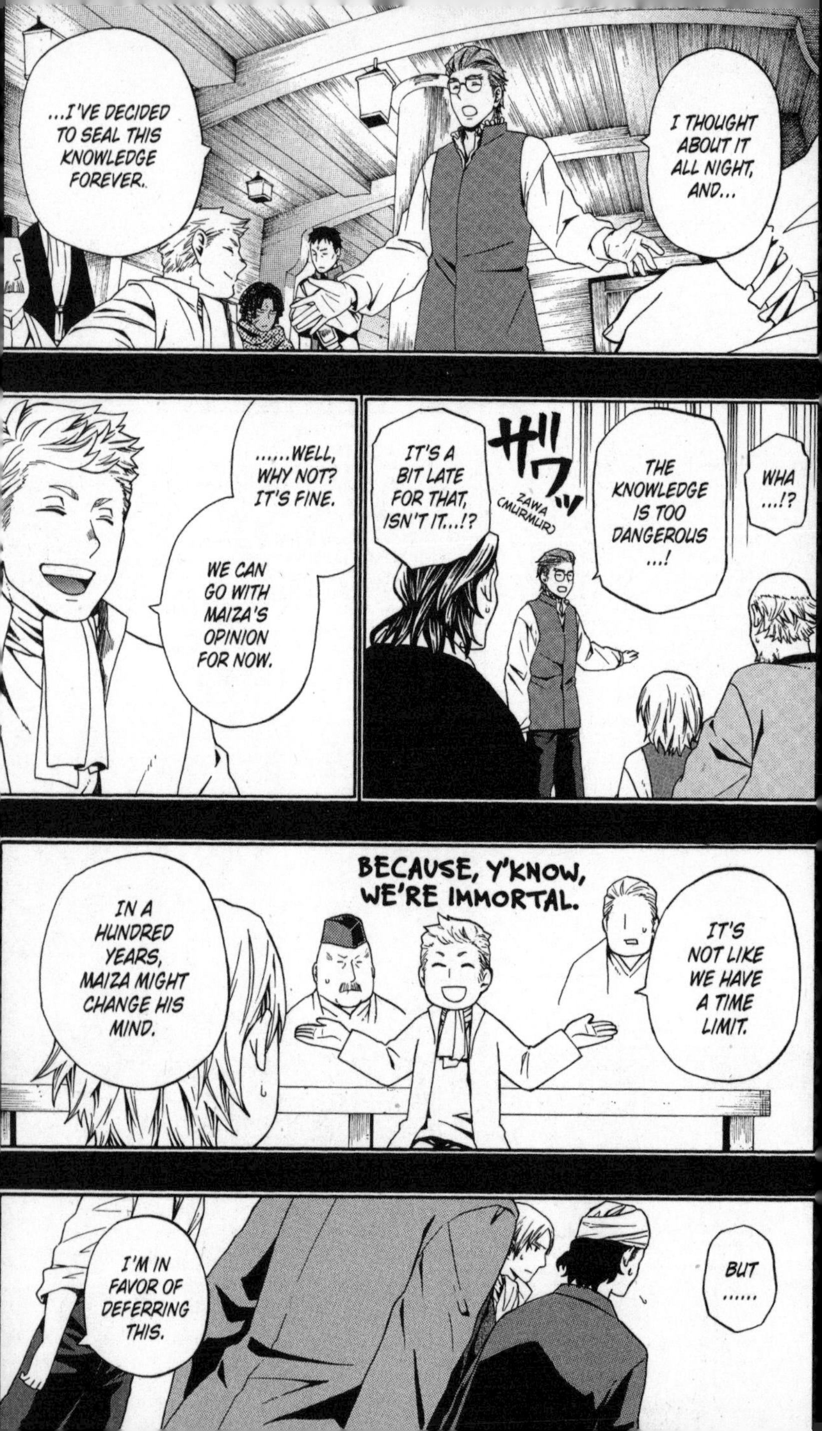
I THOUGHT ABOUT IT ALL NIGHT, AND...
...I'VE DECIDED TO SEAL THIS KNOWLEDGE FOREVER.
WHA ...!?
THE KNOWLEDGE IS TOO DANGEROUS ...!
ザワッ
ZAWA (MURMUR)
IT'S A BIT LATE FOR THAT, ISN'T IT...!?
......WELL, WHY NOT? IT'S FINE.
WE CAN GO WITH MAIZA'S OPINION FOR NOW.
IT'S NOT LIKE WE HAVE A TIME LIMIT.
BECAUSE, Y'KNOW, WE'RE IMMORTAL.
IN A HUNDRED YEARS, MAIZA MIGHT CHANGE HIS MIND.
BUT ......
I'M IN FAVOR OF DEFERRING THIS.

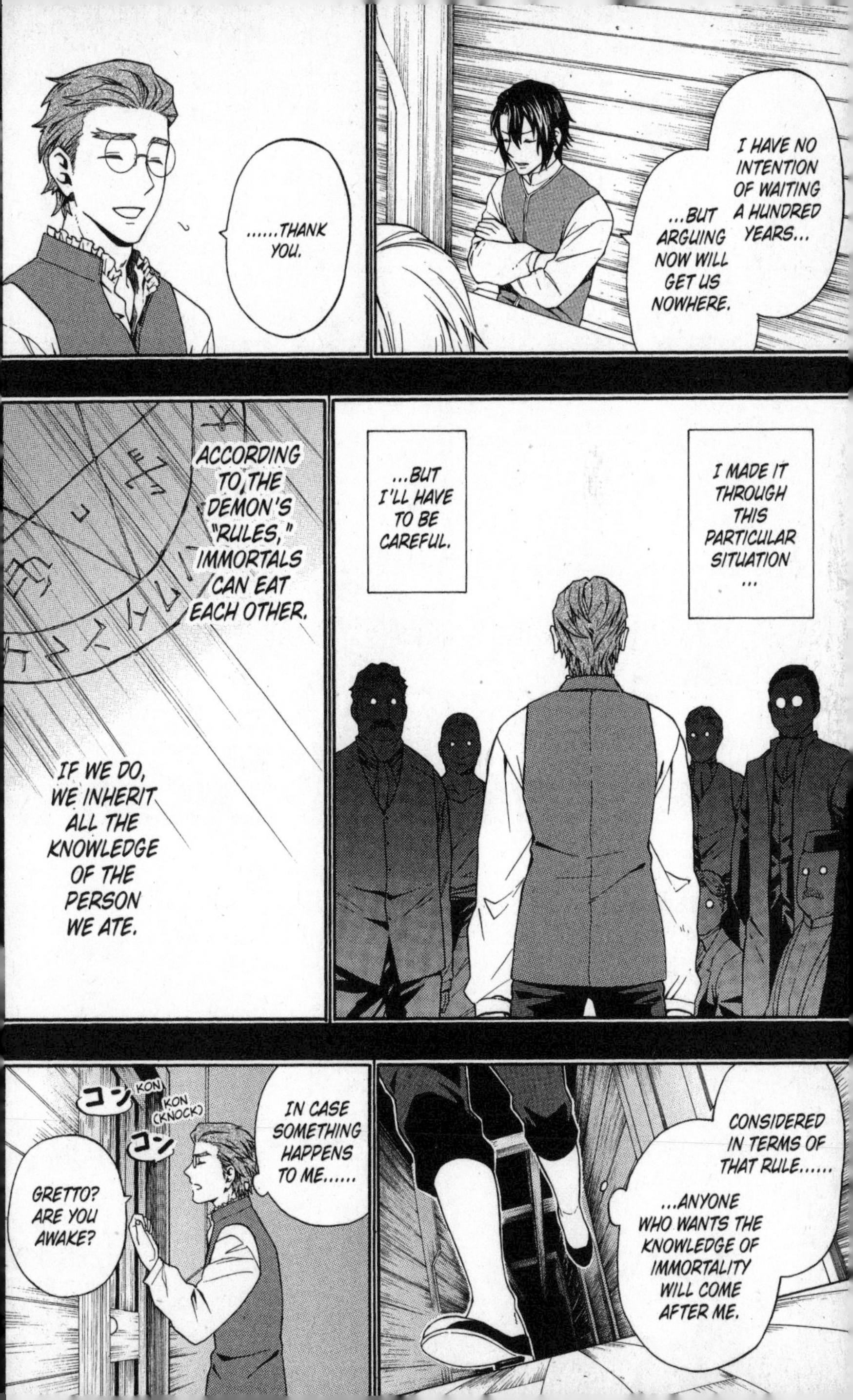
I HAVE NO INTENTION OF WAITING A HUNDRED YEARS...
...BUT ARGUING NOW WILL GET US NOWHERE.
......THANK YOU.
I MADE IT THROUGH THIS PARTICULAR SITUATION ...
...BUT I'LL HAVE TO BE CAREFUL.
ACCORDING TO THE DEMON'S "RULES," IMMORTALS CAN EAT EACH OTHER.
IF WE DO, WE INHERIT ALL THE KNOWLEDGE OF THE PERSON WE ATE.
CONSIDERED IN TERMS OF THAT RULE......
...ANYONE WHO WANTS THE KNOWLEDGE OF IMMORTALITY WILL COME AFTER ME.
IN CASE SOMETHING HAPPENS TO ME......
コン KON
コン KON (KNOCK)
GRETTO? ARE YOU AWAKE?

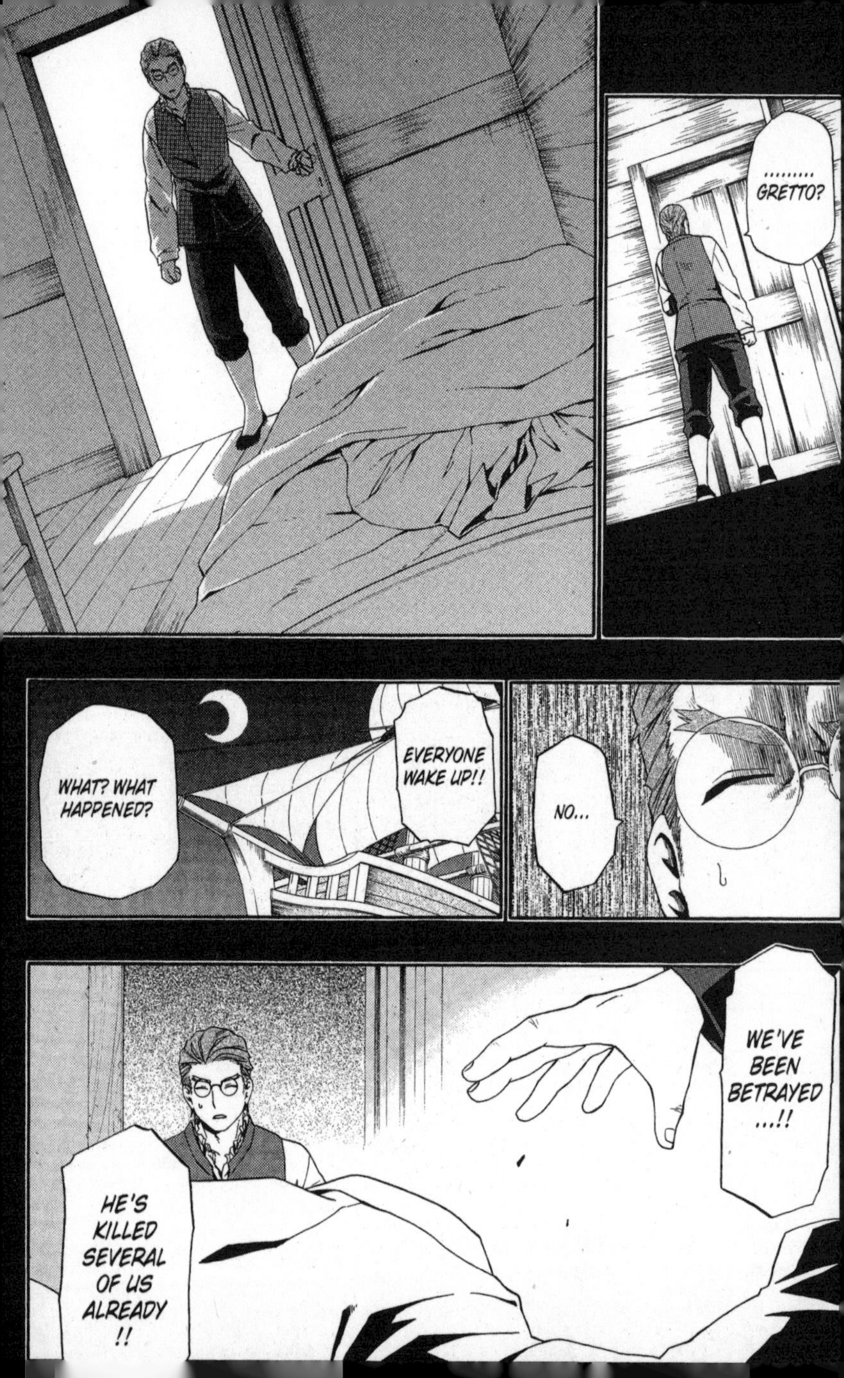
....
GRETTO?
NO...
EVERYONE WAKE UP!!
WHAT? WHAT HAPPENED?
WE'VE BEEN BETRAYED...!!
HE'S KILLED SEVERAL OF US ALREADY!!

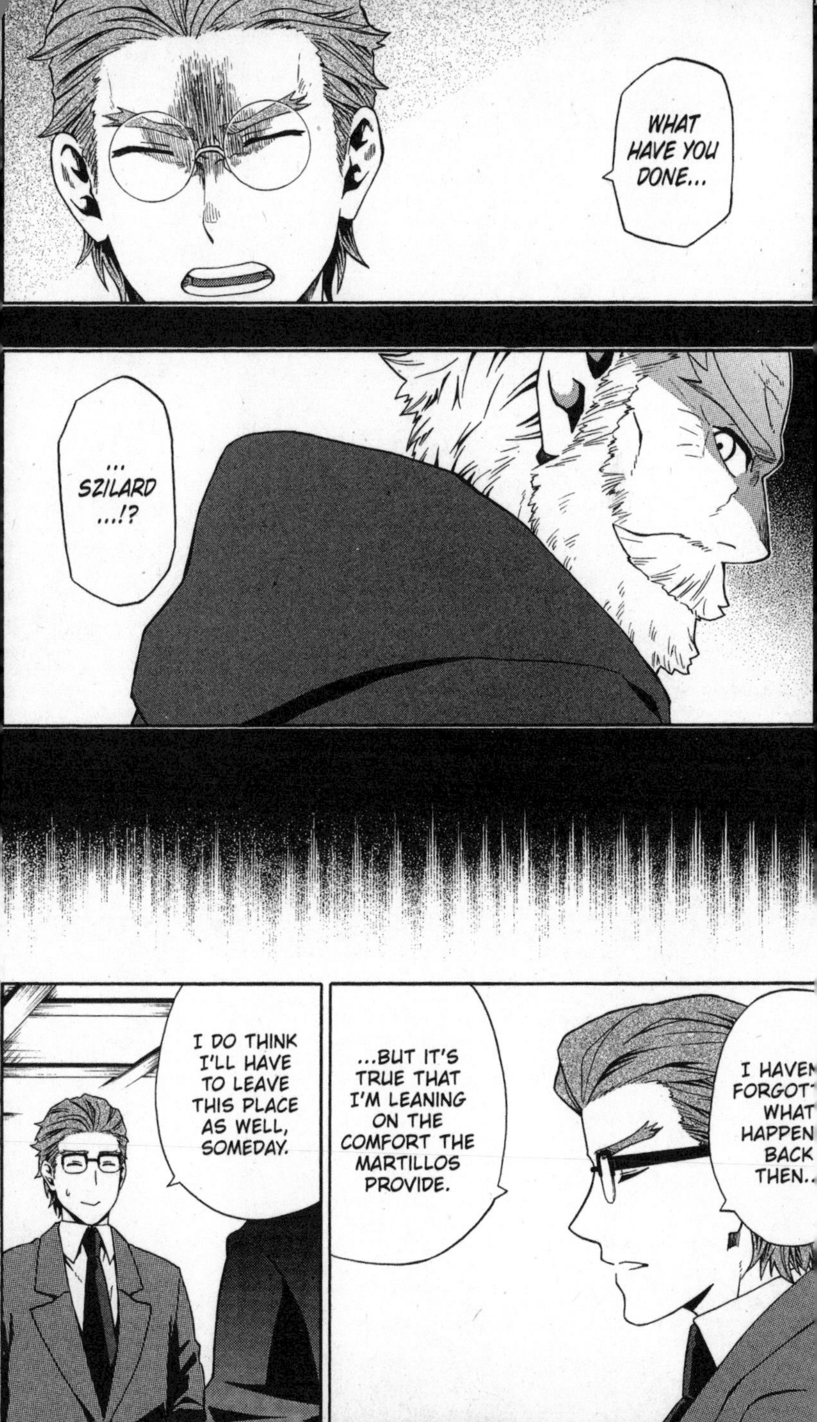
WHAT HAVE YOU DONE...
... SZILARD ...!?
I HAVEN FORGOTT WHAT HAPPEN BACK THEN..
...BUT IT'S TRUE THAT I'M LEANING ON THE COMFORT THE MARTILLOS PROVIDE.
I DO THINK I'LL HAVE TO LEAVE THIS PLACE AS WELL, SOMEDAY.

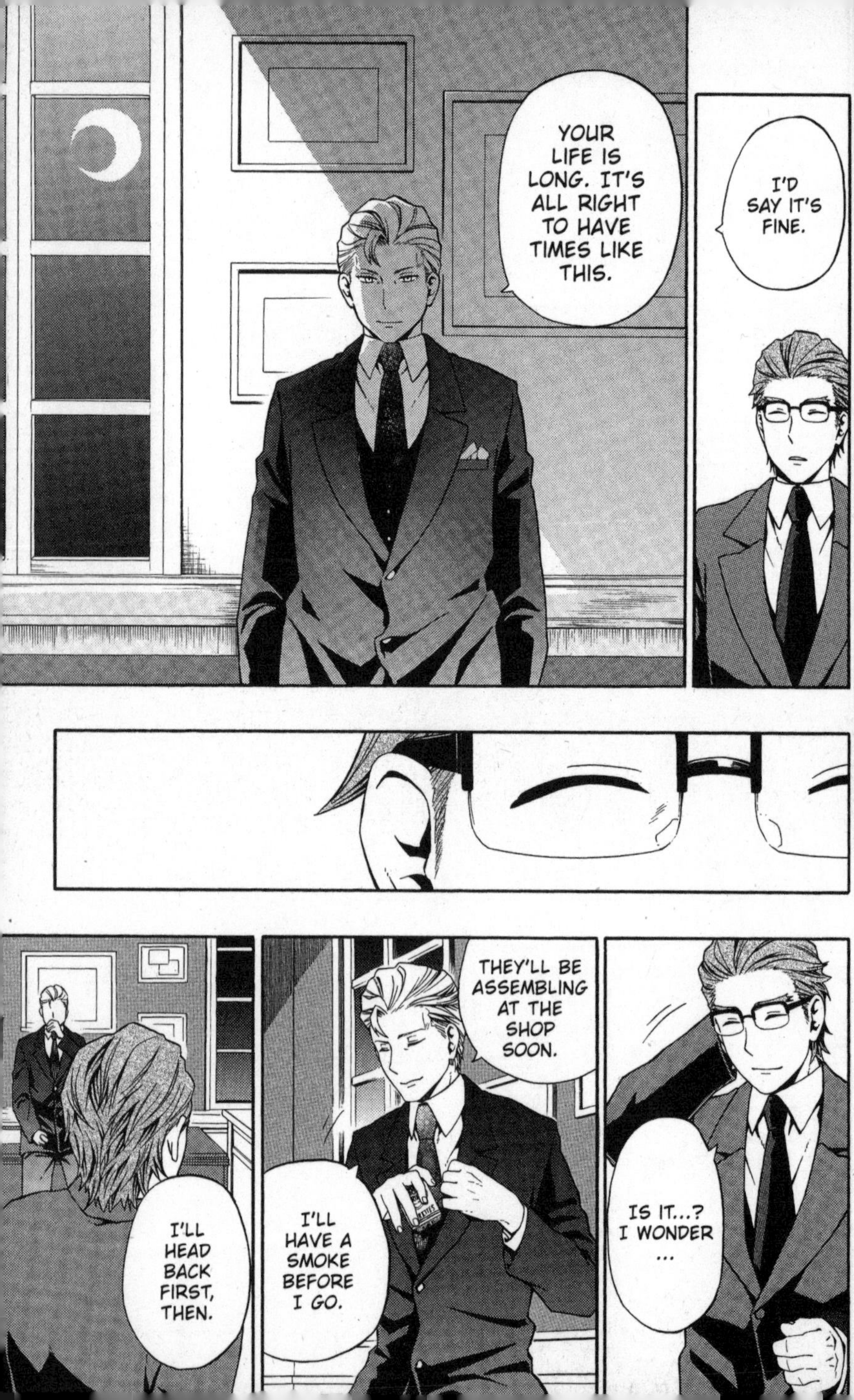
I'D SAY IT'S FINE.
YOUR LIFE IS LONG. IT'S ALL RIGHT TO HAVE TIMES LIKE THIS.
IS IT...? I WONDER ...
THEY'LL BE ASSEMBLING AT THE SHOP SOON.
I'LL HAVE A SMOKE BEFORE I GO.
I'LL HEAD BACK FIRST, THEN.

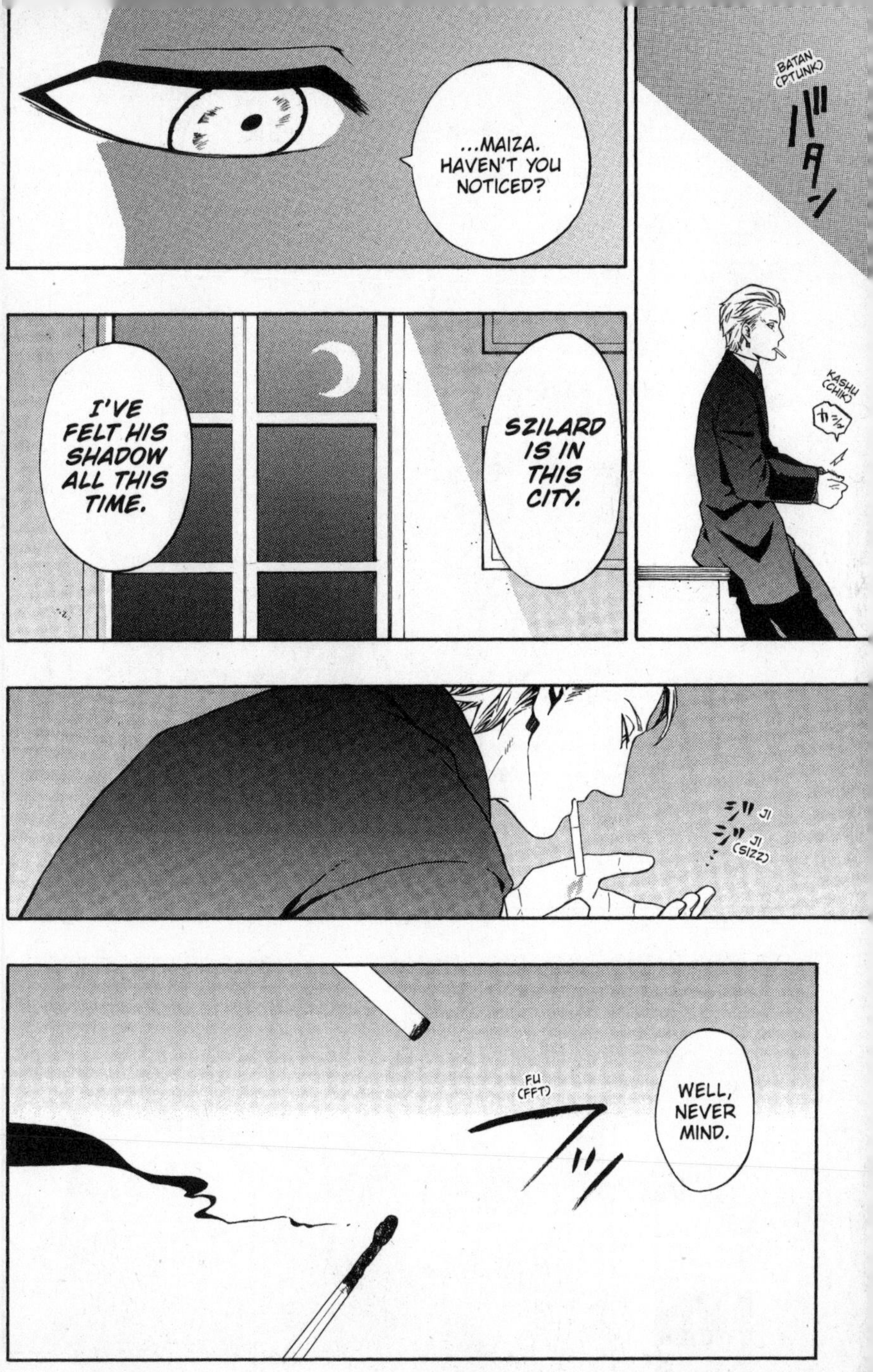
BATAN (PTUNK)
KASHU (CHIK)
...MAIZA. HAVEN'T YOU NOTICED?
SZILARD IS IN THIS CITY.
I'VE FELT HIS SHADOW ALL THIS TIME.
JI JI (SIZZ)
WELL, NEVER MIND.
FU (FFT)

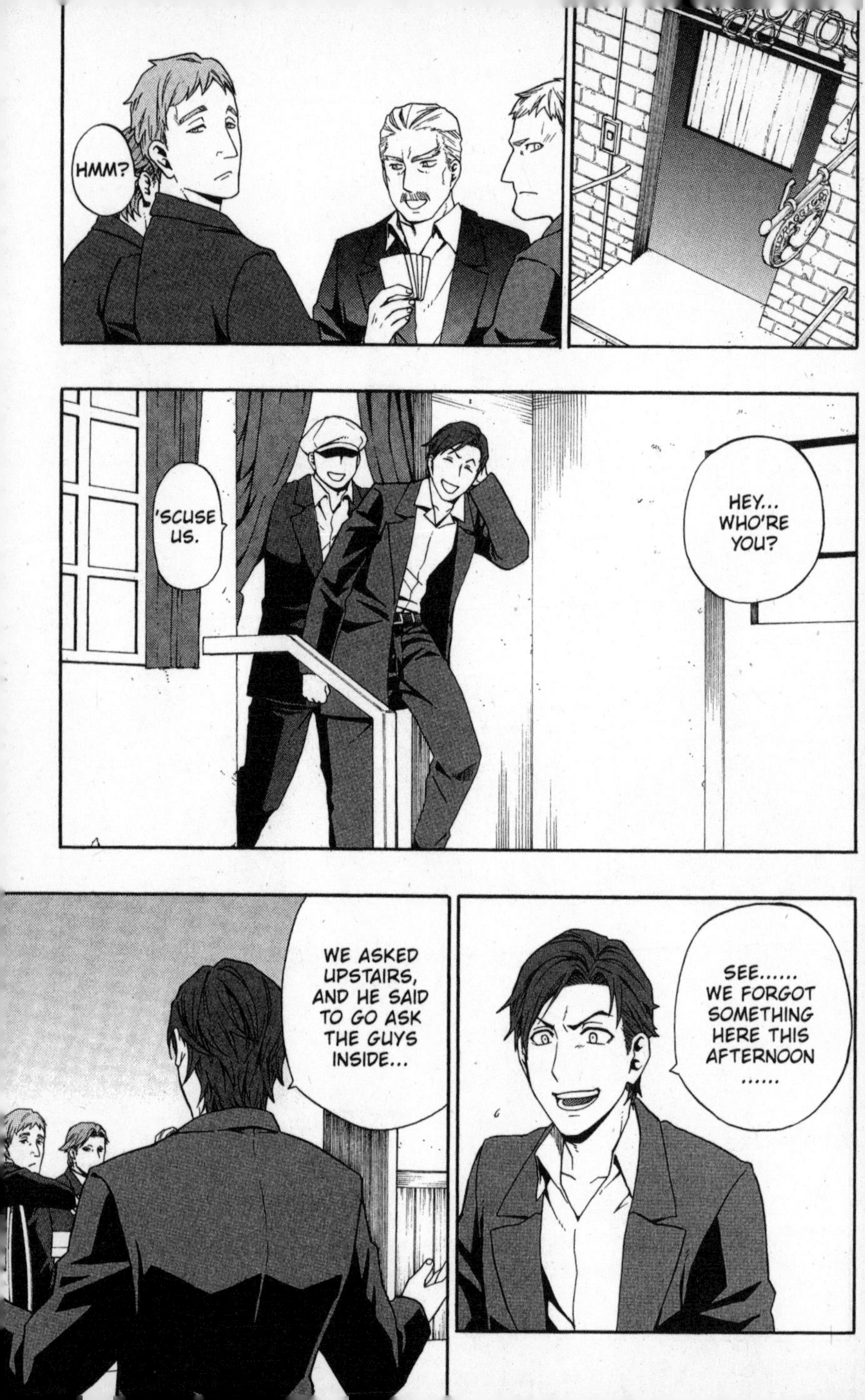
HMM?
HEY... WHO'RE YOU?
'SCUSE US.
SEE...... WE FORGOT SOMETHING HERE THIS AFTERNOON ......
WE ASKED UPSTAIRS, AND HE SAID TO GO ASK THE GUYS INSIDE...

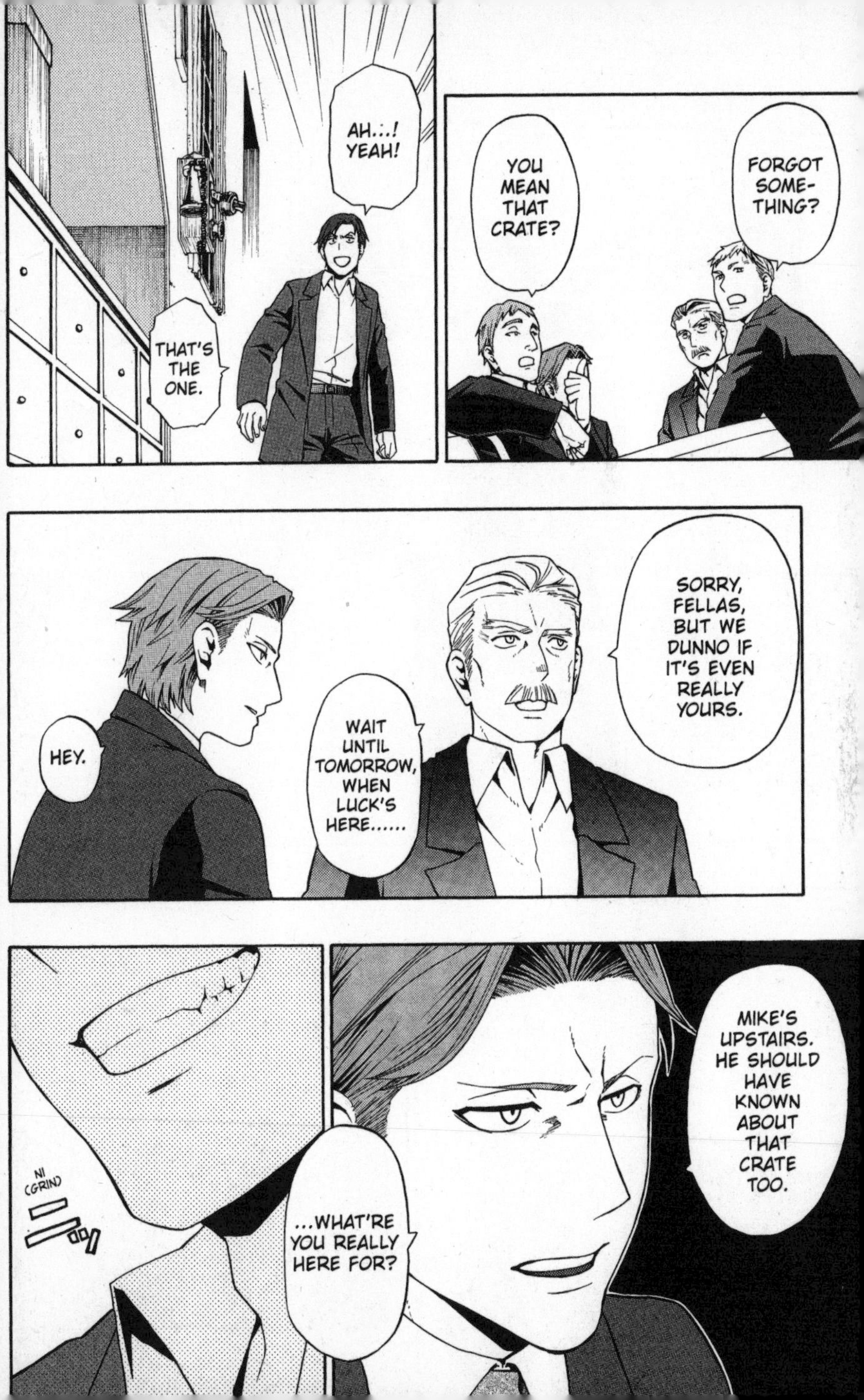
FORGOT SOMETHING?
YOU MEAN THAT CRATE?
AH...! YEAH!
THAT'S THE ONE.
SORRY, FELLAS, BUT WE DUNNO IF IT'S EVEN REALLY YOURS.
WAIT UNTIL TOMORROW, WHEN LUCK'S HERE......
HEY.
MIKE'S UPSTAIRS. HE SHOULD HAVE KNOWN ABOUT THAT CRATE TOO.
...WHAT'RE YOU REALLY HERE FOR?
NI (GRIN)

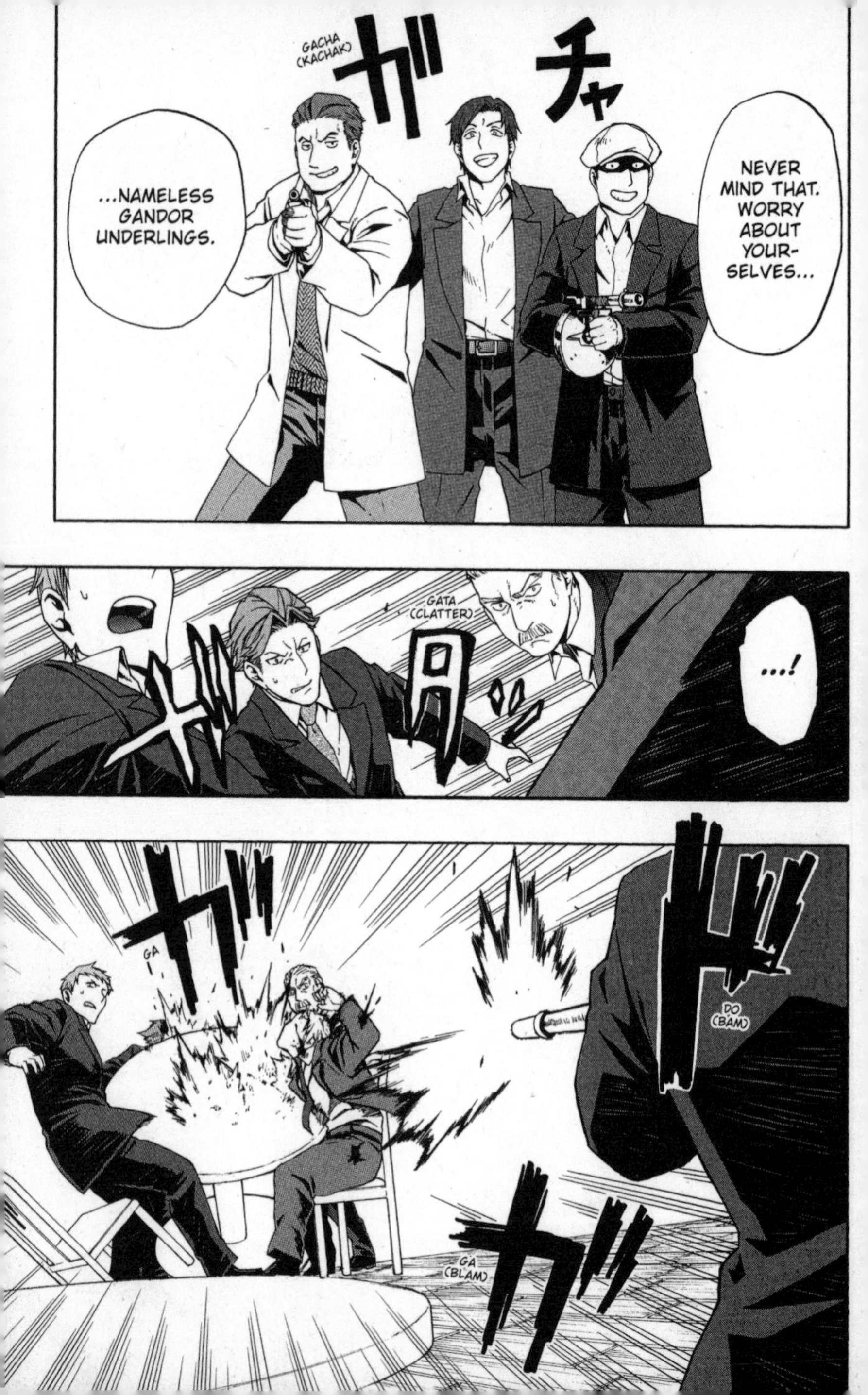
GACHA (KACHAK)
NEVER MIND THAT. WORRY ABOUT YOUR-SELVES...
...NAMELESS GANDOR UNDERLINGS.
...!
GATA (CLATTER)
DO (BAM)
GA
GA (BLAM)

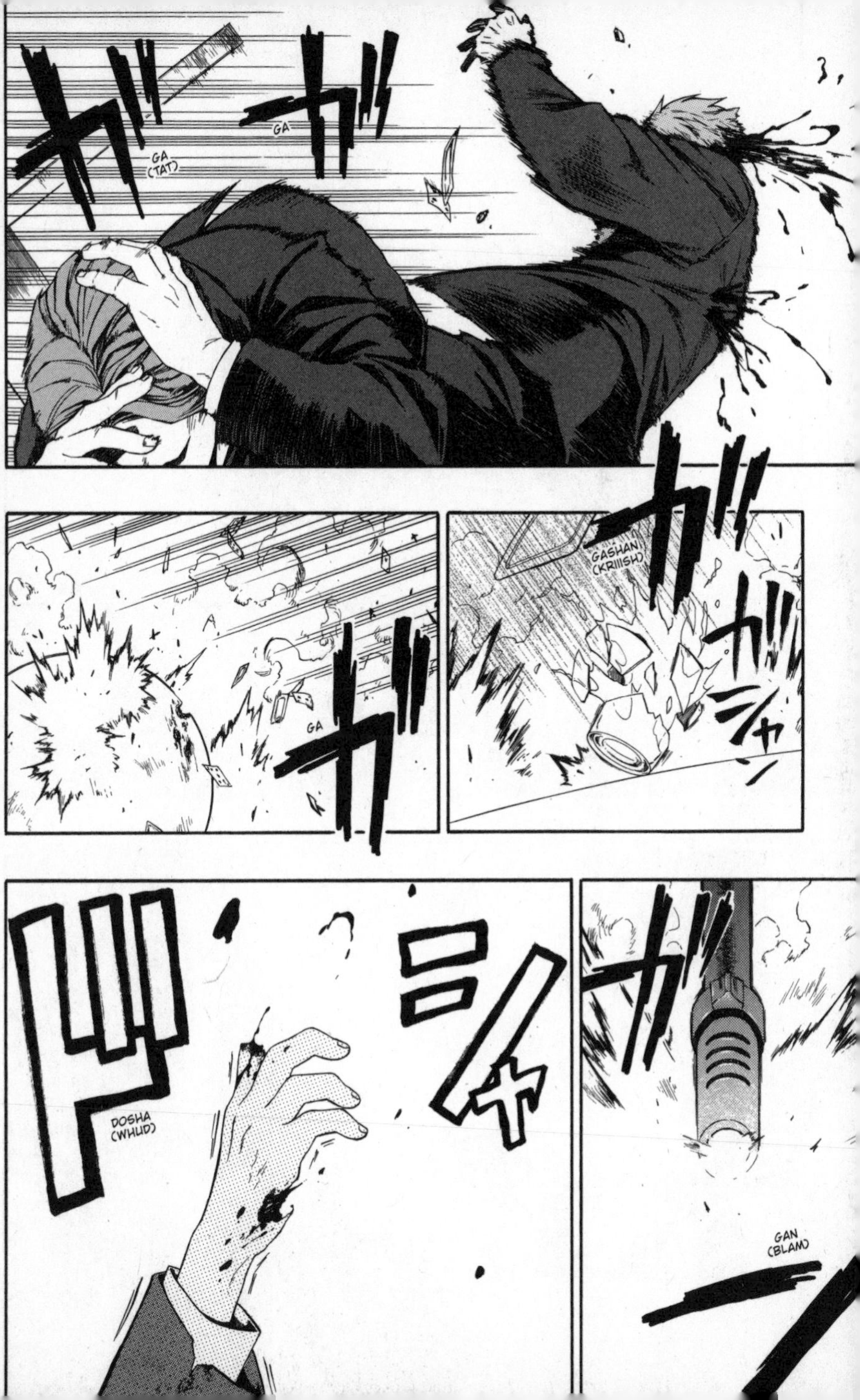
GA
GA (TAT)
GASHAN (KRIIISH)
GA
GAN (BLAM)
DOSHA (WHUD)

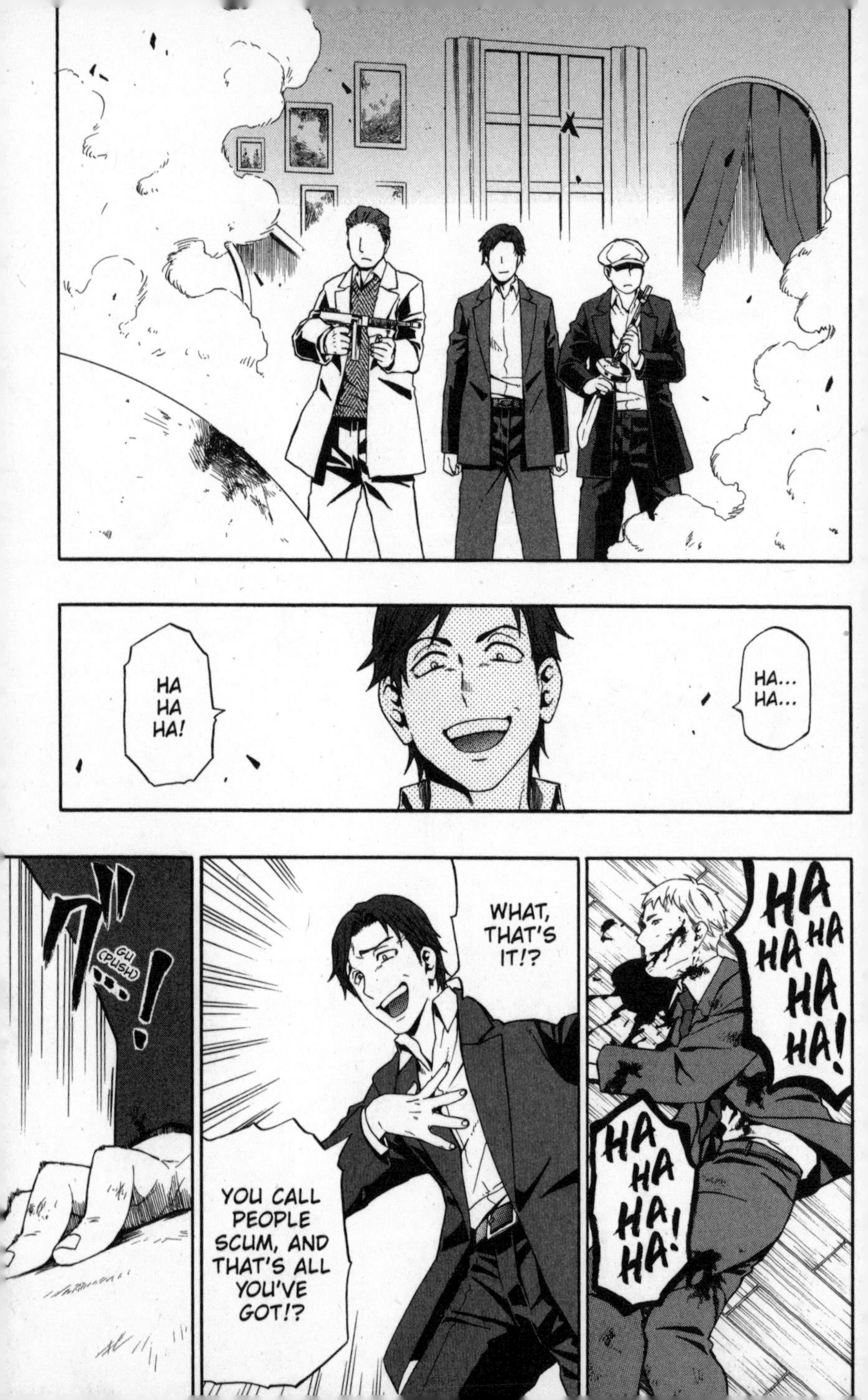
HA... HA...
HA HA HA!
HA HA HA HA HA HA HA!
HA HA HA HA! HA!
WHAT, THAT'S IT!?
YOU CALL PEOPLE SCUM, AND THAT'S ALL YOU'VE GOT!?
GU (PUSH)

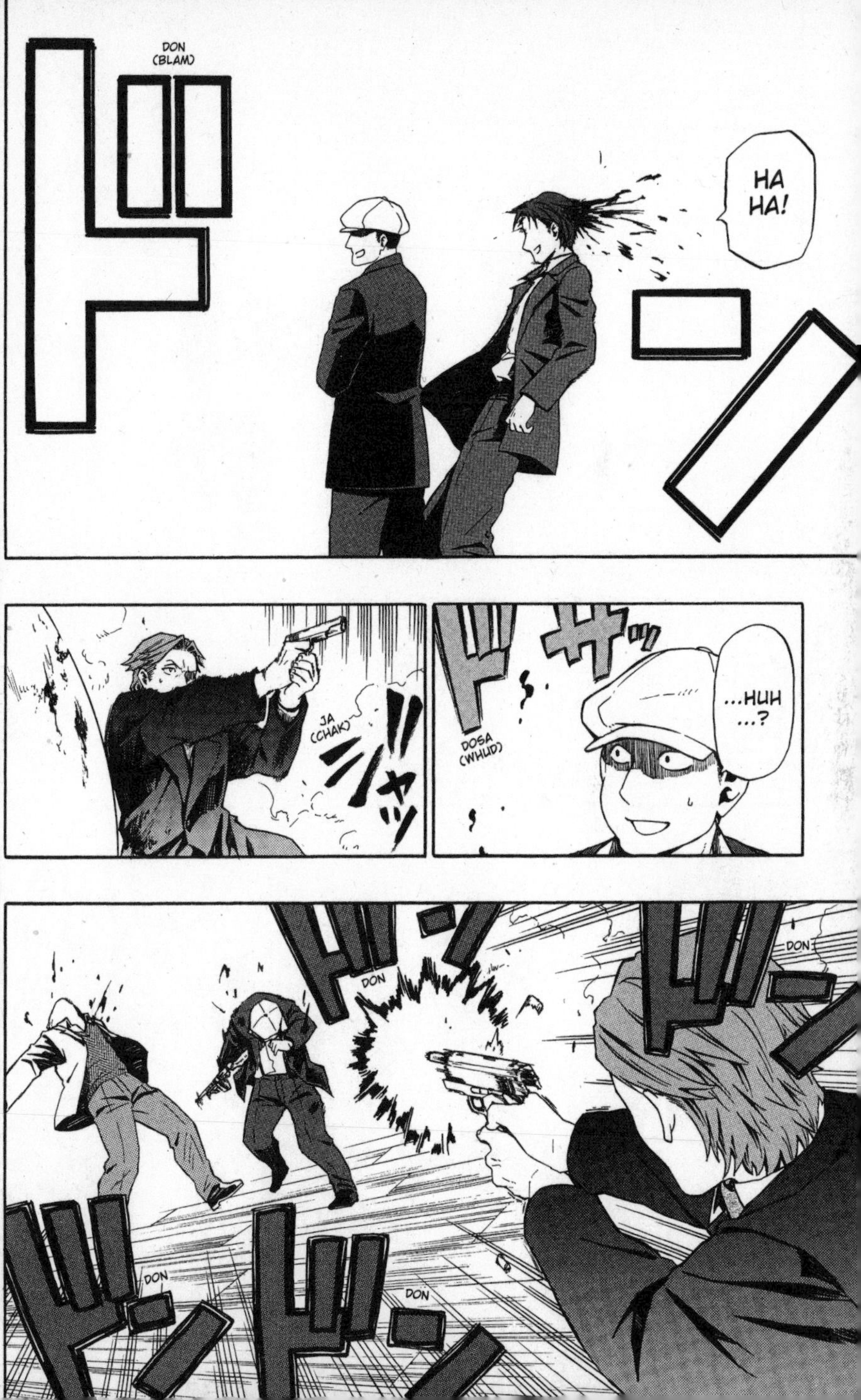
HA HA!
DON (BLAM)
...HUH ...?
DOSA (WHUD)
JA (CHAK)
DON
DON
DON
DON

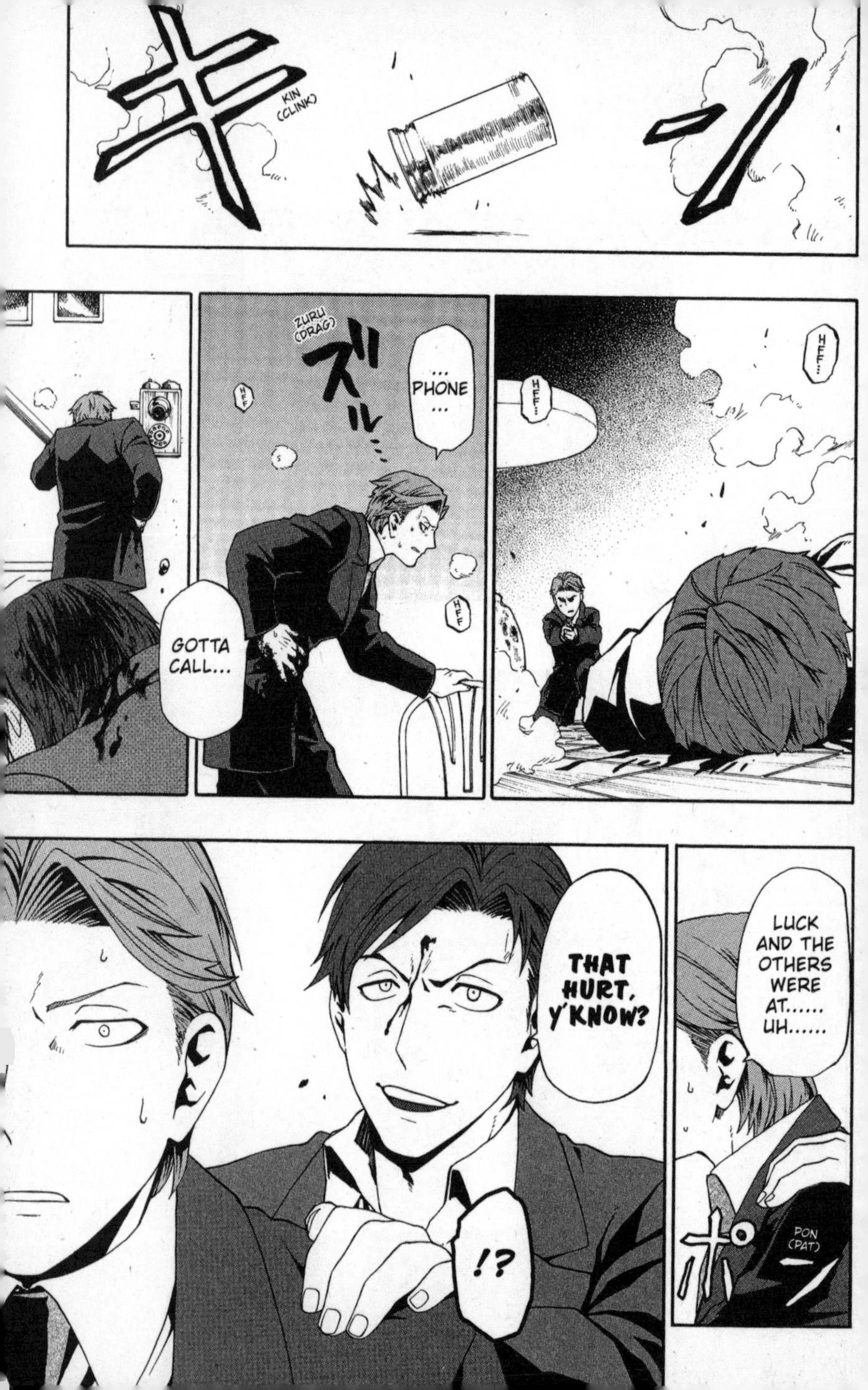
KIN (CLINK)
HFF...
HFF...
...PHONE...
ZURU (DRAG)
HFF
HFF
GOTTA CALL...
LUCK AND THE OTHERS WERE AT...... UH......
PON (PAT)
THAT HURT, Y'KNOW?
!?

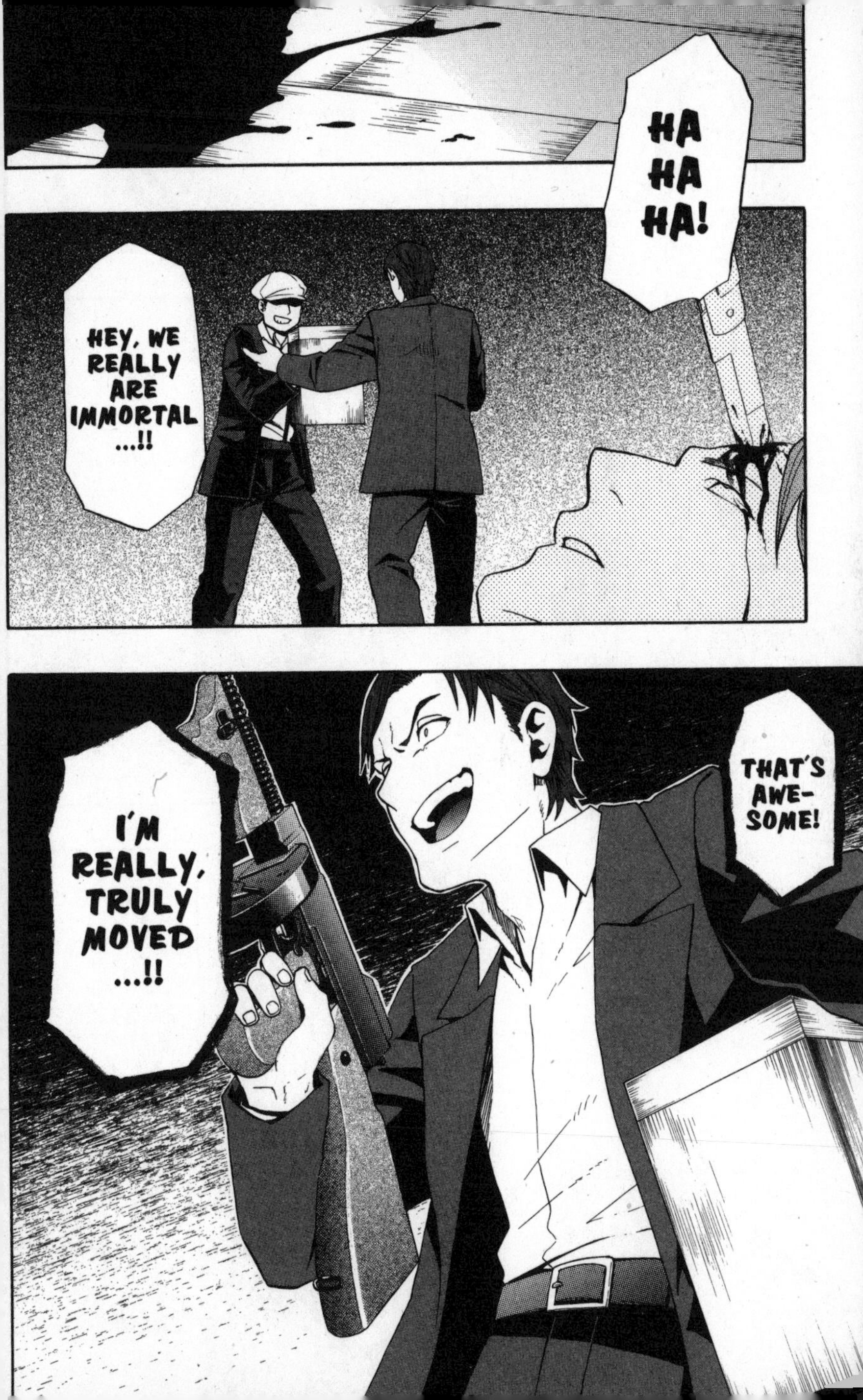
HA HA HA!
HEY, WE REALLY ARE IMMORTAL ...!!
THAT'S AWE-SOME!
I'M REALLY, TRULY MOVED ...!!

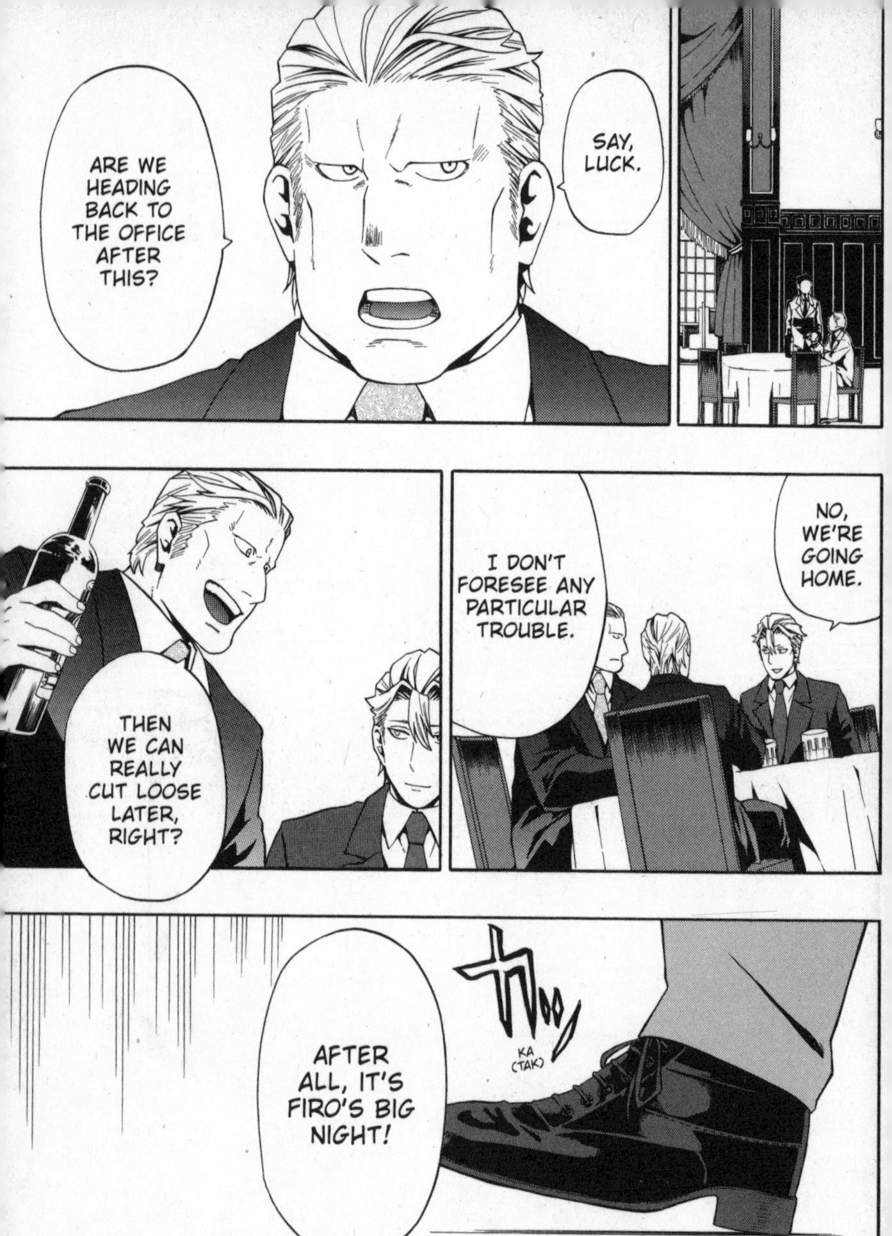
SAY, LUCK.
ARE WE HEADING BACK TO THE OFFICE AFTER THIS?
NO, WE'RE GOING HOME.
I DON'T FORESEE ANY PARTICULAR TROUBLE.
THEN WE CAN REALLY CUT LOOSE LATER, RIGHT?
KA (TAK)
AFTER ALL, IT'S FIRO'S BIG NIGHT!

...AND THE STAGE WAS SET.

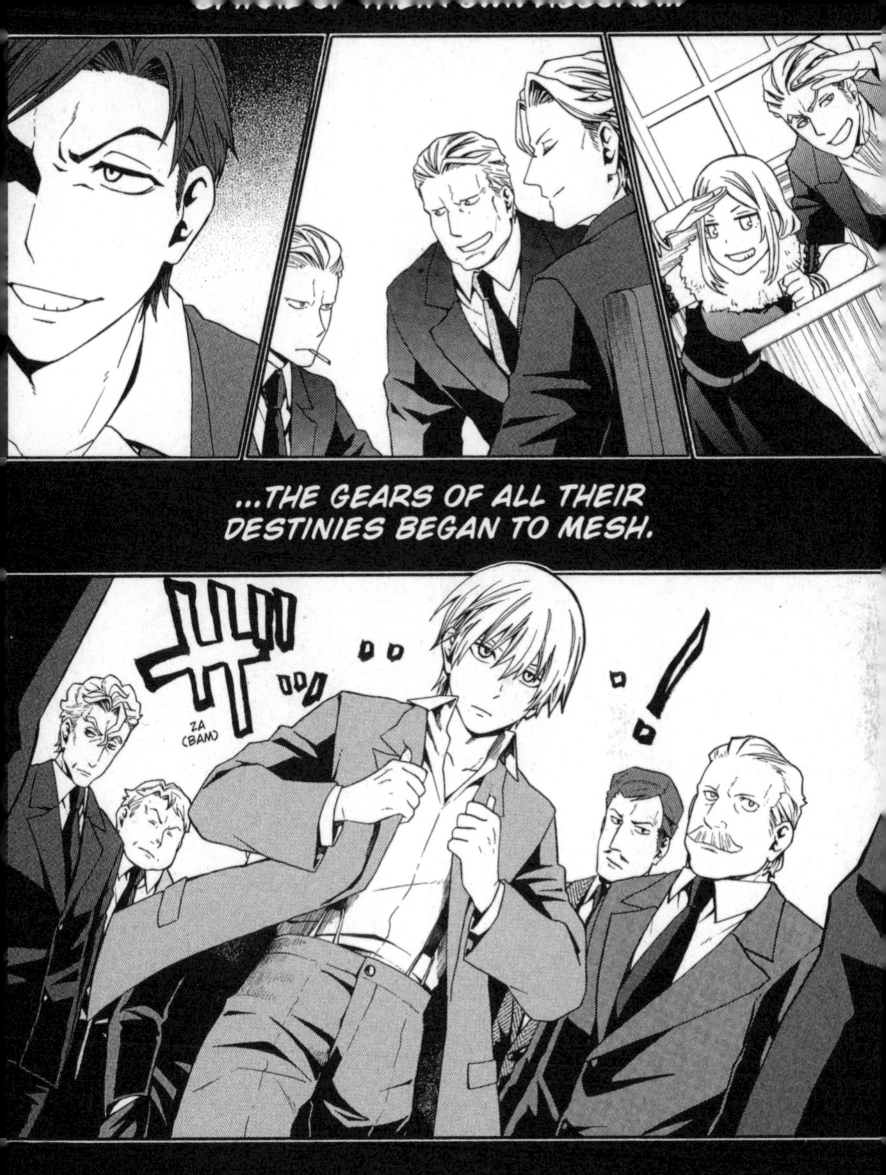
...THE GEARS OF ALL THEIR DESTINIES BEGAN TO MESH.
ZA (BAM)
AND NOW THE CRAZY RUCKUS REALLY BEGINS.

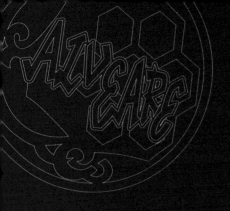

NEXT
[BACCANO!]3
————1930 DAY2
ROLLIN' ROLLIN'
ROLLIN' ROLLIN'!!

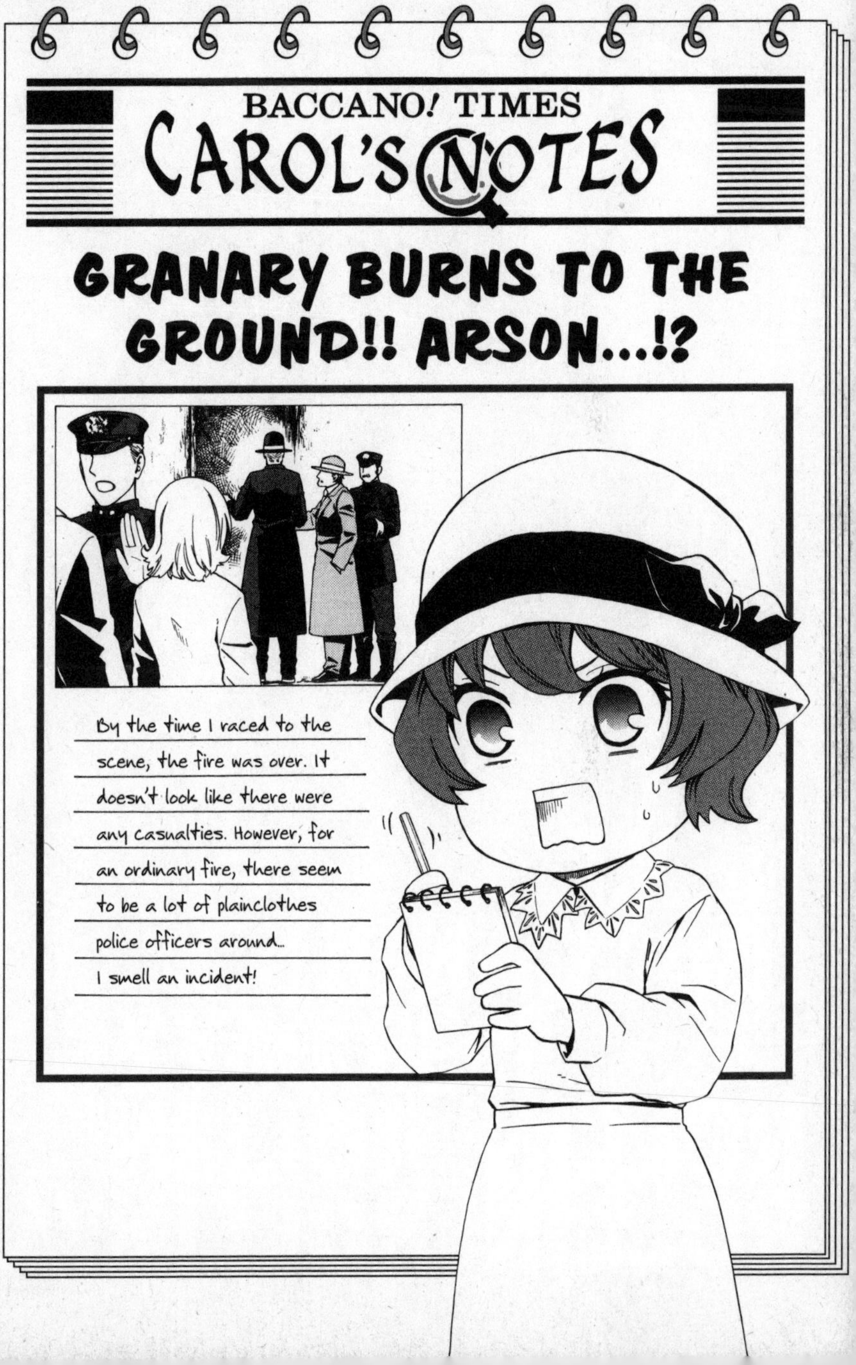
BACCANO! TIMES
CAROL'S NOTES
GRANARY BURNS TO THE GROUND!! ARSON...!?
By the time I raced to the scene, the fire was over. It doesn't look like there were any casualties. However, for an ordinary fire, there seem to be a lot of plainclothes police officers around...
I smell an incident!

Vol. 2

BACCANO!

Original Story
Ryohgo Narita
Art
Shinta Fujimoto
Character Design
Katsumi Enami

Since 1930

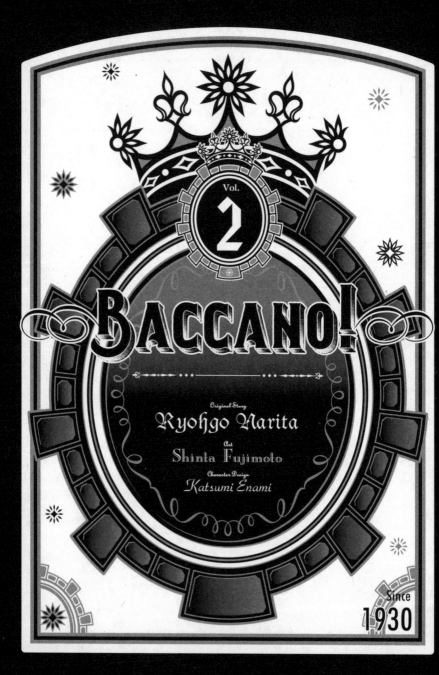

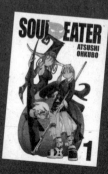

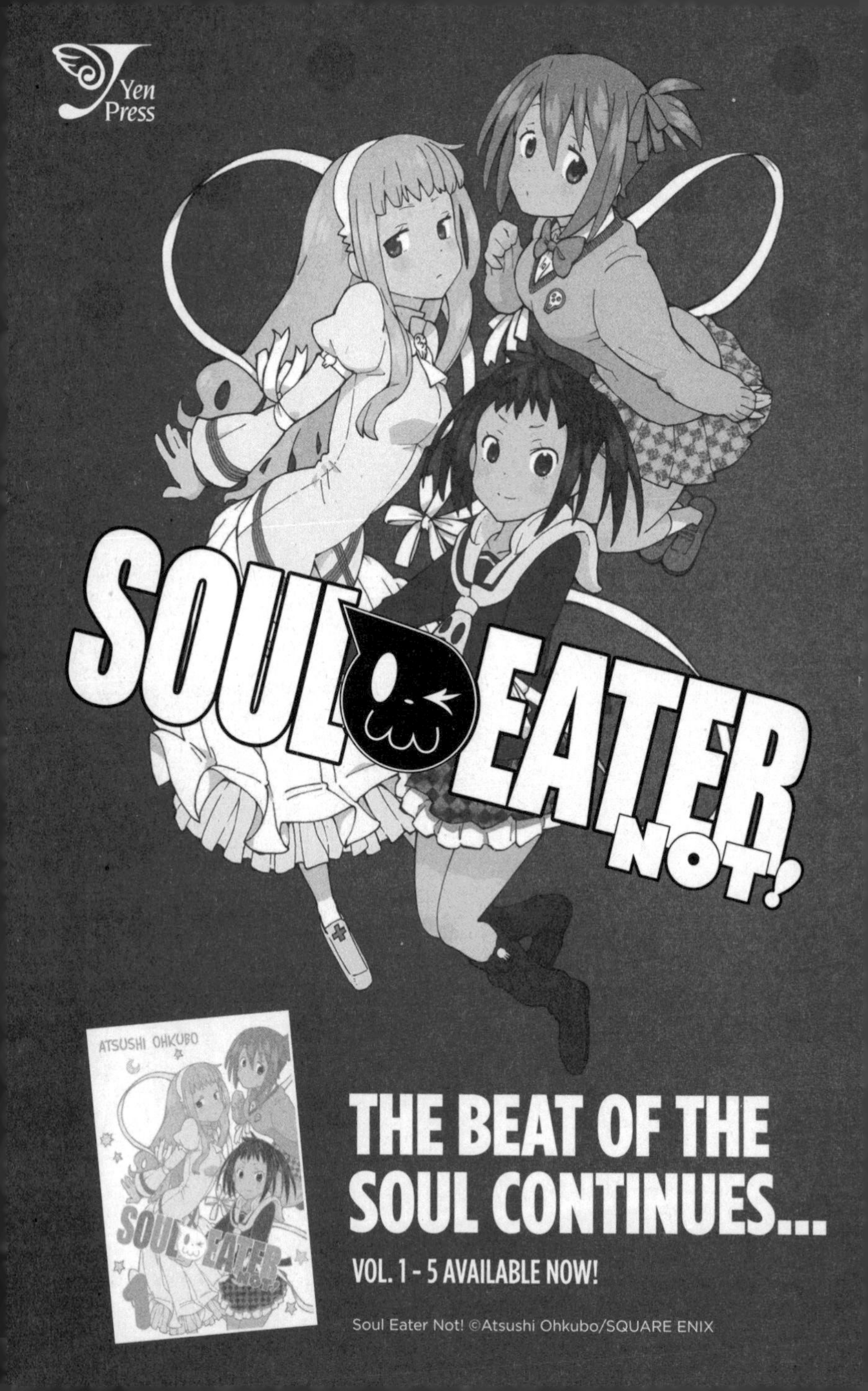
Yen Press
SOUL EATER NOT!
ATSUSHI OHKUBO
SOUL EATER NOT!
1
THE BEAT OF THE SOUL CONTINUES...
VOL. 1 - 5 AVAILABLE NOW!
Soul Eater Not! ©Atsushi Ohkubo/SQUARE ENIX

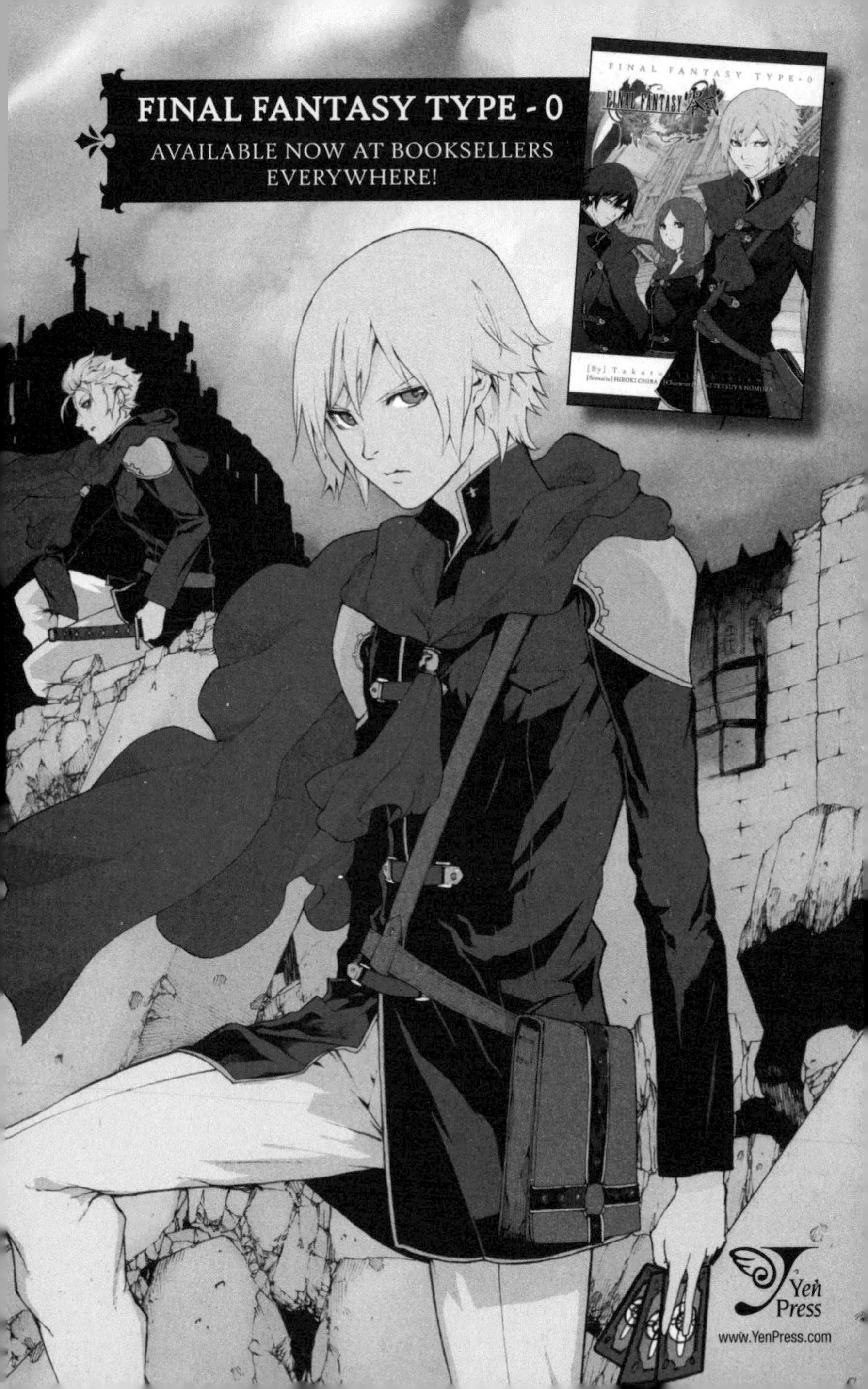
FINAL FANTASY TYPE - 0
AVAILABLE NOW AT BOOKSELLERS EVERYWHERE!
FINAL FANTASY TYPE-0
FINAL FANTASY
Yen Press
www.YenPress.com

FINAL FANTASY 零式 TYPE-0™

Art: TAKATOSHI SHIOZAWA
Character Design: TETSUYA NOMURA
Scenario: HIROKI CHIBA

The cadets of Akademeia's Class Zero are legends, with strength and magic unrivaled, and crimson capes symbolizing the great Vermilion Bird of the Dominion. But will their elite training be enough to keep them alive when a war breaks out and the Class Zero cadets find themselves at the front and center of a bloody political battlefield?!

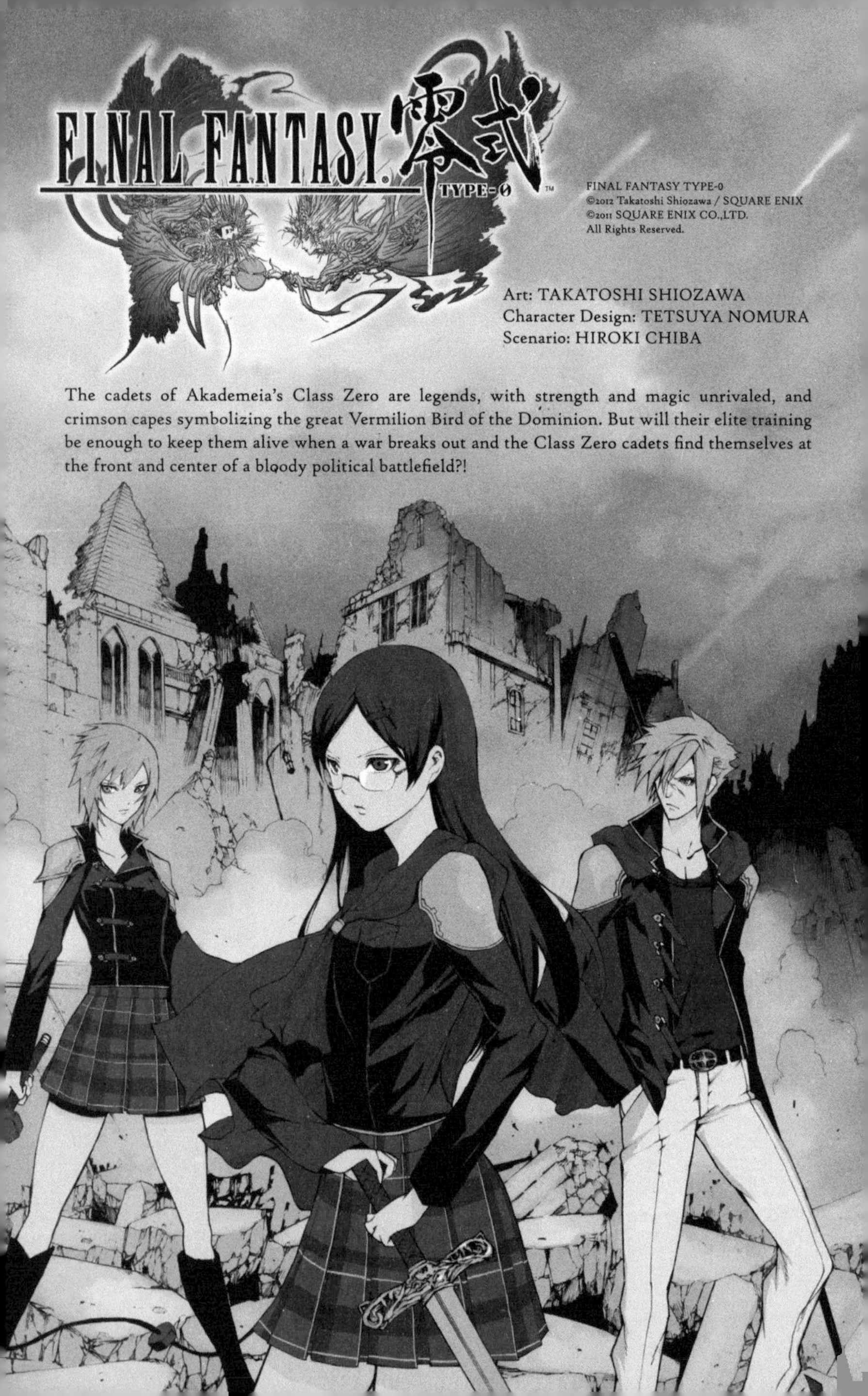

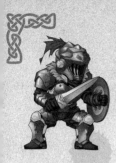
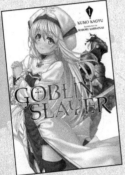
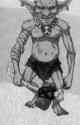
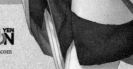

MURDERER
IN THE STREETS, KILLER
IN THE SHEETS!

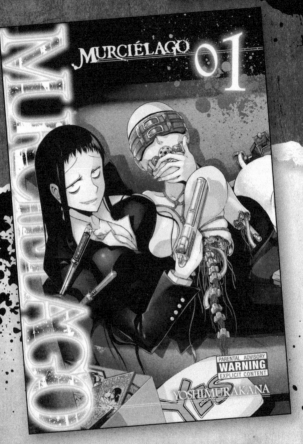

MURCIÉLAGO

VOLUMES 1-5 AVAILABLE NOW!

Mass murderer Kuroko Koumori has two passions in life: taking lives and pleasuring ladies. This doesn't leave her with many career prospects, but Kuroko actually has the perfect gig—as a hit woman for the police!

BACCANO! ②

D0999403

Translation: Taylor Engel • **Lettering: Rochelle Gancio**

BACCANO! vol.2
© 2016 Ryohgo Narita
© 2016 Shinta Fujimoto / SQUARE ENIX CO., LTD.
Licensed by KADOKAWA CORPORATION ASCII MEDIA WORKS
First published in Japan in 2016 by SQUARE ENIX CO., LTD. English translation rights arranged with SQUARE ENIX CO., LTD. and Yen Press, LLC through Tuttle-Mori Agency, Inc.

English translation © 2018 by SQUARE ENIX CO., LTD.

Yen Press
1290 Avenue of the Americas
New York, NY 10104

Visit us at yenpress.com
facebook.com/yenpress
twitter.com/yenpress
yenpress.tumblr.com
instagram.com/yenpress

First Yen Press Edition: March 2018
The chapters in this volume were originally published as ebooks by Yen Press.

Yen Press is an imprint of Yen Press, LLC.
The Yen Press name and logo are trademarks of Yen Press, LLC.

The publisher is not responsible for websites (or their content) that are not owned by the publisher.

Library of Congress Control Number: 2016910571

ISBNs: 978-0-316-44845-1 (paperback)
       978-0-316-44846-8 (ebook)

10 9 8 7 6 5 4 3 2 1

WOR

Printed in the United States of America